Assessing Children in the Urban Community

This book illuminates the process of child psychological assessment in community psychology through discussion, theory, and case studies of collaborative, systemic treatment of children and their parents. *Assessing Children in the Urban Community* presents a semi-structured form of collaborative psychological assessment, designed to help clients gain new insights and make changes in their lives. Traditional psychological assessment focuses on diagnosis and treatment but has been slow to include contextual elements, particularly social and cultural contexts into the assessment process and psychological report.

Clients receiving services in a community psychology clinic pay for their treatment through state welfare coverage. They cannot choose their providers, they cannot always determine the length and course of their mental health care, they often do not have access to transportation to begin services, to continue them, or to take advantage of follow-up recommendations. The Therapeutic Assessment model is particularly adaptable to community psychology because it allows maximum interaction in the assessment process and promotes participation in an often disempowering system.

This book will be relevant to clinical psychologists, community psychologists, social workers, family therapists, graduate students in psychology and social work, marriage and family therapists, and counseling programs.

Barbara L. Mercer, PhD, has been the Assessment Program Director and a clinical supervisor at WestCoast Children's Clinic, a community psychology clinic in Oakland, California. She has worked in community mental health throughout her career. Dr. Mercer has also been on the faculty of California School of Professional Psychology and the Wright Institute in the San Francisco Bay Area.

Tricia Fong, PhD, is a clinical child psychologist who specializes in complex trauma, trauma-informed care, and early childhood mental health. She is a clinical supervisor at WestCoast Children's Clinic where she previously worked as both an assessment psychologist and a clinical psychotherapist. Dr. Fong is also a psychologist for the Partners for Safe and Healthy Children/Prenatal to Three Initiative with Behavioral Health and Recovery Services in San Mateo County.

Erin Rosenblatt, PsyD. Dr. Rosenblatt's clinical experiences have included work with children, adolescents and adults in community settings. After five years of delivering psychotherapy and psychological assessments, Dr. Rosenblatt transitioned to the role of Director of Training at WestCoast Clinic. She is co-author of a monograph "Research to Action" which explores the needs and strengths of sexually exploited youth.

Assessing Children in the Urban Community

Edited By

Barbara L. Mercer, Tricia Fong, and Erin Rosenblatt

Routledge
Taylor & Francis Group

NEW YORK AND LONDON

First published 2016
by Routledge
711 Third Avenue, New York, NY 10017

and by Routledge
2 Park Square, Milton Park, Abingdon, Oxon OX14 0RN

Routledge is an imprint of the Taylor & Francis Group, an informa business

Library of Congress Cataloging in Publication Data
Assessing children in the urban community / edited by Barbara L. Mercer, Tricia Fong, and Erin Rosenblatt. – 1 Edition.
        pages cm
    Includes bibliographical references and index.
    1. Behavioral assessment of children. 2. Psychological tests for children. 3. Psychodiagnostics. 4. Community mental health services – Administration. I. Mercer, Barbara L., editor. II. Fong, Tricia, editor. III. Rosenblatt, Erin, editor.
    BF722.3.A84 2016
    155.4028'7–dc23   2015018597

ISBN: 978-1-138-77625-8 (hbk)
ISBN: 978-1-138-77628-9 (pbk)
ISBN: 978-1-315-77332-2 (ebk)

Typeset in Minion
by HWA Text and Data Management, London

Printed and bound in the United States of America by Publishers Graphics, LLC on sustainably sourced paper.

To children everywhere

On the seashore of endless worlds children meet. The infinite sky is motionless overhead and the restless water is boisterous. On the seashore of endless worlds the children meet with shouts and dances . . .

On the seashore of endless worlds children meet. Tempest roams in the pathless sky, ships get wrecked in the trackless water, death is abroad and children play. On the seashore of endless worlds is the great meeting of children.

Rabinranath Tagore, *Gitanjali* (1913, p. 60)

Contents

List of Illustrations   x
About the Editors   xi
List of Contributors   xii
Acknowledgements   xv

Introduction: Assessing Children in the Urban Community   1
BARBARA L. MERCER

SECTION I
Introduction to Community Psychology   9

1   Community Psychology: Managed Care, Communications,
    and Policy   11
    BARBARA L. MERCER

2   Psychological Assessment of Children in a Community Mental
    Health Clinic   19
    BARBARA L. MERCER

3   A Descriptive Analysis of Cognitive and Rorschach Variables
    of Children in a Community Mental Health Clinic   31
    HASSE LEONARD-PAGEL AND BARBARA L. MERCER

4   Assessment-Driven Intervention for Youth and Families in
    Community Service Delivery Systems   52
    JUSTIN D. SMITH, ANNE MAURICIO, AND ELIZABETH A. STORMSHAK

SECTION II
The Cultural Environment: Theory and Practice   **67**

PART 1
Cultural Experiences in Psychological Assessment   **67**

5   Collaborative Assessment and Social Justice   69
    HEATHER MACDONALD AND CHRISTY HOBZA

6   Unspeakable Fears: Exploring Trauma for Undocumented
    Immigrants   79
    CINTHYA CHIN HERRERA

7   The Ambiguous Other: Reflections on Race and Culture in the
    Assessment Relationship   89
    TRICIA FONG

8   Working with Countertransference Reactions to Treatment Team
    Members in Collaborative Assessments   96
    LISA M. NAKAMURA

PART 2
Cultural Experiences in Supervision and Training   **103**

9   Supervision: A Cross-Cultural Dialogue   105
    HASSE LEONARD-PAGEL

10 Why Are You Crying? It Didn't Happen to You?: Vicarious
    Trauma, Assessment, and Supervision   114
    CAROLINE PURVES

11 Training Assessors in Therapeutic Assessment   120
    MARIANNE E. HAYDEL WALSH, BARBARA L. MERCER, AND ERIN ROSENBLATT

12 Surface Ripples or Deep Water?: Finding the Level for Children's
    Feedback Stories   134
    CAROLINE PURVES

SECTION III
Case Studies in Community-Based Psychological Assessment **141**

13 Why Did She Put Nail Polish in My Drink?: Applying the
Therapeutic Assessment Model with an African-American
Foster Child in a Community Mental Health Setting 143
BROOKE GUERRERO, JESSICA LIPKIND, AND AUDREY ROSENBERG

14 Getting to the Heart of the Matter 159
ELISA GOMEZ AND BROOKE GUERRERO

15 The Topsy-Turvy Tearmeter: Clinical Crisis and Assessment
Intervention 165
TRICIA FONG AND ERIN ROSENBLATT

16 How Can I Stay Safe?: Assessment with a Sexually Exploited
Minor 174
BROOKE GUERRERO

17 The Case of the Bullet-Proof Vest: Complex PTSD, Racial Wounds,
and Taking Matters into Your Own Hands 184
CHRISTOPHER ARRILLAGA

18 Liberating the Butterfly Boy: Engaging the Family and System
in the Therapeutic Assessment of a Traumatized and Gender-
Nonconforming Child 196
LISA A. GREENBERG

19 Living with Danger: Complex Trauma, Attachment, and Repair
in Oakland, California 202
BARBARA L. MERCER AND KEVIN BUNCH

20 Shame: The Hidden Emotion with Tough Adolescents 215
ANKHESENAMUN BAL-MARIONI

Appendix A: Stories About Feelings 224
Appendix B: Stories About Identity 227
Appendix C: Stories About Learning 231
Appendix D: Stories About Past Hurts 233
Appendix E: Letters 237
Index 240

Illustrations

Figures

4.1 FCU Intervention Services   56
4.2 Child and Family Feedback Form   57
6.1 Luz's Projective Drawing   87
13.1 Lanice's Person-in-the-Rain   147
19.1 BENCH   210
19.2 CORNER   210
19.3 AMBULANCE   211

Tables

3.1 DAS-II Results   36
3.2 Coping Variables   37
3.3 Affective Variables   39
3.4 Self Perception Variables   41
3.5 Interpersonal Variables   42
3.6 Cognitive Triad   44
6.1 Luz's results on standardized measures   86
13.1 Paula and Jakara's Assessment Questions   146
13.2 Lanice's Structural Summary   148
15.1 Therapist's Assessment Questions   166
15.2 Mother's Assessment Questions   167
16.1 Diane's Structural Summary   179

About the Editors

Barbara L. Mercer, PhD, has been the Assessment Program Director and a clinical supervisor at WestCoast Children's Clinic, a community psychology clinic in Oakland, California, since 1986. She has worked in community mental health throughout her career. Dr. Mercer has also been on the faculty of California School of Professional Psychology and the Wright Institute in the San Francisco Bay Area where she taught psychological assessment and child therapy, and chaired a number of dissertations at both schools.

Tricia Fong, PhD, is a clinical child psychologist who specializes in complex trauma, trauma-informed care, and early childhood mental health. She is a clinical supervisor at WestCoast Children's Clinic where she previously worked as both an assessment psychologist and a clinical psychotherapist. Dr. Fong is also a psychologist for the Partners for Safe and Healthy Children/Prenatal-to-Three Initiative with Behavioral Health and Recovery Services in San Mateo County.

Erin Rosenblatt, PsyD. Dr. Rosenblatt's clinical experiences have included work with children, adolescents, and adults in community settings. After five years of delivering psychotherapy and psychological assessments, Dr. Rosenblatt transitioned to the role of Director of Training at WestCoast, where she manages a comprehensive clinical training program for psychotherapists, marriage and family therapists, social worker therapists, and their supervisors. In addition to her work at WestCoast Children's clinic, Dr. Rosenblatt has taught and presented on the topic of personality assessment.

Contributors

Ryan Adams, PsyD, is a psychologist for Kaiser Permanente in Pleasanton, California.

Christopher Arrillaga, PsyD, is an assessment supervisor at WestCoast Children's Clinic in Oakland, California. He is also in private practice in Berkeley, California.

Ankhesenamun Bal-Marioni, PsyD, is in private practice in Lafayette, California.

Julia Moon Bradley, PsyD, is an assessment supervisor at WestCoast Children's Clinic in Oakland, California.

Kevin Bunch, PsyD, is the Screening, Stabilization, and Transition Program Director at WestCoast Children's Clinic in Oakland, California.

Tricia Fong, PhD, is a clinical supervisor at WestCoast Children's Clinic in Oakland, California. She is also a psychologist for Partners for Safe and Healthy Children/Prenatal-to-Three Initiative in San Mateo, California.

Michelle Limon Freeman, PsyD, is the Assessment Director for Summit Center, Walnut Creek, Northern California. Her private practice, Neuropsychological Evaluation Center, is located in Walnut Creek, California.

Elisa Gomez, PsyD, is in private practice in Amherst, Massachusetts.

Lisa A. Greenberg, PhD, is a psychologist with Doyle Therapeutic Neuropsychological Assessment in Oakland, California.

Brooke Guerrero, PsyD, is a Clinical Supervisor at WestCoast Children's Clinic in Oakland, California.

Cinthya Chin Herrera, PsyD, is an assessment psychologist, clinical psychotherapist, and intern supervisor at WestCoast Children's Clinic in Oakland, California. She is Adjunct Professor of Graduate Psychology at John F. Kennedy University in Pleasant Hill, California, and maintains a private practice in Oakland, California.

Christy Hobza, PsyD, is Assistant Professor of Child and Adult Assessment at American School of Professional Psychology at Argosy University in Alameda, California.

Margaret Husbands, PsyD, is an assessment psychologist for the Summit Center, Los Angeles, California.

K. Benjamin Knipe, PsyD, is an assessment psychologist and intern supervisor at WestCoast Children's Clinic in Oakland, California. He also supervises doctoral students at the Wright Institute in Berkeley, California and is the Co-Director of A Home Within, East Bay Chapter, San Francisco Bay Area.

Nancy Landau, LMFT-ATR, is a clinical supervisor in the Screening, Stabilization, and Transition Program at WestCoast Children's Clinic in Oakland, California. She is also an artist, sharing her talent through her illustrations for our assessment stories and fables, available through the publisher's website.

Jessica Lipkind, PsyD, is a clinical supervisor at WestCoast Children's Clinic in Oakland, California. She is also an assessment psychologist for the Masonic Center for Youth and Families in San Francisco, California. She maintains a private practice in Berkeley, California.

Heather Macdonald, PhD, is Assistant Professor of Psychology at Lesley University in Cambridge, Massachusetts. She is also the Co-Director of the Theoretical, Historical, and Philosophical Psychology Research Lab at Lesley University.

Anne Mauricio, PhD, is Assistant Research Professor at the Institute for Research Advancing Children's Health (REACH) at Arizona State University, Tempe.

Barbara L. Mercer, PhD, is the Assessment Program Director and a clinical supervisor at WestCoast Children's Clinic in Oakland, California. She also maintains a private practice in Kensington, California.

Lisa M. Nakamura, PsyD, is an Assessment Psychologist at WestCoast Children's Clinic in Oakland, California.

Hasse Leonard-Pagel, PhD, is the Executive Director of the Psychological Services Center at Alliant International University, California School of Professional Psychology, in Oakland, California.

Kristin N. Moore, PsyD, is a psychologist for the Early Childhood Mental Health Program in Richmond, California. She is also Adjunct Professor of Graduate Psychology at John F. Kennedy University in Pleasant Hill, California, and maintains a private practice.

Margaret Owen-Wilson, PsyD, is an assessment psychologist at WestCoast Children's Clinic in Oakland, California. She also supervises doctoral students at the American

School of Professional Psychology at Argosy University in Alameda, California. She maintains a private practice in Burlingame, California.

Caroline Purves, PhD, is in private practice in Berkeley, California. She is a former clinical supervisor for WestCoast Children's Clinic in Oakland, California.

Audrey Rosenberg, PhD, is the Assistant Director of Assessment at WestCoast Children's Clinic in Oakland, California.

Erin Rosenblatt, PsyD, is the Director of Training at WestCoast Children's Clinic in Oakland, California.

Justin D. Smith, PhD, is Assistant Professor in the Department of Psychology and Neuroscience at Baylor University in Waco, Texas.

Elizabeth Stormshak, PhD, is Director of the Prevention Science Institute, Professor of Counseling Psychology in the College of Education, and the Associate Vice Provost for Research at the University of Oregon, Eugene.

Marianne E. Haydel Walsh, PsyD, is in private practice in New Orleans, Louisiana.

Acknowledgements

We are grateful to our colleagues for their skillful and sensitive work. We are fortunate to have an agency whose mission is to support historically underserved children and families, and whose work has forged a path between clinical intervention and public policy. We are thankful for our teammates at all levels of our clinic who have shared and supported a transparent and interactive process. We are appreciative of Nancy Landau, whose artistic interpretation of our clinical work is represented in the beautiful illustrations that she contributed to this project. Thank you all for being a part of our village.

We want to thank our mentors, Dr. Stephen Finn, Dr. Constance Fischer, and Dr. Deborah Tharinger, for their knowledge and wisdom in pioneering this model of assessment, and Dr. Philip Erdberg for his encouraging guidance in Rorschach and research consultation. We are grateful for their generosity in helping us find our voice and for walking with us through the complexity of our work. We would also like to thank Dr. Caroline Purves and Mark Bailie for their enthusiastic support of this project, and for their sharp eyes in providing extra editorial assistance.

Introduction

Assessing Children in the Urban Community

Barbara L. Mercer

People have always gathered in communities and organizations for aid in dealing with outside challenges. They seek close emotional relationships with others in order to help them anticipate, meet, and integrate difficult experiences. Emotional attachment is probably the primary protection against feelings of helplessness and meaninglessness; it is essential for biological survival in children, and without it, existential meaning is unthinkable in adults.

> (Bessel A. van der Kolk, Alexander C. McFarlane, Lars Weisaeth,
> *Traumatic Stress: The Effects of Overwhelming
> Experience on Mind, Body, and Society*, 1996, p. 24)

Break the pattern that connects the items of learning and you necessarily destroy all quality.

> (Gregory Bateson, *Mind and Nature*, 1979, p. 7)

Theoretical Foundations

The foundation for our approach has roots in several disciplines: the field of community psychology, the Therapeutic Assessment model developed by Constance Fischer and Stephen Finn, and psychoanalytic ideas applied to public therapy clinics (Kupers, 1981; Altman, 2009). This unique integration of ostensibly discrete systems is a radical notion, yet we show, through clinical psychological assessment work, how these concepts can be adapted to serve children and families who struggle to find resources for survival, resilience, self-efficacy, and growth.

Community Psychology

Community mental health has grown out of the parallel fields of psychology and social work. Psychology has been a human exploration since Ancient Greek times. Social work came into being in the nineteenth century as the industrial revolution spurred migration to urban areas. Social and economic conditions changed and caused an increase in social problems as well as activism to address problems. The impetus for social work was defined as a way for society to deal with poverty. In the first half of the twentieth century, psychiatry, psychology, and social work matured and often competed as ways to cope with social and mental health problems. Clinicians in the current mental health and health care climate seek to bring these practices closer together.

The field of community psychology makes theoretical links of social systems to human behavior (French & D'Augelli, 2002) postulating that people are located in social settings and communities, and that individual psychology exists in a sociocultural context. Dohrenwend's germinal work (1978) speaks to the way psychosocial stresses lead to psychopathology. Issues of prevention, advocacy, empowerment, and collaboration (Rappaport, 1981; Riger, 2002) are examined as a means to community and social change.

The "Psychological Mind" in Community Work

The Tavistock Clinic in London was founded in 1920 by a Scottish psychiatrist, Dr. Hugh Crichton-Miller, who developed pioneering psychotherapeutic methods of treating traumatized soldiers from World War I. He further focused his philosophy and treatment to work with clients of limited means (Tavistock Clinic, n.d.). Tavistock evolved into a training institute, developing pioneers in trauma and attachment such as John Bowlby (1944) and Wilfred Bion (1945), and publishing the work of child experts like D. W. Winnicott (1957). This Tavistock model of family guidance, where the child is seen but the parental/social environment is an essential participant, informed the establishment of our clinic and is a core model for the work documented here.

Neil Altman, in his book *The Analyst in the Inner City* (2009), stresses how psyche and social are linked—how psychoanalysis and psychotherapy have routinely ignored the social contexts of race, culture, socioeconomic conditions, gender, and sexual orientation. Traditional assessment overlooks how issues of trust and difference are implicit biases of which professionals are often unaware in listening to their patients (Altman, 2009). The context of community violence, abuse, neglect, and removal from family are often mentioned as background in reports, but not integrated into the results and meaning of a child's behaviors. Public clinics with limited funding have rarely been able to offer intensive treatment. In-depth treatment was only accessible for people with money and resources. When faced with a conservative political and financial climate, public clinics can sometimes prevail through more therapeutic use of behavioral techniques and psychopharmacology. Therapeutic work to cope with abandonment and ruptured attachments through abuse and neglect are rarely available to people without substantial income.

Altman reminds us that even Freud advocated offering in-depth services to everyone regardless of income. He noted that self-examination and self-reflection could be an agent for change or for understanding the obstacles to change. Operative in a psychodynamic approach are concepts and realities of transference and counter-transference, replications of parental relationships, powerful emotions, and the sequelae of traumatic experiences. Psychic states can become unthinkable, unbearable, and meaningless. Trauma generates ambivalence. A child's removal from an abusive situation can create intense polarized emotions toward a parent: a love and hate for the same person (Klein, 1975), a longing and an aversion that is raw and unprocessed, and a tension within the child of "how to love without destroying by hate" (Klein, 1975, p. 4).

Winnicott's (1963) approach was to provide a "facilitating environment" to work with the mother to learn to trust herself rather than take expert advice without question. A clinician fully present in working with people who have suffered trauma and loss must carry a portion of feelings communicated by the child or parent. These emotions projected into the work must be carried vicariously and processed by the clinicians in order to understand and assist the client. Our work "in the trenches," as Stephen Finn (2012) called it, requires the clinician to help the client process and hopefully begin to transform the raw, unthinkable emotions generated by the experience of people's everyday lives.

Often a client may tell a story in an even tone of voice, with minimal reaction, but the listener will feel the terrifying, upsetting elements in the telling. A teenager can spill out a story of early repeated molestation by a parent to a strange assessor in an initial testing session. A child doing a play assessment enacts a sadistic scene of abuse, and the assessor recoils. Genocide, famine, and natural catastrophes in Africa, Europe, Asia, and Central and South America historically have been accompanied by truth commissions. As a country, we are often blind to the traumas of our own citizens. Bion (1975) noted that disturbing emotional experiences need to be communicated to an "other" in order to transform it, and cannot be held by one mind alone (Ogden, 2009). Winnicott's concept of the "holding environment" posited that both the mother and society need to be able to "hold" overwhelming and adverse experiences as a way to build resiliency in the child as well as the wider society. MacFarlane and Van der Kolk (2007) stated, "the personal meaning of traumatic experience for individuals is influenced by the social context in which it occurs" (p. 26). They further state that although meaning is critical to the repair of trauma, "after having been traumatized, only a minority of victims seem to escape the notion that their pain, betrayal, and loss are meaningless" (p. 26). These writers share the premise that despite the indifferent face of suffering, humans have an innate need to find truth and meaning in the face of trauma.

Our therapy and assessment work with traumatized families is partially derived from the trauma-informed care model (Lanktree et al., 2012), with roots in the attachment work of Bowlby (1969) and developmental models (Stern, 1995; Hughes, 2004; Schore, 2012; van der Kolk, 2014). Our outcome research can lead to directions for future policy and research. MacFarlane and Van der Kolk (2007, p. 25) emphasized that a "core function of society is to provide people with traditions, institutions and value systems that can protect against being overwhelmed by stressful experiences." We must aspire to this challenging mandate to be, in Winnicott's term, for the "good enough mother" (never perfect), a "good enough" society.

The literature of community psychology often remains theoretical. The writings provide a meta-analysis of community, neighborhood, social change, and the impact of social systems on individuals and groups. By contrast, community mental health work in agencies has been just that, "hard work," with insufficient time for reflection, research, and outcome. The approach offered here attempts to combine a telling of this intense work with time to think and analyze, review data, and reflect on the relationship of client and assessor, supervisee and supervisor, and clinician and environment. Work in the community also demands of us to look at our own experience and biases as service providers. These include issues of counter-transference, training of clinicians, and supervision with a socially conscious humility, combined with an awareness that is profound and difficult.

The capacity of assessor/clinicians to meet clients respectfully, attentively, and doggedly allows the resilience, the stamina, the too-often-unrecognized strengths and the potential of our citizens to be revealed through the assessment process.

Therapeutic Collaborative Assessment

Our book links psychological theory with clinical practice and brings questions of community psychology, mental health, and psycho-diagnostics into focus as they apply to urban children. We demonstrate how raw testing data can uncover the experience of complex developmental trauma in ways that neither the children themselves nor traditional test reports can speak to directly. The traumas of community violence, parental substance abuse, neglect, loss of attachment figures, immigration trauma, molestation, and abuse further bring to light integral (and often invisible) social, cultural, and racial issues. From recognizing this phenomenology, solutions emerge.

Traditional psychological assessment has been slow to include contextual and cultural elements into the assessment process and psychological report. We illuminate the child psychological assessment process through discussion of diversity in both clinical work and supervision, and case studies of systemic treatment of children and their caregivers. This book presents contexts from assessments from one community mental health clinic in Oakland, California, but reflects voices from other community agencies across the country. It echoes a broader perspective on psychological services in a community context with underserved populations. Our community/clinical work adopts not just a one-person theory but also integration of community participants: a welfare system, family, school, and other providers (case managers, court appointed and wrap-around, workers, behavioral specialists). This model appeals to multicultural psychologists within and outside the United States, where a collective (rather than purely individualistic) perspective is the norm and a cultural lens is intrinsic to the psychological.

Psychological assessment has a long history dating from the late nineteenth century. The more recent Therapeutic Assessment model introduced in the past twenty years, described in these pages, is particularly adapted to meet the needs of a community agency. Interestingly, the cost and time may equal what a family with means might spend on a more traditional comprehensive assessment of a child. However, even in traditional psychological assessment practice, there is an underlying premise that the tests are powerful and the patients are unknowledgeable. Despite relational thinking gaining clinical prominence, there remains apprehension about collaboration and partnership.

In traditional psychological assessment practice, there is less transparency about results than one might think, despite an ethical mandate to provide feedback. Do parents know what instruments are being employed, and for what reasons? Do they understand the language of findings? How do they respond in hearing a variety of diagnoses from ADHD, to PTSD, to Autism Spectrum, to Attachment Disorder? One private practitioner offhandedly stated, "I don't give feedback, I send the report to the referring therapist."

The Therapeutic Assessment model originated with Dr. Constance Fischer from her phenomenological roots in Duquesne University. She describes phenomenology (Heidegger, 1926; Giorgi, 1970) as a comprehension of a person's lived experience, and a sense of the observer being in the presence of the observed but bracketing one's own assumptions so as to be as free as possible, or at least differentiated from subjective assumptions. In her 1970 article, "The Testee as Co-Evaluator," Dr. Fischer encouraged a paradigm shift from a traditional testing model by utilizing the assessment process in a relational field. This involved the unorthodox notion of sharing results and applying test data to real-life situations, thus increasing the client's participation in their own services. The model has developed over the past twenty years by Dr. Stephen Finn, who coined the term "Therapeutic Assessment" in 1993 and founded the Clinic for Therapeutic Assessment in Austin, Texas. The ideas promulgated by Finn and Tonsager (1997) emphasize that in addition to the gathering of data for diagnosis and treatment, psychological assessment can be of therapeutic value. Finn (2008) stressed the importance of empathy as an important humanistic tool in conducting assessments. The term "empathy" was used as both a careful tracking and investigation of behavior and experience (Kohut, 1959; Lerner, 1996) as well as in the more "lay" sense of sympathetic understanding (Finn & Tonsager, 2002).

The psycho-diagnostic assessments presented in this book diverge from a traditional assessment model and adapt the model of Therapeutic Assessment created and developed by Fischer (1970) and Finn and Tonsager (1992), and practiced by Finn, Fischer, and Handler (2012). Clients receiving services in a community psychology clinic pay for their treatment through state welfare coverage. They cannot choose their providers, and they cannot always determine the length and course of their mental health care. They often do not have access to transportation to begin services, to continue them, or to take advantage of follow-up recommendations.

The Therapeutic Assessment model allows maximum interaction in the assessment process and allows transparency for psychological dynamics uncovered during the evaluation. This model enlists parents or social workers in asking questions that the data can answer, involves them along the way in the findings as appropriate, and in some cases allows the caretakers to see the child "in action" during video sessions of the testing. This has the power to create change for the child and the family by allowing the parent an "in-vivo" understanding of what "lies beneath" a child's behavior.

In this time of universal health care, county funding boards are requesting a collaborative assessment model as a more efficient, long-term cost-saving method of creating change for difficult problems in community mental health clinics. For example, for issues related to kinds of attachment styles in children and caretakers, identification of traumatic material in test data can be more quickly recognized and can assist in pointing to a therapeutic direction. Our research is beginning to show that short-term intensive treatment that use test findings can deliver information in a short period of time and help children and their families.

Social workers frequently call requesting services because they want a deeper understanding of clients than they have received in more "formal" psychological reports, information that relates more closely to their personal understanding of the child. Our clinic currently is conducting an outcome study to investigate how the caretaker's perspective of their child and their parenting has changed over the course of the assessment and after six months' time. The ability to offer in-depth treatment to clients through a time-limited assessment process offers a new model of mental health care. Our assessment work has implications for training doctoral and licensed clinicians as the assessment field continues to shift. Psycho-diagnostic assessment, while a skill unique to psychologists, can become less technical and obscure to other disciplines and consumers. The use of therapeutic assessment in community psychology is a process that integrates scientific rigor with a method of communicating understanding about children's problems that embodies a cultural and human context. Systemic work needs to be attentive to the roles that can be carried out by a range of people in the environment who work together for a child or family.

In Section I, "Introduction to Community Psychology," we discuss the history of community psychology, demographics of community clinics, utilization of services, descriptive assessment data, and how to look at service effectiveness and outcome. This section also examines other nontraditional assessment methods that can aid in positive family outcomes.

Section II, "The Cultural Environment: Theory and Practice," explores theoretical constructs of the impact of race, community violence, immigration, vicarious trauma and socioeconomic status, and cultural values and background. We highlight their impact on the assessment process with children and adolescents, and in clinical supervision.

In Section III, "Case Studies in Community-Based Psychological Assessment," we present ten illustrative cases that contribute to the understanding of the systemic context of the psychological assessment process in a community setting. Case vignettes address issues of ethnicity and race, gender, poverty, and mental illness, complex trauma and attachment disruptions, and cultural mores and practices. The authors show through test measures, projective data, and clinical illustrations how these aspects play a part in the psychological assessment process and generate implications for treatment.

In the Appendices, we provide sample feedback stories created for children and adolescents. We present examples of feedback that address different types of problems related to coping with emotions, identity, learning, and past hurts.

References

Altman, N. (2009). *The analyst in the inner city: Race, class, and culture through psychoanalytic lens.* New York: Routledge, Taylor and Francis Group.

Bateson, G. (1979). *Mind and nature.* New York: E. P. Dutton.

Bion, W. R. (1975). Learning from experience. In *Seven Servants: Four Works* (pp. 1–105). New York: Aronson.

Bowlby, J. (1969). *Attachment and loss.* New York: Basic Books.

Dohrenwend, B. S. (1978). Social stress and community psychology. *American Journal of Community Psychology, 6,* 1–15.

Finn, S. E. (2008). The many faces of empathy in experiential, person-centered, collaborative assessment. *Journal of Personality Assessment, 91,* 20–23.

Finn, S. E. (2012). Therapeutic assessment "on the front lines": Comment on articles from WestCoast Children's Clinic. *Journal of Personality Assessment, 93*(1) 23–25.

Finn, S. E. & Tonsager, M. E. (1997). Information-gathering and therapeutic models of assessment: Complementary paradigms. *Psychological Assessment, 9,* 374–385.

Finn, S. E. & Tonsager, M. E. (1992). The therapeutic effects of providing MMPI-2 test feedback to college students awaiting psychotherapy. *Psychological Assessment, 4,* 278–287.

Finn, S. E. & Tonsager, M. E. (2002). How therapeutic assessment became humanistic. *The Humanistic Psychologist, 30,* 10–22.

Finn, S. E., Fischer, C. T., & Handler, L. (2012). *Collaborative/Therapeutic Assessment: A casebook and guide.* Hoboken, NJ: Wiley.

Fischer, C. T. (1970). The testee as co-evaluator. *Journal of Counseling Psychology, 17,* 70–76.

French, S. E. & D'Augelli, A. R. (2002). Diversity in community psychology. In T. A. Revinson, A. R. D'Aaugelli, S. E. French, D. L. Hughes, D. Livert, E. Seidman, M. Shenn, & H. Yoshikawa

(Eds.), *A quarter century of community psychology: Readings from the American Journal of Community Psychology* (pp. 65–86). New York: Kluwer Academic/Plenum Publishers.

Giorgi, A. (1970). *Psychology as a human science: A phenomenologically based approach.* New York: Harper & Row.

Heidegger, M. (1926). *Being and time.* New York: Harper & Row.

Hughes, D. (2004). An attachment-based treatment of maltreated children and young people. *Attachment and Human Development, 6,* 263–278.

Klein, M. (1975) Notes on some schizoid mechanisms. In *Love and gratitude and other works 1946–1963* (pp. 1–24). New York: Dell Publishing.

Kohut, H. (1959). Introspection, empathy and psychoanalysis: An examination of the relationship between mode of observation and theory. *Journal of the American Psychoanalytic Association, 7,* 459–483.

Kupers, T. A. (1981). *Public therapy: The practice of psychotherapy in the public mental health clinic.* New York: Free Press.

Lanktree, C. G., Briere, J., Godbout, J., Hodges, N., Chen, K., Trinan, L., Adams, B., Maio, C. A., & Fred, W. (2012). Treating multi-traumatized, socially marginalized children: Results of a naturalistic treatment outcome study. *Journal of Aggression, Maltreatment & Trauma, 21*(8), 813–828.

Lerner, P. (1996). Current perspectives on psychoanalytic Rorschach assessment. *Journal of Personality Assessment, 67,* 450–461.

McFarlane, A. C. & van der Kolk, B. A. (2007) Trauma and its challenge to society. In B. A. van der Kolk, A. C. McFarlane, & L. Weisaeth (Eds.), *Traumatic stress: The effects of overwhelming experience on mind, body, and society* (pp. 24-26). New York: Guilford Press.

Ogden, T. H. (2009). *Rediscovering psychoanalysis, thinking and dreaming, learning and forgetting.* New York: Routledge.

Rappaport, J. (1981). In praise of paradox: A social policy of empowerment over prevention. In T. A. Revinson, A. R. D'Aaugelli, S. E. French, D. L. Hughes, D. Livert, E. Seidman, M. Shenn, & H. Yoshikawa (Eds.), *A quarter century of community psychology: Readings from the American Journal of Community Psychology* (pp. 20–30). New York: Kluwer Academic/Plenum Publishers.

Riger, S. (2002). What's wrong with empowerment. In T. A. Revinson, A. R. D'Aaugelli, S. E. French, D. L. Hughes, D. Livert, E. Seidman, M. Shenn, & H. Yoshikawa (Eds.), *A Quarter Century of Community Psychology, Readings from the American Journal of Community Psychology* (pp. 395–408). New York: Kluwer Academic/Plenum Publishers.

Schore, A. (2012). *The Science of the art of psychotherapy.* New York: W.W. Norton.

Stern, D. (1995). *The motherhood constellation.* New York: Basic Books.

Tagore, R. (1913). *Gitanjali.* London: Macmillan & Co., Ltd.

The Tavistock Institute. (n.d.). *Our History.* Retrieved from http://tavistockandportman.uk

van der Kolk, B. (2014). *The body keeps the score: Brain, mind, and body in the healing of trauma.* New York: Viking, Penguin Group.

Winnicott, D. W. (1963). Psychiatric disorders in terms of infantile mental processes. In *The maturational processes and the facilitating environment* (pp. 230–234). Madison, CT: International Universities Press.

Section I
Introduction to Community Psychology

1 Community Psychology

Managed Care, Communications, and Policy

Barbara L. Mercer

It's better for everybody when it gets better for everybody.

Franklin Delano Roosevelt

… the conscience of society will awake and remind it that the poor man should have just as much right to assistance for his mind as he now has to the life-saving help offered by surgery.

Sigmund Freud, 1924, p. 167

Entitlement

Franklin Delano Roosevelt carried a lifelong consciousness of the masses that in 1935 led him to establish the first entitlement program known as the Social Security Act (first named the Economic Security Act). It was to be paid for by taxes of employees and employers and the states, collected by a newly formed department of the federal government to aid states in helping provide economic assistance for elderly citizens, mothers and their children, the disabled, and the unemployed. Roosevelt considered this program to be the centerpiece of his New Deal, and as Ken Burns stated in his epic documentary *The Roosevelts*, it redefined the American social contract, of "what we owe each other as a people." He saw this as a beginning of a new structure that could aid in lessening economic depression. President Roosevelt declared, "No damn politician can ever take this away" (Burns & Ward, *The Roosevelts*, 2014), but that has not prevented them from trying.

And while social security has been incorporated into the US Constitution, no such protections exist for the care of the mentally ill. There have been varying levels of investment in mental health treatment for our citizens over the past 50 years. But some more conservative politicians over the decades have tried to reduce or eradicate these services altogether, insisting that providing for people with limited resources decreases economic growth and disincentivizes our citizens.

Conversely, a San Francisco organization, the Young Minds Advocacy Project, which provides advocacy for mental health services for low-income young people and their families, defines mental health "entitlement" as a benefit that is a *legal right* to receive particular mental health care for Medicaid eligible children whose need for services is medically necessary to ameliorate their problems (Young Minds Advocacy Project, 2014).

Furthermore, the principles of the mental health system in California stress the philosophy that *everyone* has the right to equal access to mental health services, that "recovery is possible, that prevention, early intervention, education and outreach are effective, that cultural competence, consumer and family involvement in policy development are crucial in the delivery of mental health services, and that stigma and discrimination have no place in our society" (CBHDA, n.d.).

The Medicaid program, Early and Periodic Screening, Diagnosis, and Treatment (EPSDT), is a federally mandated entitlement benefit for adults and children that originated in 1967. These services are funded with a mix of federal, state, and county funds. In 1991, financial responsibility for community mental health and indigent health programs was transferred from the state to the counties with a dedicated revenue source given to the counties. These programs were partially paid for through an increased sales tax and vehicle license fee.

In the beginning, the federal government gave money (50 cents of every EPSDT dollar) to the states. It was up to the states to match that amount and decide how to administer the monies. California Health and Human Services is county administered, so the state said they would cover 45 cents of the match if the counties paid five cents of every dollar. In 2011, the structure of what was called "realignment" was adjusted so the counties were given the whole pot of money to provide the full 50 percent match. The concern with this arrangement was that, if the services exceeded their half allotment, the state would not pay out more. Mental health advocacy groups subsequently helped institute a formal agreement with the State Department of Health and Human Services, whereby the state would agree to reimburse the counties if the mental health service should exceed the county's share of the cost (Langs, Personal Communication, January 2015).

Currently, EPSDT mental health services include individual, group, and family therapy, case management services, collateral contacts, crisis intervention and medication services, behavioral management services, and day treatment. This policy has resulted in major benefits for nonprofit mental health clinics with EPSDT contracts, as it now means that clinicians can provide community/mobile services and increased systemic work through team treatment meetings, school, social worker, and caretaker collaterals. This is absolutely vital in the support of families who cannot afford to privately pay for these services, and even a greater benefit for children in foster care whose family surrogates are often "the system" and who do not have the supportive framework for development that families with resources can provide.

These policies have the potential to alter the environment of community psychology, making the premise of "community psychology" not something "radical" and "apart" but an integral part of society as a whole. Ironically, clients seeking services in community mental health may not feel a part of the societal majority "community." They may have their own smaller identity groups, often not aligned with the normative group due to income, race, language, immigration status, cultural practice, or gender nonconformity. Some clients cannot afford subway or bus fare to come for treatment.

Other families fear exposure or deportation, and too often, a parent cannot fully explain the problem or make use of the feedback given. Parents coming for treatment, often from a culture where emotional and behavioral problems are stigmatized, secretive, or shameful, may not feel empowered within a majority culture. With some families, a more respected spiritual leader may need to be brought in to assist. In other cultures the family problems may only be able to be accessed through addressing the child's problems. This mental health stigma is something still shared by all socio-economic levels of citizens in virtually all countries, yet it is "carried" more visibly by people who have fewer resources with which to "hide" it away through financial means and/or societal connections.

Community Psychology Origins

Literature on theories of community psychology and social psychology provide an overview for our work. Handbooks of community psychology (Rappaport & Seidman, 2000; Revenson et al., 2002; Kloos et al., 2011, 2012) focus on theoretical constructs of prevention, empowerment, social change, systemic reforms, research, and theoretical aspects of helping varying populations.

Social psychology came into focus following World War II with emerging concerns about issues of public health, treatment of veterans, and greater awareness and focus on combating prejudice and poverty. However, it took until 1963 for the Community Mental Health Act to be signed into law, and Medicaid had to wait until 1965. The Joint Commission on Mental Health and Illness, in publishing its intention in 1957, established a mandate for the creation of community mental health centers. However, over the decades following, the political deinstitutionalization of the mentally ill moved services into community mental health agencies, along with funding egregiously insufficient to attend to their needs. And in the 1980s, the federal government began a steady and spirited diminution of economic support from community mental health centers and other health and human services programs. The states were unable to make up the funding shortfall and were forced to restrict services.

The scope of the problem led inevitably to a failure in prevention. In 1961, it was estimated by the Joint Commission on Mental health and Mental Disabilities, that 15 to 20 percent of families in the United States—between 27 and 37 million people (based on US Census data showing almost 184 million citizens in 1961)—were in need of intensive mental health services. The fact that prevention programs were found to be effective in reducing problems, indeed even adding to tax revenue, failed to register as priorities and were often viewed more as "acceptable casualties" similar to highway deaths, school failures, homelessness, and so forth (Felner, Felner, & Silverman, 2000).

The Boston Conference in Swampscott, Massachusetts, in 1965, marked the official emergence of the community mental health field for the integration of "community" into psychology. Bennett et al. (1966) defined community psychology as "behavior in its social context" and the study of psychological processes that "link social systems with individual behavior in complex interactions" (Bennett et al., 1966, p.7). Psychological processes were viewed as necessarily linked to social systems and human behavior. The report from the Boston Conference declared that "the community psychologist should have the knowledge and skills to assess and modify the reciprocal relationships between individuals and the social systems with which they interact" (Bennett, et al., 1966, p.7) and that community psychology should be "involved with facilitating change, rather than preventing anything" (Bennett, et al., 1966, pp. 6–7). This sea change in outlook meant that mental health services, formerly inaccessible for many people with lower socioeconomic status, could finally give help with addressing problems with these people's lives, including mental illness, delinquency, poverty, the stress of poor living conditions, unemployment, and so forth. The 1960s and 1970s saw the development of residential programs for youth, innovative treatment programs (lodges) for people with mental illness, preventive programs for preschool children and the elderly, hotlines, school-based mental health, drug treatment programs, and prevention programs (Sarason, 1971). The concept of a "competent community" (Iscoe, 1974, p. 608) found traction in the Civil Rights Movement, the Women's Movement, the Community Mental Health Act, the War on Poverty, and Head Start. A body of knowledge and theories of social change emerged.

These theories included factors of resilience (Dohrenwend, 1978), the study of neighborhoods as social intervention (Chavis & Wandersman, 1990), and commitment to diversity, a premise that locates people in social settings and communities in a sociocultural context in relationship to the unequal distribution of power and privilege (Revenson & Seidman, 2002). This was based on societal problems such as racism and poverty, and there was critique of research focusing on problems faced by marginalized groups if that research reinforced negative stereotypes not balanced with strengths. Dohrenwend (1978) wrote about the ways in which psychosocial stressors lead to mental health problems. Stressors occur because of psychological characteristics of individuals, and due to environmental factors over which the person has little control. It has been shown that the occurrence of stressors can be prevented through political actions designed to change environmental conditions, by social skill–building interventions that teach individuals skills to avoid or cope with stressors, or by enhancing availability of material resources (Sandler, Gensheimer & Braver, 2002).

There is general agreement that the effects of environmental stressors vary as a function of the availability of social, environmental, and personal resources to the individual (Dohrenwend, 1978). Kelly (1990, p. 133) advocated for a community based community psychology attentive to the promotion of "competent individuals in responsive social systems." According to Levine and Perkins (1987), "Community competence building is one response to the theory that inequality, alienation, dependence and helplessness are attributable to lack of participation and self-determination" (p. 335).

Empowerment is seen as a process by which people are able to gain mastery of their lives: a process involving participation, control, and awareness. Nora Simkus (1986), in her research on social action, found that giving in to demands actually decreased the probability of escalating demands. Rappaport debated the theories of prevention, advocacy, and empowerment. Riger (1993) warned that "empowerment" can be a masculine and competitive concept, so she introduced cooperation and collaboration as a model. Social support, therefore, has become a central concept in community psychology requiring social networks—as well as interactions between individuals and their environments (Barrera, 2000).

Rappaport (1977) cited the need to have the mental health professional become a "community collaborator" rather than community expert, and that definitions of the problem and the resources needed should be provided and shaped by the community.

Mobile/Systemic Work

Mobile therapy developed out of the philosophy that people without equal access to services have the right, according to federal law, to have that access. If clients are unable to come to the clinic because of transportation obstacles, financial reasons, or illness, clinicians should meet the client where they are—be it in school, at home, or in the community. The responsible caretaking system is redefined as foster parents, adoptive parents, kinship figures, biological parents, and the larger community—social workers, case managers, therapists, psychiatrists, lawyers, judges, probation officers, neighbors, or spiritual leaders.

The optimal psychological assessment, therefore, is a collaborative process that combines psychological testing with practical interventions to help children, families, and treatment teams understand symptoms and behaviors and identify the best approach to treatment. The result is a written report—a letter to the caretaker that describes the feelings, ways of thinking, and experiences of the child—that can serve as a roadmap for how to help the youth succeed at home and school.

Utilization and Outcome

In the fiscal year 2013–14, our assessment program served approximately 200 clients with 10,000-plus hours of service. The age group of our youth ranged from ages 4 to 21 (the recent AB 12 "kin-gap" bill, effective January 1, 2012, extends over time the age of foster care youth to 21 years). More than 120 of these children seen for assessment were in the 6-to-12-year age group; the second highest was in the 13-to-17-year age group. The gender makeup was 60 percent male. Languages served in addition to English were Spanish (at 18 percent), Tagalog, Russian, and (with occasional availability to serve) Chinese-Mandarin, Cantonese, Vietnamese, Cambodian, Farsi, and Arabic. In the first half of the fiscal year 2014–15, the self-identified ethnic makeup of our population was 54 percent African American, 21 percent Latino, 18 percent White, 5 percent Pacific Islander, 1 percent Native American, and 1 percent multi-ethnic.

Statistics from our outpatient program between February 2009 and March 2014 show 940 clients served. Clients by age were 10 percent from 3 to 5 years old, 53 percent ages 6 to 12, 34 percent ages 13 to 17, and 3 percent ages 18-plus. Clients by gender were 45 percent male and 55 percent female. Clients by level of care were 54.9 percent at Level 3. "Level of care" is a summary of client needs based on a measure called the Child Assessment of Needs and Strengths (CANS) (Lyons et al., 1999), used nationwide to look at focus for treatment. Level 3 signifies "intensive outpatient with case management, wrap services, or day treatment. Level of care (LOC) does not define what level of service one is actually receiving, but rather the level of service *intensity* needed given one's scores on particular problem items (for example, anxiety, depression, suicide risk, anger, etc.). For instance, a score of 2 or 3 on the CANS is indicative of a high level of need and/or acuity for that particular item. A cluster of higher scores on the CANS then places a client in a specific LOC. The CANS measure also looks at areas of strength for child and caretaker that should be strengthened and developed.

The data on trauma exposure of our population (Basson, Personal Communication, December, 2014) reveals that 60 percent of our children have been or are currently in foster care. Sixty-seven percent of these children experienced three or more placements, with 7.1 being the mean number of placements. Data about placements are skewed because of a small (but non-negligible) number of clients with an extreme number of placements (30 or more). Placements include foster care, psychiatric hospitalizations, juvenile justice stays, and long-term AWOL youth. Of all our clients, 80 percent were exposed to interpersonal trauma. Interpersonal trauma includes emotional abuse, physical abuse, sexual abuse, neglect, and family violence exposure. Complex trauma— that is, two or more of those five interpersonal traumas—was experienced by 61 percent of these children (Basson, Personal Communication, December, 2014).

Communication and Policy

A final goal is that community psychology ought to be concerned with community change; as Phillips, Howes, and Whitebook (1992) state, *"Policy applications are natural extension of community psychology"* (p. 389).

In the climate of the Affordable Care Act, what is the future of community mental health? While health care for all should not be a threat to the Entitlement Act, the new era of managed care could change how contracts are delivered. Fee for service rates could be transformed into more bundled rates and delivery of flat amounts per level of need. Thus treatment for trauma, a specialty health need, could be equalized across consumers. Our particular county has been unique in the amount of growth and more liberal limitations than most to the authorization for children in need. The next few years will determine how states will carve out their own mental health plans.

Advocacy has helped in developing and legislating policy for foster care and transitional age youth. In 2012, our research department submitted a white paper documenting the need to address sexually exploited minors outside the judicial system (Basson, Rosenblatt, & Haley, 2012). In 2014, we worked with a coalition of advocates to secure $5 million in the 2014–15 State Budget, and $14 million thereafter, to develop the newly created *Commercially Sexually Exploited Children Program* in child welfare— the first ever state funding to help exploited youth. Of equal importance, SB 855, a bill Governor Jerry Brown signed into law on June 20, 2015, will fund prevention, intervention, and other services for children who are sexually trafficked and to provide training to child welfare and foster caregivers. The budget trailer bill clarified that a child who is sexually trafficked is a victim of child abuse (Langs, Personal Communication, January 2015). Thus children in our Transitional Age Youth Program/C-Change would receive help with a victim-centered approach rather than a delinquency model. Our research (Basson, Personal Communication, December, 2014) is developing a tool that can be used across disciplines (medical, academic, clinical) to screen for youth at risk for sexual exploitation. As mental health programs become easier to navigate and more useful in the larger community, the more outcome research can guide prevention and policy.

References

Barrera, M., Jr. (2000). Social support research in community psychology. In J. Rappaport & E. Seidman (Eds.), *Handbook of community psychology* (pp. 215–245). New York: Kluwer Academic/Plenum Publishers.

Basson, D. (December 2014). Personal Communication.

Basson, D., Rosenblatt, E, & Haley, H. (2012). *Research-to-action: Sexually exploited minors needs and strengths.* Internal paper. WestCoast Children's Clinic.

Bennett, C. C., Anderson, L. S., Cooper, S., Hassol, L., Klein, D. C., & Rosenblum, G. (1966). *Community psychology: A report of the Boston Conference on the education of psychologists for community mental health.* Boston, MA: Boston University Press.

Burns, K. (Director), & Ward, G. C. (Writer/Producer). (2014). *The Roosevelts, episode V: The rising road 1933–1939* (Series for Television). P. Burns, P. T. Baucom, & Burns, K, *The Roosevelts: An intimate history.* Arlington, VA: PBS.

CBHDA. (n.d.). *County Behavioral Health Directors Association.* Retrieved from http://www.cbhda.org.

Chavis, C., & Wandersman, A. (1990). Sense of community in the urban environment: a catalyst for participation and community development. *American Journal of Community Psychology, 18*(1), 55–81.

Dohrenwend, B. S. (1978). Social stress and community psychology. *American Journal of Community Psychology, 6,* 1–15.

Felner, R. D., Felner, T. Y, & Silverman, M. M. (2000). Prevention in mental health and social intervention: Conceptual and methodological issues in the evolution for the science and practice of prevention. In J. Rappaport, & E. Seidman (Eds.), *Handbook of community psychology* (pp. 9–44). New York: Kluwer Academic/Plenum Publishers.

Freud, S. (1955). Lines of advance in psycho-analytic therapy. In J. Strachey (Ed. & Trans.), *The standard edition of the complete psychological works of Sigmund Freud, Volume XVII 1917–1919* (pp. 157–168). London: Hogarth Press (original work published 1924).

Iscoe, I. (1974). Community psychology and the competent community. *American Psychologist, 29,* 607–613.

Kelly, J. (1990). Changing contexts and the field of community psychology. *American Journal of Community Psychology, 18,* 769–792.

Kloos, B., Hill, J., Thomas, E., Wandersman, A., & Dalton, J. H. (2011) *Community psychology: Linking individuals and communities* (2nd ed.). Belmont, CA: Wadsworth Publishing.

Kloos, B., Hill, J., Wendersman, T. E., Dalton, J., & Elias, M. (2012). *Community psychology: Uniting individuals and communities* (3rd ed.). Boston, MA: Cengage Publishing.

Langs, J. (January, 2015). Personal Communication.

Levine, M., & Perkins, D. V. (1987). *Principles of community psychology: Perspectives and applications.* New York: Oxford University Press.

Lyons, J. S., Griffin, E., Fazio, M, & Lyons, M. B. (1999). *Child and adolescent needs and strengths: An information integration tool for children and adolescents with mental health challenges (CANS-MH), Manual.* Chicago: Buddin Praed Foundation.

Phillips, D., Howes, C., & Whitebook, M. (1992). The social policy context of child care: Effects on quality. In T. A. Revenson, et al. (Eds.), *A quarter century of community psychology: Readings from the American Journal of Community Psychology (pp. 367–393).* New York: Kluwer Academic/Plenum Publishers.

Rappaport, J. (1977). *Community psychology: Values, research, and action.* New York: Holt, Rinehart, and Winston.

Rappaport, J., and Seidman, E. (Eds.). (2000). *Handbook of community psychology.* New York: Kluwer Academic/Plenum Publishers, New York.

Revenson, T. A., & Seidman, E. (2002). Looking backward looking forward: Reflections on a quarter century of community psychology. In T. A. Revenson, et al. (Eds.), *A quarter century of community psychology: Readings from the American Journal of Community Psychology* (pp.3-31). New York: Kluwer Academic/Plenum Publishers.

Revenson, T. A., D'Augelli, A. R., French, S. E., Hughes, D., Livert D. I., Seidman, E., Shinn, M., & Yoshikawa, H. (Eds.). (2002). *A quarter century of community psychology: Readings from the American Journal of Community Psychology.* New York: Kluwer Academic/Plenum Publishers.

Riger, S. (1993). What's wrong with empowerment? *American Journal of Community Psychology, 21*(3), 279–292.

Sandler, I. N., Gensheimer, L., & Braver, S. (2002). Stress: Theory, research, and action. In J. Rappaport & E. Seidman (Eds.), *Handbook of community psychology* (pp. 187–213). New York: Kluwer Academic/Plenum Publishers.

Sarason, S. B. (1971). *The culture of the school and the problem of change.* Boston: Allyn and Bacon.

Simkus, N. (1986). *Effects of improvement size on contentment aspiration level, perceived strength, perceived conflict, and instrumental action, escalation* (Doctoral dissertation, University of Western Ontario, London, Ontario, Canada). Retrieved from ProQuest, UMI Dissertation Publishing (NL33023).

Young Minds Advocacy Project. (2014). Retrieved from http://www.youngmindsadvocacy.org.

2   Psychological Assessment of Children in a Community Mental Health Clinic

Barbara L. Mercer

The history of psychological assessment highlights the ongoing and often tense dialogue between empirical and theoretical understanding, and between actuarial and clinical methods. Meehl (Dawes, Faust, & Meehl, 1989; Meehl, 1954) argued for the superiority of actuarial data and the abandonment of the clinical approach. Even Klopfer (1954) cautioned that more than superficial feedback could be destructive to the patient. Psychoanalytic assessment, illuminated by the gifted work of Lerner (2007), emphasized understanding the experience of the person being assessed, the assessment relationship, and writing in plain, interesting language. Fischer (1970, 1985, 2000), Finn and Tonsager (1997, 2002), Finn (2007), Tharinger, Finn, Wilkinson, and Schaber (2007), Handler (2008), and Hamilton and Fowler (2009) further developed the therapeutic collaborative assessment process as an integration of statistical rigor within the interpersonal context.

The growing focus of conferences, books, and articles that combine statistics with case studies (Viglione, 2003), neuropsychology with collaboration (Engleman, 2006, 2007; Smith, 2007), and analytic with structural data (Lerner, 2005, 2007) indicate that these ideas are yielding a new era of assessment. However, in a search for reference to *community psychology* in the *Journal of Personality Assessment*, not a single article emerged. Dana (1996, 1998, 2000), Dana et al. (2002), Allen (1998) and Allen and Dana (2004) have persistently interrupted our status quo assumptions with articles on the cross-cultural use of the Rorschach and MMPI (Butcher & Hass, 2009), and argued for the development of an empirical basis for multicultural assessment. The publication of international norms for the Exner Comprehensive System (Shaffer, Erdberg, & Meyer, 2007) has further awakened an understanding of a cross-cultural interpretive framework and the consideration of social values as essential to test validation.

Community Psychology: A Unique Model

Our community psychology clinic offers psychotherapeutic services to address the effects of complex trauma on children, youth, and their caregiving systems. We offer individual, group, and family therapy, psychological assessment, collateral support, case management, and coordination of care with other providers. We have programs for transitional age youth and a specialized mental health screening for all foster children in our county catchment area. These services are delivered in our clinic offices or in the client's school, residence, or other community locations (Fernando & Langs, 2009).

The program utilizes principles derived from child and adolescent development (particularly attachment theory), relational and systems theories, multicultural approaches, community psychology, and complex trauma frameworks. Our goal is to help children develop ways of coping with the impact of the maltreatment they have suffered and promote a more resilient developmental trajectory and to assist their connections with caregivers, teachers, and social supports and networks.

A Relational Psychology

Fernando (2008) noted that the purview of community psychology is a natural environment for systemic work, yet the systemic approach has fallen primarily to the social worker, whereas psychological assessment has been the tool of private practitioners and school psychologists. However, a traditional psychodiagnostic process is a less useful approach in community settings. The foster child's guardian is, in essence, a county social worker. When a child's placement changes for any reason, the social worker may change, and the report can be lost or forgotten. A biological parent may have received a report, but may frequently state, "I didn't get feedback—I have no idea what this report means." The parent may have read or even cognitively understood the language, but not been able to *therapeutically* digest the information. Part of our mission in a community psychology clinic is to collaborate with our families and the systems working with children and youth in order to understand their problems in a social context. These children are often seen by society as lost causes or unworkable. When children enter foster care, have meltdowns, and behave badly, the link of their behaviors to recent neglect, abuse, and abandonment is often minimized or forgotten. If behaviors are seen as understandable, then energy and service effort might be more willingly applied to help these children with achieving developmental progress.

Psychologists working in a public clinic cannot effectively work without a relational model. Race, class, and culture differentials are intrinsic to our understanding. When we go into the community as assessors, we experience the phenomenon of the *inner city* life (Altman, 2009) of foster children who, in many respects, are like any other children. We are asked to assess the reasons for their so-called bad behaviors—fighting, tantrums, food hoarding, poop hiding, withdrawal, attention and learning problems, social ineptness, and guarded or indiscriminate attachment. There can be a tendency to forget that one child was molested for five years; or another child had to lead his siblings out a window at night to escape one more beating; or yet another child was found wandering at twilight in the street in pajamas. These visceral stories are tormenting to hear and hard to digest. All of us find ourselves wanting to forget these distressing and gory details. We don't want to keep in our minds how children are affected by these experiences. How do these brutal facts of daily living affect the children we assess? How would any of us be impacted by any one of these events in our own lives? And, how would the impact of these events show up on a child's psychological test?

When we go into the community and leave the safety of our clinic walls, we enter a realm of trauma, poverty, and stress that some clinicians may have been fortunate to avoid in their lives. If clinicians are from a similar background or community, difficult feelings may become triggered in the process of seeing a neglected child living in a deprived or violent environment or hearing details of sexual abuse. When we conduct assessment literally on the road, we, like our clients, the foster children, face a kind of displacement and rootlessness as we attempt to create an appropriate therapeutic frame

(Fernando, 2008). While carting our WISC-IV (Wechsler, 2003) or DAS-II (Elliot, 2007) in a gigantic rolling suitcase to a child's home, shooing off a little sister in the living room as she bugs us with her own opinion of an inkblot, or calming a child in a school room after he overturns a table with his perceived failure on a subtest, we are continually challenged to both reflect therapeutically and respond in a down-to-earth manner.

How do we, deep down, view those whom we assess? As specimens to be deciphered? Problems to be corrected? Unfortunate children to be rescued? And how do those we assess perceive us? As intruders, experts, benevolent strangers, or just strangers? How are our clients, and their test results, affected if we are black, white, Spanish-speaking, talk with an accent, look rich or average, or are reserved or warm? Leary (2000) stated in her discussion on racial enactments in dynamic treatment: "it seems inevitable that each of us will, at one time or another, drift into unintended racial thoughts, feelings and actions to which we or others will later attach verbal labels and psychological meaning" (p. 642). When racial enactments occur, however, rather than an end to the communication they offer a potential for revealing more understanding and improving relationships with our clients. Yet as both white and nonwhite clinicians, are there not enactments of which we are unaware? Our origins as a psychology training clinic forecast that many of our graduate students would be white. As more diverse clinicians, supervisors, and program directors became part of the agency, the percentages still remained insufficient with respect to our 60 percent African American clientele. Currently, as we progress in bringing in diverse interns, postdoctoral residents, and staff, being a nonprofit agency with salaries lower than hospital clinics, we lose our staff of color to higher-paying employment opportunities.

What does it mean for an African American client to work with an African American assessor? In a recent assessment, a biracial adolescent concerned with her identity looked at the hair of her assessor, who was also biracial, and commented on the beauty of her curly hair. An African American assessor came back through the village square in our community with two white clinicians, and was approached by three African American men for his lunch. Although he had been saving his lunch to eat on the ride home, he gave his food to the men, without thinking. "Does this happen to you often?" his white friends inquired. "Almost every day, something like this happens," he answered. These interactions make his job meaningful. What are the pulls on an African American clinician: to be a father figure to a boy whose father has left the family? What does it mean to acknowledge his status as a professional—does it provide hope, or resignation? What are the pulls for white clinicians working with clients of different cultural or racial backgrounds? Is there a pull to be "tough" or "knowledgable"? Is there still a fear of engaging and exploring the community outside the clinic doors as a total environment, not just a place where a client receives therapy? These are the underlying questions and emotions we struggle with as we engage in psychological assessments with our clients.

The questions abound. Will we get different data with a different assessor? We have many times found that assessors in our clinic have completed work with children who were described as 'untestable'. Even among our own clinicians, we have noted differences in a particular clinician/client match. Recently, a predoctoral intern with a fearless relational capacity and ability to use down-to-earth language was able to complete an assessment with a guarded adolescent who had boycotted a previous experienced assessor. When another child was to be brought to our clinic for testing, he had to be restrained. When the assessor instead went to the group home to assess him, they began a conversation about his reservations ("I'm not crazy," he told her) that ended not only in a successful assessment, but in psychotherapy.

Dr. Francine Cornos, a professor of psychiatry at New York City's Columbia University, herself a former foster child, spoke of being referred for a psychological evaluation at 14 years of age after her mother died of cancer and there was no one to take her in:

> "What's that?" the psychologist asked me. We sat together in a small room at the foster care agency headquarters. She was pointing to an inkblot with two dancing figures that seemed clearly to have both penises and breasts, but her finger was on the penis. "I don't know" I replied. She seemed incredulous and challenged my answer. Don't waste your time, I was thinking. Of course any teenage girl knows what a penis is, but I'm never going to tell you that word ... I was on strike ... from the social worker who came to our foster home too much for my taste and who lay in wait for me as I returned from school ... . "Do you have friends?" she inquired. "Yes I have friends," I replied knowing full well that I merely went through the motions and lost all ability to feel genuinely close to anyone new. "Why don't you hang up pictures of your mother?" She nagged again. I was totally silent. "You fool don't you know I don't even own a picture of my mother? Don't you know I was sent to this place without any of my mother's possessions? Don't you see that my foster mother is in a rage at me for not embracing her as my new mother? ... " But I said nothing. She talked on and on. "Shut up! Shut up!" I finally screamed ... after all my carrying on, she referred me for a psychological evaluation.
>
> (2004, p. 150)

Psychological assessment in a community clinic must integrate both traditional methods with standardized scores and diagnoses, designed for describing behaviors to a third party (e.g., social worker, court, psychiatrist, group home staff) as well as provide a way to access the lives of children who have experiences outside the norm. Although it is important to summarize data in talking about attachment difficulties, mood problems, attentional difficulties, and the impact of trauma, it is equally important to delineate a context for these problems. This is necessary so that the social worker or foster parent can be helped to understand why, for example, a girl's acting out might increase after visitation with her mother who neglected her; or that loyalty issues to a parent, however abusive, might affect a child's adjustment to foster care; or why an adolescent might sabotage a placement as she begins to get closer to her foster mother. One foster parent had returned her foster-adoptive teen to the assessment-holding center, but after reading a thorough psychological assessment report, called the social worker to say, "I want her back ... I never understood her acting out before." With increased depth of understanding, these pieces of information often take on useful applicability. They can be consciously thought about, talked about, and used to begin to work with the child, foster parent, treatment team, and parent.

Therapeutic Collaborative Assessment Model

Demographics and Impact of Foster Care

The numbers of children placed in foster care in the United States have doubled from approximately 280,000 in 1987 to 600,000 in 2006 (Needell et al., 2008). According to the Department of Health and Human Services, the median age of children in foster care is 10.1 years old, with 52 percent being male, 42 percent African American, 36 percent Caucasian, and 15 percent Latino (Wulczyn, Brunner, & Goerge, 2002). Disproportionate numbers of African American children in foster care may relate to the consequences of disenfranchisement, racism, under-scrutiny of white families, and insufficient preventative and supportive services. Studies indicate that foster children are not only at greater risk for behavioral and psychological problems related to attachment, depression, and chronic post-traumatic stress reactions, but many more report significant difficulties in maintaining age-appropriate grade level achievement, completing high school, and finding employment (McDonald & Allen, 1996). Other common features of former foster children are criminal involvement, poor health, substance abuse, further victimization, early parenthood, and having their own children in foster care. While some youth removed from their biological parents achieve stability, productivity, and well-being, research has suggested that the population as a whole is highly vulnerable and in need of social policy and programs to support them in many aspects of their lives (Wulczyn, Brunner, & Goerge, 2002).

Like foreign refugees, our foster children often find themselves traveling from one impermanent home to another without notice, with nothing more than a garbage bag to carry their belongings. Aunts and grandparents, making ready for retirement, find themselves thrust into unwanted parental roles with small, dysregulated children. They are confronted with the realization that if they want to prevent their grandchildren from going into professional foster care, they must undertake raising them by themselves.

Structural and Projective Data

Kelly (1999) wrote that on the Rorschach, abuse and trauma produce high Lambda, an increase in m's and Y, elevated de-repressed contents, and disordered thinking. On the Thematic Apperception Test (TAT), Murray (1943) found physically and sexually abused children showed affective pathology and significantly more impairment on object-relations scales than their nonabused counterparts. This in-depth understanding of abuse and trauma in children who must nevertheless move toward adulthood and attempt to find a place in our society has added to the literature on the lives of children in unusual or extreme circumstances. Kelly (1999) discussed the "lives compromised and dreams finally dashed by the harsh realities of adulthood" (p. ix), despite being removed from the source of trauma. Although these children have survived, like war refugees, Kelly (1999) commented that they "rarely complained and hardly talked of abuse" (p. x). They do, however, reveal these horrors in the test material and the de-repressed contents: *bloody cockroaches running for their lives*, sexual images such as *busted babbs* and *vajayjays*, and *slimy monsters, dead penguins, spitting rats, sheep on fire, red-eyed vampires, geckos who pull out people's teeth and eat them* shock the assessor. As supervisors, we have to challenge our staff to make these nasty thoughts *thinkable* (Bion, 1962; Alvarez, 1992) so that they can take the data and the graphic material and translate the intolerable into tolerable feedback. We must transform despair into "contact with emotional life rather than disowning it" (Gin, 2008, p. 83).

Studies of foster children suffering the additional trauma and insult of removal from their families are only the beginning. Our own clinic's Rorschach research (Goldblatt, 2003) showed Mutuality of Autonomy object relation scales in a range similar to a severe PTSD population. Traumatized children perceive relationships as threatening and damaging. However, in contrast to individuals with severe psychopathology, traumatized children also exhibit a capacity for mutuality. Eshom's foster care sample (2006) showed a higher Ego Impairment Index-2 (Viglione, Perry, & Meyer, 2003) than a normal sample. This sample of children who went through multiple foster care placements had significantly more minus form Human Movement responses and fewer Good Human responses than children who remained with their original kinship caretakers. Another study by Kim (2005) showed that foster children referred for aggressive behaviors demonstrate features of disordered thinking at a level similar to in-patient samples of conduct disordered and psychotic children. In a recent demographic study of sexually exploited foster care minors, Rorschach data of girls involved in prostitution revealed high Traumatic Content Score (Armstrong & Loewenstein, 1990), and significance on the isolation index (Crowell, 2009). An exploratory internal review of their protocols also showed Kwawer object relations scores (Kwawer, 1980) reflective of predatory damage and malignant internal processes.

In a descriptive study conducted with 72 of our clinic's foster children (Mercer, 2003), 92 percent had an Egocentricity Ratio over one standard deviation below their age norm; 78 percent had a W:M ratio (a ratio of a person's aspirations to available resources) outside the norm; 42 percent had DEPI positive (an index measuring depressive symptoms); and 39 percent had CDI positive (an index of a pervasive sense of helplessness). Projective material reveals the emotional meaning of these scores. One girl with an .09 Egocentricity Ratio gave responses on the Rorschach ranging from butterflies, rabbits, and "happy mouths" to "scribble-scrabble," fish dying in oil, graveyards, and knives slamming down. Themes repeated consistently in projective storytelling material describe so-called bad kids who can never escape badness because they have lost a home base of parents, food, security, and sense of future. These children often feel they have caused the trauma that led to foster home placement and later to severe self-hate and the potential for self harm. One 9-year-old boy spoke of a foster child's future on Roberts Apperception Card (McArthur & Roberts, 1982) Card 13:

> This is about a boy who thought heaven was good and the devil was bad but he switched them around because his parents always told him heaven was bad and the devil was good ... and then he started acting up until his parents gave him up to a foster home, and when he was 21 he went to jail and said, "I am going to kill myself to get away from me" ... and when he went to heaven God said, "why do you do all these bad things?"

A 12-year-old boy described the fallout from the absence of attachments and role models on Card I of the Children's Apperception Test (CAT; Bellak & Bellak, 1949):

Their mom died when they were born and they didn't have anyone to teach them to fly. They had to depend on themselves. The father has worms and dies of heart disease. They die too because they haven't learned how to depend on themselves.

Children store their early experiences in a childlike place where their hope for a better life is fragile and can be snatched away, as in this story of 13-year-old Natasha with a .17 Egocentricity Ratio, no Human Movement responses, and only three Whole responses, told on Card 7 of the Roberts Apperception Test:

She scared because she in the dark alone. She is in a black-out alone. She's all scared in Brooklyn. Then her mom started singing her a song—"things are going to be easier" … She's feeling lonely, lonely now because her mommy said I'm leaving because I hate you. She said mommy don't leave. Now she's dead because her Mommy left and she got nowhere to go and nothing to eat so she is dead.

What they hope for is not beyond reality, as with this 9-year-old girl who decided (in her projective story) to study Black History even though she is mad, and passes her test. This is her description of her human figure drawing:

That's a girl. She is happy. Her name is Sharena. I'll make her a brain. She has a little brain. Empty at first, but every time she goes to school, she got more brain, little by little. She practiced it, practiced it, practiced it, and finally she got all filled up. She knows how to spell. She wants to be a teacher.

The Use of Data in Collaborative Assessment

The assessor must interpret test results to social workers, foster parents, teachers, and even to reunifying parents originally responsible for abusive or neglectful behavior (and themselves suffering trauma or community violence). It can be difficult and overwhelming for parents to hear feedback. However, without bringing the assessment to life, it is likely to be forgotten, ignored, or found too overwhelming to be useful. From the statement of the problem, we reach the point of examining our own W:M (aspiration to resource) ratios (Exner, 1969) as therapists and assessors, envisioning potential interventions with the resources available to us and to our clients.

Feedback Stories

One of the barriers to useful assessment reports is that the language is more technical than the words used by clients. We often find that the story written for the child provides the most dynamic and understandable information, even to the parent or the social worker. In one feedback story, an intern wrote about a young buck with the most beautiful antlers of all the deer in the forest—but instead of making him proud, his "angry" antlers caused him worry. In the feedback session, the foster family worker heard for the first time through this fable, that the boy was angry. "That can't be right, you haven't gotten in trouble for fighting have you?" the worker asked. "Yes I have," the boy replied. Although the sympathetic worker had read the court reports about past severe physical beatings and maternal abandonment, he admitted: "I didn't know all this had happened to you or rather I guess I *forgot* or didn't want to see it."

Foster children go through their lives in the system with few people remembering who they are. Our feedback stories to our children speak in metaphor and fable, and to our surprise, our young clients frequently say, "That girl sounds just like me." A story told to a 6-year-old girl, once sexually abused, recounted the tale of "Princess Pinky who was hurt and banished from her home," and to a boy with a learning disability came the tale of "Baller Bobby who could shoot hoops but couldn't do math." A behaviorally acting-out boy became "Exo Man" in his story, a boy who had to be willing to lower his robotic shield to really be strong. Daisy the Kangaroo from Hopscotch Hollow, a kangaroo who escaped out the window from abusive parents to look for her kangaroo aunt, had a "confusing case of the opposites: she was glad to be safe from harm, but missed her mother." A boy diagnosed with a pervasive developmental disorder was told about "Henry the Hangman Helper of Puzzle Place" who had to solve the "Great Feelings Puzzle" by learning the names and faces of four feeling words: sad, happy, angry, and scared. These are the companion pieces to our traditional reports. A 13-year-old developmentally delayed girl called her assessor on the phone after receiving her feedback story in the mail about Callie who felt just "a little bit different" and asked "did you write this story for me ... it sounds just like me. I told my foster parents and teacher about it because I think they should know so they can help me." Neither the social worker nor the foster parent had been able to make time to come for feedback. But the child got it and was now advocating for herself!

A 15-year-old boy diagnosed with bipolar disorder asked the following questions: "Who am I?"; "Why do I fight with the people I love?"; and "Why do I hate myself?" He was given feedback in a letter and a discussion about what kinds of things caused his emotions to fluctuate, and how he used his anxieties and temper to prevent risking new social contacts. The assessor told him he fights with loved ones because he wants them to protect him against things that are hard to do for himself, because he wants to feel powerful instead of helpless. She told him he "hates" himself because he gets stuck on the bad things and has a hard time seeing the good things when he feels down. She told him that he is smarter than he thinks, that he cares about global warming and his family, that he is proud of his biracial ethnicity, and that he wants to feel connected to people. His mother, who resisted getting him evaluated at first because she felt no one understood either her or her son, and felt she could no longer handle him at home, became invested when she felt her experience was understood and that she could get help in handling his tantrums, and that a day treatment program could help provide structure and help him develop. The youth was able to feel understood by this feedback without sulking or having a tantrum.

Parent Participation

There has been a mystery surrounding psychological assessment, especially the Rorschach. The diagnosis and understanding are left to the experts, and the parents are rarely brought in on the process. Tharinger et al. (2007) have introduced the live feed technique, which allows the caretakers to watch the assessment on video from an adjoining room with a second clinician who can help the parent understand what the child might be experiencing that leads to the problematic behaviors. Young and latency-age children do not necessarily expect total privacy. They sometimes use the assessment to communicate something that needs saying to their parents.

Our screening requirements for a caretaker to view an assessment "in vivo" include having a stable caretaker and placement, logistical availability to our clinic, and an investment by the caretaker with an explicit desire to better understand his or her child. We have flagged variables that might promote caution or in some cases prohibit direct caretaker involvement. A crisis that destabilizes the system or decreases the parent's ability to utilize the assessment information resulting in an increase in punishment, blame, or self-blame can lead us to limit the collaborative aspects of the assessment process. However, even when the parents have suffered their own traumas or mental breakdowns, we have noted significant gains, especially with the support of treatment team members. In one case, a mother, watching her child struggle with reading, herself started to blame his problem on her own past domestic violence. The assessors reevaluated the decision to continue in this collaborative feedback to this vulnerable mother about her son's anxieties and reflected upon how to let her know that his acting out might reflect his need to heal her depression. The assessor's concern increased toward the end of one projective testing session when the boy seemed overwhelmed, but the mother, unable to find her own boundaries, insisted, "Ask him *right now* what he feels about his grandmother, about his father." In a subsequent session, the boy himself was able to talk clearly to his mother about his worry due to past domestic violence. His mother recognized the truth of this and could take in the feedback. This problem had originally seemed insurmountable. It was much more powerful for her to hear results of testing through her son, than from the assessors at a final feedback session, as is often the case in traditional models of assessment. The assessors were able to reassure her that many children had problems with reading, unrelated to family conflict. In the final session, she felt more empowered to cope with his problems and expressed gratitude for being allowed to participate in the assessment.

In another case, during the process of the evaluation, a mother was hospitalized and diagnosed with a mood disorder. Using the collaborative process, the treatment team, including the child's therapist from an outside agency, was able to meet in support of the family. The team was able to bring in extended family members for support and to discuss their belief that the child carried the family genetics for mental illness. The assessment data helped the family to understand the child's behavioral problems in the context of the mother's illness and the recent severe family stress.

The collaborative assessment model includes generating questions from both parents or caretakers and the child, administration of traditional test instruments, planning a school or community intervention and feedback, and finally, conducting feedback sessions with the family and writing a feedback story or letter for the child or youth to communicate the results of the testing. Work with clients receiving public funds for mental health services, adapted from the Therapeutic Assessment model, highlights the necessity for a relational, culturally aware, family oriented, systemic model in providing psychological assessment services to children and families in a community setting.

References

Allen, J. (1998). Personality assessment with American Indians and Alaska Natives: Instrument considerations and service delivery style. *Journal of Personality Assessment, 70*(1), 17–42.

Allen, J., & Dana, R. H. (2004). Methodological issues in cross-cultural and multicultural Rorschach research. *Journal of Personality Assessment, 82*(2), 189–206.

Altman, N. (2009). *The analyst in the inner city.* Boca Raton, FL: The Analytic Press Taylor & Francis Group.

Alvarez, A. (1992). *Live company.* London: Routledge.

Armstrong, J. G., & Loewenstein, R. J. (1990). Characteristics of patients with multiple personality and dissociative disorders on psychological testing. *Journal of Nervous and Mental Disease, 178,* 448–454.

Bellak, L. & Bellak, S. S. (1949). *The Children's Apperception Test.* Larchmont, NY: CPS.

Bion, W. R. (1962). *Learning from experience.* London: Marsfield.

Butcher, J. N., & Hass, G. (2009, March). *Considering culture, race & ethnicity in personality assessment.* Paper presented at the meeting for Society for Personality Assessment, Chicago, Illinois.

Cornos, F. (2004). Parental death and foster care: A personal and professional perspective. *Journal of Infant, Child and Adolescent Psychotherapy, 3*(3), 342–355.

Crowell, K. (2009). *Understanding the trauma of child prostitution: An exploratory examination comparing child sexual abuse victims to commercially sexually exploited minors.* (Unpublished doctoral dissertation, Pacific Graduate School of Psychology, Redwood City, CA).

Dana, R. H. (1996). Culturally competent assessment practice in the United States. *Journal of Personality Assessment, 66*(3), 472–487.

Dana, R. H. (1998). Cultural identity assessment of culturally diverse groups. *Journal of Personality Assessment, 70*(1), 1–16.

Dana, R. H. (Ed.). (2000). *Handbook of cross-cultural and multicultural personality assessment.* New Jersey: Lawrence Erlbaum Associates, Inc.

Dana, R. H., Aguilar-Kitibutr, A, Diaz-Vivar, N., & Vetter, H. (2002). A teaching method for multicultural assessment: Psychological report contents and cultural competence. *Journal of Personality Assessment, 79*(2), 207–215.

Dawes, R. M., Faust, D., & Meehl, P. E. (1989). Clinical versus actuarial judgment. *Science, 243,* 1668–1674.

Elliot, C. D. (2007). *Differential abilities scale II (DAS-II®).* San Antonio, TX: Pearson Education, Inc.

Engleman, D. H. (2006, March). *Using a neuropsychological evaluation as the basis for a therapeutic story.* Paper presented at the meeting of the Society for Personality Assessment, Washington, DC.

Engleman, D. H. (2007, March). *Advantages of collaboration in a complicated adolescent neuropsychological assessment.* Paper presented at the meeting of the Society for Personality Assessment, Washington, DC.

Eshom, J. (2006). *An examination of the impact of trauma and multiple placements in foster children using the ego impairment index-2 on the Rorschach.* (Unpublished Dissertation, The Wright Institute, Berkeley, CA).

Exner, J. E. (1969). *The Rorschach systems.* New York: Grune & Stratton.

Fernando, A. D. (2008). Examples from the road: Mindlessness in-home. *Journal of Infant, Child, and Adolescent Psychotherapy, 7,* 88–99.

Fernando, A. D., & Langs, J. (2009). *MEGA RFP-23-2009: Child, youth and family system of care, adult and older system of care, behavioral health services.* Submitted grant proposal.

Finn, S. E., & Tonsager, M. E. (1997). Information-gathering and therapeutic models of Assessment: Complementary paradigms. *Psychological Assessment, 9,* 374–385.

Finn, S. E., & Tonsager, M. E. (2002). How therapeutic assessment became humanistic. *The Humanistic Psychologist, 30,* 1022.

Finn, S. E. (2007). *In our client's shoes.* New York: Psychology Press Taylor & Francis Group.

Fischer, C. T. (1970). The testee as co-evaluator. *Journal of Counseling Psychology, 17,* 70–77.

Fischer, C. T. (1985). *Individualizing psychological assessment.* Hillsdale, NJ: Lawrence Erlbaum Associates.

Fischer, C. T. (2000). Collaborative individualized assessment. *Journal of Personality Assessment, 74,* 12-14.

Gin, K. B. (2008). Demands upon the mind for work: Fostering agency within an organization. *Journal of Infant, Child, and Adolescent Psychotherapy, 7,* 79–87.

Goldblatt, N. G. F. (2003). *Assessment of object relations phenomena in foster children.* (Unpublished dissertation, The Wright Institute, Berkeley, CA).

Hamilton, A. M., & Fowler, J. L. (2009). "Why won't my parents help me?": Therapeutic assessment of a child and her family. *Journal of Personality Assessment, 91*(2), 108–120.

Handler, L. (2008). Supervision in therapeutic and collaborative assessment. In A. Hess, K. Hess, & T. Hess (Eds.), *Psychotherapy supervision* (pp. 200–222). New York: Wiley.

Kelly, F. (1999). *The psychological assessment of abused and traumatized children.* New Jersey: Lawrence Erlbaum Associates, Inc.

Kim, K. H. (2005). *An exploratory study of disordered thinking with aggressive children in foster care.* (Unpublished dissertation, The Wright Institute, Berkeley, CA).

Klopfer, W. G. (1954). Principles of report writing. In M. D. Ainsworth, W. G. Klopfer, & R. R. Hold (Eds.), *Developments in the Rorschach technique: Vol. 1 technique and theory* (pp. 601–610). New York: Harcourt, Brace & World.

Kwawer, J. (1980). Primitive interpersonal modes, borderline phenomena, and Rorschach content. In J. Kwawer, A. Sugarman, & P. Lerner (Eds.), *Borderline phenomena and the Rorschach Test* (pp. 89-105). Madison, CT: International Universities Press.

Leary, K. (2000). Racial enactments in dynamic treatment. *Psychoanalytic Dialogues 10*(4), 639–655.

Lerner, P. (2005). Red beavers and building bridges between assessment and treatment. *Journal of Personality Asseessment, 85*(3) 271-279.

Lerner, P. (2007). When we were comrades together: A note on the language of assessment. *Journal of Personality Assessment, 88*(3), 255–263.

Meehl, P. (1954) *Clinical versus statistical prediction: A theoretical analysis and review of the evidence.* Minneapolis, MN: University of Minnesota Press.

McArthur, D. S., & Roberts, G. E. (1982). *Roberts Apperception Test for children: Manual.* Los Angeles, CA: Western Psychological Services.

McDonald, T. & Allen, R. (1996). *Assessing the long-term effects of foster-care: A research synthesis.* Washington, DC: CWLA Press.

Mercer, B. L. (2003, March). *Rorschach variables of children in foster care: W:M ratio, egocentricity ratio, and projective metaphor.* Paper presented at the meeting of the Society for Personality Assessment, San Francisco, CA.

Murray, H. (1943). *Thematic Apperception Test manual.* Cambridge, MA: Harvard University Press.

Needell, B., Webster, D., Armijo, M., Lee, S., Dawson, W., Magruder, J., et al. (2008). *Child welfare services reports for California.* Retrieved from University of California of Berkeley Center for Social Services research website, http://cssr.berkeley.edu/ucb_childwelfare/.

Shaffer, T. W., Erdberg, P., & Meyer, G. J. (2007). Introduction to the JPA special supplement on international reference samples for the Rorschach comprehensive system. *Journal of Personality Assessment, 89*(1), S2–S6.

Smith, S. R. (2007, March). *Collaborative therapeutic neuropsychological assessment: What has been learned one year later?* Paper presented at the meeting of the Society for Personality Assessment, Washington, DC.

Tharinger, D. J., Finn, S. E., Wilkinson, A. D., & Schaber, P. M. (2007). Therapeutic Assessment with a child as a family intervention: A clinical protocol and research case study. *Psychology in the Schools, 44,* 293–309.

Viglione, D. J. (2003). *New ventures in Rorschach interpretation: Systematic methods for case studies.* Paper presented at the meeting of the Society for Personality Assessment, San Francisco, CA.

Viglione, D. J., Perry, W., & Meyer, G. (2003). Refinements in the Rorschach ego impairment index incorporating the human representation variable. *Journal of Personality Assessment, 81*(2), 149–156.

Wechsler, D. (2003). *Wechsler Intelligence Scale for Children, 4th edition (WISC-IV®).* San Antonio, TX: Harcourt Assessment.

Wulczyn, F., Brunner, K. & Goerge, R. (2002). *Multistate foster care data archive.* Chicago, IL: University of Chicago Press.

3 A Descriptive Analysis of Cognitive and Rorschach Variables of Children in a Community Mental Health Clinic

Hasse Leonard-Pagel and Barbara L. Mercer

Literature on children in foster care and low-income urban children has primarily been the purview of social sciences and the humanities, and specifically the field of social work and public health policy. The inclusion of literature with this population specific to psychological assessment, however, is limited. Most of the discussion about foster care, loss of parental care, child trauma, and abuse is related to training caregivers for children placed in their care, stability of placement, educational support, attachment needs, targeted intervention and case management, delinquency, substance abuse, and resilience issues of transitional age youth.

Foster Care Studies

It is encouraging to note that many doctoral dissertations in the past few years have addressed issues specific to foster youth and their caregivers and the post-foster-care future of transitional age youth. These important topics include improving foster-care engagement (Dorsey, Conover, & Revillion Cox, 2014) and placement stability (Hernandez-Mekonnen, 2012). This placement study found that less than one-third of foster care placement disruptions are due to actual youth behavioral problems but are primarily due to system or other circumstances. Policy and practice interventions can potentially mitigate foster parent/foster child communication and attachment dilemmas (McKinney, 2014). This latter interesting investigation into foster-care relationships found that foster parents tend to identify their wards as "a person of a certain sort" and interpret their actions accordingly. By contrast, the foster child is engaged in a communicative struggle to identify as an "acceptable person." Social research has examined the long-term effects of foster placement (McDonald et al., 1996; Meloy & Phillips, 2012) and investigated the ingredients for better outcomes in foster care (Berrick, 2008).

Psychological Assessment and Urban Youth

Few articles have reviewed psychological assessment with low-income and foster-care youth. One study, "Are Two Voices Better Than One?" (Toche-Manley et al., 2014), found that using multi-informant mental health and strength data, including the youth as an informant, significantly improved permanency for minority youth in mental health settings.

Another study analyzed the Differential Ability Scales, Second Edition (Elliot, 2007a) General Conceptual Ability scores with low SES and high SES preschool-age children (Christensen, Schieve, Devine, & Drews-Botsch, 2014). The premise behind the study suggests that disparities in children's achievement and cognitive performance are a function of poorer or better health and overall functioning created by social and economic advantage. The researchers found that individual-level SES status scores (higher and lower) were associated with DAS scores.

Rorschach With Urban Youth and Trauma

Studies exploring the Rorschach and foster youth and urban poor youth are few. One study (Crowell, 2001) compared the Rorschach of sexual abuse victims to inner-city, commercially sexually exploited minors and found more trauma content in the Rorschach protocols of the sexually exploited minor (SEM) group. Another compared adolescent female offenders to female offenders engaged in prostitution and found increased symptoms on multiple scales. Significant symptoms noted in the sexually exploited population included dissociation, post-traumatic stress, distress, negative self-concept, and sexual concerns and problems (Lerach, 2008). Other dissertations focused on psychological testing with trauma, multiple foster placements, and parental separations (Cohon & Cooper, 2002; Hagino, 2002; Goldblatt, 2003; Kim, 2005; Eshom, 2006). In a descriptive study conducted with 72 clinic foster children (Mercer, 2003), 92 percent had a Rorschach Egocentricity Ratio (a ratio related to a solid sense of self) over one standard deviation below their age norm; 78 percent had a W:M ratio (a ratio of a person's aspirations to available resources) outside the norm; and 42 percent were DEPI positive (an index measuring depression). Several studies and literature look at Rorschach and traumatized children and youth. Kelley (1999) was one of the first to contribute to an in-depth exploration of the inner world and object relations of traumatized children. Other studies include a Rorschach investigation of childhood sexual abuse severity with results correlating sexual abuse severity with problems in affect regulation (Zodan et al., 2014). Resnick (2012) examined profiles of traumatized inner-city children, and children referred for reported child abuse with and without diagnosed PTSD. He found dissociative symptoms and constriction to be a prominent feature of children who had been abused as well as children who lived in communities with violence. He connected constriction symptoms to a numbing of trauma, and a flooding presentation and more complexity of response to attempts to work through acute trauma exposure. Armstrong (2002) noted that the Rorschach is a valuable instrument when attempting to access both traumatic intrusive material as well as the defensive dissociative process resulting from trauma. Doctoral researchers explored Rorschach variables of attachment achievements related to foster children (DellaCorte, 2008), and found a security of attachment on an attachment technique measure (George, Soloman & deJong, 1995) correlated with emotional regulation and good human representation on the Rorschach. Another dissertation study used seven Rorschach attachment and object-relations variables to discriminate risk factors related to violent and nonviolent African American inner-city adolescents (Caswell, 2001). More foundational research differentiated chronic trauma responses from psychotic symptoms (Viglione, 1990), guided the development of the Trauma Content Index (Armstrong & Loewenstein, 1990) and its use with different populations (Kampuis, Kugeares, & Finn, 2000), and its incorporation into the new Rorschach structural system, R-PAS (Rorschach Performance Assessment System, 2011)

Documenting the psycho-diagnostic data of low-income, minority, foster care children and adolescents, and comparing them to the majority population, is way overdue. Our research and this project is an attempt to add to a limited body of literature. This descriptive study provides cognitive, coping, affective, and self/other personality variables of 120 children using the DAS-II and the Rorschach. We examined results from DAS composite scores (Verbal Composite Scores, Nonverbal Composite Score, and the Spatial Composite Score) and Rorschach scores of children and adolescents between 6 and 16 years of age. These children were referred for a psychological evaluation at our community mental health clinic between the years of 2006 and 2010. This sample includes primarily children of color from lower socioeconomic backgrounds, and a high percentage of our sample was living in foster care during the time of the evaluation. Data was compared to normative data of the DAS and Rorschach variables of coping, affect, interpersonal, self-perception, and thought processes. The purpose of the study is to delineate descriptive psychological assessment data that can illuminate the experience of low-income urban children in relation to a normative experience, and give direction to further research.

Methodology

Participants

One hundred and twenty children and adolescents' archival assessment data were used in this study. Archival assessment data from children and adolescents were analyzed. These children's ages ranged from 6 to 16 and they were assessed during a four-year period, between 2006 and 2010. These children and adolescents were 80 percent African American, 10 percent Hispanic/Latino, 6 percent Asian (Samoan, Filipino, Hawaii Native, Chinese), 3 percent Caucasian, and 1 percent Native American; 83 percent had resided or currently were residing in a foster care placement and were from a low-income urban community.

Procedures

Archival data was used from the administered DAS-II and Rorschach of children and adolescents ranging from ages 6 to 16 and who sought services at our community clinic in the Bay Area of Northern California between the years of 2006 and 2010. Licensed psychology staff, postdoctoral fellows, and doctoral interns administered the DAS-II and the Rorschach. Only school-aged battery data was included in this study. Staff and trainees all received intensive training in child assessment and the Rorschach. All scoring on cognitive and Rorschach measures was reviewed and approved by licensed psychologist supervisors. The Rorschach was administered using the Comprehensive System standardized instructions.

For inclusion criteria, completed and scored DAS-II core subtests were required along with valid Rorschach protocols. All caregivers and legal guardians gave consent for data to be included in research at our community clinic.

Measures

Differential Ability Scales, Second Edition (DAS-II) (Elliot, 2007a) is a comprehensive cognitive measure that assesses cognitive abilities and processing as it relates to learning (Elliot, 2007b). The DAS-II provides an in-depth analysis of both children and adolescents' cognitive strengths and weaknesses. Similar to the Wechsler Intelligence Scale for Children IV (Wechsler, 2004; FSIQ), the DAS-II General Conceptual Ability (GCA) is based on the Cattell-Horn-Carroll Theory (CHC) measure of g. The DAS-II composite scores provide information about a child and/or adolescents Verbal Ability, Nonverbal Ability, Spatial Ability, and Special Nonverbal Composite. Diagnostic subtests are available to tease out specific cognitive issues that might be impeding a child's ability to learn.

According to the author (Elliot, 2007b), the "DAS-II helps you find out why a child isn't learning, and targets the specific nature of the problem, so that appropriate intervention strategies can be identified. It's a well-rounded assessment of a child's strengths and ability that also enables measuring change over time, in order to monitor progress." "The Das-II measures the g factor only by those sub-tests that are the best estimates of g, in contrast to virtually all other cognitive batteries. The DAS does not refer to g by the terms intelligence of IQ, but by the term General Conceptual Ability" (Pearson Clinical, n.d.).

This cognitive assessment measure was chosen in order to meet the needs of the population served at the community clinic where the archival data was collected. More commonly used IQ measures are not employed for African American children in public schools in the Bay Area due to Larry P. v. Wilson Riles (1979 [1974]). The court determined that individual intelligence tests could not provide a fair assessment of minority children and prohibited the use of individual IQ tests with African American Children. "The DAS-II is appropriate for diverse populations as it can predict achievement on the basis of ability equally well for African-American, Asian, Hispanic, and White/Non-Hispanic children" (Pearson Clinical, n.d.).

The Exner Comprehensive System (Exner, 1974, 2003) has been in popular use for 40 years; it is used widely both clinically and academically to understand the psycho-diagnostic picture of a client. Another interpretive system (Rorschach Performance Assessment System, 2011) grounded in an evidence-based meta-analysis of Rorschach research studies, has been developed based on international norms (Meyer, Erdberg & Shaffer, 2007). Normative data for children is continuing to be gathered for both clinical and nonclinical population.

The data in this study was collected and analyzed prior to the development of the new interpretive procedures. However, in our study, we chose one variable from each cluster of the Rorschach that was also found among the most strongly supported variables in a meta-analysis of 65 variables (Mihura et al., 2012) in the Comprehensive system, and now incorporated into the R-PAS system (Rorschach Performance Assessment System, 2011).

. The following variables from the Rorschach were chosen: Lambda, or F% (part of the Coping Cluster), is a measurement of nuance or multiple ideas (versus avoidance and emotional constriction and suppression); Blends and Synthesis Responses, or DQ+ (part of the Cognitive Triad), are measures of engagement and complexity of information processing; MOR (from the Self-Perception Cluster) is a measure of feelings about the self; Affective Ratio (from the Affect Cluster) is related to emotional style; and GHR:PHR (part of the Interpersonal Cluster) is a reflection of one's representation of others and expectations for relationships.

Lambda, DQ+, and Blends all relate to the factors of complexity, components that have a high correlation with the first factor of the Rorschach factor analysis (Meyer & Viglione, 2006). These variables are particularly associated with complex thinking or the ability to think in cause-and-effect terms. The Affective Ratio is related to emotional engagement and the Morbid variable is related to the presence of morbid thoughts images or feelings, resulting in a damaged sense of self. Morbid responses were found to have more correlation with dysphoria than the Depression Index on the Comprehensive Structural Summary (Rorschach Performance Assessment System, 2011). The GHR:PHR ratio relates to the understanding of relationships with others, whether healthy and adaptive or distressed and maladaptive.

Results

Findings from the DAS-II only include the Verbal Composite Scores, the Nonverbal Composite Score, and the Spatial Composite Scores. The General Ability Composite Scores was not included due to the Core Subtests variability or too much scatter between the Composite Scores. The findings from the DAS-II are shown in Table 3.1

Verbal Composite Score

Children in the 6 to 8 age group's Verbal Composite Scores ranged from 65 to 123. The median for this age group was 96. The 9- to 11-year-old group's Verbal Composite Scores ranged from 54 to 115. The median for this age group was 89. The 12- to 14-year-old group's Verbal Composite Scores ranged from 37 to 109. The median for this group was 88. The 15- to 16-year-old age group ranged from 57 to 119. The median for the older group was 88.

Nonverbal Composite Score

Children in the 6 to 8 age group's Nonverbal Composite Scores ranged from 70 to 111. The median for this age group was 90. The 9-to 11-year-old group's Nonverbal Composite scores ranged from 59 to 129. The median for this age group was 89. The 12-to 14-year-old group's Verbal Composite Scores ranged from 69 to 103. The median was 84. The 15- to 16-year-old age group ranged from 64 to 107 on the Nonverbal Composite score. The median was 84.

Spatial Composite Score

Children in the 6 to 8 age group's Spatial Composite Scores ranged from 83 to 130. The median for this age group was 95. The 9- to 11-year-old group's Spatial Composite Scores ranged from 64 to 132. The median for this age group was 90. The 12- to 14-year-old group's Spatial Composite Scores ranged from 63 to 105. The median was 83. The 15- to 16-year-old age group ranged from 68 to 102. The median was 83.

Table 3.1 DAS II Results

Age in Categories		Verbal Composite Scores	DAS Nonverbal Composite Scores	DAS Spatial Composite Scores	DAS GCA Scores	DAS WM Scores	DAS PrSp Scores
6 to 8	Median	95.50	90.00	95.00	94.00	86.00	94.00
	Grouped Median	95.50	90.20	95.00	93.71	86.00	94.00
	Minimum	65.00	79.00	83.00	76.00	40.00	73.00
	Maximum	123.00	111.00	130.00	109.00	98.00	102.00
	Range	58.00	32.00	47.00	33.00	58.00	29.00
9 to 11	Median	89.00	89.00	90.00	89.00	88.00	96.00
	Grouped Median	89.00	88.33	90.00	88.75	87.00	95.67
	Minimum	54.00	59.00	64.00	61.00	35.00	62.00
	Maximum	115.00	129.00	132.00	132.00	105.00	121.00
	Range	61.00	70.00	68.00	71.00	70.00	59.00
12 to 14	Median	88.00	84.00	83.00	84.00	83.00	82.00
	Grouped Median	87.67	84.33	83.00	83.67	84.50	82.00
	Minimum	37.00	69.00	63.00	57.00	56.00	49.00
	Maximum	109.00	103.00	105.00	101.00	112.00	128.00
	Range	72.00	34.00	42.00	44.00	56.00	79.00
15 to 16	Median	88.00	84.00	83.00	86.00	89.50	83.00
	Grouped Median	88.00	84.33	83.00	86.00	89.33	84.33
	Minimum	57.00	64.00	68.00	63.00	76.00	65.00
	Maximum	119.00	107.00	102.00	107.00	105.00	106.00
	Range	62.00	43.00	34.00	44.00	29.00	41.00
Total	Median	90.00	88.00	87.00	88.00	87.00	92.00
	Grouped Median	89.80	87.57	87.67	88.00	86.67	92.00
	Minimum	37.00	59.00	63.00	57.00	35.00	49.00
	Maximum	123.00	129.00	132.00	132.00	112.00	128.00
	Range	86.00	70.00	69.00	75.00	77.00	79.00

Lambda

Findings from the t-test (Table 3.2) indicated that children in the age groups of 6 to 8 and 9 to 11 significantly differed from children in their normative group when endorsing Pure Form responses, which produced a high Lambda. In the older age groups of 12 to 14 and 15 to 17, there was no statistically significant difference between this sample and the normative group.

Table 3.2 Coping Variables

Coping Variables : Age 6 to 8

	t	df	Sig. (2–tailed)	Mean Difference	95% Confidence Interval of the Difference	
					Lower	Upper
Lambda	2.991	26	.006	.5592926	.174931	.943654
D	.353	26	.727	.053	−.26	.36
M−	.637	26	.529	.083	−.19	.35
EA	−6.307	26	.000	−3.0455	−4.038	−2.053
CDI	17.389	26	.000	3.519	3.10	3.93
m	1.311	26	.201	.397	−.23	1.02
FM	−7.836	26	.000	−2.683	−3.39	−1.98

Coping Variables : Age 9 to 11

	t	df	Sig. (2–tailed)	Mean Difference	95% Confidence Interval of the Difference	
					Lower	Upper
Lambda	2.775	32	.009	.8648485	.230109	1.499588
D	−1.427	32	.163	−.350	−.85	.15
M−	1.914	32	.065	.481	−.03	.99
EA	−5.571	32	.000	−3.1121	−4.250	−1.974
CDI	14.414	32	.000	3.121	2.68	3.56
m	1.808	32	.080	.568	−.07	1.21
FM	−6.400	32	.000	−1.834	−2.42	−1.25

Coping Variables : Age 12 to 14

	t	df	Sig. (2–tailed)	Mean Difference	95% Confidence Interval of the Difference	
					Lower	Upper
Lambda	3.169	36	.003	.7930297	.285537	1.300523
D	−1.425	36	.163	−.329	−.80	.14
M−	2.466	36	.019	.539	.10	.98
EA	−7.393	36	.000	−3.4244	−4.364	−2.485
CDI	15.934	36	.000	3.216	2.81	3.63
m	.413	36	.682	.097	−.38	.57
FM	−5.578	36	.000	−1.948	−2.66	−1.24

continued …

Table 3.2 continued

Coping Variables : Age 15 to 16

	t	*df*	*Sig. (2–tailed)*	*Mean Difference*	95% Confidence Interval of the Difference	
					Lower	*Upper*
Lambda	1.150	17	.266	.2633333	−.219863	.746530
D	.914	17	.373	.158	−.21	.52
M−	2.980	17	.008	1.228	.36	2.10
EA	−1.700	17	.107	−1.7894	−4.010	.431
CDI	8.751	17	.000	2.722	2.07	3.38
m	.679	17	.506	.234	−.49	.96
FM	−5.526	17	.000	−2.200	−3.04	−1.36
Lambda	1.150	17	.266	.2633333	−.219863	.746530

Affective Ratio

Across all of the age groups, the Affective Ratio was statistically significant when compared to the normative group (Table 3.3). This sample had fewer responses to chromatic cards; they pulled away from emotional stimuli or situations.

Morbid Responses

There was not a significant difference (Table 3.4) between the 6 to 8 age sample group and the normative sample when endorsing Morbid content. The 9 to 11 age group, 12 to 14 age group, and the 15 to 16 age group were all statistically significantly different when compared to the normative population, indicating that they reported more Morbid content in their responses.

GHR:PHR

Results from the t-test from the variable GHR:PHR, found that there was a statistically significant difference between this sample and the normative group (Table 3.5). This finding suggests that children and adolescents within this sample reported fewer Good Human Responses (GHR) and reported more Poor Human Responses (PHR). In the 15 to 16 age group, there were almost four times as many PHRs to GHRs responses.

Blends and Synthesis Responses

Results from the t-test indicated that the age groups of 6 to 8, 9 to 11, and 12 to 14 had fewer Blends when compared to the normative group (Table 3.6). Only the older adolescents showed some comparable flexibility to their normative counterparts.

The DQ+ yielded statistically significant differences across all age groups, with fewer synthesis responses when compared to the normative group.

Table 3.3 Affective Variables

Affective Variables: Age 6 to 8

	t	df	Sig. (2–tailed)	Mean Difference	95% Confidence Interval of the Difference	
					Lower	Upper
SumC'	.554	26	.584	.142	−.38	.67
Sum V	2.431	26	.022	.185	.03	.34
SumT	−11.462	26	.000	−.799	−.94	−.66
Sum Y	−2.074	26	.048	−.267	−.53	.00
Mor	1.902	26	.068	.420	−.03	.87
Affect Ratio	−4.462	26	.000	−.3140407	−.458724	−.169357
An+xy	4.082	26	.000	.770	.38	1.16
AG	−3.836	26	.001	−.423	−.65	−.20
S−	3.661	26	.001	.703	.31	1.10
WSmC	−5.037	26	.000	−2.0215	−2.846	−1.197
Pure C	−1.325	26	.197	−.268	−.68	.15
FC	−.651	26	.521	−.249	−1.03	.54
Cf+C	−6.272	26	.000	−2.152	−2.86	−1.45

Affective Variables : Age 9 to 11

	t	df	Sig. (2–tailed)	Mean Difference	95% Confidence Interval of the Difference	
					Lower	Upper
SumC'	.702	31	.488	.215	−.41	.84
Sum V	1.278	32	.210	.054	−.03	.14
SumT	−5.546	32	.000	−.660	−.90	−.42
Sum Y	.286	32	.777	.054	−.33	.44
Mor	2.851	32	.008	1.144	.33	1.96
Affect Ratio	−4.294	32	.000	−.2733333	−.402998	−.143668
An+xy	1.753	32	.089	.535	−.09	1.16
AG	−3.852	32	.001	−.665	−1.02	−.31
S−	2.786	32	.009	.480	.13	.83
WSmC	−7.688	32	.000	−2.3406	−2.961	−1.720
Pure C	.193	32	.848	.023	−.22	.27
FC	−2.546	32	.016	−.851	−1.53	−.17
Cf+C	−7.680	32	.000	−1.944	−2.46	−1.43

continued …

Table 3.3 continued

Affective Variables : Age 12 to 14

	t	df	Sig. (2–tailed)	Mean Difference	95% Confidence Interval of the Difference	
					Lower	Upper
SumC'	.248	36	.805	.059	−.42	.54
Sum V	.795	36	.432	.049	−.08	.17
SumT	−10.647	36	.000	−.730	−.87	−.59
Sum Y	−1.378	36	.177	−.321	−.79	.15
Mor	4.491	36	.000	1.394	.76	2.02
Affect Ratio	−3.864	36	.000	−.1967000	−.299931	−.093469
An+xy	−.436	36	.665	−.102	−.58	.37
AG	−6.747	36	.000	−.829	−1.08	−.58
S−	1.930	36	.061	.263	−.01	.54
WSmC	−5.687	36	.000	−1.7505	−2.375	−1.126
Pure C	1.337	36	.190	.138	−.07	.35
FC	−6.954	36	.000	−1.511	−1.95	−1.07
Cf+C	−5.314	36	.000	−1.385	−1.91	−.86

Affective Variables: Age 15 to 16

	t	df	Sig. (2–tailed)	Mean Difference	95% Confidence Interval of the Difference	
					Lower	Upper
SumC'	.531	17	.602	.332	−.99	1.65
Sum V	.917	17	.372	.148	−.19	.49
SumT	−8.110	17	.000	−.818	−1.03	−.61
Sum Y	.268	17	.792	.108	−.74	.96
Mor	3.848	17	.001	1.662	.75	2.57
Affect Ratio	−2.698	17	.015	−.1938889	−.345504	−.042273
An+xy	.108	17	.915	.034	−.64	.71
AG	−2.611	17	.018	−.564	−1.02	−.11
S−	1.254	17	.227	.251	−.17	.67
WSmC	−3.638	17	.002	−1.8483	−2.920	−.776
Pure C	4.022	17	.001	.576	.27	.88
FC	−4.230	17	.001	−1.785	−2.68	−.89
Cf+C	−2.264	17	.037	−.906	−1.75	−.06

Table 3.4 Self Perception Variables

Self Perception Variables: Age 6 to 8

	t	df	Sig. (2–tailed)	Mean Difference	95% Confidence Interval of the Difference	
					Lower	Upper
Egocentricity Index	−15.271	26	.000	−.5274407	−.598434	−.456447
Mor	1.902	26	.068	.420	−.03	.87
An+xy	4.082	26	.000	.770	.38	1.16
(H)+Hd+(Hd)	1.219	26	.234	.443	−.30	1.19

Self Perception Variables: Age 9 to 11

	t	df	Sig. (2–tailed)	Mean Difference	95% Confidence Interval of the Difference	
					Lower	Upper
Egocentricity Index	−8.816	32	.000	−.3721545	−.458142	−.286167
Mor	2.851	32	.008	1.144	.33	1.96
An+xy	1.753	32	.089	.535	−.09	1.16
(H)+Hd+(Hd)	1.684	32	.102	.751	−.16	1.66

Self Perception Variables: Age 12 to 14

	t	df	Sig. (2–tailed)	Mean Difference	95% Confidence Interval of the Difference	
					Lower	Upper
Egocentricity Index	−9.027	36	.000	−.3000000	−.367402	−.232598
Mor	4.491	36	.000	1.394	.76	2.02
An+xy	−.436	36	.665	−.102	−.58	.37
(H)+Hd+(Hd)	1.498	36	.143	.561	−.20	1.32

Self Perception Variables: Age 15 to 16

	t	df	Sig. (2–tailed)	Mean Difference	95% Confidence Interval of the Difference	
					Lower	Upper
Egocentricity Index	−1.918	17	.072	−.1272222	−.267157	.012712
Mor	3.848	17	.001	1.662	.75	2.57
An+xy	.108	17	.915	.034	−.64	.71
(H)+Hd+(Hd)	2.214	17	.041	1.082	.05	2.11

Table 3.5 Interpersonal Variables

Interpersonal Variables: Age 6 to 8

	t	df	Sig. (2–tailed)	Mean Difference	95% Confidence Interval of the Difference	
					Lower	Upper
COP	−8.617	26	.000	−1.239	−1.53	−.94
AG	−3.836	26	.001	−.423	−.65	−.20
GHR	−8.726	26	.000	−2.456	−3.03	−1.88
PHR	4.849	26	.000	1.804	1.04	2.57
H	−2.439	26	.022	−.640	−1.18	−.10
Isolation Index	−5.885	26	.000	−.1529963	−.206433	−.099559
active	−6.770	26	.000	−3.095	−4.04	−2.16
passive	−1.237	26	.227	−.381	−1.01	.25

Interpersonal Variables: Age 9 to 11

	t	df	Sig. (2–tailed)	Mean Difference	95% Confidence Interval of the Difference	
					Lower	Upper
COP	−4.632	32	.000	−.955	−1.38	−.54
AG	−3.852	32	.001	−.665	−1.02	−.31
GHR	−9.836	32	.000	−2.724	−3.29	−2.16
PHR	5.255	32	.000	2.761	1.69	3.83
H	−2.591	32	.014	−.744	−1.33	−.16
Isolation Index	−2.466	32	.019	−.0863303	−.157648	−.015013
active	−4.013	32	.000	−2.009	−3.03	−.99
passive	−1.917	32	.064	−.735	−1.52	.05

Interpersonal Variables: Age 12 to 14

	t	df	Sig. (2–tailed)	Mean Difference	95% Confidence Interval of the Difference	
					Lower	Upper
COP	−7.239	36	.000	−.996	−1.28	−.72
AG	−6.747	36	.000	−.829	−1.08	−.58
GHR	−9.553	36	.000	−2.951	−3.58	−2.32
PHR	4.183	36	.000	1.841	.95	2.73
H	−6.161	36	.000	−1.535	−2.04	−1.03
Isolation Index	−2.260	36	.030	−.0437270	−.082964	−.004490
active	−6.383	36	.000	−2.530	−3.33	−1.73
passive	−3.443	36	.001	−1.078	−1.71	−.44

Interpersonal Variables: Age 15 to 16

	t	df	Sig. (2-tailed)	Mean Difference	95% Confidence Interval of the Difference	
					Lower	Upper
COP	−3.827	17	.001	−.792	−1.23	−.36
AG	−2.611	17	.018	−.564	−1.02	−.11
GHR	−2.991	17	.008	−1.928	−3.29	−.57
PHR	4.464	17	.000	2.746	1.45	4.04
H	−.778	17	.448	−.627	−2.33	1.07
Isolation Index	−1.854	17	.081	−.0594444	−.127077	.008188
active	−2.860	17	.011	−2.461	−4.28	−.65
passive	.685	17	.503	.543	−1.13	2.22

Discussion

This is a descriptive naturalized study, unlike a quasi-statistical experiment. We did not randomly assign children to groups; they were sorted by their life circumstances. The DAS-II findings suggest that our sample's range of composite scores are not uncommon for other children who experience poverty, move from place to place due to being in foster care, or who have had limited access to a consistent education. Our findings all suggest that even with many risk factors, some children and adolescents in our sample also represent the higher end of the DAS-II composite scores, suggesting there are also many resilient factors that protect their cognitive abilities.

In reporting t-test scores for the Rorschach, we were interested in how our sample differed significantly from the normal sample. In looking at the Exner normative data, it is important to consider the demographics of this group. In the 1970s, the normative sample was procured from children of Midwest faculty, who would be classified today as "super normal kids" from high functioning, intact, upper middle class families (Exner & Weiner, 1995). The Exner Comprehensive child norms have not been updated since the 1980s. Findings from a study of private school parochial children with predominantly intact families (Hamel, Erdberg & Shaffer, 2007) found that their sample looked "unhealthy" most specifically related to reality convergence (Xo% and X-%) when compared to the existing Exner Comprehensive norms. As a result of this study, and others that provided a wide variability of results when comparing different samples of children from the United States and abroad to the Exner's normative group children, a group of researchers developed a new scoring system for the Rorschach, the R-PAS, (Rorschach Performance Assessment System, 2011). The developers of the R-PAS are currently working on gathering international child and adolescent norms in order to have a more balanced and updated normative group. Our study was initiated prior to the R-PAS; however, we have since insured that the variables chosen matched the variables supported by the meta-analysis of the journal studies. We also chose variables that looked at emotional variables and the quality of self and other representations (as opposed to reality convergence).

Table 3.6 Cognitive Triad

Cognitive Triad: Age 6 to 8

	t	*df*	*Sig. (2–tailed)*	*Mean Difference*	95% Confidence Interval of the Difference	
					Lower	*Upper*
WSUm 6	1.970	26	.060	6.479	−.28	13.24
Lvl 2	3.171	26	.004	1.369	.48	2.26
DQ+	−3.859	26	.001	−1.678	−2.57	−.78
DQv	−4.504	26	.000	−.949	−1.38	−.52
Blends	−6.946	26	.000	−2.013	−2.61	−1.42
X–%	3.197	26	.004	.1425593	.050909	.234209
Zd	3.818	26	.001	2.7252	1.258	4.192
P	−5.364	26	.000	−1.928	−2.67	−1.19

Cognitive Triad: Age 9 to 11

	t	*df*	*Sig. (2–tailed)*	*Mean Difference*	95% Confidence Interval of the Difference	
					Lower	*Upper*
WSUm 6	1.935	32	.062	4.088	−.22	8.39
Lvl 2	3.170	32	.003	.716	.26	1.18
DQ+	−5.170	32	.000	−2.838	−3.96	−1.72
DQv	−.751	32	.458	−.199	−.74	.34
Blends	−5.887	32	.000	−2.437	−3.28	−1.59
X–%	1.978	32	.057	.0896970	−.002655	.182049
Zd	.658	32	.515	.4524	−.947	1.852
P	−8.217	32	.000	−2.455	−3.06	−1.85

Cognitive Triad: Age 12 to 14

	t	*df*	*Sig. (2–tailed)*	*Mean Difference*	95% Confidence Interval of the Difference	
					Lower	*Upper*
WSUm 6	.755	36	.455	.879	−1.48	3.24
Lvl 2	.819	36	.418	.112	−.17	.39
DQ+	−11.724	36	.000	−4.214	−4.94	−3.49
DQv	−.727	36	.472	−.095	−.36	.17
Blends	−3.096	36	.004	−3.016	−4.99	−1.04
X–%	2.587	36	.014	.0944054	.020391	.168419
Zd	−1.135	36	.264	−.8995	−2.507	.708
P	−7.901	36	.000	−2.491	−3.13	−1.85

Cognitive Triad: Age 15 to 16

	t	df	Sig. (2-tailed)	Mean Difference	95% Confidence Interval of the Difference	
					Lower	Upper
WSUm 6	2.871	17	.011	8.764	2.32	15.21
Lvl 2	2.244	17	.038	.809	.05	1.57
DQ+	−2.468	17	.024	−2.354	−4.37	−.34
DQv	−.671	17	.512	−.153	−.64	.33
Blends	−.583	17	.567	−1.225	−5.66	3.21
X−%	2.817	17	.012	.1033333	.025931	.180736
Zd	.391	17	.700	.4528	−1.989	2.894
P	−4.850	17	.000	−2.617	−3.76	−1.48

Lambda

When a Rorschach protocol has primarily pure form responses (a high Lambda) it suggests that an individual or sample has provided very concrete responses or has not used a great deal of sophistication or complexity in responding. This is common in a population who has experienced developmental trauma including parental loss, abuse, attachment disruptions and lack of stable home environment. In previous studies, (Resnick, 2012; Lerach, 2008; Armstrong, 2002) looking at the impact of personal and/or community trauma on children and adolescents, findings support dissociation, constriction, and avoidance of trauma-related distress. When children are removed from their homes and their parents—their secure environment—no matter how distressful or untenable the situation has been, they continue to yearn for their early attachments. They can't risk feeling the intensity of the loss and trauma, nor can they trust forming new relationships because doing so calls up the risk of losing the desired parent, feelings of self-blame for the removal, and the reality that the new person can also disappear. Their navigation system goes on "shut-down." High Lambda on the Rorschach precludes or depresses the presence of more complex variables such as stress and distress (shading responses), ability for planning, imagining, and directed action (Movement responses), and Self and Other representation (Aggression, Cooperative responses). Therefore, the ability to self-regulate, skills in cause and effect thinking, problem solving, and flexibility are compromised. Their circumstances put them at a disadvantage. Navigating school years, home life, friendships, social relationships, and later intimate relationships becomes difficult, and decreases their potential for success in school and beyond. While a high Lambda creates a defensive wall, it is at a great cost to flexible functioning and learning. One adolescent, a victim of molestation from a male relative, gave this second response after seeing an anatomy response of pure form on Card IV: "a chest, the kidneys, half the body"; "I have no clue what this is. I don't wanna do this. (Examiner: Do you need more time?) Nope." As this population moves into adolescence, they may at least have the potential to be more engaged with complexity and provide more flexible sophisticated responses, although not necessarily healthy responses. Here are some adolescent complex, less adaptive examples: "Two men grabbing on two women that have their arms in the air"; Two women birds with boobs, long legs, and super long knee caps and they both have heels on. It looks like they are holding half a penis"; "Cotton candy with trees are here and these are their stumps and there's fire on top"; "Death because it's all black, with feelings under it, this is the heart here inside it"; "Looks like the Titanic about to crash into an iceberg." And with the potential for more adaptive adolescent responses: "Two girls dancing around the lake, the light is shining on them and reflecting off the water"; "Two people each holding a green leaf and bringing it to the ocean"; "a rocket ship with engine things and a landing pad and these are the windows."

Affective Ratio

The Affective Ratio across all age groups points to an emotional pulling away from affective stimuli in the environment. This supports the Complex Development Trauma (van der Kolk, 2005) profile documented in lives of the children in our study. There is a psychic numbing and dissociation (Armstrong & Loewenstein, 1990) of internal and external emotional responsiveness. The avoidance of reminders of trauma then can produce the difficulty with self-regulation when situations or relationships surrounding those memories are triggered. In our study, we found that across all age groups in this sample, age groups reported fewer Aggressive responses when compared to their normative group. While this may be an artifact of their high Lambda, constriction suggests that children and adolescents who experience this suppression of normal anger and intense emotion are denying their anger, thus making them more susceptible to dysregulation and behavioral and relational problems. Studies of children in high conflict divorce show a strong tendency to withdraw from emotionally tinged events (to wall off on one's own). There is no opportunity to be self-reflective about thoughts or feelings. It is part of a survival reaction, and as a result they often feel that things are being done to them rather than feeling like they have control over their lives. In our sample, even with a high Lambda, there were persistent intrusions of traumatic material throughout their protocols. This is consistent with research about the vacillation from constriction to flooding with post-trauma reactions (Armstrong, 2002; Resnick, 2012). Here are some responses from the children in our sample: "Like a heart that got cut in half or something went through it, something went through it to make it deformed"; "looks like a spirit being dragged in hell, with the little flames are bringing it down"; "Two rabbits playing paddy-cake but someone shot them in the leg."

Morbid Responses

Only the youngest group endorsed Morbid content at the same rate as the normative sample. Children and youth from 9 to 16 had significantly more Morbid content responses, indicative of a pessimistic, fragile and damaged sense of self. Examples from our sample include: "Moldy disgusting meat"; " a broken wing"; "a scary face with blood"; "an otter, all bloody"; "aborted babies"; "a rat on a stick"; "a man without a head"; "a piece of useless track"; "a corrupted Mickey Mouse"; "a person this is their bow but their head is cut off"; Researchers have documented that the Rorschach is a useful instrument for capturing the impact of trauma on an individual. Unlike in a self-report measure developed specifically to assess for symptoms associated with traumatic experiences, the Rorschach is more sensitive to tapping into these associations or traumatic images because of the projective nature of the instrument (Armstrong, 2002; Viglione, 1990). These morbid responses are associated with a dysphoric sense of self and outlook on life.

Human Representation

Across all age groups, our sample showed a predominance of Poor Human Representations over Good Human Representations. Poor Human Responses have been correlated with difficulty with disorganized attachment (DellaCorte, 2012; Rorschach Performance Assessment System, 2011). Good Human Representation responses in the comprehensive system are described as human or quasi-human images that are "logical, benign, and undamaged" (Mihura, et al., 2012). Some examples from our sample include: "Two monks bowing to each other," or "Two mermaids playing underwater flute together"; "two boys giving each other some awesome high fives." These examples produce the likelihood of a healthy and adaptive understanding of others. This creates the potential for reciprocity in relationships. Poor Human Representation responses are classified as human or quasi-human images that are "illogical, damaged, aggressive or poorly formed creating a disturbed or maladaptive understanding of relationships" (Mihura, et. al, 2012); for example, the following came from a six-year-old boy in our clinic sample: "This is blood. They killed each other. They're standing up doing it. They killed a boy so they can have a date." From an adolescent boy: "A bear being crucified, and two bears being hanged," from a sexually exploited adolescent girl: "here are skeletons with blond hair, and here's their cockroach body"; "Two dudes got shot in the leg and they're laying down … they hit their heads, and all that, the rest up there is their blood"; "a skeleton with fire coming out." As we see from our results, there is more of a distortion of relationships as children in our sample move into mid-adolescence. This finding suggests that although there is more sophisticated responding in the Rorschach for these youth, their internal object representations are rooted in hopelessness and distrust. For children under five, this finding speaks to how early a disrupted attachment with a parent can derail the hope for loving care and the belief in self. The five-year-old who saw many trains on the Rorschach and "a useless piece of track" had been abandoned by his mother who left on a train and didn't return. The only way to repair this internal sense of despair and self-blame is to find other stable and caring relationships that can endure this painful "living past" and help with new experiences. For older children, it is a reminder that their experience of what happens in interpersonal relationships does not generate conventional test data, given that their upbringing and stability is not conventional. PHR can reflect children's social stimulus value, and thus the way they come across to people can be off-putting. Their interpersonal competence is undeveloped, the likelihood of missing social cues and relational ability. Relationships are often construed as threatening and harmful, with an imbalance of power. These perceptions impact children's ability to navigate school, friendships, and competence in life.

Synthesis and Blends

Results of Synthesized and Blend Responses in this study show a significant statistical difference from the normative sample. This substantiates the finding related to Lambda, more specifically complexity, in our population. Even mid-adolescents have fewer synthesized responses, although they are beginning to show a normal number of Blend responses. We can see as youth mature, their emotional engagement resembles conventional adolescents. They are beginning to have the capacity to engage in the world in a more flexible manner. There is an opening for them to be more present in their environment, although they still need to develop the ability to make meaning of their experience and integrate information in an organized way. For example, one adolescent responded to a card stating: "A totem pole with the tribe moving all around it"; "A butterfly and foxes on the outside and nature, the mountain top and green trees, maybe they're all connected." From a ten year-old boy: "Two bats hugging or flying towards each other"; "I see those trees in the Savannah, those Baobab trees all spread out, how the light green fades out and goes to dark green." These responses reflect the findings of Goldblatt (2003) who found that the object relations of foster children were similar to an acute PTSD population (and dissimilar to a psychiatric child population) where both damaged and healthy mutuality of autonomy responses exist in individual protocols.

Limitations of Study and Future Research

The norms used in this study are derived from the original child standardization sample (Exner & Weiner, 1995) and are not representative of norms that are representative of the current population. Some researchers continue to use the original child norms as the best reference to interpret their findings. Other researchers have accumulated norms from international child samples at each age group. When we initiated this study, there were not sufficient international data to accurately represent children and adolescent from urban communities. Future research will look at clinical groups in contrast to updated international norms and compare a variety of clinical populations. With the increased utilization of the Child Assessment of Needs and Strengths Checklist (Lyons, Griffin, Fazio, & Lyons, 1999) in documenting problem areas for treatment planning and care acuity, it would be beneficial to look at the relationship of this external criterion of symptom severity to assessment data and diagnostic categories in foster care and urban population. It would be useful to look at diagnostic categories of our population related to the Developmental Trauma Diagnosis (van der Kolk et. al, 2009) versus the strict DSM-V Post-Traumatic Stress Diagnosis.

The other vital area of research is to examine the psychological variables that contribute to a child's ability to engage in more competent problem solving. How do we support children's psychological complexity, flexibility, and problem-solving ability? How do we assist in building optimism, more emotional engagement, less numbing and distancing, and more trusting and adaptive feeling about relationships. Research in treatment outcome of foster and urban youth, as well as youth and caregiver data related to strength and needs, is the next step for increasing knowledge and generating resources for our children.

Van der Kolk (1996) describes societies holding differing definitions regarding the mutual obligations between individuals and society. With acute trauma, the social environment responds, for example, with cultural or religious ceremonies, disaster relief for hurricanes, tsunamis, floods, and evolved social and religious structures to help distressed people in rebuilding and resuming their lives. External validation about the reality of trauma in a supportive environment is vital in preventing and treating stress. As children, youth, and families receive acknowledgment of their experiences as reality, there is an increased possibility on the local and national levels that the need for treatment and intervention is required in order to be able to function and participate successfully as members of our society.

As Joan Kelly stated in summarizing the challenge for understanding and changing our social system:

> Our social institutions allow us to express and share so little of our real human needs that we are forced to lock them up inside ourselves. We all bear witness to the results: the explosions and implosions of these pent-up feelings are the stuff of the private tragedies and public violence and the disorder of our everyday life. Let us acknowledge, then ... that the personal is political; that the test of a social system is its ability to translate the personal into the public and at the same time to make community a real part of one's daily, personal life through meaningful participation in the decisions that shape us all.

(Kelly, 1984, p. xvii)

References

Armstrong, J. G. (2002). Deciphering the broken narrative of trauma: Signs of traumatic dissociation on the Rorschach. *Rorchachiana, 25*, 11–27.

Armstrong, J. G. & Loewenstein, R. J. (1990). Characteristics of patients with multiple personality and dissociative disorders on psychological testing. *Journal of Nervous and Mental Disorders, 178*, 448–454.

Berrick, J. D. (2008). *Take me home: Protecting America's vulnerable children and families.* New York: Oxford University Press,

Caswell, D. P. (2001). *A proposed method of discrimination between violent and non-violent African American adolescents.* The Chicago School of Professional Psychology, Proquest, UMI Publishing, 3024542.

Christensen, D. L., Schieve, L. A., Devine, O. & Drews-Botsch, C. (2014). Socioeconomic status, child enrichment factors, and cognitive performance among pre-school-age-children: Results from the follow-up of growth and development experiences study. *Research in Developmental Disabilities, 35*, 1789–1801.

Cohon, J. D., & Cooper, B. A. (2002). A first look: Foster parents of medically complex, drug-exposed, and HIV+ infants. *Children and Youth Services Review, 15*, 105-130.

Crowell, K.D. (2001). *Understanding the trauma of child prostitution: An exploratory examination comparing child sexual abuse victims to commercially sexually exploited minors.* Dissertation abstract international: Science and Engineering, Volume 72 1-B 526. The Chicago School of Professional Psychology, ProQuest, UMI Dissertations Publishing, 3024542.

DellaCorte, M. R. (2008). *An exploratory investigation of attachment and selected variables of the Rorschach in a sample of referred foster children.* The Wright Institute ProQuest, UMI Dissertation Publishing, 3318652.

Dorsey, S., Conover, K. L., & Revillion Cox, J. (2014). Improving foster parent engagement: using qualitative methods to guide tailoring of evidence-based engagement strategies. *Journal of Clinical Child and Adolescent Psychology, 43*(6), 887–889.

Elliot, C. (2007a). *Differential Ability Scales-II (DAS-II).* San Antonio, TX: Pearson.

Elliot, C. (2007b). *Differential Ability Scales-II (DAS-II): Introductory and technical handbook.* San Antonio, TX: Pearson.

Eshom, J. A. (2006). *An examination of the impact of trauma in multiple placements in foster care children using the ego impairment index II on the Rorschach.* The Wright Institute, ProQuest, UMI Dissertations Publishing, 3230476.

Exner, J. E. (1974). *Rorschach comprehensive system, volume I: Basic foundations.* New York: Wiley & Sons.

Exner, J. E., (2003). *Rorschach comprehensive system, volume 1: Basic foundations* (3rd ed.). New York: Wiley & Sons.

Exner, J. E., & Weiner, I. B. (1995). *Vol. 3 Assessment of children and adolescents,* (2nd ed.). New York: Wiley & Sons.

George, S., & deJong, A. (1995). Children classified as controlling at age six: evidence of disorganized representational strategies and aggression at home and school. *Development and Psychopathology, 7,* 447–463.

Goldblatt, N., (2003). *A study of object relations phenomena in foster children.* The Wright Institute, Berkeley, ProQuest, UMI Dissertations Publishing, 3084475.

Hagino, K. K. (2002). *Early separation from primary caretakers: The effects of foster care on perceptions and expectations of interpersonal relationships.* The Wright Institute, ProQuest, UMI Dissertations Publishing, 3044817.

Hamel, M., Erdberg, P., & Shaffer, T. W. (2007). Rorschach Comprehensive System data for 100 nonpatient children from the United States in two age groups. *Journal of Personality Assessment, 89* (Suppl. 1), S174–S182.

Hernandez-McConnen, R. (2012). *Foster care: An analysis of factors that impact placement stability.* University of Pennsylvania, ProQuest, UMI Dissertations Publishing, 3551691.

Kampuis, J. H., Kugeares, S. L., & Finn, S. E. (2000). Rorschach correlates of sexual abuse: Trauma content and aggression indexes, *Journal of Personality Assessment, 75*(2), 212–224.

Kelley, F. (1999). *The psychological assessment of abused and traumatized children.* Mowath, NJ: Lawrence Erlbaum Associates.

Kelly, J. (1984). *Women, history, and theory.* Chicago: University of Chicago Press.

Kim. K. (2005). *An exploratory study of disordered thinking of aggressive children in foster care.* The Wright Institute, ProQuest, UMI Dissertations Publishing, 3188700.

Lerach, S, (2008). *An investigation into the psychological constructs of adolescent female offenders who prostitute as compared to other adolescent female offenders.* Alliant University, San Diego, CA, UMI Dissertations Publishing, 3335153.

Larry P. *v.* Wilson Riles. (1974). 343 F. Supp. 1306 (N.D. Cal. 1972) (preliminary injunction), affirmed, 502 F. 2d 963 (9th Cir. 1974), opinion issued No. C-71-2270 RFP (N.D. Cal. October 16, 1979).

Lyons, J. S., Griffin, E., Fazio, M, & Lyons, M. B. (1999). *Child and adolescent needs and strengths: An information integration tool for children and adolescents with mental health challenges (CANS-MH) Manual.* Chicago: Buddin Praed Foundation.

McDonald, T. P., Allen, R. I., Westerfelt, A., & Piliavin, I. (1996) Assessing the long-term effects of foster care: A research synthesis. *Child Welfare League of America,* Washington, DC.

Meloy, M. E., & Phillips, D.A. (2012). Foster children and placement stability: the role of childcare. *Journal of Applied Developmental Psychology, 33*(5), 252–259.

Mercer, B. L. (2003, March). *Rorschach variables of children in foster care: W:M ratio, egocentricity ratio, and projective metaphor.* Paper presented at the meeting of the Society for Personality Assessment, San Francisco, California.

Meyer, G. J., Erdberg P., & Shaffer, T. W. (2007). Toward international normative reference for the comprehensive system. *Journal of Personality Assessment, 89* (Suppl. 1), S201–S216.

Meyer, G. J., & Viglione, D. J. (2006, March). *The influence of R, form%, R-Engagement, and complexity on interpretive benchmarks for Comprehensive System variables.* Paper presented at the annual meeting of the Society for Personality Assessment, San Diego, CA.

Mihura, J. L., Meyer, G. J., Dumitrascu, N., & Bombel G. (2012). The validity of individual Rorschach variables: Systematic reviews and meta-analysis of the comprehensive system. *Psychological Bulletin, 139*(3), 548–605.

McKinney, J., (2014). Speaking of self: "Winners" and losers in therapeutic foster care. *Children and Youth Services Review, 39*, 84–90.

Pearson Clinical (n.d.) Differential Ability Scales®-II. Retreived from http://www.pearsonclinical.com/education/products/100000468/differential-ability-scales-ii-das-ii.html

Rorschach performance assessment system. (2011). Toledo, OH: Rorschach Performance Assessment System.

Resnick, J. D. (2012). *Rorschach profiles of traumatized inner city children with or without PTSD*, vol. 62, 11B, p. 5388, PsycINFO Database Record (c) APA.

Toche-Manley, L., Dietzen, L., Nanhen, J., & Beigel, A. (2014). Are two voices better than one? Prediction permanency in minority youth using multi-informant mental health and strength data. *The Journal of Behavioral Health Services & Research, 41*(3), 56–369.

van der Kolk, B., McFarlane, A. C., & Weisaeth, L. (Eds.). (1996). *Traumatic stress: The effects of overwhelming experience on mind, body, and society*. New York: The Guilford Press.

van der Kolk, B. A. (2005). Developmental trauma disorder. Toward a rational diagnosis for children with complex trauma histories. *Psychiatric Annals, 35*, 401–408.

van der Kolk, B. A., Pynoos, R. S., Cicchetti, D., Cloitre, M., D'Andrea, W., Ford, J., et al. (2009). *Proposal to include a developmental trauma disorder diagnosis for children and adolescents in DSM-V.* Unpublished manuscript, the National Child Traumatic Stress Network Developmental Trauma Disorder Taskforce, University of California Los Angeles, Los Angeles, CA.

Viglione, D. (1990). Severe disturbance or trauma induced adaptive reaction: a Rorschach child case study. *Journal of Personality Assessment, 55*(1&2), 280–295.

Wechsler, D. (2004). *The Wechsler intelligence scale for children – fourth edition*. London: Pearson Assessment

Wechsler, D. (2008). *Wechsler fourth edition (WISC-IV)*. San Antonio, TX: Pearson.

Zodan, J., Hilsenroth, M., Chamas, J., Goldman, R., & Bornstein, R. (2014). Rorschach assessment of childhood sexual abuse severity, borderline pathology, and their interaction: An examination of criterion validity. *Psychological Trauma: Theory, Research, Practice, and Policy, 6*(4), 318–327.

4 Assessment-Driven Intervention for Youth and Families in Community Service Delivery Systems

Justin D. Smith, Anne Mauricio, and Elizabeth A. Stormshak

Community-Based Services for Children and Families in the United States

The percentage of children in the United States who meet criteria for a mental health disorder is estimated at 46 percent with 21 percent meeting criteria for a disorder that results in severe impairment (Merikangas et al., 2010). Research indicates that as few as 20 percent of children with mental health disorders actually receive services (Kataoka, Zhang, & Wells, 2002). Moreover, although children exposed to poverty and corresponding risk factors have an increased vulnerability to mental health problems (Larson, Russ, Crall, & Halfon, 2008), children from families with limited economic resources have less access to mental health services (Kataoka et al., 2002; Wang et al., 2005). In addition to income-related barriers such as transportation that impede the utilization of community mental health services (Reyno & McGrath, 2006), poor families, traditionally overrepresented by ethnic minority families, are less likely to have health insurance coverage for mental health–related concerns (Wang et al., 2005). When low-income families do engage in services, poverty-related life stressors increase vulnerability to premature termination, further contributing to the unmet need for mental health services among low-income and ethnic minority families (Snell-Johns, Mendez, & Smith, 2004).

The quality of services that are available to low-income or uninsured families exacerbates the problem (Nelson, 2002). Publicly funded community mental health centers balance the high demand for services with limited resources, and caseworkers must manage excessively high caseloads with limited supervisory support, contributing to burnout and turnover, thus offering less than optimal quality of care (Aarons & Sawitzky, 2006). Further, despite the explosion of evidence-based interventions in recent decades, their uptake in community mental health has been poor (Novins, Green, Legha, & Aarons, 2013). Increased utilization of evidence-based interventions in publicly funded behavioral health centers could help reduce disparities in the quality of services by ensuring that services are best practices. Improving the availability of these culturally sensitive services that can be adapted to meet the unique needs of families is also critical, as it would likely enhance the utilization and quality of mental health services (Griner & Smith, 2006). Empirically informed collaborative assessment intervention models exemplify culturally responsive services that should be integrated into community service delivery systems (Guerrero, Lipkind, & Rosenberg, 2011). These models are effective in engaging families, as they can be tailored to meet the needs and preferences of each family while empowering the client as a collaborator in the change process

(Finn, Fischer, & Handler, 2012). Because of the focus on empowerment, collaborative assessment models may be particularly impactful for low-income, ethnic minority families, who are too often marginalized in society (Smith, Knoble, Zerr, Dishion, & Stormshak, 2014). In the context of the 2012 Affordable Care Act that mandates delivery of evidence-based clinical practices, it is an opportune time to promote dissemination of collaborative assessment models in community settings (Mechanic, 2012). In order to meet the changing landscape of mental health care for children, evidence-based practices must be delivered in service systems that are readily accessible to low-income and minority families, including community mental health, primary care, social service programs, and public schools.

The Current State of Assessment

The predominant view among mental health professionals is that the clinical utility of traditional psychological assessment—the extent to which the assessment leads to demonstrable improvements in clinical services, and in turn, improvements in client functioning—has yet to be satisfactorily demonstrated (Hayes, Nelson, & Jarrett, 1987; Hunsley & Mash, 2007). These concerns have contributed to a diminished focus on assessment training (Clemence & Handler, 2001) as well as a decline in the professional practice of psychological assessment (Norcross, Karpiak, & Santoro, 2005). However, the growing prominence of the collaborative models mentioned above—those that use assessment to drive the intervention process, explicitly aiming toward clinically meaningful change—increases the effectiveness of services for children in community contexts. In this vein, we offer our definition of an assessment-driven intervention approach.

Assessment-driven interventions typically focus on a specific problem behavior or area of concern. The tests administered and constructs assessed are specifically chosen to address the referring problems and are linked to related follow-up interventions. Assessment batteries for child and family cases are multi-method, comprising questionnaires (self and other reports) and videotaped observational assessment that the clinician rates and scores. Existing assessment-driven interventions place significant emphasis on a collaborative feedback session, in which the provider leverages the norm-based results of the assessment to increase motivation to change, address ambivalence and resistance, and develop an intervention plan that is individualized to the family's needs identified by the assessment and the family context.

The Family Check-Up

In the remainder of this chapter, we discuss this process using an evidence-based, assessment-driven intervention approach for families called the Family Check-Up (FCU; Dishion & Stormshak, 2007). The FCU is the result of an effort to develop an effective and efficient intervention for families using a parent management training approach to intervention for youth age 2 to 17. Parent management training refers to programs that train parents to be more effective at managing their children's behaviors both in the home and in the school contexts. Broadly speaking, the primary goal of the FCU is to accurately assess the ecology of the family, motivate caregivers' use of family management skills implicated in the prevention of problem behaviors, such as positive behavior support and monitoring, and motivate participation in indicated follow-up intervention services. In this way, the assessment-driven model acts as both a brief intervention and as the entry point for indicated follow-up services to meet the needs of individual families. This chapter provides a concise description of the FCU model, reviews the empirical findings from FCU trials germane to community mental health for children, and briefly discusses the ways the FCU model can address the challenges of community mental health systems serving youth and families.

As will become evident in the following description, the FCU differs from traditional psychological assessment. The FCU is a brief assessment-driven intervention and was developed in part to couple with evidence-based family management treatment programs that address the family factors implicated in the development and maintenance of a broad array of child psychopathology (see Smith & Dishion, 2013). This focus differs somewhat from the traditional practice and foci of a child-centered psychological assessment in which diagnostic clarification, case conceptualization, and referral for indicated services are the primary goals. During the FCU, if the therapist identifies a potential area requiring further testing, such as an autism spectrum disorder, learning disorder, or psychosis, a referral results. This process individualizes care and aids in the allocation of services to those children and families with indicated need.

Procedures

The FCU is an individually tailored approach to family intervention. The results of an ecological assessment, which includes questionnaires and observed family interaction tasks, are the foundation for empirically informed clinical decisions concerning individualized treatment planning and referral to indicated services. Figure 4.1 shows the three-steps of the FCU model: (1) the initial intake interview; (2) the ecological assessment; and (3) the feedback and motivation session. The FCU can be accomplished in two to three meetings with the family, depending on the needs of the family and the demands of the service delivery context and other factors (e.g., managed care considerations). As will be elaborated in the section on implementation, the FCU was designed with community-based delivery in mind. Thus, each step can fit within the typical 50-minute billable therapy hour. If desired, the intake interview and assessment can be completed in one 75 to 90 minute meeting.

Initial Intake Interview

A cornerstone of the FCU is framing caregivers' presenting concerns and intervention goals using a family management focus, viewing caregivers as the active agents in the change process. In the initial intake interview, sometimes referred to as the "get to know you" session, the therapist uses motivational interviewing techniques and rapport-building strategies to engage parents in the change process (Miller & Rollnick, 2002). The primary aims of the session are: (1) for the therapist and caregiver to arrive at a shared perspective about family challenges and concerns that motivated participation in the FCU; and (2) for the therapist to prompt dynamics critical to the change process, such as motivation and self-appraisal (Dishion & Stormshak, 2007).

Consistent with the principles of motivational interviewing, the collaborative, interpersonal partnership between the therapist and the caregivers functions as the catalyst for creating a shared perspective. Establishing a collaborative relationship and perspective enhances commitment to change while maintaining respect for the parent's autonomy in the change process (Miller & Rollnick, 2002). This collaboration minimizes the likelihood that caregivers will feel judged, which can diminish readiness to change and be a strong deterrent to actively engaging in the intervention process (Dishion & Stormshak, 2007). Motivational interviewing and rapport-building strategies reduce resistance, enhance parent commitment to the change process, increase parent perceptions that change is important, and build parent confidence that they can successfully create change (Burke, Arkowitz, & Menchola, 2003). This is particularly important for parents who feel ambivalent about participating in behavioral health services due to feeling marginalized after receiving less than optimal care for themselves and their children. Regardless of the reasons for ambivalence, it is important to recognize where a caregiver is in the change process. The FCU therapist has the opportunity to gauge readiness to change during the intake and, if needed, address ambivalence and orient the feedback to align with the needs of the caregiver in moving toward the desired changes.

Ecological Assessment

The second step of the FCU is a brief norm-based, multi-method, multi-rater ecological assessment focused on the broad domains of family background and support, youth adjustment, and family management and relationships. Constructs germane to family-based intervention for youth behavior problems are assessed within each domain (Figure 4.1). Consistent with the theoretical bases of parent management training programs, FCU interventionists aim to increase the effectiveness of core parenting skills to improve child adaptation indirectly (see Reid, Patterson, & Dishion, 1997). Thus, the FCU assesses the domains that influence youth outcomes in the individual child (e.g., behavioral inhibition), in the family context (e.g., parent-child conflict), and in the peer environment (e.g., deviant peer influence), as well as the factors that inhibit or promote effective family management practices (e.g., parent mental health, partner support, residence in a dangerous neighborhood). These domains are primarily assessed using brief questionnaires administered to caregiving adults and teachers (when the youth is school aged), as well as the youth directly (beginning around age 10). Administration and scoring of the questionnaires can be done via an Internet-based system. Paper and pencil measures are also available. The FCU uses well-established measures of various domains, such as the Strengths and Difficulties Questionnaire (Goodman, 1997), and also developed new psychometrically sound and brief measures of constructs including early childhood parenting skills (McEachern et al., 2012) and early adolescent peer relationships (Dishion, Kim, Stormshak, & O'Neill, 2014). To meet the demands of community practice, the FCU questionnaires are brief, requiring less than 30 minutes for caregivers to complete and 15 to 20 minutes for youth and teachers.

The ecological assessment also includes a predetermined set of short-videotaped observation of three to five semi-structured family interaction tasks. Videotaped observation and macro-social coding of family dynamics was necessitated by research findings indicating that self-report measures failed to adequately capture salient and

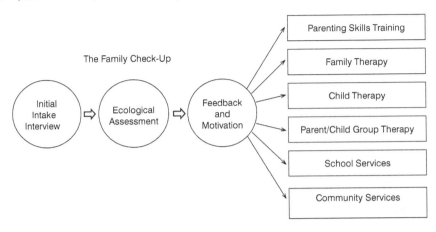

Figure 4.1 FCU Intervention Services

nuanced interaction patterns, such as coercion, which often occur automatically and outside the conscious awareness of those in the interaction (Dishion, Patterson, & Kavanagh, 1992). Similarly, family management skills, such as monitoring, are more predictive of child outcomes when assessed observationally (Dishion, Nelson, & Kavanagh, 2003). There are distinct FCU interaction tasks specifically designed for the developmental requirements of young children (2 to 5 years), school-age children (6 to 10 years), or preadolescent and adolescent youth (11 to 17 years). For example, family management skills and the parent-child relationship are assessed via a child-directed play task for young children, whereas the caregiver-adolescents interaction task may involve discussing a time when the caregiver was unaware that the teen was without adult supervision. FCU interventionists then code each interaction for relationship quality, positive behavior support, and monitoring and limit setting, which are key family management practices targeted in a subsequent parent training intervention. Clinical and nonclinical norms are provided for the questionnaire data and observational ratings through the FCU website.

Feedback and Motivation

The culmination of the three-session FCU intervention is a feedback session to the caregivers. The feedback session is a collaborative discussion of the findings of the ecological family assessment; it builds on the initial contact and is intended to motivate behavior change, thus serving as a bridge to other services and intervention resources (Dishion & Stormshak, 2007). In accordance with the motivational interviewing model, the feedback process involves a comparison of the family's results to normative data to initiate a discussion of current areas of strength and areas that could benefit from additional attention. For ease of presentation, the therapist plots the assessment findings on the Child and Family Feedback Form (Figure 4.2) along a visual continuum ranging from "area of strength" to "needs attention."

During discussion of the findings, the therapist uses techniques from motivational interviewing to reframe caregivers' appraisals of the child and the problem. Within this framework, the therapist aims to increase motivation to change behavior by exploring

Child and Family Feedback Form

Family Background and Support

Family Stress	
Parent Well-Being	
Parent Coping Strategies	
Caring Adults/Support Network	
Partner Support	
Parent Substance Use	
Other:	

Area of Strength   Needs Attention

Youth Adjustment

Behavior	
Emotional Adjustment	
Peer Relationships	
School Success	
Coping and Self-Management	
Other:	

Area of Strength   Needs Attention

Family Management and Relationships

Relationship Quality	
Positive Behavior Support	
Monitoring & Limit Setting	
Other:	

Area of Strength   Needs Attention

Figure 4.2 Child and Family Feedback form

ambivalence and resistance to change through empathy. The feedback is beneficial for all families because it was designed to motivate caregivers to both maintain current effective practices and reduce those parenting practices and parent-child interactions that undermine healthy child adaptation. At the end of the discussion, caregivers should have a sense of self-efficacy about their parenting, which is accomplished through collaboration concerning behavior-change goals and available resources that can be accessed to support these changes, which, in the FCU, takes the form of a menu of intervention options that is presented to the family and discussed. This is a key aspect of the FCU model's individual-tailored intervention process.

As illustrated in Figure 4.1, the menu of options on the far right comprises a variety of services for the family, youth, and parents. In many circumstances, the FCU therapist will provide these services, though often community and school-based referrals, as well as referral to other professionals with specialized training, are needed to support the youth and family. The *Everyday Parenting* curriculum (Dishion, Stormshak, & Kavanagh, 2011) can be used for brief parenting interventions that might focus on one or two parent-management skills that need attention (e.g., monitoring, positive behavior support) or for a more comprehensive parent training treatment. Other evidence-based interventions are integrated into the menu of services dependent upon availability in the agency or in the community, where referral would be appropriate. Leijten et al. (2014) evaluated the effects of this individually tailoring approach to intervention with a randomized trial of families with young children. In the trial, referred to as the *Early Steps Project*, 731 families were randomized to the FCU or services as usual. All families in the study were assessed each year when the target child ranged in age from 2 to 5, during which time families randomized to the FCU condition were offered the intervention (i.e., meeting with a therapist for an initial contact and a feedback session). Participants were then reassessed when the target child was 7.5. Leijten et al. (2014) examined families' service usage in the period between age 5 and 7.5 when the FCU wasn't offered to the families. Results indicated that families from the FCU condition accessed more services than the control group. This effect was strongest for families that were lower socioeconomic status and had children exhibiting higher levels of behavior problems, demonstrating that those families at highest risk for adverse developmental outcomes accessed more services. This is a critical finding in support of integrating the FCU into existing community mental health systems of care in order to achieve sustainable change for the highest-risk youth.

Clinical Example

A brief clinical example will illustrate how the FCU is used in practice. Gill, Hyde, Shaw, Dishion, and Wilson (2008) wrote about the process of the FCU with a Caucasian family with a 2-year-old girl. The interested reader can access the original publication for more details. This particular family was drawn from a large randomized trial of families with young children who were recruited based on the presence of sociodemographic, child, and family-risk factors. The biological parents, both in their mid-30s, were not employed at the time of the assessment; neither had received a high school diploma; five children lived in the home, two from the current marriage and three from previous marriages of the mother. In brief, the results of the ecological assessment and information obtained in the initial interview indicated a number of strengths as well as areas that warranted attention. Among the strengths were the child's language development, a supportive relationship between the mother and the father, high confidence in their ability to parent, and significant social support for the parents. The child, however, exhibited serious behavioral problems including not following directions well, some aggressive behaviors, and a lack of positive play. The parents had difficulty setting effective, age-appropriate limits, lacked proactive parenting strategies, and had high levels of mother-daughter conflict. As well as living in a high-crime neighborhood, the parents reported many daily hassles, maternal depression, and stress concerning their employment and financial situation, and harassment from the mother's ex-husband.

The feedback session began with a rapport-building introduction and a check-in with the parents regarding anything they had learned about their daughter during the interview and assessment steps of the FCU. They reported that her behavior was much better when others were present. Her behavior in the videotaped interaction tasks was much better than what was typical in the home. The therapist then oriented the parents to the feedback form and discussed the areas of strength and concern in each domain. The therapist presented the "story" that emerged from the assessment using the family management focus of the FCU; this illustrated that the child's problem behaviors were directly linked to the effectiveness of the parent's family management strategies (e.g., lack of positive behavior support, poor limit setting). In turn, the factors affecting family management skills were then discussed. For this family, the issue of the mother's depression was central. She reported that this was definitely linked to her level of parenting stress. The mother became tearful when discussing her mood and agreed that intervention for her depression was something she wanted to pursue. The therapist then highlighted the family and couple's strengths as parents, at which point the mother smiled and verbalized her appreciation for the therapist noticing their efforts. This focus on strengths was used to instill hope for successful changes in the family. The final task of the feedback session was to set goals and offer a suggested course of action to achieve them. Working on parenting skills to reduce their daughter's temper tantrums and aggressive behaviors was one of the goals.

Following this session, the therapist met with both parents biweekly for a total of 10 sessions. The interventions focused first on the mother's depression and managing the harassment from her ex-husband, as these were deemed to be more immediate needs. They then shifted toward skills-based training in the effective use of praise, incentives, encouragement, and time out to manage their daughter's problem behaviors.

Assessments conducted one and two years after the parents participated in the FCU indicated that the child's behavior problems had improved to the extent that they were no longer in the clinical range. Two years after the FCU, the mother's self-reported depression had also fallen below the clinical range. Observational assessments (videotaped interaction tasks conducted at age three and four) revealed improved child behavior as well as improved limit setting and use of proactive parenting skills.

Empirical Support

Randomized trials of the FCU have been conducted in public middle schools (ages 12 to 15); community mental health agencies (ages 5 to 17); and as a home visiting model (ages 2 to 12). The FCU has intervention effects on (1) problem behaviors in early childhood (e.g., Dishion, Brennan, et al., 2014; Dishion et al., 2008) and in adolescence (e.g., Connell, Dishion, Yasui, & Kavanagh, 2007; Stormshak, Dishion, Light, & Yasui, 2005; Van Ryzin & Dishion, 2012); (2) substance use during adolescence (e.g., Connell, Dishion, & Deater-Deckard, 2006; Dishion, Kavanagh, Schneiger, Nelson, & Kaufman, 2002); (3) school readiness in young children (Lunkenheimer et al., 2008); (4) academic outcomes in middle and high school (Stormshak, Connell, & Dishion, 2009); (5) parent-child relationships and other family factors (e.g., Sitnick et al., in press; Smith, Dishion, et al., 2014); and (6) the prevention of obesity in childhood (Smith, Montaño, Dishion, Shaw, & Wilson, 2014) and young adulthood (Van Ryzin & Nowicka, 2013). The effectiveness of the FCU does not vary for families from different racial/ethnic backgrounds (e.g., Smith, Knoble, et al., 2014). The varied intervention effects that have been found attest to the trans-diagnostic nature of the FCU's underlying mechanisms of action, which improve youth mental health and adaption in multiple domains of functioning (see Smith & Dishion, 2013).

Delivering the FCU in Community Mental Health

In contrast to many of the prevailing family-centered treatment models for youth behavior problems, which are typically time and resource intensive, the FCU was designed for implementation in service delivery systems that serve high volumes of youth and families (Dishion & Stormshak, 2007). For example, (1) Internet-based administration and scoring of questionnaires reduces the time required of providers; (2) the individual tailoring of intervention components, as indicated by the FCU's ecological assessment, more effectively allocates resources; and (3) delivery of the model by Master's and Bachelor's level providers makes it scalable. The FCU model also explicitly allows for adaptation of various components to meet the needs and challenges of specific systems and implementation sites more effectively. Delivering the model in a community mental health clinic required adaptations so that model components, such as videotaping of family interactions, could be accomplished. These site-specific adaptations are made in consultation with FCU developers to ensure that fidelity to the model is maintained. They are identified early in the implementation process through a readiness assessment that identifies potential barriers and facilitators to implementation, or later in the implementation process as the system encounters challenges to delivering aspects of the model with fidelity.

In a pragmatic effectiveness trial, Smith, Stormshak, and Kavanagh (2014) demonstrated the successful implementation of the FCU in community mental health agencies serving children and families. In this study, 40 Master's level therapists employed at three community mental health agencies were randomly assigned to the FCU condition, where they were trained in the model, received consultation, and provided the service to new client families, or to a treatment as usual condition. Therapists in the FCU condition received training in the model in a four-day workshop format and received elective ongoing consultation with FCU developers, which was initiated by the therapist. The agencies were selected because they served a high volume of ethnically, culturally, and economically diverse children and families from a large catchment area (urban, suburban, rural) and received funding through a state safety net managed care organization. Seventy-one families (43 in the FCU condition) with children ranging in age from 5 to 17 (Mean = 11.6, SD = 2.6) were enrolled in this study and completed pretreatment assessments.

The results revealed significant reductions in youth and parent-reported conduct problems from pre- to post-intervention. Further, observational ratings of fidelity to the FCU model were similar to those obtained in randomized trials of the efficacy of the FCU. Specifically, 77 percent of therapists in the study were able to achieve a score above the a priori fidelity benchmark. Previous research has shown that ratings of fidelity to the FCU are related to long-term changes in parenting practices and child outcomes (Smith, Dishion, Shaw, & Wilson, 2013). Further, drift in fidelity over time was related to improvements in child problem behaviors, with less drift being associated with clinically significant improvements from age 2 to 7.5 (Chiapa et al., under review). These findings concerning fidelity to the FCU are quite promising considering the challenge associated with training providers to fidelity in EBPs (McHugh & Barlow, 2010). Findings also indicated high treatment acceptability, therapist adoption, and feasibility of delivering the FCU in community mental health agencies. Further, families reported high satisfaction with the FCU. Last, compared to families in the control condition that completed three sessions, families who completed the three-session FCU attended significantly more subsequent sessions at the agency. This is a promising finding to counter the typical problem of high drop-out and low engagement in community mental health where the families served have a high need for services.

This pragmatic effectiveness trial of the FCU (Smith et al., 2014), although successful in many ways, also identified the significant challenges for assessment-driven interventions in real-world community mental health systems. Two of the more important challenges involved staff turnover and billing for services. Frequent turnover of therapists and other staff in community mental health agencies is a known problem that affects efforts to embed and deliver evidence-based practices (Aarons & Sawitzky, 2006). In our trial, therapist turnover necessitated ongoing training in the FCU model by the treatment developers, which came at a significant cost. Ideally, therapists demonstrating skill in the model would have received additional training on how to train and supervise their colleagues on the FCU model. Unfortunately, skilled therapists more often than not remained at the agency for too brief a time to advance to the level of a trainer. The train-the-trainer approach to sustained implementation can be successful (Forgatch & DeGarmo, 2011), but it requires continuity at the therapist and administrative levels to support such a model. Second, billing managed care for assessment-driven services for families can be challenging, particularly when the child is the identified client but services are primarily delivered to the caregivers. For example, some barriers include billing protocols that require the child ("identified patient") to be in the session when the most effective treatment may involve working only with the caregivers as well as no available billing or financial support for supervision. Additionally, managed care paperwork and administrative tasks that are requisite for billing and must be completed in the clinical hour may limit in-session time for delivering the intervention protocol with adequate fidelity. It is important that pre-implementation assessments of agency readiness identify potential billing restrictions and that the intervention model is adapted to overcome these constraints.

Conclusions

In this chapter, we provided a rationale for and definition of an assessment-driven approach to child and family intervention that can be delivered in community mental health systems. We illustrated this approach using the evidence-based FCU program. We also presented the supporting empirical evidence of the FCU with an emphasis on the applicability to community mental health. The FCU model was developed with the goal of scalability in service delivery systems such as community mental health where practitioners and administrators face many challenges, including engaging culturally and socioeconomically diverse families in services, efficiently allocating sparse resources, and delivering evidence-based intervention programs, primarily by Master's level therapists (Hoagwood, Burns, Kiser, Ringeisen, & Schoenwald, 2001). Recent changes to healthcare policies in the United States encourage and will likely facilitate the use of empirically supported programs on a large scale, and we hope that assessment-driven interventions such as the FCU will be prominently featured as this country enters the next era of community mental health service delivery. FCU developers and scientists continue to adapt and refine the model to meet the ever-changing landscape of community mental health, most notably funding structures, training, and sustainability.

Acknowledgements

This work was supported by Centers for Disease Control grant CE001389-01 to Elizabeth A. Stormshak. Justin Smith received support from the National Institute on Drug Abuse through a pilot study grant awarded by the Center for Prevention Implementation Methodology for Drug Abuse and Sex Risk Behavior (P30 DA027828).

References

Aarons, G. A., & Sawitzky, A. C. (2006). Organizational climate partially mediates the effect of culture on work attitudes and staff turnover in mental health services. *Administration and Policy in Mental Health and Mental Health Services Research, 33*(3), 289–301. doi: 10.1007/s10488-006-0039-1.

Burke, B. L., Arkowitz, H., & Menchola, M. (2003). The efficacy of Motivational Interviewing: A meta-analysis of controlled clinical trials. *Journal of Consulting and Clinical Psychology, 71*(5), 843–861. doi: 10.1037/0022-006X.71.5.843.

Chiapa, A., Smith, J. D., Kim, H., Dishion, T. J., Shaw, D. S., & Wilson, M. N. (under review). A longitudinal study of fidelity to the Family Check-Up: Drift and relationship with clinical improvement in child problem behavior. *Journal of Consulting and Clinical Psychology.*

Clemence, A. J., & Handler, L. (2001). Psychological assessment on internship: A survey of training directors and their expectations for students. *Journal of Personality Assessment, 76,* 18–47.

Connell, A. M., Dishion, T. J., & Deater-Deckard, K. (2006). Variable- and person-centered approaches to the analysis of early adolescent substance use: Linking peer, family, and intervention effects with developmental trajectories. *Merrill-Palmer Quarterly, 52,* 421–448.

Connell, A. M., Dishion, T. J., Yasui, M., & Kavanagh, K. (2007). An adaptive approach to family intervention: Linking engagement in family-centered intervention to reductions in adolescent problem behavior. *Journal of Consulting and Clinical Psychology, 75*(4), 568–579. doi: 10.1037/0022-006X.75.4.568.

Dishion, T. J., Brennan, L. M., Shaw, D. S., McEachern, A. D., Wilson, M. N., & Jo, B. (2014). Prevention of problem behavior through annual Family Check-Ups in early childhood: Intervention effects from home to early elementary school. *Journal of Abnormal Child Psychology, 42*(3), 343–354. doi: 10.1007/s10802-013-9768-2.

Dishion, T. J., Kavanagh, K., Schneiger, A., Nelson, S. E., & Kaufman, N. (2002). Preventing early adolescent substance use: A family-centered strategy for public middle school. *Prevention Science, 3*(3), 191–201. doi: 10.1023/A:1019994500301.

Dishion, T. J., Kim, H., Stormshak, E. A., & O'Neill, M. (2014). A brief measure of peer affiliation and social acceptance (PASA): Validity in an ethnically diverse sample of early adolescents. *Journal of Clinical Child & Adolescent Psychology, 43*(4), 601–612. doi: 10.1080/15374416.2013.876641.

Dishion, T. J., Nelson, S. E., & Kavanagh, K. (2003). The Family Check-Up for high-risk adolescents: Preventing early-onset substance use by parent monitoring. *Behavior Therapy, 34,* 553–571. doi: 10.1016/S0005-7894(03)80035-7.

Dishion, T. J., Patterson, G. R., & Kavanagh, K. (1992). An experimental test of the coercion model: Linking theory, measurement, and intervention. In J. McCord & R. Tremblay (Eds.), *Preventing antisocial behavior: Interventions from birth through adolescence* (pp. 253–282). New York: Guilford.

Dishion, T. J., & Stormshak, E. A. (2007). *Intervening in children's lives: An ecological, family-centered approach to mental health care.* Washington, DC: American Psychological Association.

Dishion, T. J., Stormshak, E. A., & Kavanagh, K. (2011). *Everyday parenting: A professional's guide to building family management skills.* Champaign, IL: Research Press.

Finn, S. E., Fischer, C. T., & Handler, L. (Eds.). (2012). *Collaborative/therapeutic assessment: A casebook and guide.* Hoboken, NJ: John Wiley & Sons, Inc.

Forgatch, M. S., & DeGarmo, D. S. (2011). Sustaining fidelity following the nationwide PMTO™ implementation in Norway. *Prevention Science, 12*(3), 235–246. doi: 10.1007/s11121-011-0225-6.

Gill, A. M., Hyde, L. W., Shaw, D. S., Dishion, T. J., & Wilson, M. N. (2008). The Family Check-Up in early childhood: A case study of intervention process and change. *Journal of Clinical Child & Adolescent Psychology, 37*(4), 893–904.

Goodman, R. (1997). The Strengths and Difficulties Questionnaire: A research note. *Journal of Child Psychology and Psychiatry, 38*(5), 581–586. doi: 10.1111/j.1469-7610.1997.tb01545.x.

Griner, D., & Smith, T. B. (2006). Culturally adapted mental health intervention: A meta-analytic review. *Psychotherapy: Theory, Research, Practice, Training, 43*(4), 531–548. doi: 10.1037/0033-3204.43.4.531.

Guerrero, B., Lipkind, J., & Rosenberg, A. (2011). Why did she put nail polish in my drink? Applying the Therapeutic Assessment model with an African-American foster child in a community mental health setting. *Journal of Personality Assessment, 93*(1), 7–15.

Hayes, S. C., Nelson, R. O., & Jarrett, R. B. (1987). The treatment utility of assessment: A functional approach to evaluating assessment quality. *American Psychologist, 42*(11), 963-974. doi: 10.1037/0003-066X.42.11.963.

Hoagwood, K., Burns, B. J., Kiser, L., Ringeisen, H., & Schoenwald, S. K. (2001). Evidence-based practice in child and adolescent mental health services. *Psychiatric Services, 52*(9), 1179–1189.

Hunsley, J., & Mash, E. J. (2007). Evidence-based assessment. *Annual Review of Clinical Psychology, 3,* 29-51. doi: 10.1146/annurev.clinpsy.3.022806.091419.

Kataoka, S. H., Zhang, L., & Wells, K. B. (2002). Unmet need for mental health care among U.S. children: Variation by ethnicity and insurance status. *American Journal of Psychiatry, 159,* 1548–1555. doi: 10.1176/appi.ajp.159.9.1548.

Larson, K., Russ, S. A., Crall, J. J., & Halfon, N. (2008). Influence of multiple social risks on children's health. *Pediatrics, 121*(2), 337–344.

Leijten, P., Shaw, D. S., Gardner, F. E. M., Wilson, M. N., Matthys, W., & Dishion, T. J. (2014). The Family Check-Up and service use in high-risk families of young children: A prevention strategy with a bridge to community-based treatment. *Prevention Science,* 1–10.

Lunkenheimer, E. S., Dishion, T. J., Shaw, D. S., Connell, A. M., Gardner, F. E. M., Wilson, M. N., & Skuban, E. M. (2008). Collateral benefits of the Family Check-Up on early childhood school readiness: Indirect effects of parents' positive behavior support. *Developmental Psychology, 44*(6), 1737–1752. doi: 10.1037/a0013858.

McEachern, A., Dishion, T. J., Weaver, C. M., Shaw, D. S., Wilson, M. N., & Gardner, F. E. M. (2012). Parenting Young Children (PARYC): Validation of a self-report parenting measure. *Journal of Child and Family Studies, 21*(3), 498–511.

McHugh, R. K., & Barlow, D. H. (2010). The dissemination and implementation of evidence-based psychological treatments: A review of current efforts. *American Psychologist, 65*(2), 73–84. doi: 10.1037/a0018121.

Mechanic, D. (2012). Seizing opportunities under the Affordable Care Act for transforming the mental and behavioral health system. *Health Affairs, 31*(2), 376–382.

Merikangas, K. R., He, J.-P., Burstein, M., Swanson, S. A., Avenevoli, S., Cui, L., et al. (2010). Lifetime prevalence of mental disorders in US adolescents: results from the National Comorbidity Survey Replication–Adolescent Supplement (NCS-A). *Journal of the American Academy of Child & Adolescent Psychiatry, 49*(10), 980–989.

Miller, W. R., & Rollnick, S. (2002). *Motivational interviewing: Preparing people for change* (2nd ed.). New York: Guilford Press.

Nelson, A. (2002). Unequal treatment: confronting racial and ethnic disparities in health care. *Journal of the National Medical Association, 94*(8), 666–668.

Norcross, J. C., Karpiak, C. P., & Santoro, S. O. (2005). Clinical psychologists across the years: The Division of Clinical Psychology from 1960 to 2003. *Journal of Clinical Psychology, 61*(12), 1467–1483. doi: 10.1002/jclp.20135.

Novins, D. K., Green, A. E., Legha, R. K., & Aarons, G. A. (2013). Dissemination and implementation of evidence-based practices for child and adolescent mental health: A systematic review. *Journal of the American Academy of Child & Adolescent Psychiatry, 52*(10), 1009–1025. doi: 10.1016/j.jaac.2013.07.012.

Reid, J. B., Patterson, G. R., & Dishion, T. J. (1997). *Antisocial boys*. Portland, OR: Castalia.

Reyno, S. M., & McGrath, P. J. (2006). Predictors of parent training efficacy for child externalizing behavior problems–a meta-analytic review. *Journal of Child Psychology and Psychiatry, 47*(1), 99–111.

Sitnick, S. L., Shaw, D. S., Gill, A., Dishion, T. J., Winter, C., Waller, R., et al. (in press). Parenting and the Family Check-Up: Developments and changes in observed parent-child interaction during early childhood. *Journal of Clinical Child & Adolescent Psychology*. doi: 10.1080/15374416.2014.940623.

Smith, J. D., & Dishion, T. J. (2013). Mindful parenting in the development and maintenance of youth psychopathology. In J. T. Ehrenreich-May & B. C. Chu (Eds.), *Transdiagnostic mechanisms and treatment for youth psychopathology* (pp. 138–160). New York: The Guilford Press.

Smith, J. D., Dishion, T. J., Shaw, D. S., Wilson, C., Winter, C., & Patterson, G. R. (2014). Coercive family process and early-onset conduct problems from age 2 to school entry. *Development and Psychopathology, 26*(4), 917–932. doi: 10.1017/S0954579414000169.

Smith, J. D., Dishion, T. J., Shaw, D. S., & Wilson, M. N. (2013). Indirect effects of fidelity to the Family Check-Up on changes in parenting and early childhood problem behaviors. *Journal of Consulting and Clinical Psychology, 81*(6), 962–974. doi: 10.1037/a0033950.

Smith, J. D., Knoble, N., Zerr, A. A., Dishion, T. J., & Stormshak, E. A. (2014). Multicultural competence and the Family Check-Up: Indirect effect on adolescent antisocial behavior through family conflict. *Journal of Clinical Child & Adolescent Psychology, 43*(3), 400–414. doi: 10.1080/15374416.2014.888670.

Smith, J. D., Montaño, Z., Dishion, T. J., Shaw, D. S., & Wilson, M. N. (2014). Preventing weight gain and obesity: Indirect effects of a family-based intervention in early childhood. *Prevention Science*, Available ahead of print. doi: 10.1007/s11121-014-0505-z.

Smith, J. D., Stormshak, E. A., & Kavanagh, K. (2014). Results of a pragmatic effectiveness-implementation hybrid trial of the Family Check-Up in community mental health agencies. *Administration and Policy in Mental Health and Mental Health Services Research*, Available ahead of print. doi: 10.1007/s10488-014-0566-0.

Snell-Johns, J., Mendez, J. L., & Smith, B. H. (2004). Evidence-based solutions for overcoming access barriers, decreasing attrition, and promoting change with underserved families. *Journal of Family Psychology, 18*(1), 19–35. doi: 10.1037/0893-3200.18.1.19.

Stormshak, E. A., Connell, A., & Dishion, T. J. (2009). An adaptive approach to family-centered intervention in schools: Linking intervention engagement to academic outcomes in middle and high school. *Prevention Science, 10*(3), 221–235. doi: 10.1007/s11121-009-0131-3.

Stormshak, E. A., Dishion, T. J., Light, J., & Yasui, M. (2005). Implementing family-centered interventions within the public middle school: Linking service delivery to change in problem behavior. *Journal of Abnnormal Child Psychology, 33*(6), 723–733.

Van Ryzin, M. J., & Dishion, T. J. (2012). The impact of a family-centered intervention on the ecology of adolescent antisocial behavior: Modeling developmental sequelae and trajectories during adolescence. *Development and Psychopathology, 24*, 1139–1155.

Van Ryzin, M. J., & Nowicka, P. (2013). Direct and indirect effects of a family-based intervention in early adolescence on parent–youth relationship quality, late adolescent health, and early adult obesity. *Journal of Family Psychology, 27*(1), 106–116. doi: 10.1037/a0031428.

Wang, P. S., Lane, M., Olfson, M., Pincus, H. A., Wells, K. B., & Kessler, R. C. (2005). Twelve-month use of mental health services in the United States: results from the National Comorbidity Survey Replication. *Archives of General Psychiatry, 62*(6), 629–640.

Section II
The Cultural Environment
Theory and Practice

Part 1
Cultural Experiences in Psychological Assessment

5 Collaborative Assessment and Social Justice

Heather Macdonald and Christy Hobza

In his book, *Constructing the Self, Constructing America: A Cultural History of Pyschotherapy*, Philip Cushman (1995) proposed the idea that people are products of specific cultural frameworks shaped by moral understandings and local politics. He also argued that clinicians in the field of psychology are all too eager to demonstrate the universality of the psychological processes such as motivation, perception, and emotion and have ignored the individual in his or her own context. In the zest for universal psychological structures, the social, moral, and political constructs of a person have become a threat or impediment to the clinician who strives for more "objective" and "apolitical" psychotherapeutic or assessment process. However, as assessors working with African-American children, adolescents, and families in foster care and impoverished situations, we have found Cushman's ideas to be true. It is impossible for the assessment process to remain entirely "apolitical" or "ahistorical." It is difficult to ignore the fact that there is an extremely inequitable distribution of power between assessor and client that creates a question about social justice right from the start. Race, ethnicity, social class, education, age, and language are just some of the ways that the assessor or therapist often differs from their clients and their families, therefore the question becomes how to hold onto the differences while not missing the similarities. This chapter will look at what happens when cultural, political, and social justice issues emerge in the assessment process through two case studies. As the assessments by design often strongly impact a person's treatment at the very least, we look at how the social and political can be reintegrated into the assessment process. As Samuda (1975/1998) pointed out so long ago, assessments can be very damaging to minorities if the tests are not normed on a sample that is representative of the person being tested as well as if the interpretation does not take environmental factors into account.

Many assessors, including but not limited to Stephen Finn (2007), Constance Fischer (1985/1994), and Leonard Handler (2007), have argued for a collaborative model of assessment. Through this model, they have emphasized that nothing is more fundamental than experiences and events in the lived world of the client and that everything in the assessment must refer back to that world, including test results and diagnosis. The individualized assessment gives a portrait of the person and characterizes his or her point of view and approach to situations, which allows for openness and a sense of cultural humility on the assessors part. This removes the potential for the assessor to be seen as or to see him or herself as an oracle, and "truth" in this instance becomes part of a larger meaning-making process and where worldviews contextualize the data. Even with this idea of individuality and collaboration, there still appears to be little mention in any previous collaborative assessment literature on the issues of political power, defined as the sense of relationship where one person may appear to have more "power and control"; this may inadvertently reproduce and extend the larger political structures at play within society (Collins, 2004) and social justice within the context of working with ethnic minority populations while conducting psychological evaluations. Counseling psychology appears to have taken to the idea that assessment is a tool that can be used to achieve social justice. The American Counseling Association clearly supports utilizing a social justice framework for assessments (West-Olatunji, 2010; Wood & D'Agostino, 2010). There have been a few book chapters published since 2010 on this idea of assessment and social justice, and it is clearly a direction that psychology can move toward in the future (Enns, 2012; Newell & Coffee, 2013; West-Olatunji, 2010; Yeh & Kwan, 2010)

We are (for the most part) well aware as psychologists and assessors that culture must be taken into account in treatment and diagnosis. For years, scholars have argued that psychologists conducting psychological testing and assessment with clients in a multicultural setting must understand the complex role that cultural diversity plays in their professional activities (Sue & Sue, 1990). It is not new to consider the challenges of understanding clients in multicultural assessments as described by Dana (1998) regarding test fairness and the impact of the testing instruments themselves with clients from diverse groups. The emphasis of neutrality, objectivity, and universal norms within mainstream psychology makes it difficult for psychologists to grapple with the nuance of cultural differences (Dana, 1998) or even more complex moral topographies that define what is good, what is right, and how we should relate to one another (Geertz, 1973; Taylor, 1989). We argue that just taking culture into account when doing an assessment fails to fulfill the potential for portable social justice. Social justice is about equality in economics, politics, opportunities, and rights. Holding onto the aspirations of attaining equality during an assessment gives the clinician the opportunity to actively not promote oppression as the psychological assessment moves forward.

The traditional models for psychological assessment and the use of the test data, as it is applied to the client, involve Quantitative and Empirical Paradigms (Wiggins, 2003) that uphold the science and philosophy of the Western archive with stringent rigor. These paradigms involve the use of objectivism that traditionally gives no play to historical contingency, cultural identity, or political forces. This can give a sense both within the assessor and the client that the assessor and tests have almost oracular power. Taking a collaborative approach removes much of the need to hold historical, cultural, or political issues at bay and provides a forum to think with the client. Deeper questions of human existence, such as the construction of reality by those in power (Fanon, 1967, 1963/1986; Foucault, 2008), domains of difference and displacement (Bhabha, 1994), and engagement of the voices of the subaltern (Spivak, 1988) can be brought into the testing and the capitalistic structures of the pharmaceutical and insurance companies (Huett & Goodman, 2012), as a certain diagnosis prescribes what insurance companies will or will not cover.

Traditional psychological practice (assessment in particular) still carries with it many forms of racial oppression and violence as outlined by previous scholars (Du Bois, 1903/1994; Fanon, 1967; Foucault, 2008; wa Thiong'o, 2009) but it is also a potential site of reversal, open contingency and transformation. That this unique and often bizarre form of inter-subjective space (giving and taking psychological tests) can be loaded with affirmative agency for political power and can support processes of becoming and recognizing the evolution of a person in context.

We look at two cases to see how politics, social oppression, economics, opportunities, and rights can come into play in an assessment. The first case outlines the assessment process with a 17-year-old African American female named Dedra, who was pregnant at the time of the assessment. The second case describes a 9-year-old African American male named Henry, who was referred for an evaluation due to symptoms of hyperactivity and severe tantrums. In both cases, the assessor was White, a doctoral-level clinician, historically mid-SES, and had not experienced family or community violence on par with their client's experience. This highlights the weight of social justice or oppression potential in each assessment case in that the privilege level of the assessor was readily apparent but without a formal protocol in place to account for the unequal distribution of power within the framework of the assessment process.

Case Example 1

Reason for Referral

The county social worker who had made the referral explained to me that she had concerns about the presence of a possible mood disorder, such as bipolar disorder, since Dedra had exhibited symptoms of extreme irritability, depression, and impulsive behaviors that had started prior to pregnancy. Dedra had returned home to her mother after over a year in foster care, and since that time she had become "obsessed with death." However, the worker could not explain to me over the phone exactly what she meant by Dedra's "obsession."

It was fortunate that I worked at an agency that often encouraged clinicians to have initial meetings in the home of the client in order to gather background and experience in the context of the client's world.

Testing Session 1

Dedra sat down on a kitchen stool and looked at me from across the table. I noticed for the first time the features of her face. Her eyes were a deep brown color with eyelashes that curled perfectly above them. Her belly was enormous beneath a bright yellow cotton t-shirt. She said, "I am having a boy." She picked up her phone and sent a text while appearing to ignore me. A knot formed in the middle of my chest as I pulled out the Minnesota Multiphasic Personality Inventory, Adolescent (MMPI-A; Butcher, Dahlstrom, Graham, Tellegan, & Kaemmer, 1992) and a battery of cognitive tests. A text came back to her with a ring tone I recognized and I said, "Hey, that is Lil' Wayne." She gave me a brief upward glance and with several keystrokes on her phone, the whole song played.

We talked for sometime about her love of music and various rap and hip-hop legends. Although we shared some ideas about music, I felt like an intruder. I felt like she knew something that I did not; that I could give her those tests and it would not matter since I would still be the one who did not know or could not know.

In this first session Dedra was willing to complete the Wechsler Abbreviated Scale of Intelligence, Second Edition (WASI-II; Wechsler, 1999). Dedra's overall performance indicated that she was functioning in the average range overall. Dedra appeared to enjoy the cognitive testing as she completed the tasks with ease. However, during this initial testing session she refused to complete the MMPI-A (Butcher et al., 1992). She stated, "These are the tests that will put you in jail. You are trying to make me look crazy!"

She had mentioned to me before that she had wanted "White people" out of her business and that this assessment would finally get the White people "off my back." I was confused about what to do next. Dedra paused before asking the next question, "Do you know about the death of Oscar Grant?" I replied, "Yup. He was shot a week ago by a police officer just outside the office where I work."

Dedra nodded and then looked away in a manner that told me I had missed the point. The fact of the matter was that I did not know her experience at all, nor could I ever really understand it. Then Dedra took me into her bedroom because she wanted me to see her dresser mirror. It became apparent that this related to the original referral question regarding her "obsession with death." On the left side of the mirror was a column of five newspaper obituaries she had cut out and shoved into the edge of the wood. I leaned in close to read each one. All five people who died were African-American and male. Oscar Grant was the last in line; a policeman had shot Mr. Grant while he was facedown on the ground with his hands cuffed behind his back.

When I looked up I observed Dedra's reflection in the mirror, with her swollen belly and her baby boy about to come into the world; I felt my whole body flush with emotion. She wanted me to know the odds. This was not about pity, sentimentality, helplessness, or liberalism. Dedra existed in the quickly disappearing space right between birth and death, and she knew it. Dedra wanted me to get the message: there is an inequitable distribution of power in our culture, a loaded dice game wagered with human lives. I said, "Dedra—this is so cold." She nodded, "You better be cold. Because that's how it is."

Test Results

The more I was able to be with Dedra and to listen to her explain, from her perspective, the social and cultural context, the more she was willing to complete the testing that included a sub-clinical MMPI-A profile (with an L score = 70 and F2 score = 40) and a valid Rorschach Comprehensive System protocol (Exner et al., 2005). Given my initial testing session with Dedra, I fully expected that the MMPI-A and the Rorschach would reveal some kind of post-traumatic response and some signs of depression given the amount of loss she had experienced in her life; however, the testing revealed that Dedra had a defensive coping strategy for keeping painful feelings out of her awareness. In particular, her Rorschach profile revealed intense emotional constriction. This is evidenced on the Rorschach by a C' = 3 and the FC:CF+C ratio (0:0). Also of note was that the Coping Deficit Index was positive (D = -1, Adj D = -1), which meant that Dedra needed to increase both her internal psychological resources as well as external support so that she could meet her daily demands without becoming overwhelmed. Her positive CDI also made sense in light of the fact that she was in her third trimester of pregnancy and just emerging from the foster care system.

Dedra's emotional coping strategy and affective constriction made sense from a "street" perspective where to expose yourself emotionally was too much of a risk when your survival was at stake. Any form of vulnerability, tenderness, or need has to be kept out of range so that people would not take advantage of that weakness.

It seemed that Dedra tried to integrate the violence and death that had been prevalent in her community through the numerous obituaries up on her mirror. If she was unable to express herself verbally, she at least could use the images that represented the pain and/or the losses in her life and in her community. At times there is simply no language for the trauma, no way to express the unsayable or unspeakable. In short, her overall testing profile was one of bitter resilience.

Feedback Letter

I wrote a long feedback letter to Dedra in which I attempted to stay true to the data and true to the issues of social justice. In the final paragraphs, I wrote:

> In the opening statement of his autobiography *Blues All Around Me*, B. B. King (1996) states, "When it comes to my own life, others may know the cold facts better than me … . Truth is, cold facts don't tell the whole story … I'm not writing a cold-blooded history. I'm writing a memory of my heart. That's the truth I'm after— following my feelings no matter where they lead. I want to try to understand myself, hoping that you … will understand me as well." [p. 2] Your baby boy will be learning about his heart through yours. He will want to know how to live in this world, not just to survive, but how to really share himself and his dreams with others. He will want to know how to become his full potential by following his own truth and you can teach him.

As soon as we finished the final feedback session I gathered up my things and prepared to leave. She walked me to the door and waited for me to exit with her hands on her hips. It was an awkward farewell and an extremely intimate moment across an abyss of distance, across the unknowable. Once outside, I looked back at her through the closed rebar screen door. She smiled and waved goodbye.

Case Example 2

Reason for Referral

Henry was referred for an assessment by his mother, Terry, who described Henry's symptoms as follows: a bad temper, laying down on the ground kicking and screaming, hitting walls, interrupting people, being fidgety, getting suspended for fights, poor academics, and saying "om" repeatedly. Terry asked to meet in the clinic, rather than her home, to discuss Henry's history and symptoms further. Terry explained later that she and her family were essentially homeless. Terry had been evicted from her subsidized housing due to not paying rent in an effort to demand that her landlord address a severe mold and mildew problem, where the floor was peeling up and the walls were covered in mold. I also learned over time that Henry and his family were living with Terry's alcoholic grandmother who did not tolerate any kind of noise and that they spent most of their days out of the house.

Meeting with Terry

Terry called to cancel our first meeting. She very apologetically stated, "My god-brother was shot in the face today. I have to help my mother and auntie. I am so sorry that I can't make it in. I tried to get on the bus to see you but I started crying." I was struck by how important our meeting was for Terry, even in the face of this horrific family tragedy.

When we met the following week, Terry was still understandably visibly upset by her god-brother's death. She shared some graphic details of seeing his body on the street. I was quite shaken by the details she shared because, while random shootings do occur with some regularity in Oakland, it was not something that I am used to dealing with. It was my first glimpse at how she took care of herself and her family with limited resources—Terry as a pillar trying to hold up her three children and to keep them from toppling over into the muck she was trying to escape.

Terry shared more family tragedies with me. She knew that while the police were doing their best, they often meted out justice in ways that were unfair and biased against African Americans. "Take what is going on with Oscar Grant," she shared with me. "If that had been a black man who had shot a white man, he would be convicted of first degree murder." I wondered aloud if she feared for her son, since he was growing up to be a black man. "Yes," she responded, quickly followed by, "He is a good boy you know."

Meeting with Henry

Henry was a delight to work with. I often bring a lot of snacks to a first session to use as sustenance or motivators and this was no exception. Henry appeared excited and asked if the snacks were all for him, and when I told him yes, he ate some and then saved some to share with his family. Henry's sister was also receiving an assessment at the same time, and Terry would schedule these appointments in succession with one another. Terry would "camp out" in our waiting room all day with her youngest daughter, reading books and playing with toys. It seemed like a way for her to have a safe place for her children to play.

Henry shared that he cried every day and had nightmares all of the time, but both Henry and his mother denied any specific traumatic experiences for Henry. Yet, as I gave him the Behavior Assessment System for Children, Second Edition parent report and self-report (BASC-2; Reynolds & Kamphaus, 2004), his eyes became glassy and I saw the look of dissociation familiar with traumatized children. I knew that Henry heard gunfire regularly and was aware of different people getting shot, and when I asked Henry about this, he told me about his god-uncle's open-casket funeral and seeing the hole in his head. I also knew that his sister had recently suffered third degree burns due to an accident with a candle, and they had tried to hide the fire from their mother so as not to worry her. I came to understand that while Henry had no one identifiable trauma, his family was constantly traumatized by their environment.

Test Results

I administered a long battery of tests to Henry that included the Wisconsin Card Sorting Test (WCST; Heaton, Chelune, Talley, Kay, & Curtis, 1993), Conners' Continuous

Performance Test, II (CPT-II; Conners & MHS Staff, 2000), California Verbal Learning Test – Child (CVLT-C; Delis, Kramer, Kaplan, & Ober, 1994), Clinical Evaluation of Language Fundamentals, Fourth Edition (CELF-4; Semel, Wiig, & Secord, 2003), Differential Abilities Scale, Second Edition (DAS-II; Elliott, 2007), Wechsler Individual Achievement Test, Third Edition (WIAT-III; Wechsler, 2009), BASC-2 (Reynolds & Kamphaus, 2004), Rorschach Comprehensive System (Rorschach CS; Exner et al., 2005), Rosenzweig Picture-Frustration (Rosenzweig P-F; Rosenzweig, 1953), a sentence completion task, and a house-drawing task. Henry's cognitive results indicated that he had some executive functioning difficulties, language difficulties, impulsivity, and hyperactivity. The results from the CPT-II did not indicate that Henry had any difficulties with attention, but the dissociation that I observed indicated that he became inattentive when emotionally aroused. While Henry's previous cognitive results indicated that he functioned in the average to low-average range, my DAS-II test results suggested that Henry's cognitive functioning was below average across all domains. Of note, my testing also occurred after Henry had gone through multiple traumas, including homelessness, witnessing his sister get severely burned, and learning that his god-uncle had been shot in the face.

Henry's Rorschach CS results indicated that he withdraws from the world and clamps down his emotions to keep himself safe (C '= 2, FC:CF+C = 6:3). Henry's performance also indicated that he is hyper sensitive to the emotions of others (Afr = 2.0). Due to this awareness he seemed to keep his feelings inside so as not to burden his mother with his pain. His mother worked diligently to pull their family out of poverty and violence and wanted to see her son and daughters grow up. Henry's hyperawareness of his mother's fear that he could become the next victim of an unlawful police shooting led him to say that he is okay even though he cried and had repeated nightmares. Henry wanted and needed to be okay (Adj D = +2; Morbid Responses = 2; M minus = 1). His Rosenzweig-P-F responses also showed excessive minimizing of problems in situations that often incite anger in others. Alternatively he would take the frustrations out on himself with responses such as "It's okay" and "I'm sorry."

Henry's desire to be "good" also emerged in his projective stories. For one story, he stated, "Once there was a boy and he was sad and he was crying and his mom asked him was if was he okay. He said, 'no.' [Then] he went to take a nap. [His mom felt] happy." While Henry pretends to be okay like the boy in the story he is not okay. He lives in a world of chaos where he is near homeless and surrounded by danger. His way of coping with this dichotomy is to interpret the world in fantastical ways (WSum6 = 23 and M- = 1) as evidenced by his Rorschach CS responses. However, he ends up feeling like he is less than and damaged in some way (MOR = 2). Henry's intense and controlled emotions left him with limited recourse. Like a young child, he would throw a tantrum on the floor because it provided him with emotional release. He also used dissociation as a viable way to escape the intense world around him.

Feedback

While waiting for the report to be completed, Terry called me and told me that Henry had urinated on the play structure at school. "I don't know why he did that. He is a good boy!" she explained to me. I reassured Terry that I saw goodness in Henry and she expressed relief. This was the best feedback I could give to Terry. She wanted someone else to see that her son was good.

I wrote a comprehensive report for Terry and I wrote a story for Henry about a boy who struggled with emotions. As we read the story together with Terry, Henry expressed that he saw none of himself in the story. "I think this sounds like you," Terry told Henry. As Terry mirrored Henry's goodness to him, he visibly relaxed and agreed that the story could be true.

By happenstance, the day that I met with Henry to give him his story was also the day that Oscar Grant's shooter was sentenced. During our meeting, a knock sounded on our playroom door. A supervisor poked her head in and said that as a precaution, our clinic was closing for safety due to protests and potential rioting. Again, trauma had touched Henry and his family as they quickly packed up their things and headed for the bus.

Conclusion

In both cases, the assessors struggled with issues of oppression and justice, and questions about how to include these issues in the assessment process. To ignore these issues would have ignored core aspects of the referral questions. By taking time to listen and recognize our positioning as assessors, we were able to relinquish some notions of being "experts." By increasing our awareness of the oppressive paradigms that ordinarily stay hidden in the discourse of assessment, we seek to join with our clients and acknowledge the meaning of their experiences. Henry or Dedra may have found this power on their own; however, had we moved forward without taking into account the reality of their daily lives and the fears they experienced, our clients may have felt unheard. Oppression is real. As psychologists, we are trained, as Ken Hardy (2008) described, to be "pretty good, decent white therapist[s]" and as such we are trained to continue the oppression that comes with the majority population.

We as assessors need to look at how political and social situations impact people. We need to be concerned with the assumption that our knowledge is systematically prioritized over local worldviews and understandings. In these two cases, two mothers faced fears that their children would become young victims of injustice. Dedra looked to the future of her unborn child and wondered about the prescription society had written for him. Her way of coping was to hide her emotions, a streetwise and adaptive strategy. In Henry's case, he and his mother were facing the world with its potential tragedies. Following his mother's lead, Henry kept his feelings of anxiety and depression to himself so that he could be "okay." We need to look at the sociopolitical atmosphere in which our clients live in to see if the symptoms they exhibit are adaptive. We hold the ability to use our awareness to work and collaborate more sensitively with our clients.

References

Bhabha, H. K. (1994). *The location of culture*. London/New York: Routledge.

Butcher, J. N., Dahlstrom, W. G., Graham, J. R., Tellegan, A., & Kaemmer, B. (1992). *MMPI-A: A Minnesota multiphasic personality inventory-adolescents: Manual for administration and scoring*. Minneapolis, MN: University of Minnesota Press.

Cushman, P. (1995). *Constructing the self, constructing America: A cultural history of psychotherapy.* Cambridge, MA: Perseus Publishing.

Collins, A. (2004). Critical Psychology: The basic co-ordinates. In D. Hook (Ed.), *Introduction to critical psychology* (pp. 10–24). South Africa: University of Cape Town Press.

Conners, C. K., & MHS Staff. (2000). *Conners' Continuous Performance Test II (CPT II).* North Tonawanda, NY: Multi-Health Systems.

Dana, R. H. (1998). *Understanding cultural identity in intervention and assessment.* Thousand Oaks, CA: Sage Press.

Delis, D. C., Kramer, J. H., Kaplan, E., & Ober, B. A. (1994). *California Verbal Learning Test: Children's Version.* San Antonio, TX: The Psychological Corporation.

Du Bois, W. E. B. (1903/1994). *The souls of black folk.* New York, NY: Dover Publications.

Elliott, C. D. (2007). *Differential Ability Scales, second edition.* San Antonio, TX: Harcourt Assessment.

Enns, C. Z. (2012). Feminist approaches to counseling. In E. M. Altmaier & J. C. Hansen (Eds.) *The Oxford handbook of counseling psychology* (pp. 434–459). New York: Oxford University Press.

Exner, J. E., Jr., Colligan, S. C., Hillman, L. B., Metts, A. S., Ritzler, B. A., Rogers, K. T., et al. (2005). *A Rorschach workbook for the comprehensive system* (5th ed.). Asheville, NC: Rorschach Workshops.

Fanon, F. (1967). *Black skin white masks.* New York: Grove Press.

Fanon, F. (1963/1986). *The wretched of the earth.* New York: Grove Press.

Finn, S. E. (2007). *In our client's shoes: Theory and techniques of therapeutic assessment.* Mahwah, NJ: Lawrence Erlbaum Associates.

Fischer, C. T. (1985/1994). *Individualizing psychological assessment.* Mahwah, NJ: Lawrence Erlbaum Associates.

Foucault, M. (2008). *The birth of biopolitics: Lectures at the Collège de France 1978–9.* Basingstoke: Palgrave.

Geertz, C. (1973). *The interpretation of cultures.* New York: Basic Books.

Handler, L. (2007). The use of therapeutic assessment with children and adolescents. In S. R. Smith, & L. Handler (Eds.), *The clinical assessment of children and adolescents: A practitioner's handbook* (pp. 53–72). Mahwah, NJ: Lawrence Erlbaum Associates.

Hardy, K. V. (2008). *Kenneth V. Hardy on multiculturalism and psychotherapy. An interview with Randall C. Wyatt.* Psychotherapy.net. Retrieved from: http://www.psychotherapy.net/interview/kenneth-hardy.

Heaton, R. K., Chelune, G. J., Talley, J. L., Kay, G. G., & Curtis, G. (1993). *Wisconsin Card Sorting Test (WCST) Manual Revised and Expanded.* Odessa, FL: Psychological Assessment Resources.

Huett, S. & Goodman, D. (2012). Levinas on managed care: The (a)proximal, faceless third-party and the psychotherapeutic dyad. *Journal of Theoretical and Philosophical Psychology, 32*(2), 86–102. http://dx.doi.org/10.1037/a0026698.

King, B. B. (1996). *Blues all around me.* New York: Avon Books.

Newell, M. L., & Coffee, G. (2013). A social justice approach to assessment. In D. Shriberg, S. Y. Song, A. H. Miranda, & K. M. Radliff (Eds.), *School psychology and social justice: Conceptual foundations and tools for practice.* (pp. 173–188) New York: Routledge/Taylor & Francis Group.

Reynolds, C. R., & Kamphaus, R. W. (2004). *Behavior assessment system for children* (2nd ed.). Circle Pines, MN: American Guidance Service.

Rosenzweig, S. (1953). *The Children's Form of the Rosenzweig Picture-Frustration Study.* St. Louis, MO: Rana House..

Samuda, R. J. (1975/1998). *Psychological testing of American minorities: Issues and consequences.* Thousand Oaks, CA: Sage Publications Inc.

Semel, E., Wiig, E. H., & Secord, W. A. (2003). *Clinical evaluation of language fundamentals* (4th ed.). Toronto: The Psychological Corporation/A Harcourt Assessment Company.

Sue, D. W., & Sue, D. (1990). *Counseling the culturally diverse: Theory and practice.* New York: Wiley.

Spivak, G. (1988). Can the subaltern speak? In C. Nelson & L. Grossberg (Eds.), *Marxism and the interpretation of culture* (pp. 271–313). Basingstoke: Macmillan Education.

Taylor, C. (1989). *Sources of the self: The making of the modern identity.* Cambridge, MA: Harvard University Press.

wa Thiong'o, N. (2009). *Something torn and new: An African renaissance.* New York: Basic Civitas Books.

West-Olatunji, C. A. (2010). ACA Advocacy Competencies with culturally diverse clients. In M. J. Ratts, R. L. Toporek, & J. A. Lewis (Eds.), *ACA advocacy competencies: a social justice framework for counselors* (pp 55–63). Alexandria, VA: American Counseling Association.

Wiggins, S. J. (2003). *Paradigms of personality assessment.* New York: The Guilford Press.

Wechsler, D. (1999). *Wechsler Abbreviated Scale of Intelligence Test, second edition: Examiner's manual.* San Antonio, TX: Psychological Corporation.

Wechsler, D. (2009). *Wechsler Individual Achievement Test* (3rd ed.). San Antonio, TX: Pearson Assessments.

Wood, C., & D'Agnostino, J. V. (2010). Assessment in counseling: A tool for social justice work. In M. J. Ratts, R. L. Toporek, & J. A. Lewis (Eds.), *ACA advocacy competencies: a social justice framework for counselors.* (pp. 55–63). Alexandria, VA: American Counseling Association.

Yeh, C. J., & Kwan, K. K. (2010). Advances in multicultural assessment and counseling with adolescents: An ecological perspective. In J. G. Ponterotto, J. M. Casas, L. A. Suzuki, & C. M. Alexander (Eds.), *Handbook of multicultural counseling* (pp. 637–648). Thousand Oaks, CA: Sage Publications, Inc.

6 Unspeakable Fears

Exploring Trauma for Undocumented Immigrants

Cinthya Chin Herrera

A successful therapeutic process hinges on a number of factors: therapeutic alliance, empathy, and mutual goals. At the foundation of these factors is trust. A client's ability to trust their mental health professionals is essential to gathering information pertinent to the reasons they are seeking services or support. This trust enables a strong working relationship, a necessary condition to effective therapeutic intervention. This holds true both in therapy and in assessment, but it can be particularly challenging when working with certain populations that may have difficulty trusting new or unfamiliar individuals, agencies, and systems.

The vulnerability of immigrant clients is co-created, both through the dynamics imposed by those in positions of power, and through the inherent impotence of the immigrant in a less powerful role. Immigrants' level of vulnerability, influenced by their perception of the sociopolitical climate of immigration, can in turn affect their ability to trust others as a manner of self-preservation and protection. Often these dynamics are further complicated by additional obstacles immigrant clients face in securing care. In mental health, factors such as long wait lists, geographically inaccessible services, linguistic barriers, or a lack of understanding of patient rights can affect access and utilization of services. These numerous dynamics and barriers are navigated in order for clients to obtain mental health services.

Trusting the mental health system can seem like a risk for many immigrant families who may need to guard against various American systems. This is a justifiable position, given that practitioners, in addition to having the power to help, are also capable of harm. Service providers, in the role of mandated reporter, have the power to divide families. In the role of assessor and diagnostician, clinicians have the power to stigmatize through our pathologizing labels and measures of health. In the act of conceptualizing and intervening, they can disempower through theories designed around dominant cultural values or perpetuate the dynamic of disempowerment that exists in interactions with other systems. It is no wonder why many immigrant clients and families have difficulty trusting the mental health system. As brokers of an institution of wellness, mental health providers must examine our potential to contradict the messages of safety, equality, and well-being that we attempt to promote. It is for this reason that all treatment, but especially treatment with immigrant families, must begin with the assessment and development of trust.

Every immigrant has a unique story that influences the assessment process. Tales of overcoming tremendous obstacles in order to begin a new life in the United States of America shape the context of the information gathered in the assessment. The tenuous stability established in this country is often overshadowed by the mere anxieties from the potential interactions with the public child welfare system, police, or being detained or deported by US Immigration and Customs Enforcement (ICE). Added to the challenges of acculturation, language acquisition, prejudice and discrimination, inequality, and lack of access to adequate care, these realities prove difficult to address for many families and clinicians. However, these factors have an undeniable influence on the information or clinically relevant data provided by a parent or caregiver.

Health agencies across the United States are experiencing an increasing demand for services for immigrant clients due to the increase in immigrant populations in many of the most populated states (US Census Bureau, 2007). Agencies often struggle to keep up with the demands of this population while offering high quality, culturally sensitive, and linguistically appropriate services. Our community mental health agency, while addressing the issues of trauma, attachment, transition, and instability, is also tasked with providing trauma-informed care to immigrant populations. Clients who may wait months on waitlists with various mental health agencies often find that the clinician who begins working with them is the first port of entry into mental health services. The first clinical interactions with a family establish contact, trust, and the therapeutic frame for a safe space in which treatment will occur. These initial interactions also are a point of triage to determine the immediate needs of a client or family, and to provide them with information regarding any auxiliary services that might be needed, such as a psychological assessment, case management, or guidance around navigating the educational system.

The discussion of legal status demands the existence of trust in the relationship and safety in the frame of therapy. Often at the start of treatment, and possibly during the first session while reviewing informed consent and confidentiality, the topic of immigrant legal status is embedded into the conversation and discussed as part of what remains confidential in the work. Determining explicitly the legal status of important family members is a necessary component of the initial assessment of a client and their environment, as necessary as it might be to know if an important family member has a chronic illness or whether one might own weapons. During the clinical interview, information about the family's history, including their history of immigration, is also important to assess. Details about where each parent is from, how they met, and how they arrived to the United States can begin to provide a rich history and engage the parents in recounting their immigration story. This discussion of immigration history can uncover a range of information about the family's narrative about their existence in the United States as well as the context for the child's environment and reality. Understanding why a family immigrated to the United States, or emigrated from their home country, how the migration has affected each family member, and the many losses and gains in culture, relationships, and community can be important for determining whether these contextual circumstances have influenced the child's presenting problems of the present day.

A Case Example: The Family

In this following section, a composite case study is presented in which a number of themes from client lives are woven together to depict facets of treatment that may arise with many immigrant children and families. The assessment process begins long before the client is referred for formal psychodiagnostic or therapeutic assessment.

When the Tenoch family was referred for psychotherapy to address their 6-year-old daughter's difficulties at school, parents Elena and Memo were not entirely certain how therapy could help. However, Elena, who was open to any service that might help her daughter, expressed great interest in meeting and seemed eager to share all of her concerns about their daughter Luz.

Despite her initial desire to share a thorough family history, gathering this data from Elena was challenging and occurred over the course of several months. Elena described a multi-step immigration history. Raised by a loving family in central Mexico, Elena shared that the thought of leaving home was not an easy one. Convinced that the opportunities for work might be better in the United States than in her hometown, she came to the United States alone in her early twenties with a student visa—Elena wanted to become a teacher. She arrived in Los Angeles, driven by a desire to care for others and a hope for her new future in the United States. At the time of Elena's migration, Mexico's violence and crime had increased and worsened. Though she had been accustomed to traveling back to Mexico to visit family regularly, doing so was becoming an undesirable risk.

On one visit home to Mexico, Elena reconnected with Memo, her childhood sweetheart. They married and decided to raise a family in the United States. Memo, also interested in job opportunities in California, convinced a then-pregnant Elena to return with him to the United States. They moved to the San Francisco Bay area where Memo was able to find work without providing papers. Their daughter Luz was born soon thereafter. They attempted to settle into their new community while remaining connected to family in Mexico. During their sporadic phone conversations, Elena and Memo learned of several instances where family members had been faced with the increasing violence and corruption in the country. Christmas presents were stolen. Family spoke of their fears of being held at gunpoint when traveling. At one point, Elena's uncle was kidnapped and held for ransom, then subsequently released when the family was able to provide the equivalent of $3,000 USD to the kidnappers. Perhaps due to limited finances or from a subconscious fear of returning to Mexico, Elena allowed her visa to expire. This rendered Elena and Memo unable to return to Mexico without being discovered as undocumented and subsequently banned from returning to the United States. The emotional toll of the combined stressors of their recent migration and their worries about family abroad seemed insurmountable. When Memo's father died the following year, Elena and Memo were flooded by a wave of suffering and grief that was exacerbated by their inability to pay their respects, or provide and receive direct emotional support, due to the miles and barriers that were now between them.

Elena and Memo felt an increasing distance from their families, able to only contact them by phone. Reflecting back on this time, Elena described the sensation that she and Memo seemed to experience as an immense sense of loneliness. This was compounded by isolation from their home community. Though the Mexican immigrant community in their new city was present and active, it consisted of a heterogeneous group of Mexicans and other Latinos from diverse regions that honored separate traditions, holidays, and customs. In addition to their grief around the death of Memo's father, Elena and Memo also fell into a different grief process, cultural bereavement (Eisenbruch, 1991), from the physical, social, and cultural uprooting that had disrupted all aspects of their lives and self-identity.

These events served as a backdrop for the family history that Elena perceived as relevant to her daughter's current struggles. Her narrative contained traces of the family's trauma history—of being vicarious victims of the violence in the country they called "home," of the disillusionment of a "happy ending" promised in the American dream, and of the unanticipated losses and sacrifices that would occur along the way. With few exceptions, immigration is often not discussed under the umbrella of trauma, and may not come up in interview questions about traumatic events of the past unless raised explicitly by the clinician. It is often easier to acknowledge that an exposure to traumatic events occurs for refugees, who may have fled their native country due to a war, police corruption, or gangs. Similarly, there are some immigrants who seek asylum because of fear of persecution. But even for those who sought opportunities for better work or food security, there is often a rude awakening when the economic problems in this country affect the immigrant community the first and worst. These immigrants are often faced with losing family, community, country, security, language, culture, and way of life. The effects of these losses reach deep into the lived experiences of the children and grandchildren raised in immigrant families.

It is worth noting that the information shared by Elena regarding their troubled migration history was uncovered slowly over many sessions as she "remembered" key details she realized could be relevant. Although the focus of treatment was on Luz, initially for her academic struggles, there was an importance of entertaining the deep discussion of pertinent family events as a way of utilizing an ecological model to assess "from the outside in" all the factors that could hold importance in determining the root cause of Luz's current struggles.

As Elena continued to disclose details about relevant history, she shared that she believed Luz had a fairly "normal" development during her early childhood years, except for the fact that she did not talk much. Elena believed Luz preferred English as a language, though she was not certain the extent to which Luz had mastered English since both parents were monolingual Spanish-speakers and perceived this to be the reason they had limited communication with Luz.

Working with Luz

Developing a therapeutic environment that allows individuals to experience an inclination of trust is not an easy endeavor, but it is crucial to better understanding the family's experience as well as the work that lies ahead. Although Luz was referred through her elementary school for significant struggles with maintaining focus in the classroom, her challenges surpassed what the school had reported.

Through the course of the clinical interview with her therapist, it became clear that Luz would frequently bite her nails, struggle to fall asleep, have nightmares, have frequent episodes of encopresis, and was easily agitated. She often worried about her family in Mexico, and was especially nervous regarding the whereabouts of her parents if they were slightly late when picking her up from school. Through thoughtful history gathering, it was clear that the family's fear for their relatives' safety in Mexico, daily concerns about interacting with immigration authorities, and the history Memo had faced with police, all were family stressors that heightened Luz's lack of feeling safe. Luz's symptoms and their triggers painted a clearer picture of a world filled with anxiety that had been impacting her daily life for some years.

Luz's parents were not entirely conscious or perhaps not entirely convinced of the ways that the family history was impacting Luz's daily functioning. They often described Luz as *rebelde*, or rebellious, for not wanting to participate in school. When her parents were asked to reflect on how Luz might be navigating the delicate topic of immigration and family history with others outside of her family, they responded that Luz was instructed to keep those details as family secrets. Because, they added, people outside of the family should not know those details.

Survival Secrets

One of the many issues that arises with immigrant families is the importance of knowing the documentation status of clients, and the members of their immediate family, while carefully determining how the family has integrated this aspect of identity into the narrative they hold of themselves and the presenting problem. In clinical work, the fear of a parents' legal status being discovered can underlie the child's double-bind, resulting in problematic symptomatology while having been coached to hold family secrets. In this case example, Luz, who was instructed to never speak of sensitive details about her family by her parents and warned of the terrors that could ensue if she did, could not reconcile that mandate with the conflicting request to speak at school. As a result, she was singled out and punished for her poor participation at school. As can be expected, the clinical implications of these circumstances can have a profound impact on a client's perceptions of self and cultural identity.

It was due to this very fear that the Tenoch parents, labeled as resistant by teachers for failures to seek a psycho-educational evaluation promptly and to participate consistently in parent-teacher meetings, took a substantial amount of time to initiate psychotherapy and later the assessment. Mrs. Tenoch admitted regretfully at a later date that she had avoided therapy for far too long out of fear that the school or mental health system might expose her as undocumented and lead to her or her husband's deportation. It made sense, however, that if this family's survival were based on keeping big secrets, then of course they would always be inclined to report that Elena's development was "normal" and that a larger problem did not exist. However, as the question of why Elena continued to struggle with participation in school continued to come up in meetings, the need for a formal assessment became more evident. With some convincing due to their continued pattern of hesitation, Elena and Memo agreed to have Luz assessed.

One task for a mental health provider aware of family members' legal status then becomes how to delicately balance the family's trust while creatively explaining the needs of the client to the treatment team and teachers without disclosing documentation status. The provider becomes triangulated in a dynamic of secrecy maintained between the parents and the party who does not know and, in effect, becomes yet another individual holding one of the family's secrets in a narrative that is fragmented. This position can become especially challenging as it may mean omitting relevant history that could be incriminating, or being asked to remedy inconsistencies from the "facts" and history provided by the family.

This is where a collaborative assessment model can be important in that it allows for co-treatment through the concerted efforts of both the therapist and assessor. Having a therapist involved already in a case can provide a value of gathering information and can help the client and family develop a better relationship with the mental health system. This ultimately allows the family and the client to utilize the assessment to greater degrees of therapeutic depth.

The established therapeutic relationship has often played an intricate role in supporting the assessment process and can give space for a greater narrative that facilitates the psychological assessment. Parents are more likely to trust, disclose, and utilize the assessment if they already have an established relationship through the therapeutic services offered to them.

There can be additional complications that can arise when there are multiple team members and multiple systems involved, such as whether the family is "out," so to speak, in regards to their legal status with all the members of their treatment team or the school. It can be difficult in the assessment process to gather accurate information, as the function of secrets are powerful and not easily bypassed. For a child like Luz, one false step or one misspoken lie could create instability, separation, and loss, as her parents had warned her all too well. How then, as a mental health provider, is one to undo what may be a survival strategy—the act of secret keeping—for the sake of unearthing, exploring, and processing a child's internal experience? This clinical and ethical dilemma is further complicated when a crisis involving the secret begins to unfold.

In all of the initial interviews and the months of therapy that had followed, the Tenoch family had failed to disclose Memo's history with alcoholism. Perhaps ashamed, or perhaps believing these details irrelevant to Luz's struggles, it was not until Memo was involved with police that the secret came to light. Elena contacted her therapist one late night, crying. Her voice was filled with fear as she reported that Memo had been arrested for driving while intoxicated. The trauma of detention and separation that follows inevitably impacts the parent's well-being and mental health as well as their children's. Within days, Memo was moved from the county jail to a detention facility where a deportation process would begin. Memo had suddenly become a statistic—one of the 400,000 immigrants that would be deported by the United States that year in order to meet its quota that had reached record-breaking levels several years in a row. But the family did not need the statistics. They needed hope. And they needed stability.

As the therapist worked with Elena and Luz through their time of panic and fear, advocacy and case management helped Elena and Luz return to a tolerable emotional state. Elena and Luz were seen for some time at home, fearing the risk of being racially profiled and stopped by police. Elena's reality that her daughter could be taken away by child protective services if she too were detained, rendering her without rights to speak or have contact, had paralyzed and imprisoned them in their own home. Days after Memo's arrest, Luz seemed filled with fear, clinging to her mom, unable to leave her side. Elena, appearing sleep deprived and emotionally drained, hugged Luz close to her side. Memo's abrupt absence greatly impacted the psychological and physical well-being of the entire family. Elena reported that both she and Luz were crying often and experiencing a loss of appetite along with sleep disturbances and fearfulness. Luz slept on the floor next to the entrance doorway to their home, sometimes clinging to an article of her father's clothing, waiting for him to return.

Given that more than 5 million children in the United States have at least one undocumented parent (Passel & Cohn, 2011), many communities have seen families with undocumented parents pulled apart in the aftermath of deportations. A parent who is detained or consequently deported may find it virtually impossible to participate in child welfare case plan requirements or family court proceedings, increasing the likelihood that their parental rights will be inappropriately or prematurely terminated. In 2011, at least 5,100 children were estimated to be living in foster care due to having at least one detained or deported parent (Wessler, 2011). Unfortunately, detention by Immigration and Customs Enforcement (ICE) obstructs participation in Child Protective Services' plans for family unity (Cervantes & Lincroft, 2010). Most child welfare departments lack systemic policies to keep families united when parents are detained or deported. The political climate involving undocumented parents and what would be considered their parental rights, related to their US-born children, is a bleak and an unbearable reality for many caregivers. This reality was not lost on Elena, who was determined to fight for Memo's release. However, Elena needed help in learning to navigate the justice system in this foreign land and foreign language. Memo was in fact released after one month in detention. However, the family felt the long-lasting effects of this traumatic separation long afterward.

It is important to understand during circumstances like the ones the Tenoch family faced that time is critical, as is the collaboration between therapist and assessor. In order to support the process of father's return, clinician and assessor must fight the pull to succumb to the family's fear, panic, powerlessness, and vulnerability. Despite the uncertainty of the Tenoch family's future, providers and family alike were fueled to action by a determination and an unspoken, firm belief that despite the minor offense committed, the family did not deserve to be torn apart in this way.

Although Luz was unable to separate from her mother to attend school or speech therapy, she eventually managed to attend therapy and testing sessions at the clinic. In the battery of tests Luz was given, her results on the Preschool Language Scale-5 Spanish version (Zimmerman, Steiner, & Pond, 2012) confirmed significant impairments in verbal language, both receptive (SS: 76) and expressive (SS: 52). These results were in contrast to her scores on the KABC-II (Kaufman & Kaufman, 2004) Nonverbal Index (NVI: 93) showing average levels of ability when factoring out language, through nonverbal tests assessing her visual perception, nonverbal reasoning and abstraction, spatial relations, short-term visual memory, and sequencing skills. With regard to adaptive functioning, Elena's responses on the Vineland Adaptive Behavior Scales-II (Sparrow, Cicchetti, & Balla, 2008) showed functioning in the average range on all scales except communication. Similarly, concerns reported by Elena and Luz's teachers on the Behavior Assessment System for Children-II (Reynolds & Kamphaus, 2004) suggested that aside from Luz's communication struggles, the primary concerns others had for her pertained to Luz's struggles with emotional functioning. Their concerns specifically centered around Luz's high level of anxiety, emotional reactivity, and her withdrawal from social interactions (Table 6.1).

In test measures used to assess Luz's emotional functioning, it was recognized that Luz had completed some of the testing during a period of high distress due to her father's detention that had ultimately challenged her coping abilities. According to the reports of her mother, teacher, and speech therapist, Luz had shown markedly different behaviors

Table 6.1 Luz's results on standardized measures

Test	Standard Score	T–Score	Percentile Rank
PLS–V Spanish Receptive Language	76	–	5
PLS–V Spanish Expressive Language	52	–	0.1
KABC–II Nonverbal Index	94	–	34
Vineland–II Communication Scale	69	–	2
BASC–II Parent Rating Scale – Anxiety	–	76	99
BASC–II Parent Rating Scale – Depression	–	73	97
BASC–II Parent Rating Scale – Withdrawal	–	52	67
BASC–II Teacher Rating Scale – Anxiety	–	65	91
BASC–II Teacher Rating Scale – Depression	–	58	84
BASC–II Teacher Rating Scale – Withdrawal	–	63	90

in the time of her father's absence. She refused to attend school for nearly two weeks due to extreme separation anxiety, and had to be accompanied by her mother during her speech therapy sessions in order to keep Luz from throwing a tantrum or crying.

Luz found ways to express, often nonverbally, through projective test measures, themes of separation that she struggled to understand and a sense of independence she hoped to master. Her projective test data supported the observations and concerns reported by her mother and teacher. During a sand tray interview, Luz placed figurines equidistant from each other in the sand. The figures were related and included a mother, a daughter, and a father. But the characters did not interact. The mother and daughter stood alone on one end of the sand tray while the father stood on the other end, facing in the opposite direction.

In another example, Luz was asked to complete a projective drawing of a Person-In-The-Rain (Verinis, Lichtenberg, & Henrich, 1974). Luz initially drew a girl with no hands, without an umbrella, and missing the most basic protective gear. With extensive efforts on the part of the assessor thorough questioning and extended inquiry, Luz came to the realization that the girl could be given tools to help her manage her immediate need to stay dry, and therefore began to draw an umbrella. Luz described the girl in the drawing as "happy," despite her initial unmet need for protection. Her drawing and explanation alluded to her own emotional experience involving her attempts to keep negative feelings at bay and present herself in a positive light, despite the evident metaphorical storm that had been raining down on her (Figure 6.1).

Although Luz's responses suggested that she was making great efforts to appear unaffected by the stressors within her family, she showed occasional glimpses into an underlying emotional distress and sadness. One projective story from the Robert's Apperception Test for Children (McArthur & Roberts, 1982) depicted a girl embracing her mother. According to Luz, "The girl and mom has bad news. They hug because they sad."

Discussion

In light of testing data suggesting limited receptive and expressive language abilities, Luz could not fully process the environmental and family stressors that she and her mother were experiencing. Luz could not inquire about the changes in the home in a way that

Figure 6.1 Luz's Projective Drawing

would satisfy her need for this knowledge. At times, it was easier for Luz to withdraw and avoid others, particularly when she did not feel that they would understand what she wanted to communicate and convey. Thus, the "rebellious" behaviors that occurred when Luz would refuse to follow instructions were her way of firmly conveying what she could not express verbally. Withdrawal and refusal of tasks, coping strategies even before her father's separation from the family, were a way for Luz to create a safe emotional distance from those things that reminded her of the often intolerable challenges she faces throughout her day.

The collaboration between therapist and assessor, especially at the end of the assessment, becomes useful for allowing a better understanding of symptoms, coping strategies, strengths, and weaknesses. Feedback provided to the parents can be held and carried by the therapist who ensures a longer-term approach to navigating the challenges to their readiness for implementing recommendations and acquiring a comprehensive understanding of the child. The goal involves finding ways for the family to integrate the different pieces of a child's experience to create a new understanding within the context of the family and their collective history. It involves helping the family put the fragmented pieces of a child's story together to create a new narrative that includes more of the child's lived experiences. The child brings into a therapeutic space their fragmented self, and through the therapeutic work, arrives at a more genuine and complete understanding of self in return. Whether during the assessment, or in therapy, uncovering the underlying truths and realities of a child involves giving voice and space for expressing the unspeakable fears fighting for acknowledgement. It is only by allowing children and their family members to speak of these inconceivable tragedies that a clinician can begin to facilitate their emotional process, allow them to grieve for the chaos that they had not expected to have survived, and explore the unexpected resiliency that can surface in the face of such adversity. Through this empowerment, our clients can begin to acknowledge their abilities, their humanity, and the strength in their voice so that they may begin to overcome the fears and struggles that are inherent in their stay in this country.

Our clinical role does not include being rescuers, saviors, or heroes. But we can use our knowledge and power in our work by preparing immigrant parents to address the injustices they might encounter in the justice system or child welfare system—systems that often do not have the family's best interest in mind. An invaluable goal for immigrant clients is to shift their narrative of victim and perpetrator so that immigrant children and parents can feel a sense of agency and control over their world with the tools to be advocates for themselves and their families.

References

Cervantes, W., & Lincroft, Y. (2010). *The impact of immigration enforcement on child welfare.* First Focus. Retrieved from https://www.ils.ny.gov/files/Effect%20Of%20Immigration%20 Enforcement%20On%20Child%20Welfare.pdf.

Eisenbruch, M. (1991). From post-traumatic stress disorder to cultural bereavement: Diagnosis of Southeast Asian refugees. *Social Science & Medicine, 33*(6), 673–680. doi:10.1016/0277-9536(91)90021-4.

Kaufman, A. S., & Kaufman, N. L. (2004). *Kaufman Assessment Battery for Children* (2nd ed.). New York: American Guidance Service.

McArthur, D. S., & Roberts, G. E. (1982). *Roberts Apperception Test for Children: Manual.* Los Angeles: Western Psychological Services.

Passel, J. S., & Cohn, D. (2011, February 1). *Unauthorized immigrant population: National and state trends, 2010.* Pew Hispanic. Retrieved from http://www.pewhispanic.org/files/reports/133.pdf.

Reynolds, C. R., & Kamphaus, R. W. (2004). *Behavior Assessment System for Children* (2nd ed.). Circle Pines, MN: American Guidance System.

Sparrow, S. S., Cicchetti, D. V., & Balla, D. A. (2008). *Vineland Adaptive Behavior Scales* (2nd ed.). New York: American Guidance Service.

US Census Bureau. (2007). *American community survey.* Retrieved from http://factfinder.census.gov/.

Verinis, J. S., Lichtenberg, E. F., & Henrich, L. (1974). The draw-a-person in the rain technique: Its relationship to diagnostic category and other personality indicators. *Journal of clinical psychology, 30*(3), 407–414.

Wessler, S. F. (2011). *Shattered families: The perilous intersection of immigration enforcement and the child welfare system.* Applied Research Center. Retrieved from https://www.raceforward.org/research/reports/shattered-families.

Zimmerman, I. L., Steiner, V. G., & Pond, R. E. (2012). *Preschool Language Scales,* fifth edition Spanish. San Antoni, TX: Pearson Clinical.

7 The Ambiguous Other

Reflections on Race and Culture in the Assessment Relationship

Tricia Fong

"You're Chinese!" my young, non-white assessment client proclaimed somewhat disdainfully. "How do you know?" I inquired. "Because of your name," she stated. "And your eyes," she added tentatively. "What are you?" I asked curiously. "I'm … I'm regular," she replied.

Race and ethnicity create powerful dynamics in any clinical relationship (Cardemil & Battle, 2003; Leary, 1997). As psychologists, we are tasked with understanding the deep meanings of race, ethnicity, culture, power and oppression within the context of psychological structures and interpersonal interactions. My training years stressed a cognitive understanding of a myriad of cultures. While well intentioned, this study of diversity (in its infant years as a curriculum mandate) neglected to adequately prepare me for the experience of my ethnicity as it occupies important but ambiguous space in the room. As clinicians, we are asked to do more than simply acknowledge racial difference. We find ourselves sitting with its totality—its weight, power, histories, pain, and ambiguity. We are required to negotiate its implied and unconscious meanings as they unfold in already complex therapeutic or assessment relationships, and are thus asked to understand the humanity of the client and of ourselves in the context of racially charged interactions.

Literature regarding the interaction of race and ethnicity within the clinical relationship has primarily focused on the negotiation of race between the white therapist and the ethnic minority client. However, consideration of race in the clinical relationship between the ethnic minority therapist and the white or ethnic minority client brings about its own unique issues, at times immediately catalyzing race-related transference and countertransference reactions (Comas-Diaz & Jacobsen, 1991). Kimberlyn Leary (1995) writes, "To talk about race and ethnicity involves immersion, however temporary in a body whose sight, texture, and even smell may be alike or dissimilar from one's own. Thus, talk about race can arouse powerful affects and key human concerns" (p. 128). This clinical immersion is unique in that it elicits distinct and at times immediate transference and countertransference that can set the stage for clinical interactions to follow. While meaningful, the negotiation of race and ethnicity becomes one of power and privilege, oppression and subjugation. This process can be crude, often evoking a deep human vulnerability within the minority clinician. In a separate article, Leary (1997) notes, "the fact that I am a person of color carries important social meanings. Race and ethnicity—particularly when they are observable features of the analyst's self—represent a kind of self-disclosure. Although I have not conveyed anything about myself, the fact that race is written on my face shapes the clinical dialogue to follow" (pp. 165–166). This chapter attempts to explore these complicated dynamics through discussion and reflection on my work as an Asian American clinical psychologist serving ethnically diverse children who are traumatized or otherwise disenfranchised. This chapter will examine a psychological assessment case of a youth assessment client in the community setting.

Portholes for Race-Related Transference and Countertransference

It is important to set the stage for my own personal and cultural narrative in order to understand the entry points that were primed for countertransference in the assessment case that I will discuss. I am a third-generation Chinese American. My grandmother immigrated to the United States in the 1920s. Her family had once been wealthy, but they struggled after political and economic unrest. Their financial struggles prompted an arranged marriage for my grandmother to a man almost twenty years her senior. My grandmother was detained on Angel Island and recalled those days as humiliating imprisonment. Once allowed to enter the country, she settled into a tenement in San Francisco's Chinatown and raised eight children on meager wages earned in an alley sweatshop. My mother was one of those children. Because she was neither male nor the youngest child, she was denied a college education as the family's finances could only cover tuition for two of the eight children. My father was also raised in San Francisco's Chinatown. His own father had passed during his adolescence. As the eldest son, he assumed the role of head of household, running the family's barbershop at the age of 15. My psychological roots are, in part, embedded in my parents' hard-won efforts to move out of Chinatown into the outer lands of San Francisco. It was only a few miles in distance but a world away from the pain of their childhoods and the struggle of their immigrant parents. As a child, I felt palpably their press for assimilation. The Chinese culture was held at an ambivalent distance. My parents did not encourage my acquisition of the Chinese language. I was enrolled in a nearly all-white, wealthy Catholic preschool from which some of my earliest memories derive. I remember the *feeling* of difference, whether it was my hair and skin color, the shape of my eyes, or my second-hand clothing. I *knew* deeply that something was amiss, that I was being seen and treated as different despite my perfect English or place of residence. San Francisco has always had a large Asian American population, and my elementary years onward in the public education system thankfully recalibrated my earlier experiences, grounding them in relationships with those like me. When we traveled outside of San Francisco, however, I was reminded of my ethnic difference whether through direct racial slurs, crude jokes, or refusal of service. My parents and relatives, all strong and successful people, seemed small and helpless in their silence. In these moments, I learned that to be Chinese meant to be irregular, if not unfavorable. These overt experiences of racism capitalized on the sense of difference that I had felt as a young child. Together, they shaped a deep sense of ethnic inferiority and ambiguity in my childhood and youth.

While I have since become anchored in and proud of my Chinese American heritage, these dark internal places are the entry points for my countertransference to a client's racially charged interactions. My clinical interactions have ranged from a child client insidiously mocking the Chinese language to becoming a psychological trigger for a Vietnam veteran's traumatic memories of his war crimes against Asian women. These instances are clear examples of how my ethnic appearance can immediately determine or shape the therapeutic course. Other times, the race-related projection surprises me, making a late appearance in the clinical relationship. After several months of working with a young foster child and her caregiver, her caregiver insisted that she, herself, was a "black-Asian mother." She had just finished reading Amy Chua's controversial piece on the "Tiger Mother." While I appreciated her efforts to ally, I deeply resented the perception that I would naturally share in these harsh childrearing beliefs simply because I, too, am Chinese. I struggled between my human impulse to correct her misgivings about my Chinese-ness and an inclination to clinically experiment with the projection. In this short moment, I had been "raced," implicated into a narrowly defined set of cultural assumptions and shortchanged in my capacity to respond (Leary, 2007). During these many years of clinical practice, I have learned that cultural sensitivity is not necessarily a skill to be mastered, but an attunement to the dynamic that is created when I, as an Asian American woman, step into the clinical space. May Tung (1981) writes, "countertransference lies … in the fact that the content of our interaction touched the very root of my existence. We can discuss cultural and racial issues, but our roots are, by definition in our unconsciousness" (p. 661). As evidenced in the following case, the experience of my racial being, with its deep and conflicted roots, as a vehicle for client transference is an exercise of strength and stamina. On a good day, I am patient with the interaction, ready for the emotional stabs of its charge, angst, and intensity, and eager to make clinical sense of the process. Other times, I am weary, unwilling, or ill prepared to "go there." These opposing stances are illustrated in the following case.

The Case of Adam

Adam was a 14-year-old high school freshman referred for a psychological assessment by his therapist. He self-identified, almost insistently, as multiracial, though his intake paperwork denoted his ethnicity as Caucasian. He was at risk for expulsion due to truancy and repeated behavioral disruptions in the classroom. Of primary concern were repeated themes of physical violence, molestation, and rape in his classwork assignments. According to school administration, Adam had twice placed the school on lockdown when he started rumors of bombs on campus. These behaviors were incongruent with his therapist's experience of him and alarming to his great aunt and caregiver who insisted that nothing was wrong.

Adam's family history was marked by recurrent family stress, exposure to parental substance use, witness to domestic violence, physical abuse, and moves of residence due to both mandated out-of-home placement and voluntary kinship care. Prior to his birth, Adam's mother had suffered from a traumatic brain injury after a drug deal had gone awry, which left her wheelchair bound. Adam was exposed to substances in utero and spent his early years raised by both parents in an urban, impoverished neighborhood. Adam's father was described as unpredictable and enraged, and Adam's early and middle childhood years were plagued by repeated episodes of severe domestic violence, intermittent neglect, and violent physical abuse. As the assessment progressed, Adam's great aunt shifted from guarded and vague disclosures to vivid memories of a young Adam who witnessed and was victim to his father's violent rages and his mother's lifelong addiction. Additionally, Adam had been forced to obtain and distribute drugs on behalf of his parents and had been threatened with weapons or witness to life-threatening situations. At the age of ten, Adam himself requested to live elsewhere and transitioned to the long-term care of his great-aunt and her then partner. His great aunt had served as an auxiliary protector throughout Adam's young life. She had been cued by the sights or sounds of Adam's distress from her nearby window and intervened during many incidents when his physical safety was urgently compromised. Her partner had been a close, sober, and consistent figure for Adam, whose later passing Adam frequently spoke of during the assessment.

By all accounts, Adam was described as smart and intellectually capable. However, his grades began to decline in middle school. His academic work came to the attention of his high school instructors due to the repeated, violent nature of the writing that he authored. Adam's violence potential became a central theme throughout the assessment, manifesting in the assessment questions, the clinical relationship, and serving as points of tension between the assessor and the collateral service providers. His aggression befuddled others, prompting those in either authority or in close emotional relationship to him to engage in a perplexing interchange of alarm and distance. The testing had occurred in the school setting. While the school staff was cordial and logistically helpful, questions around the validity of Adam's distress and aggression had been a source of tension between this assessor and the school staff. This tension was most palpable after Adam's disclosure during a self-report clinical symptom inventory prompted a crisis hospitalization. During this process, the staff had obliged this clinician's request for assistance while minimizing the validity of his statements, stating that he "exaggerates," "likes to tell stories," and "just wants attention."

Testing Adam: Racism as Experiential Data

Throughout the assessment, Adam struggled to maintain attention and concentration. He fidgeted, moved about the room, and initiated breaks either by requesting one or simply leaving and returning. Adam's manner of relating vacillated between cooperation and anger and hostility. At times, he was genuine in his efforts to build rapport, emotionally honest in his responses, and mindful of his manners. In other instances, Adam became verbally hostile, yelling, "Shut up!" or proclaiming, "You're so stupid!" At its extreme, he screamed, "You cunt!" or provocatively discussed his white supremacist relatives. His blatant verbal hostilities occurred consistently throughout the testing, with more or less frequency depending on his mood. He struggled to display aggression and test boundaries, and simultaneously attempted to maintain this examiner's favor.

The emotional testing sessions were difficult and taxed both Adam's psychology and the clinical relationship. During these moments, he was anxious and oppositional, as his anxiety and hostility ran side by side. Adam would burp loudly, blow the air toward this assessor, and yell, "Ahh! Don't you smell that?" While Adam's behaviors were obnoxious, off-putting, distracting, and limit-testing, they were tempered by his vulnerability, and thus somewhat manageable. However, Adam began to use racial epithets and other racially charged language. The manner in which he did so vacillated between impulsive curiosity, compulsive and aggressive hatred, and naively echoed mantra from the white supremacy beliefs to which he had been exposed. Adam impulsively yelled, "Ahh! Black people!," told racist "jokes," and created swastikas with the blocks used for intelligence testing. Most disturbingly, he repeatedly responded with "nigger" to the Rorschach cards then immediately claimed that he was "only kidding."

This assessor consulted with the primary people in Adam's life. Adam's therapist, an African American woman, followed each session as the energy and rage behind his statements escalated. Adam's behavior surprised her, and she gasped at my report of his charged hostility and racist remarks. At school, any inappropriate remark was met by quick and immediate discipline. As his assessor, I witnessed Adam's confusion and was subjugated to his rage about race, power, and relationship. I struggled both in session and outside of it. When I directly confronted him, Adam would deny, minimize, become visibly uncomfortable, and avoid. Without an immediate boundary, however, the frequency and intensity of these racially charged outbursts increased. This assessor became Adam's receptacle for his race-laden rage and angry outbursts. I was grossly offended, agitated, and frustrated. "He's such a racist!" I frequently blurted out in supervision, exasperated at having to tolerate his spewing hatred, angry about having to maintain a semblance of neutrality, and defeated by the power of his whiteness. It mattered little to both himself and to me that he only once made a direct racist remark about my Asian ethnicity. I had become the target of his aggressive othering. His racism was all about me and not about me, hidden beneath his words yet exposed in its generalities. It was indirect, insidious, obvious through tone, and hurtful through intention.

There are a myriad of clinical responses to Adam's racist or racially charged statements. Clinical theory or orientation would need to be the guidepost or roadmap. Having previously trained in behaviorally oriented child settings, I knew that I could implement a hard line. I could strongly assert that his statements were inappropriate, that his behavior was not okay or that we would end early if he continued. However, I was no longer working in this setting and had professionally forayed into an analytically informed community clinic. The lived experience of this assessment case had become an exercise in transference and countertransference. The assessment space had become deeply clinical, forged by interpersonal interactions between client and clinician. It was created by moments of rage and vulnerability, and its intensity was only tempered by fleeting compassion when Adam spoke of his early childhood.

While the test data exposed Adam's deep conflicts and complex rage, my attempt at a relatively neutral stance came at the compromise of my ethnic self. At a fundamental human level, I neither protected myself nor stood up for the minority community at large. I had reconciled my actions as sound clinical decisions, one that gave voice to Adam's internal rage that had either been hidden from or dismissed by others. Yet, I felt a strong sense of shame and betrayal of myself as a minority woman. I had acted within my clinical psychologist role and the frame of therapeutic assessment. Yet, I simultaneously failed to act on behalf of my own humanity, silenced by his oppression, and immobilized by my own subjugation.

This case exhausted me and toward its end, I questioned if I was strong enough to do *this* work in *this* dynamic way. I was emotionally and psychologically taxed by holding Adam's racism and by tolerating his anger and racism, risk, and suicidal ideation. Moreover, I held this alone in a system of providers who either refused to see it or with whom Adam would not allow their witness. I struggled to find the clinical meaning of his interactions, often pondering if the interpretation was worth his assault on my already conflicted cultural self. The clinical interactions with Adam were emotionally distinct from other transferences, entangled by his difficult early history and notable for their exchanges of oppression and subjugation.

Toward Holding the Rage and Anger

Leary (1995) writes, "The psychoanalytic situation may offer a unique opportunity for elaborating the meaning of race and ethnicity to the extent that the analytic clinician can focus on the amalgams of fantasy and reality to which talk about race is heir and discover the idiosyncratic purposes to which it has been put" (p. 133). When I understood the clinical interactions with Adam within the assessment space as discovery, I felt them to be less of an affront to my personhood. This stance neutralized my impulsive need to fiercely protect my ethnic self. Adam's racist and racially charged interactions were windows to his own pain and his early experiences of interpersonal horror and helplessness. While he offered glimpses of his early memories of neglect, violence, abuse, and separation, he was adamant on protecting the semblance of his parents as good. Adam carried great confusion about relationships and struggled to make sense of his opposing early experiences of intimacy and violence.

Concluding Remarks

My maternal uncle was a pioneer in accessing public education for Chinese immigrant children. In his published doctoral dissertation, he writes, "Each step gained chipped away at a tenaciously held stereotyping of the Chinese as unassimilable, passive, inscrutable, and 'unimpressible'" (Low, 1982, p. 192). The perception of the Chinese as "unimpressible" was a direct quote by George Tait, the San Francisco School Superintendent who, in his 1864 annual report, referred to the city's Chinese people as unprogressive, apathetic, and otherwise unimportant. In a handwritten note inside the front cover of the copy he gifted to my parents, my uncle wrote, "With all good wishes. May our children and theirs be less unimpressible."

In this chapter, I have attempted to briefly explore the complex dynamics of race-related transference and countertransference in the assessment relationship. One of my primary goals was to identify the distinct responses racially charged interactions evoke in the assessor as demonstrated in the case of an adolescent client who had experienced multiple traumas and had been exposed to a white supremacist group as a young child. In the assessment relationship, Adam's racism became a vehicle for him to express his aggression and victimization. It was an opportunity for him to explore his confusion around his primary interpersonal conflicts of affability and hate, and his earliest attachment experiences of intimacy and rejection. The assessment data gave voice to Adam's deep anxieties about relationship, conflicts that he either hid in his daily interactions or that erupted in big and threatening ways.

While the assessment garnered needed information regarding Adam's interpersonal dilemmas and the traumas that had constructed them, the neutral clinical stance that helped to usher his racism into conversation, data responses, or the assessment space came at a high personal cost. My work with Adam required that I wrestle with my own experiences of subjugation as he spewed either racially charged or blatantly racist remarks toward me. My responses were clumsy at best, and fraught with feelings of anger and empathy, and resentment and compassion. In retrospect, I had confused my neutral stance with being silenced. In this misperception, I felt a deep sense of betrayal to my family and cultural roots. Had I become passive and apathetic? Had I become unimpressible?

In an article about a child's projections onto her Chinese ethnicity, Tung (1981) writes, "The innocence of children seems to show up in the bluntness of cruelty" (p. 661). I had been hurt by the cruelty of Adam's racism. Adam's innocence had, however, been evidenced in his central questions for the assessment. "Am I crazy?" he wondered. "Why don't I tell people how I feel? Why are my feelings so strong?" he added. His innocence had also emerged in moments when he shared his favorite music or opened the door for his great aunt. Adam's interactions with me were clinical data, a porthole into his internal chaos and a glimpse into the tragedies of his early life. He was resistant to verbalizing or processing his racially charged statements, and instead demanded that they occupy space in the room. The challenge for me, the assessor, was to allow its presence while prohibiting it to take residence in my personhood. I needed to tolerate his words without being tortured by them. Perhaps Adam's unconscious intentions were not to obliterate me or position me into the passivity that I feared. Perhaps his intentions were to activate and mobilize me to better understand the darker parts of him and the roots of their existence.

Consistent with the assessment data, Adam navigated the ending of the assessment service with ambivalence. He listened to the feedback letter with both interest and opposition. His ability to tolerate my responses to his initial questions was greatly impacted by the loyalty conflict that had been inadvertently created when I had invited his therapist to the reading of his feedback letter. When the ending approached, he begged for an additional meeting. However, at this last meeting, he was flippant and dismissive. In these final days, I had become less of an object for his racism and more of a receptacle for his disorganized attachment. These processes are not discrete but rather representative of one another, working in concert to evidence the deep impact of interpersonal and complex trauma.

References

Altman, N. (2010). *The analyst in the inner city: Race, class, and culture through a psychoanalytic lens.* New York: Routledge.

Cardemil, E. V. & Battle, C. L. (2003). Guess who's coming to therapy? Getting comfortable with conversation about race and ethnicity in psychotherapy. *Professional Psychology: Research and Practice, 34*(3), 278–286.

Comas-Diaz, L. & Jacobsen, F. M. (1991). Ethnocultural transference and countertransference in the therapeutic dyad. *American Journal of Orthopsychiatry, 6*(3), 392–402.

Leary, K. (1995). "Interpreting in the dark"; Race and ethnicity in psychoanalytic psychotherapy. *Psychoanalytic Psychology, 12*(1), 127–140.

Leary, K. (1997). Race, self-disclosure, and "forbidden talk": Race and ethnicity in contemporary clinical practice. *Psychoanalytic Quarterly, 36,* 163–189.

Leary, K. (2007). Racial insult and repair. *Psychoanalytic Dialogues, 17*(4), 539–549.

Low, V. (1982). *The unimpressible race: A century of educational struggle by the Chinese in San Francisco.* San Francisco: East-West Publishing.

Tung, M. (1981). On being seen as a "Chinese" therapist by a Caucasian child. *American Journal of Orthopsychiatry, 51*(4), 654–661.

8 Working with Countertransference Reactions to Treatment Team Members in Collaborative Assessments

Lisa M. Nakamura

The psychologist who performs evaluations of children in community mental health typically produces a report that is given to the referring party, often a social worker, or the legal guardian. These results, which are directly based on the questions posed by this referral party, may be further discussed over the phone or in a meeting. Other members of the child's treatment team are included primarily to provide the psychologist with background information. The model is one of limited involvement with the other parties in the child's life—it is one of getting in, getting the job done, and getting out. However, therapeutic collaborative assessments in community mental health settings inherently call for closer collaboration of many treatment team members, an aspect that can be fraught with its own set of complexities and challenges.

Stephen Finn created a model for therapeutic collaborative assessments, which we draw upon at our agency (Finn, 2007). The model encourages the client, the caregiver, and his or her treatment team to generate their own referral questions. The assessor actively engages with the various caregiver's perceptions about a client's test results, to the point that the report would act as a summary of what was already discussed. Discussion of the results is tiered into Level 1, 2, and 3 corresponding to the degree in which a caregiver can integrate these results into their current perception of a client. Level 1 encompasses feedback that is already within the caregiver's understanding and thus easily accepted. Level 2 involves feedback that the caregiver can reasonably accommodate into their current understanding. Finally, Level 3 feedback consists of those findings that are so outside of the realm of the caregiver's understanding that they would likely trigger a defensive response. Finn outlined many dynamics to consider in working with other treatment team members of a case (Finn, 2007). I have found Finn's chapter invaluable in working with treatment team members in community mental health. This chapter will further explore the role of countertransference reactions amongst treatment team members in therapeutic collaborative assessments in these settings through a case study. Countertransference refers to a clinician's own intense emotional reactions with a client that may reflect an (typically unconscious) aspect of the client's inner world and/or the clinician's triggers from his or her own personal history.

Many foster children have no stable caregiver. Treatment teams often fill the role of a surrogate parent; yet because of staff turnover or the child's change of placements, these teams are inherently unstable. In some cases where a foster child is frequently removed from placements, it is challenging to work collaboratively with a treatment team that is in flux—new members coming in and old members leaving. Moreover, the sheer panoply of treaters is daunting: a foster child can work with therapists, Court Appointed Special Advocate (CASA) workers, group home case managers, county social workers, Foster Family Agency (FFA) workers, education attorneys, and Therapeutic Behavioral Services (TBS) workers; and the list goes on.

In this context, the evaluator is in the awkward position of being yet another new and temporary member of a team working with a child with complex issues. I liken this role to being an obnoxious new roommate of a treatment team, loudly voicing how the furniture could be rearranged.

Because community mental health assessments often work across multiple systems which can involve a myriad of service providers, countertransference reactions and splitting are more likely to arise. Splitting is the phenomenon in which sharp divisions within a treatment team are often seen as good versus bad. Even within an agency, an evaluator may have little time and space to process countertransference and splitting dynamics within a case over the bread-and-butter priorities of interpreting test results and making recommendations. When countertransference and splitting dynamics are discussed, it is usually within the context of working with a client and the caregiver, rather than another service provider.

In my own work with treatment team members, I discovered how my countertransference reactions that have to do with my own history could interfere with my collaboration with treatment team members. Over time, I tried to pay closer attention to these issues. In this case study of a 13-year-old African American young man, "Devone," I was thus able to avoid enactments when I held strong disagreements with an outside agency's treatment approach. Devone had been in treatment at different residential settings of the highest level in security. He had experienced major setbacks from his earliest years. His history was rife with trauma: significant sexual and physical abuse, neglect, and loss. There was history of severe out-of-control behaviors including fire setting, driving stolen cars, smoking illicit substances, aggression, frequent stealing, threatening peers with a weapon, and suicidal and homicidal ideation, which had begun early. His significant out-of-control behaviors threatened his safety and that of the community. He was moved to numerous placements and school settings, none of which had much success in containing him.

In light of his history, it is no surprise that Devone struggled with school. These struggles emerged from the beginning, when he could not be contained in preschool. School records reveal a litany of problems: oppositional behaviors, serious aggression, emotional lability, hyperactivity, low frustration tolerance, and short attention span. As he grew older, he often refused to do any schoolwork; he was particularly resistant to reading. He once told a teacher, "I'm not fit to read." He was far below grade level in all areas and seemed to engage best when given one-on-one support.

When I first started testing him, he was stabilizing at a residential facility for the first time in his life. He had developed positive relationships with some staff, and over time, the incidents of his running away became few and far between. Many staff persons described Devone as "sweet," despite one concerning incident of aggression with one staff member. Because of funding issues, this residential facility was forced to close, upending his stability and transferring him to another placement. The next placement struggled, similarly to all of his previous placements, with containing his initial delinquent and out-of-control behaviors.

These behaviors also challenged the testing. I frequently had to set limits on these aggressive behaviors. During one of our breaks in testing, for example, Devone managed to steal a valuable item belonging to a staff member. The item he took would have enabled him to run away if the group home staff had not intervened. It was no wonder that staff at this residential facility viewed him as manipulative, sophisticated, and conduct disordered. Moreover, after that incident took place, I had the feeling that one staff member viewed me as naïve and unable to be firm enough to handle Devone's behaviors. This made my position in collaborating with the treatment team more complicated, especially as it was Devone's county social worker who had referred his case for assessment, not his group home.

In testing, Devone showed incredibly low frustration tolerance and significant emotional dysregulation. He was easily overwhelmed. He could manage only two subtests at a time before becoming agitated, physically restless, oppositional, and at times verbally aggressive or threatening. His aggressive behaviors escalated when doing the Rosenzweig Picture Frustration Study (Rosenzweig, 1978).[1] Devone vacillated in his response between being appropriate and even empathic to being verbally aggressive and expressing homicidal ideation. Agitated with his responses on the Rosenzweig, he then repeatedly struck a piece of furniture with an electrical cord. When given the Thematic Apperception Test (TAT; Murray, 1943) projective cards, Devone became upset and surprised by his stories and asked to discontinue testing, worrying about how the county might use such information to keep him from reuniting with his family. I gave him the audiotape recording of his TAT stories so that he could be reassured that the information was destroyed. He aborted the Conners' Continuous Performance Test (Conners & MHS Staff, 2000) and was unable to complete Wisconsin Card Sorting Test (Heaton, Chelune, Talley, Kay & Curtis, 1993) where he had punched the computer and immediately apologized.

Because of the magnitude of Devone's low frustration tolerance, testing had to be administered over a more extended period of time than is usual, thus giving me an opportunity to develop a relationship with him. With time, I also saw the positive parts of Devone that the former group home had experienced. As an incentive for testing, I made an agreement to give him a small amount of fast food with each testing session. In one instance, I had forgotten my wallet and had to tell him the reason I could not give him some hash browns. Devone was angry. He accused me of lying and removed a wheel from a nearby chair. I told him that I felt bad about the mishap and wondered how it made him feel. I was transparent in exactly what events took place, such as canceling the order I placed with the cashier after realizing I did not have my wallet. Devone exhibited empathy and protectiveness with me, "That's awkward! You shouldn't have driven here without your license. You can get into trouble." After giving him the option of whether he would like to continue testing today or not, Devone agreed to proceed with testing and, after finishing, thanked me as he left the room.

Experiencing these positive aspects of Devone made me want to disagree strongly with his group home staff who seemed to perceive him mostly in manipulative, negative ways. Furthermore, as someone who identifies as a person of color, I struggled with my countertransference reactions because Devone was Black and all of the group home staff who viewed him negatively and worked closely with him were White. This situation triggered my own anger about my experiences and my family history of being perceived negatively by Caucasians. It also made me keenly aware of the research that indicate that African American youth tend to be disproportionately diagnosed with Conduct Disorder (Mizock & Harkins, 2011), experiencing racial bias in treatment systems. However, at the same time, I felt that being Asian American placed me in an awkward position to speak about issues of race, a discussion that is often polarized between being Black and White. I did not know whether the Caucasian staff and even Devone would recognize me as a person of color, White, or something alien altogether in race-based discussions. I took the first opportunity I had to do a brief consultation with Dr. Kenneth Hardy, an African American professor of family therapy at Drexel University and Director of the Eikenberg Institute for Relationships. He had presented numerous workshops on diversity, multiculturalism, and cultural competency at our agency. After discussing my case with him, he underscored the importance of helping Devone celebrate and develop the "kind parts" of himself in treatment and suggested that I review his chapter on addressing issues of loss in his book (Hardy & Laszloffy, 2005). His recommendation emboldened me to figure out some way to highlight these aspects with his treatment team, recognizing the challenges of it being Level 3 feedback.

Devone's testing results brought out additional challenges in collaborating with his new group home treatment team. His findings indicated that he had pervasive deficits that made effective school functioning a serious challenge. He exhibited significant problems with impulsivity, problem solving, and planning with a considerable difficulty maintaining rules.[2] He struggled in most areas of intellectual functioning, particularly with vocabulary.[3] His results also confirmed significant reading issues.[4] Yet surprisingly, these areas of weakness were also what Steve Finn would label as Level 3 findings for his group home staff, or findings so discrepant from what they thought of Devone that it would likely trigger a defensive response. Indeed, when I shared how low his cognitive results were, members of his team rejected the findings, noting how savvy Devone was in his manipulative behaviors.

This was helpful feedback from his current caregivers, because as the evaluator, I had to understand how Devone could be manipulative in some ways and completely helpless in others in order to make sense of the complexities of his presentation for the treatment team. I shared with them how Devone was the most engaged in testing when he was provided with one-on-one support and modeling. For instance, I described how Devone was motivated to learn how to do the DKEFS Tower subtest after he completed it (Delis et al. , 2001). He asked me to show him how to do the more difficult items. He watched closely in amazement and then proceeded to do the next two items after learning its strategy. Devone could have learned to drive those stolen cars the same way, watching people closely many times. It can explain how he can be "savvy." At the same time, his ability to learn through observation also could be an important tool for learning skills in school. I discussed how one-on-one support and modeling could help Devone establish a sense of mastery in school, given that his trauma history and cognitive deficits make him feel helpless and incompetent.

In thinking about how to collaborate with the group home staff and avoid acting on my reactions, I decided that the best approach for me would be to treat staff as the client's caregiver, deserving of the same need to humanize their own position in working with the client while trying to gently introduce additional ways in perceiving the client. Thus, when a key residential staff member characterized Devone again as antisocial and manipulative, I agreed with him, addressing him in the same way as I would with caregivers in a therapeutic collaborative assessment. I then talked about how I indeed knew how severe his behaviors could be since he stole items on my watch and displayed aggressive behaviors. Then I discussed how I also saw these other sides to him, when there was no incentive for him to be manipulative, sharing the interactions I had with Devone when I forgot my wallet. This staff person agreed with my perception. I acknowledged how difficult it would be for the residential facility to provide opportunities for him to show these kind parts of himself outside of their incentive-based programs, given his other behaviors. In the report, I detailed the bind that service providers would be in treating Devone, since they have to be both vigilant to his manipulative and out of control behaviors while at the same time open and vulnerable enough to give him opportunities to further develop and show the kind and trusting aspects of himself.

Later, the same staff person called to tell me that Devone was in tears after given a significant consequence for refusing to meet with me for testing earlier in the week. He noted with Devone the impact of his decision would have on me as I travelled a long distance to his site. As a result, he was barred from seeing family members as planned. I felt extremely sad for Devone. Again, treating the staff person like a caregiver, I discussed how Devone really needs firm limits for his behaviors and have appreciated that the group home has been so on top of that. I acknowledged how his behaviors can be manipulative but explained how, in this case, I had made an agreement with Devone that he could change his mind about testing in order to give him a sense of control over the process. I added that to Devone's credit, despite the extensive number of testing sessions we have had, this was his first time refusing testing and wondered aloud if other clients would be as patient as he had been. The staff person was open and agreed with this point. I wondered about the specific circumstances that made him refuse testing with me, which in this case was his first week of fall vacation. I also raised that though the staff person was so good about setting the firm limits needed, unfortunately, in this particular case, there seem to be ethical issues in giving him consequences because Devone has the right to refuse testing at any point of the process. The staff member wondered what would make Devone so afraid of testing that he would need to control the process. I related his fears of being permanently separated from his biological family. The staff member agreed and expressed empathy for him. He later had a very kind conversation with Devone about his right to refuse testing at any time and worked immediately to arrange another time for him to see family members.

I cannot say whether my assessment had any significant impact on his treatment staff's perceptions of Devone or in his treatment since I did not have an opportunity to hear from staff after the assessment was completed. As I shared my work with him in case conference, whose members were both people of color and White, I found some of my colleagues in tears. They were moved by the severity of his history of trauma and the considerable out of control behaviors he was exhibiting from such a young age. They grieved about the loss of his previous residential facility and the struggles he had at the current one. They expressed their upset about the considerable barriers he would have to overcome in order to function in school and thus in life. In so many ways, their reaction reflected my own deep sadness about Devone's history, missed treatment opportunities, and prognosis. At the same time, I felt content that I avoided further complicating his situation with my own enactments, given my strong conflicted feelings toward his new group home staff.

In my last feedback session with Devone, I immediately sensed that he was feeling more at ease that day. He knew it would be our last session. We both waived the need for an extra staff to help monitor his behaviors. He asked that I follow him to get a set of cheese and crackers before we started our session. For feedback with our clients, evaluators at our agency often either write a letter or create a story about what we learned about them in following Steve Finn's model of therapeutic collaborative assessments. However, for Devone, a story or a letter would be challenging, given his difficulties with reading. I thought he deserved an award, something he probably had never received before. So I made a special award certificate for him, with an image of a young African American student at a computer. I presented it to him, telling him that I did not know of any other youth to complete 15 testing sessions for an assessment and how remarkable he was in sticking with it. I read it to him, "Devone, A Hard Worker." He studied it carefully and reflected that the young man, "looks just like me." He tenderly rolled it up. Devone finished spreading cheese on his crackers, carefully folded a napkin around them and handed them to me. "This is for your ride back," he said. I thanked him. I commented on how kind he was in doing that and how I would think about him as I ate the crackers on my drive back.

In summary, conducting therapeutic collaborative assessments within community mental health settings can trigger countertransference issues with other treatment team members, particularly with those from other outside agencies and systems. Discussing these issues with supervisors, consultants, and peers can be a way to gain support and clarity about how to avoid reacting to one's own countertransference feelings. Locating those aspects of countertransference reaction that were mine helped me greatly in raising awareness of these issues. Realizing what approach was more adaptive for me in working with treatment team members was also essential. I discovered that I was better working with treatment team members from other agencies when I viewed them as concerned caregivers, just as vulnerable as anyone else in managing their own reactions and feelings with a particular client, rather than as peer professionals, with whom I was at risk of having less patience and empathy. Because our time with treatment team members is limited, raising awareness of these issues can be crucial in our ability to bridge any disagreements about our understanding of our clients, given that there may be no interest or investment in the relationship between an assessor and the rest of the treatment team. It could have been so easy for me to write off Devone's group home staff or, even worse, react negatively. Taking risks in engaging thoughtfully with other treatment team members can open possibilities in treatment for our clients. The moment of success I had in helping one staff person have empathy for Devone's fears and engage in kindness toward him helped humanize Devone. In doing so, that staff person became more humanized in my eyes as well.

Notes

1 The Rosenzweig Picture Frustration Study is formatted like a comic book where the client is asked to fill in their response to frustrating situations with others.
2 NEPSY (Korkman, Kirk & Kemp, 2007) Inhibition-Inhibition Combined Scaled Score (ss) = 3, Percentile Rank (PR) = 1; DKEFS Tower ss = 6, PR = 9; DKEFS Tower Total Rule Violations' Cumulative Percentile Rank = <1. The average value of a scaled score = 10 with a standard deviation of 3.

3 DAS (Elliot, 2007) Verbal Standard Score (SS) = 59, PR = 0.3, Nonverbal Reasoning SS = 67, PR = 1, Spatial SS = 72, PR = 3. The average value of a standard score = 100 with a standard deviation of 15. Word Definitions T = 22, PR = 0.2. The average value of a T-score = 50 with a standard deviation of 10.

4 WIAT-III (Wechsler, 2009) Reading Comprehension and Fluency SS = 60, PR = 0.4.

References

Conners, C. K. & MHS Staff. (2000). *Conners Continuous Performance Test II (CPT II).* North Tonawantda, NY: Multi-Health Systems.

Delis, D. C., Kaplan, E. & Kramer, J. H. (2001). *Delis Kaplan Executive Function System (D-KEFS).* San Antonio, TX: The Psychological Corporation.

Elliot, C. (2007). *Differential Ability Scales-II (DAS-II).* San Antonio, TX: Pearson.

Finn, S. (2007). *In our clients' shoes: Theory and techniques of therapeutic assessment.* New York: Psychology Press.

Hardy, K. & Laszloffy, T. (2005). *Teens who hurt: Clinical interventions to break the cycle of violence.* New York: The Guilford Press.

Heaton, R. K., Chelune, G. J., Talley, J. L., Kay, G. G., & Curtis, G. (1993). *Wisconsin Card Sorting Test (WCST) Manual Revised and Expanded.* Odessa, FL: Psychological Assessment Resources.

Korkman, M., Kirk, U. K., & Kemp, S. (2007). *NEPSY-II: A developmental neuropsychological assessment.* San Antonio, TX: The Psychological Corporation.

Mizock, L. & Harkins, D. (2011). Diagnostic bias and conduct disorder: Improving culturally sensitive diagnosis. *Child & Youth Services, 32(3),* 243–253.

Murray, H. (1943). *Thematic Apperception Test (TAT) Manual.* Cambridge, MA: Harvard University Press.

Rosenzweig, S. (1978). *The Children's Form of the Rosenzweig Picture-Frustration Study.* St. Louis, MO: Rana House.

Wechsler, D. (2009). *Wechsler Individual Achievment Test (WIAT-III)* (3rd ed.). San Antonio, TX: Pearson.

Section II
The Cultural Environment
Theory and Practice

Part 2
Cultural Experiences in Supervision and Training

9 Supervision

A Cross-Cultural Dialogue

Hasse Leonard-Pagel

The night is beautiful,
So the faces of my people.
The stars are beautiful.
So the eyes of my people.
Beautiful, also, is the sun.
Beautiful, also, are the souls of my people.
"My People," by Langston Hughes

As I think back over my supervision through the years, this poem gives me the opportunity to reflect, entering a world where the population I served often looked like me but my supervisees looked less like me. I know this is not the first chapter or article that anyone has written about the difference of supervisor–supervisee matches. It is also not the first time an author has written about the impact of countertransference issues on the ability to have a multicultural dialogue. I hope this chapter helps all supervisors, no matter what their ethnic makeup, feel more confident in having a dialogue about racial scripts, narrative storytelling, the influence of our social context in the world, and the impact of our own personal identity that informs us on how we navigate the world.

Introduction

Growing up with a strong single mom made me realize the importance of independence and working hard. Education was very important in my family, not just in my immediate family but my extended family as well. My mother was a Civil Rights Attorney and my father a System Analyst (before the IT industry became so big) for a government institution. Their siblings were also highly educated, along with their siblings' children. In my hometown in the Midwest, Black people, as we were called in the '70s, '80s, and '90s, were hard working, educated, and had a strong sense of community. Although my parents divorced when I was young and we lived with my mother, it was important for my father to be a present figure in my life. When my mother ran for Judge, my dad was there to ensure that my sister and I ate dinner and did our homework so that my mother could focus on her campaign. My grandmother was also very present in our lives and was a strong force in the community, being a teacher and a strong political activist. My extended family was very close. We would spend holidays together and run around and play while the adults would sit around the table discussing political issues and debating about their favorite politicians' ambitions or choices and whether they believed they were right or wrong. There were moments throughout the evening when my youngest cousin and I would run into the "grown-up room," as we called it, so we could get a hug from our parents or grandparents. They would smile and continue to talk. We realized after about ten minutes that their conversation was "boring"—of course we would. The volume at which our family debated, which was not uncommon for a lot of Black houses and Jewish houses in the Midwest, was quite loud. Being heard and demonstrating your passion over a subject was very important. Strong affect and putting your whole self into how you felt about an idea or issue indicated that you were committed to your knowledge and ideology. If you were meek, quiet, or seemed to vacillate between one idea or another, you would be devoured by intellectual minds that were a force to be reckoned with. As we got older, my cousins would join the table in the "grown-up room" trying to find their voices. They would share their views on issues but were often left watching the ongoing passionate debate and ideas about social issues swirl around the room. My youngest cousin and I would continue to go in getting hugs from our parents and grandparents and sit with them. As we got older, we sat longer. What amazed me the most was how interrelated our family was, given the multiple disagreements.

I would like to revisit this notion of how important education was for my family and the Black community that surrounded me. My siblings, cousins, and I often reflect that we were never told, "you must go to college to make something of yourself," but we always knew that we would go to college. What was communicated unconsciously was that we had the right to go to college! My siblings, cousins, and I are all highly educated and hold esteemed positions in our respective fields. I don't share this to brag, albeit I am proud of all of them, I share this to demonstrate an African American's story, one that is not filled with community violence, drugs, or substance abuse, or the negative impact of the justice system. The former are stories that are often forgotten and the latter is what is shared in the media. If people who are not from the Black community don't know the range of stories from members of my community, they are often only left solely with the impact of oppression and trauma on the Black community, causing them to overlook the positive and influential legacy that Blacks have had on the world as we know it today.

Race and Identity in the Professional Realm

Opportunity, Passion, and Commitment

As I think about my journey to the field of psychology, I reflect on the many individuals who have influenced me, supported me, encouraged me, and demanded that I continue my path even with the challenging and painful experiences of racism and oppression. I often reflect on my experience as an elementary school-age child coming from the Midwest, where I began my education, to the heart of the Bay Area, where I ended my education. As I left the comfort of my community to venture west with my mother, we landed in a small affluent community that was predominately White. While in school in the Midwest, I was classified as "gifted," which had no real meaning to me other than that I had the opportunity to be in a class with my favorite teacher for three years. This woman, whom I will call Mrs. A, a Caucasian woman, had a great impact on me. She was kind, loving, and pushed all of her students to think critically, and she opened our eyes to new ways of thinking about Greek Gods, algebraic terms, and famous Black writers and poets. I was in her class from the third grade to the fifth grade. Mrs. A worked in an environment where the majority of the children were Black and the majority of the teachers were White. She never made any of us feel less than our white counterparts and told us that we had the capacity to do great things. I remember one school assembly that I have shared with my own children: Rosa Parks came to our school. She was from my city in the Midwest, so she was asked by someone who knew her to come in and tell her story; oral tradition is very important in the Black community. We were bright-eyed elementary students waiting to hear what this woman, who was not very tall but seemed bigger than life, had to say. I looked over at Mrs. A and saw her wipe a tear from her face and wondered, "Why is she so sad? Mrs. Parks is telling us a story about when she was strong and stood up to someone." Mrs. A, as an adult, heard the entire story, the story of racism and oppression that I did not understand at that time.

Rosa Parks seemed larger than life to me. As I went up to shake her hand, she said to me, "Hello beautiful little girl, you can be anything you want to be ... bless you child." With that I found myself in her arms embracing her; she reminded me a lot of my own grandmother, who I loved dearly.

Now, I would like to fast forward to the story of moving to a small, affluent White community in California. As I entered my new school, I quickly realized that I was one of two Black children in all of my middle school classes. I was perplexed by this, as I had seen other Black children on the playground. Looking back, I realized that my teachers were surprised that I was in their mainstream and advanced classes. After having a discussion with my mother one day, I realized that this school was not used to having Black children in higher-level classes and they were often placed in remedial classes. This was so foreign to me, given that I had come from an environment where all of my classmates were Black and considered very smart. How could they segregate students in California? Wasn't this supposed to be a place where they were more integrated? I realize that even today, after the milestone case of Larry P. v. Wilson Riles (1979) (Lambert, 1981), California still has more Black children placed in special education in the Bay Area than any other ethnic group. I share my own narrative because it has had a strong influence on how I negotiate the world and think about opportunities for social justice dialogues, teaching in academia, and supervising in the clinical and assessment realm.

From Student to Professional

Entering graduate school, I looked for mentors to help me continue my voyage on understanding the world I lived in. I symbolically saw myself standing on the shoulders of my champions: my mother, grandmother, and my teacher from elementary school. I wanted to continue to connect with other students and hear their stories to find out who influenced them to be in the field. My mentor at the time, Dr. J-M, had great influence on me. She was smart, encouraging, and taught me one of my passions, psychological assessment. I watched her navigate a predominately White system in academia. She never seemed to waiver in her commitment and ability to be present as students from the Black Student Association came in charged with anger, resentment, and sorrow about injustices that occurred in their classrooms. Dr. J-M kept me on my course, encouraging me to continue my passion in assessment. Under her supervision, I reassessed many

Black children who were misdiagnosed during former assessments and were often classified as learning disabled. This became my charge!

Thinking about the impact of oppression and trauma on your own people can be devastating and hard to communicate to others who are not from your community. Working in a field where you are destined to come across other psychologists from different ethnic backgrounds is commonplace. As an African American psychologist working in a community psychology setting, it is also highly likely that the clinical population that you will be working with will be African American, Latino, or some other group of people of color. You have to pause and contemplate, "How can I contain my pain after hearing about so many heartbreaking stories related to community violence, oppression, and trauma and still maintain my composure to be an effective supervisor?" I must confess that there have been many moments that have been difficult to be present and not experience tremendous sorrow. Luckily, I have been successful at reaching out to colleagues to get support in the same way, we as supervisors require our supervisees to reach out for support.

Theory as a Guide for Synthesizing Personal Experience and the Professional Role of Supervision: Conceptual Frameworks

Privileged Self Vs. Subjugated Self and Vicious Circles

Dr. Ken Hardy's concept (2001) of the privileged self versus the subjugated self is a useful framework when trying to understand the power in relationships. He purports that in a relationship, it is important to know what power dynamic is at play. The two roles that he defines are the "privileged self" and the "subjugated self." The privileged self, which is based on the status you hold in society, the most powerful being Caucasian, then male, heterosexual, and, of course, your class status. The subjugated self, which is also based on ethnicity (nondominant culture), gender (women), sexual orientation (gay or lesbian), and class (lower SES) and is experienced by a marginalized or a devalued group of people. The role of the subjugated position is to "regain one's voice." The role of the privileged position is to acknowledge that there is unfairness and work toward not using one's own privilege as power while simultaneously countering the idea that everyone and everything is equal. Another important component of this conceptual framework is that individuals can hold different positions in different situations. When you are in an authority position, no matter what your race, gender, sexual orientation, or class, you may be in a privileged position. Here is a personal, albeit professional vignette that captures my moving between these two positions.

I think back to a difficult supervision when I had a young male Caucasian supervisee say to me, "I don't understand why that mother (who happened to be African American with five children and had recently left an abusive relationship) just won't get a job already. She needs to demonstrate to her kids that she is going to make something of herself!" My initial reaction was to say, why don't you try leaving an abusive relationship and taking care of five kids, getting them ready every morning for school, and making sure they have enough food to eat!" I also was gathering from this student that he thought this mother needed to get off government assistance, which she had just applied for after leaving her abuser. Prior to that she was gainfully employed. Thank goodness for

Executive Functioning and training! I replied instead with, "Let's look at this mother's ego strength and her resources. Now, let's look at what her priorities are and how she is currently bringing the kids in weekly for therapy, getting them to school everyday and looking for work. Now, let's take a look at your countertransference to this mother ... " Although I was this young man's supervisor, putting me in a privileged position, I heard this student's unsympathetic comment from my subjugated self (An African American woman). Therefore, my initial response was anger, however, given my ability to take some distance and be in my supervisory role, I was able to leverage my privileged position in a positive way by requiring this trainee to look at his own countertransference reaction to this client, which was related to her not having a voice.

Critical Race Theory and Relational Theory

Critical Race Theory (Delgado, Stefancic, & Liendo, 2012), or the CRT movement, stems from activists and scholars interested in continuing to study the impact of racism and power on people of color. This movement and its ideas have roots that link back to W. E. B. Dubois' work; European philosophers such as Michel Foucault; notable iconic activists like Sojourner Truth and Frederick Douglass; the important legal case of Brown v. Board of Education; and civil rights movement leaders such as Dr. Martin Luther King, Rosa Parks, and Cesar Chavez. This theory stresses the importance of the "voices of color" and that people of colors' narratives or "storytelling" are an opportunity for others to better understand the impact of racism and oppression on them (Treviño, Harris, & Wallace, 2008). Rather than classifying their experience as an illusion or an excuse to not take responsibility for their life circumstances, understanding narratives and racial scripts as communicating the context of someone's experience (Jenkins-Monroe, 2012) is imperative in order for groups of people to truly move into a cross-cultural dialogue. Another idea or term that is useful in understanding the person of color's storytelling are micro aggressions. A micro aggression (Shiegenmatsu, 2010) is a subtle comment or statement that is not easily identifiable as a "racist statement" but when analyzed more deeply invokes a very strong visceral response for the person on the receiving end. Micro aggressions happen in academic settings (Butler-Boyd, 2010; Flores-Ortiz, 2012; Curtis-Boles, 2012), in supervision (Shiegenmatsu, 2010), in other professional contexts, and in every day life. It is our job as supervisors to address these micro aggressions when they come up in our supervision. When the clinician and client are from different ethnic backgrounds or social classes, micro aggressions tend to increase.

Altman's (1995) relational theoretical concept of the three-person model further illuminates the importance of understanding who you are as the psychologist in the room, based on your social context and framework, when working with your patients. The three-person model is an expansion from the traditional one- or two-person relational approach. This traditional approach puts great emphasis on the interaction between the individuals involved in the relationship and uses the transference and countertransference reactions of the dyad as a way of bringing meaning to the relationship. This interaction is still important when working from a relational perspective, but what Altman offers is the inclusion of the impact of the dyad's social context outside of the room on the therapeutic relationship. This is, of course, a very simplistic and brief explanation of Altman's model but one that I think is important to highlight when understanding the impact of race, culture, and class on our projections as professionals and how micro aggressions can seep into the clinical space. Without the consciousness of race, culture, and class informing our roles in the larger social context, we fall prey to maintaining a privileged position, continuing the vicious circles of stigma, racism, and oppression (Wachtel, 2001).

Bringing It All Together: Therapeutic Collaborative Assessment and the Opportunity for a Cross Cultural Dialogue

Therapeutic Collaborative Assessment (TCA; Finn, Fischer, & Handler, 2012), as mentioned earlier in this book, takes the traditional assessment model and integrates the family system's narrative therapy framework as a way of conceptualizing the symptoms in the family and intervening throughout the assessment. At the end of the assessment, the child or adolescent is provided with a fable, letter, rap, poem, or other creative work, depending on the age and interest of the child or adolescent. The caregiver is provided with a letter addressing their questions in a way that is not judgmental but that integrates the new narrative of the system that supports the cultural identity of the family. I will share a brief description of the full Therapeutic Colllaborative Assessment model that is used at our clinic. In this model, the caretaker watches the assessment through video feed and a separate assessor works with the child. Below is a clinical vignette that demonstrates this model and how a supervisee and I were able to move from a traditional dialogue about assessment into a cross-cultural dialogue. In this vignette, we discussed the impact of racial scripts (Adams, 2012), our social context (Altman, 1995), micro aggressions, and understanding the "voices of color" as narrative storytelling (Delgado, et. al., 2012; Jenkins-Monroe, 2012).

My supervisee, a Caucasian female, brought in all of her data for a 10-year-old African American male who she was assessing and stated, "I am confused by the data ... all his paternal grandmother reports is that he is 'hard headed' and doesn't listen ... he is just lazy like his father!" My supervisee also shared that her client's father was in prison and his mother is currently using both crack cocaine and alcohol. This is not an uncommon story for the community we work in. She continued to be puzzled by the fact that his cognitive scores were within average range. I recognized her dismay and commented, "You seem puzzled." She replied, "Well, I am just surprised that his cognitive scores are in the average range, you don't see that often with this population!" "Hmm," I said, "I am not sure what you mean!" Of course, I knew what she meant but wanted to give her a chance to explain herself. "Well," she said, "most of the children that I have tested here are below average in their cognitive abilities." "So," I calmly replied, "are you saying that because he is an African American child from a lower income area, his cognitive scores should be lower?" "Well ... his father is in jail and his mother is a drug addict so I don't know, I just figured that he would have some learning difficulties," she said relatively quietly. This seemed like a great opportunity to challenge her privileged position by discussing the social context at which this child lived in as well as her own social context. "Well," I said, "let's take a step back and look at this child's academic upbringing in the context of his community for a moment. What is your understanding of his grandmother's experience with the educational system and what do we know about his own mother and father's experience in school? This is important information when we begin talking about narratives and racial scripts (which I explained to her). Also, I want to discuss micro aggressions." This conversation was on the heels of a recent training we had on race, class, and micro aggressions. I could have responded right away to her comment about her confusion about why her client was not experiencing learning difficulties and cognitive issues given his ethnicity, but I did not want to foreclose the cross-cultural dialogue that was about to take place.

Me: "So, let's return back to his grandmother's comment about him: 'He is hardheaded and doesn't listen … he is just lazy like his father!' What does this mean to you?"

Supervisee: "Well, I think she is saying he doesn't listen, not sure what she means by hard-headed. I also think she believes that he is not working hard enough."

Me: "Yes, that is part of it. So hard-headed in the African American culture means a child is not listening to their parent or elder's wisdom and is choosing to either ignore them or make decisions on his or her own without taking into consideration the consequences. Now, in terms of the laziness, this is a common fear of many women about their male children. She fears that if she doesn't get him to understand the importance of being motivated, getting educated, and making something of himself, the dominant culture is going to classify him as just another ignorant Black man; she don't want him to end up in prison like his father. What do you think?"

Supervisee: (She looked at me blankly, and then sighed.) "Wow, I guess I missed a lot. I was not even understanding it as her fear, I thought she was just being mean to him!"

Me: "Now, I want to look back at your comment as a way to understand why his grandmother has this racial script. Remember when you said, given his circumstances, his parents are unable to care for him, he is from a lower socioeconomic status of the African American community, and that you were puzzled by the fact that his cognitive abilities are in the average range?" (Again, I want to pause here and acknowledge that I would not have gone directly to this point if we had not just had a training on this topic.)

Supervisee: "Oh no! That was a micro aggression! It makes me think of the comments that his teacher made as well, which were more focused on my client's behavior rather than his cognitive ability, even though that was the referral question. I can't believe I thought that … even worse, I said it! It makes me think about when his grandmother was saying all of those negative things in front of him … I was so uncomfortable watching him while she said this, that he was not going to be anything and is lazy and doesn't realize what he has … she was letting me know about her own experience raising her son and being saddened by the outcome of his life as well as her own experience being raised by her great aunt."

Me: "Yes! I am glad that you felt comfortable enough to say it in our supervision rather than just think it because it gave us an opportunity to have a dialogue around misperceptions and how these micro aggressions are part of our daily life. It is the absence of this dialogue that continues oppression and racism. Now, how do we bring this information into the collaborative assessment?"

Supervisee: "I want to talk to the assessor who is working with the grandmother and debrief in our team meeting."

After our team meeting, which included my supervisee, the other assessor, the supervisor of the assessor working with the caregiver, and myself, my supervisee was able to write a fantastic story for her client. She was able to highlight his emotional overwhelm while he was in school because he was constantly thinking about the loss of both of his parents. This behavior got him in trouble and caused him to go to the office often because his behavior would overwhelm the teacher. His projective tests identified a lot of aggression, fear, and anxiety, which illuminated the impact that his family story had on him. My supervisee also highlighted the fact that he is a bright kid, allowing him to pick up on the nuances of his grandmother's concerns even when she believes she is protecting him from her worries about his future. The feedback to the grandmother included a letter and oral feedback about how much she cared for her grandson and feared that he would make the same choices that his father has made. It also included her attempt to prepare him, even when it felt like a harsh criticism, for a very difficult and racial world. The little boy's reaction to the story was, "I can't believe that you understand me that well!" The grandmother teared up in her feedback with the assessor who was working with her and said, "You know, I really love him and I know that he is a good boy who is smart!" As supervisors of this model, we were able to watch the feedback session and give feedback to our supervisees along the way as needed. Watching the feedback session, the grandmother moved closer to her grandson and said, "You know I love you … I just worry … I know that you are a good kid!" which made the whole team once again realize the impact that this model, which allows for a very dynamic and culturally relevant dialogue, has on the families we provide services to. It, of course, has a strong impact on us as well as providers of the assessment services, affording us the opportunity to understand narrative storytelling from the "voices of color," which positions us to have a cross-cultural dialogue.

This is only one example of many opportunities for cross-cultural dialogues in supervision. As any psychologist knows, theory is important to the foundation of what we do. Relational theory has guided me in my understanding of the therapeutic space and how to understand the transference and countertransference issues that arise from our clinical work. Traditional theories fall short on the impact of cultural and social context. Altman's three-person model expands this conceptualization to include who we are as patient and psychologist in a social context. For me as a clinician and supervisor, understanding my own narrative and the impact that it has had on me as an African American woman has helped strengthen my sense of who I am as a psychologist and supervisor of color. The therapeutic collaborative assessment model offers a nice medium to allow for assessors to enter into a cross-cultural dialogue. The treatment team works closely over the course of the week and meets before and after every assessment session. The journey that we all take together gives us the opportunity to develop trust and further our commitment to the children, teens, and families that come into our clinic.

I dream a world where man
No other man will scorn,
Where love will bless the earth
And peace its path adorn.
I dream a world where all
Will know sweet freedom's way,

Where greed no longer saps the soul
Nor avarice blights our day.
A world I dream where black or white,
Whatever race you be,
Will share the bounties of the earth
And every man is free,
Where wretchedness will hang its head
And joy, like a pearl,
Attends the needs of all mankind—
Of such I dream, my world!

"I Dream a World," by Langston Hughes

References

Adams, D. (2012). Racism, trauma, and being the other in the classroom. In H. Curtis-Boles, D. Adams, & V. Jenkins-Monroe (Eds.), *Making our voices heard: Women of color in academia* (pp. 35–46). New York: Nova Science Publishers, Inc.

Altman, N. (1995). *The analyst in the inner city: Race, class, and culture through a psychoanalytic lens.* Hillsdale, NJ: The Analytic Press.

Butler-Boyd, N. M. (2010). An African-American supervisor's reflections on multicultural supervision. *Training and Education in Professional Psychology, 4*(1), 11–15.

Curtis-Boles, H. (2012). An African-American woman's experience in the academy: Negotiating cultures. In H. Curtis-Boles, D. Adams, & V. Jenkins-Monroe (Eds.), *Making our voices heard: Women of color in academia* (pp. 9–20). New York: Nova Science Publishers, Inc.

Delgado, R., Stefancic, J., & Liendo, E. (2012). *Critical race theory: An introduction* (2nd ed.) (pp. 113-142). doi: 83528025a30d8c34c9e34c9953ca19d.

Finn, S., Fischer, C., & Handler, L. (2012). *Collaborative-Therapeutic assessment: A casebook and guide* (pp. 1–24). Hoboken, NJ: John Wiley & Sons.

Flores-Ortiz, Y. (2012). How many Latinas does it take? Reflections of 30 years if life in the academy. In H. Curtis-Boles, D. Adams, & V. Jenkins-Monroe (Eds.), *Making our voices heard: Women of color in academia* (pp. 145–154). New York: Nova Science Publishers, Inc.

Hardy, K. V. (2001). African-American experience and the healing of relationships. In D. Denborough (Ed.), *Family therapy: Exploring the field's past, present & possible futures.* Retrieved from http://dulwichcentre.com.au/articles-about-narrative-therapy/african-american-experience/.

Jenkins-Monroe, V. (2012). How I got over: Supports and life lines in my journey to the academy. In H. Curtis-Boles, D. Adams, & V. Jenkins-Monroe (Eds.), *Making our voices heard: Women of color in academia* (pp. 89–98). New York: Nova Science Publishers, Inc.

Lambert, N. A. (1981). Psychological evidence in Larry P. v. Wilson Riles: An evaluation by witness for the defense. *American Psychologist, 36*(9), 937–952.

Shiegenmatsu, S. M. (2010). Microaggressions by supervisors of color. *Training and Education in Professional Psychology, 4*(1), 16–18.

Treviño, J. A., Harris, M. A., & Wallace, D. (2008). What's so critical about critical race theory? *Contemporary Justice Review: Issues in Criminal, Social, and Restorative Justice, 11*(1), 7–10.

Wachtel, P. (2001). Racism, vicious circles, and the psychoanalytic vision. *Psychoanalytic Review, 88*(5), 653–672.

10 Why Are You Crying? It Didn't Happen to You?

Vicarious Trauma, Assessment, and Supervision

Caroline Purves

The check-in in our assessment case conference was going smoothly. The last person to speak said,

> I don't know if this is the right place but I wanted to share something with you. I have been testing one of three adopted children, the seven-year-old. She's been difficult but the parents have been great, supportive, and reliable. Shockingly, the father died unexpectedly five months ago and since then, the mother has changed completely. She's confused, unable to follow up on appointments, sleeping for hours, and neglecting the children. My child had been awful, fighting with everyone, exploding, just her worse self. The kids have been removed temporarily to the "shelter" (where children stay until a placement is settled), and the staff are having a terrible time with her. She's resistant to everything, and having wild tantrums. So I went to see her, somewhat apprehensive about what would greet me. When she saw me, she gave me a glare, almost daring me to ask her questions or give her a task. We looked at each other for what seemed like a long time, but was probably only a few seconds. For a few moments I felt paralyzed. What was my role here? I was the assessor, not her therapist. But because I had worked with the family in a collaborative, therapeutic way for several weeks, I was the person she knew best. And the only one who was right there. So I listened to my gut and just took a chance. I said, I bet what you need right now is a hug. She threw herself into my arms and broke down in sobs.

As the group leader it was my task to help with the moment, but I found myself unable to speak, holding back my own sobs. Everything about this story seemed both utterly tragic and utterly powerful. It was so unfair, first of all. That this child, who had already been traumatized before she came into the family, was now dealt a blow she could barely understand, much less manage. Her wild behavior was a regression and a defense against unbearable feeling, which, the one person who could help, her mother, herself had fallen apart. And now she is back in the shelter, the assessment center—again a homeless, parentless child. We could understand her nasty, temper-ridden behavior as a last ditch attempt at having some control in her world. But the cost was great in terms of getting the real help that she needed.

Into this mess steps the assessment clinician. Instead of backing out by hiding behind a "white coat" of assessor professionalism, she took on the child's immediate pain, to the great relief of the little girl. Obviously it was tremendously healing. Trying to understand my own reactions, I suggest that I was responding to the clinician's sense of overwhelm as much as the child's. Not only had she contained her own empathic sadness during the weeks after the father's death as she tried to complete the assessment, she was also feeling the relief that her offer of sustenance had been a catalyst for the little girl. At the same time there was the uncertainty that she had described a possible "breaking the boundaries" in front of her colleagues. She was hesitant to share this moment because it wasn't the usual assessor role, and while the group members generally have an open and trusting relationship with each other, it wasn't necessarily obvious to her that there would not be criticism aimed her way. Furthermore, that I might fault her for not holding the "correct stance."

Introduction

Vicarious trauma is a concept whose time has come. Since the bombing of the World Trade Center in September 2001, and the number of extreme natural disasters here and throughout the world, the public face of mental health responders has come under scrutiny. Their need for training, how and when to help, and what kind of help is effective has lead to the development of protocols of how best to work in crisis situations. The effect on these mental health responders of working with many people who have been terribly affected by catastrophe has been much written about and labeled to the extent that vicarious trauma, or secondary trauma or compassion fatigue, now has its own set of initials, VT. However, long before the catastrophic events of 9/11, the effect of working nonstop in situations that are saturated with pain and trauma has been recognized in such books as Isobel Menzies Lyth's *Containing Anxiety in Institutions* (1992). Her team examined the reasons why young, competent nurses were leaving in significant numbers. Much of the early research comprised attempts to understand and mitigate burn-out, the premature leaving of positions by competent and experienced practitioners. Vicarious trauma is now understood to be a major factor in burn-out.

Secondary trauma is defined in the 2003 article "Secondary Traumatization in Mental Health Care Providers" by Rose Zimering, James Munroe, and Suzy Bird Gulliver as indirect exposure to trauma through a firsthand account or narrative of a traumatic event. The vivid recounting of trauma by the survivor and the clinician's subsequent cognitive or emotional representation of that event may result in a set of symptoms and reactions that parallel Post-Trautmatic Stress Disorder (e.g., re-experiencing, avoidance, and hyperarousal). Apparently, controversy has developed over this description. Detractors of the secondary traumatization phenomenon in health care professionals claim that labeling clinicians with secondary PTSD is pathologizing and best described as a reaction, not a disorder. Rather than argue over definitions, we can state that, in brief, vicarious trauma is a constellation of reactions both conscious and unconscious that may develop in those who bear witness to someone else's traumatic experience.

While this phenomena is discussed in terms of first responders, medical workers, and therapists of all disciplines, I have not found anything written about those who conduct psychological assessments. Certainly there is nothing written about those who supervise the assessors.

I will attempt to remediate this oversight by describing examples of this vicarious traumatic reaction in assessors and their supervisors, giving examples both as a group phenomena as well as an individual one. The idea of secondary trauma, once I began to think about it, was obvious, but it was a long time before I began to put reactions of the assessing staff into this context. From time to time, particularly in the case conference, certain subjects would take hold, and like forest fires become intense until gradually the topic would die down. For instance, after a particularly horrific crime in our city, one in which four policemen were shot, members of the group began talking about safety. The neighborhood was one in which several of the clinicians had gone to make home visits, even conducting their assessments in clients' homes. While their fear and anger in the case conference discussion seemed reasonable, the topic of personal safety expanded to rage at the clinic and the administrative staff for not taking care of them. This was beyond the immediate reaction to the crime and had a quality of unconscious panic. Safety measures had, in fact, been much discussed, and usually paid scant heed. In retrospect, I can understand this reaction as the coalescing of many, many instances of the clinicians swallowing their own fears and anxieties as they listened to their clients who experienced these events and feelings on a daily basis. Having to be stalwart in the face of visiting unsafe neighborhoods, learning histories of the children who experienced shootings, often in their own families as well as in their neighborhoods, while being strong and thoughtful, had taken its toll. Once there was an opportunity to express some harsh and painful feelings in a relatively safe environment, the lid came off. The usually calm and often humorous atmosphere had metamorphized into one of blame and fear.

The lid did not stay off, however. Very soon the protective mechanisms were back in place; both clinicians and supervisor were able to slip back into our more self-protecting roles as competent professionals who could hold no end of compassion with professional ease. Various tropes that helped us be sturdy in the face of seemingly endless trauma came into play. These ranged from serious examination of the data, thoughtful suggestions for dealing with the families of the children, and various theories that help make sense of a lot of confusion, along with a fair amount of gallows humour and shared understanding of outrageous predicaments. A scared kid who hides under the testing table joined by the assessor brings common affection for the beleaguered psychologist. A teenager who has threatened the group home staff, who almost purrs with the understanding brought by his assessor elicits admiration from the others in the group. Once again, the defenses that allow us to be effective in our roles come into play and the momentary personal affective responses go underground.

The Clinician Experience

To understand why vicarious trauma might even be relevant to assessment, let us examine closely the nature of the work. One of the joys of private practice is that one can pick and choose the kinds of people to whom services are offered. Often, there is a lot of variablility, of age, of socioeconomic status, of severity of the problem, and of the referring sources. Even when there is a specialty, such as neuropsychological testing, or a particular diagnostic category, such as the autistic spectrum, if the psychologist wants to take a break for a while, he can just say no. The level of trauma also varies from none to severe.

The WestCoast community-based clinicians can make some choices for client caseload regarding age and gender but they cannot decide to take someone without a trauma history. This is because the clients referred to the clinic almost always have some history of trauma; even if they are still with their biological parents, the backgrounds resonate with serious problems. And the case loads are unrelenting. To keep the clinic afloat, a certain amount of work has to be going at all times. As you have just heard from the samples presented earlier, our population represents, in the general way, the failures of our society to protect a significant minority of its children and families. In societal terms our child clients' suffering can be connected to poverty, racial scars, political oppression, the legacy of the advent of crack cocaine in the inner city in the '80s, the loss of manufacturing jobs, and limited resources in our public schools. To add to these stressors, we are seeing more of our families losing their homes. Furthermore, when we look at the specifics of families, we see—to put it in the most generous terms—many, many parents who are unable to do the job of the most basic protection of their families. Even in families in which the parents are trying their best, or those in which the foster parents are committed to the child, often such attachment damage has occurred that the child presents with serious development problems, both cognitively and behaviorly.

A brief survey of what makes the assessors most reactive varies. As the traumatic reactions of clients varies with their history of vulnerability, so the secondary trauma experienced by our assessors and supervisors also reflects our areas of vulnerability. One person finds herself fuming when she learns of a very young child's history of abuse—finding herself furious with the thought that there was no way for the child to protect himself, and no one there who stepped in. The deficits in learning and problems with regulation are ones that were not there at birth, but were brought on by the early developmental trauma. The sadness and loss of this is sometimes so affecting for the clinician that unconsciously she finds herself taking an inordinately long time to write up the material. Her fury and feelings of helplessness lead her to retreat, at least for a while until she can regroup.

Another clinician is most affected when he reads the case files and learns that sexual molestation is what caused the young person to be removed from the home. Then, when he reads further that the molester was back in the home and the child is not, he becomes even more upset. Well, of course, all of us have some level of upset by these events, but this clinician, who tends to be able to cope with the most outrageous situations with aplomb, cannot even think about the case for days at a time. Eventually, after recognizing and working through his experience with supervision and the group in the case conference, he can become aware of his own transference overwhelm and get back to work on the case.

The Supervisors' Experience

How about supervisors' reactions? Basically, supervisors aren't supposed to have reactions, other than an empathic holding of the assessor and the difficulties inherent in all aspects of assessment. After all, the supervisor rarely even sees the client, unless accidentally bumping into them in the hallway. We are offered data, histories, test results, drafts of the reports, and can offer suggestions, open up possibilities, notice the assessor's unconscious lapses, call attention to transference and countertransference issues (yes, even in assessment!), and in general act the part of the experienced helper. Or not even act, actually be a helping, even calming voice, for the clinician. Until, that is, one is suddenly gobsmacked by a response; for example, to the Rorschach protocol that is so primitive and uncontained that it grabs hold of the mind and won't let go. A supervisor told me that she has struggled for days to get certain images out of her head so that she can find her way back to objectivity.

One of our supervisors emailed me the following example when I told her about this chapter:

> Last week I was reviewing an assessment report. I kept putting it off. I knew there was an issue with me not being "ready" to review it with the kind of depth and care I knew it deserved. The child, aged ten, has experienced lots of neglect, deprivation, and trauma—and now, despite having good intellectual and learning abilities, he is really in trouble interpersonally and emotionally. In spite of having some resources and good intellect, he appears to be hell-bent on destroying whatever good relationships and attachments might come his way. He might be destined for a residential fully-controlled treatment center—that is, if one is available.

I took the time to throroughly review the report and data, and offered necessary comments and revisions. But to make this happen, I ended up waking very early on two separate days to take time to really think about things and work with the emotions brought up in me by the child's story and data.

I wrote her back wondering why at this time the child had affected her. Was it because there was potential that the child was being placed in jeopardy? She replied:

> Yes, I think it is because I see the potential in him but also the seriousness of the disturbance. He is destroying all that he needs to heal – his educational path (school has expelled him and won't let him back in) – and the relationships that could lead him to a better life. I fear that residential treatment will not address his attachment issues – my experience seeing kids in residential treatment has been mixed, but for the ones with serious attachment problems, residential treatment does not seem like a good solution.

She found herself so caught up in the child's dilemma and her worries about his future that she needed to regroup before she could help the assessor.

Now, with the collaborative/therapeutic model, supervisors can watch a video of many parts of the assessment, keeping us less removed from the experience of our supervisees. Another of our supervisors, again experienced in both testing and supervising for many years in foster care agencies, asked me to join her in a mutual collaborative assessment meeting with the two assessors. She found herself so triggered by watching the video of the adoptive mother of a young girl with serious attachment difficulties that she had lost her sense of empathy and was basically enraged at this mother. It was only after much discussion with the team and helpful family interventions, which softened the mother's approach to the child, that she was able to regain her usual empathic and thoughtful stance. Later she was able to understand why she had such a strong reaction to this particular case, which was connected to her own childhood history.

Protective Strategies

What do assessing psychologists and their supervisors do to ward against these vicarious reactions? A brief sampling, again from the case conference, suggests that finding a way to compartmentalize work from the rest of one's life is very important. One person said that she never tells people what exactly she does. If they already know and start to question more deeply, she deflects the attention to something else. Sympathy is unwelcome; as she says, "they have no idea." Others take off for weekends, take care of themselves through exercise or participating in music, theatre, or retreats—activities completely unrelated to the work. They seem to recognize that they must allow enough positive experiences into their own lives not to be swallowed up by the constant exposure to other people's trauma.

Conclusions

There are two aspects to think about when exploring vicarious trauma. One is the underground constant hum of the pain in the lives of the children with whom we work, the relentlessness and amount of trauma that they have endured. The other is the sudden, unexpected punch in the stomach experienced by the assessors and by their supervisors. For the first, I would suggest that the means of self-protection described and the rewards of being able to make a difference to many of the children and their families are protections against being overwhelmed. The second kind is of a different nature.

Gordon Allport (1937) said that neurotic symptoms have a secondary unconscious function. I believe that these unexpected reactions also have unconscious functions. First, they break down that protective barrier, that "I can handle a lot" part of our professional makeup that does, indeed, allow us to continue working. But those moments of destabilization bring us back to the reality of the child in a truly empathic experience. We can understand it as a moment of projective identification, but one, because of our own vulnerabilities, we are ready to receive. So not only do these moments of vicarious trauma tell us something about the child, they show us where we might learn more about ourselves. Finally, rather than think of vicarious trauma in pathologic terms, in the work of assessment I prefer to think of the experience as a reaction, one that is painful to experience, that should be identified and explored within the case and within oneself, and ultimately used for greater understanding.

References

Allport, G. W. (1937). *Personality: A psychological interpretation.* New York: Holt, Rinehart, & Winston.

Menzies Lyth, I. (1992). *Containing anxiety in institutions: Selected essays, volume 1.* London: Free Association Books.

Zimering, R., Munroe, J., & Gulliver, S. B. (2003). Secondary traumatization in mental health care providers. *Psychiatric Times.* Retrieved from http://www.psychiatrictimes.com/ptsd/secondary-traumatization-mental-health-care-providers.

11 Training Assessors in Therapeutic Assessment

Marianne E. Haydel Walsh, Barbara L. Mercer, and Erin Rosenblatt

The case reported in this chapter was conducted as part of an advanced training in Therapeutic Assessment (TA). In this training, we applied what we had learned through previous TA workshops to two live cases in an advanced training under the supervision of Stephen E. Finn, PhD. In learning TA, assessors usually begin with an introductory workshop in which the principles and techniques are introduced and video portions of actual assessments are viewed. Assessors then participate in an intermediate workshop, during which workshop participants engage via video feed in a live assessment conducted by Dr. Finn or another clinician. They are asked to participate in planning an assessment intervention session as well as a summary discussion session. Finally, assessors can participate in an advanced level workshop during which the assessors conduct a TA under the close supervision of Dr. Finn. The clinicians that participated in our training had completed beginning and intermediate workshops and had begun utilizing components of therapeutic collaborative assessment in their everyday work. Another unique aspect of our training was that the clinical team consisted of one supervisor and two assessment clinicians. The role of the supervisor was akin to a "team leader" who participated fully in the assessment process.

Personality assessment training and supervision typically begins with reading and studying texts. The process can be highly structured and focused on the more practical and technical aspects of conducting psychological testing, such as administration, scoring, and interpretation (Berant, Saroff, Reicher-Atir, & Zim, 2005; Potash, 1998). Often, the supervisors and experts teach the theory and techniques of psychological assessment, and the student administers, measures, and reports back to the supervisor. Learning personality assessment can bring up fears, defenses, and personal resistances that can impact the assessment process (Fowler, 1998). Additionally, authors have described the importance of exploring the interpersonal elements that emerge during the course of a psychological assessment and that these interactions provide additional data to be considered in clarifying the client's functioning (Berant et al., 2005; Fowler, 1998). A more collaborative model of teaching, supervising, and training addresses these potential issues and facilitates learning in a number of ways (Handler, Hess, Hess, & Hess, 2008). Utilizing the TA model increases engagement of the participants, decreases feelings of anxiety and powerlessness in participants, and increases motivation (Finn, 2007). This model of training makes the process more transparent and allows fears and resistances to be conscious, making it possible to process feelings that provide additional data over the course of the assessment. The advanced training reported here differed from traditional models of training because the supervisor and clinician worked together, provided consultation, and helped to bring varying perspectives that facilitated and shifted the family dynamics. There were several levels of consultation in our learning process. The team of three clinicians consulted with the parent, the supervisor and assessors consulted as a team, the three clinicians consulted with Dr. Finn, and near the end of the week, the clinicians received input from their agency colleagues. We found that learning within a TA model invited greater participation and collaboration and enhanced our experience in the ways mentioned above.

Training Structure

One aspect that differentiates TA from traditional assessment with children is that parents are encouraged to observe the standardized testing sessions to help the parents or caregivers better understand the child's functioning (Finn, 2007; Hamilton et al., 2009; Tharinger, Finn, Wilkinson, & Schaber, 2007). This can occur by the assessor, child, and clinicians working with the parent or caregiver (the mother in our case) being in the same room. With this configuration, the assessor conducts the testing with the child while the caregiver and the clinician working with the caregiver are observing in the same room. This configuration was used for our case, with Dr. Haydel testing the child, and Dr. Mercer and Dr. Rosenblatt observing and processing with the mother. Before each session, Dr. Mercer and Dr. Rosenblatt met with the mother to discuss any thoughts, observations, or updates. Additionally, at the end of every testing session, Dr. Mercer and Dr. Rosenblatt met with the mother again to discuss observations and begin to develop hypotheses that might inform the assessment questions. While the clinicians met with the mother during these brief consultation sessions, Dr. Haydel met with the child in a separate room, engaging in free play or administering additional measures. The session procedures differed somewhat from those described by Finn, Tharinger, and colleagues (Finn, 2007; Tharinger et al., 2007). Typically in the TA model, all assessors meet for *mini consultations* with the parent(s) before and after the observed testing of the child. However, the families at our clinic are often from single-parent homes without reliable childcare, and it is not possible to have additional meetings with the parent or family member separately. Therefore, our solution was to have Dr. Haydel continue with the assessment of the child while Dr. Mercer and Dr. Rosenblatt consulted with the parent.

This configuration with the parent in the same room as the child during the assessment can be beneficial when the child is younger or when the assessor does not have access to a one-way mirror, live video feed, or video equipment. It is typically best for parents in the room to observe inconspicuously and to discuss insights and reactions during the consultation sessions. However, in our case, the child was highly attuned to the mother's presence and her reactions and interacted with her nonverbally throughout the testing sessions. Being able to observe their interactions provided useful information about the family dynamic that was impacting the child's functioning.

Background and Presenting Problems

Joey is a 6-year-old biracial White and Latino boy who was referred for an assessment by his mother who was concerned about his learning, his emotional meltdowns, and "out of control" behaviors at home. He had been retained in kindergarten due to lack of academic progress. His mother reported concerns that he may have a learning disability, but indicated that the school was refusing to test him. In addition, the family had recently experienced a tremendous loss when Joey's sister, who was older by one year, died from cancer. The mother reported that this had been a serious, devastating strain on the family and that at the end of the sister's illness, the family had moved into the hospice with her and was there when she passed away.

Joey's mother reported that he had good days and bad days at home. She stated that he would tantrum for up to 20 minutes when he couldn't have things his way. The mother had tried many things, but stated that only time-outs and taking things away improved his behaviors. The mother reported that her boyfriend and his mother (who lived in the home) believed that the boy was doing things on purpose and frequently stated, "That boy has too much energy."

The mother described their regular homework routine as being exceedingly stressful. She stated that she felt bad because he doesn't like to do it and has so much trouble, and that she can only work with him for five minutes at a time. She stated that she didn't want to make him feel worse about himself. At the time of referral, Joey was taking medication for anxiety, which the mother reported was not helpful. He, as well as the mother and younger sister, had been seen in family therapy to help cope with the death of his sister, but were not in treatment at the time of the assessment.

The following were the questions generated by the mother for the assessment:

1   Why isn't he learning at the same pace as other kids his age?
2   Why is he so jumpy?
3   Why is he different at school and at home?
4   Why does he get out of control?
5   How has everything that has happened at home affected him?
6   Why doesn't he play with other kids?
7   How can I help him to do better?

Additional concerns were revealed during our meetings with Joey's mother. She described him with autistic and Asperger's-like features and explained that he would come home and run around the house making odd noises, like "meep meep meep," and squealing and saying "whoopee" to no one in particular. However, during his sand play interview, he told the story of a boy who fought pirates and sailed away all alone. "He likes to be alone," Joey said, and then said, "No he doesn't like to be alone; he's lonely; he wants a friend." In the incomplete sentences he repeatedly referred to his desire to play and have friends. In the beginning of testing, he had a difficult time making eye contact; however, as time went on, he looked at us more and more, and was highly reciprocal and related. Further, he seemed to love the attention of his mother and the three clinicians over the course of the assessment.

The current family system consisted of the boy, his 8-year-old sister, his younger sister, the mother's boyfriend, and the boyfriend's parents, who all lived together in the home. Joey's mother and father divorced when he was 3 years old. After the divorce, Joey's biological father was reported to live in a car in front of his mother's house. The mother reported that Joey had a younger brother who lived with his paternal grandmother. The mother handed over custody of Joey's younger brother when his sister was diagnosed with cancer because she felt he was too aggressive to stay in the home. The parents originally had joint custody of all the children, but eventually the mother obtained full custody. It was reported that

Joey saw his father two weekends a month and even more frequently if the mother allowed it. When Joey visited with his father, he stayed in his paternal grandmother's home, who didn't allow Joey's father to enter the home except to put Joey to bed because she didn't want him to become "too comfortable."

Over the course of our consultation sessions with the mother, the intensity of what the family had been through was revealed to us. Although there was a great deal of grief and loss that Joey and his mother were struggling with, we also learned how much the mother's own history of trauma and disrupted family relationships continued to impact her ability to parent Joey and his siblings. In one session, in which we completed a genogram with the mother, she disclosed her own traumatic past. She described her own mother as "mentally and physically abusive." Her mother was mentally ill and had been psychiatrically hospitalized several times. Joey's mother was kicked out of the house at age 16 by her mother and began a relationship with Joey's biological father. She and her brother received the brunt of the physical abuse. She stated that she raised her five younger siblings and that one brother died as an infant. Her mother was White, and although she didn't know her biological father, she decided to get genetic testing herself, which revealed that she is Puerto Rican, Mexican, and White.

The mother acknowledged domestic violence by Joey's biological father, particularly that she was beaten when she was pregnant with Joey's sister. The mother reported that Joey did not witness violence but may have heard it. The mother decided to pursue a divorce from Joey's biological father, but her family aligned with Joey's biological father and provided little to no support. Joey's mother started a relationship with her boyfriend after the divorce. She became strong in her role as a caretaker of both her siblings and her children. This role appeared to be a core part of her identity, and yet she felt alone in this responsibility as a mother.

Hypotheses Developed

As the information emerged through the course of the assessment, we gleaned a better understanding of the mother's story about herself. We hypothesized the following:

1   Because the mother always had to take care of herself as well as others and was unable to rely upon anyone for support or to trust others with what was important to her, a dynamic was created between mother and son that made it difficult for him to be a 6-year-old boy.

2   In the context of many family losses as well as a traumatic past, the mother had developed a close and nurturing relationship with her son, but the dynamic that was created limited his ability to develop as a capable 6-year-old boy, and it made it more difficult for the mother to set limits with Joey. As the mother clearly articulated, she did not want to make Joey feel any worse about himself nor did she want to harm or put him at risk in any way. She could not bear to lose another child or to see another child in so much pain.

3   In the context of the mother's history of abuse and betrayal, her difficulty trusting others prevented her from enlisting or utilizing the support of her partner, his parents (who lived in the home), or even available community supports. This only reinforced her feelings of isolation and resentment of having to take care of everyone, yet she

remained committed to her role, which created a bind for her that was difficult to resolve.

In making hypotheses about the family dynamic, the TA training model allowed us to utilize each other to reflect on what was being revealed and to increase our understanding of Joey and his family system. We used our training consultation sessions to debrief, begin to develop hypotheses, and to brainstorm ways to explore them through various interventions over the course of the assessment. We wanted to highlight the relationship between Joey and his mother and to increase Joey's self-expression during the sessions. To reach that goal, we commented on their sensitivity to each other and provided encouragement and modeling to help Joey express himself.

In our initial session with Joey and his mother, we asked Joey to draw a picture of a family. Feelings of loss and anxiety were triggered that resulted in Joey commenting on his sister who had passed away. During this part of the session, Joey's mother began to cry. Joey immediately shifted into a caretaking role, sitting in his mother's lap and attempting to provide her with comfort. These interactions highlighted how attuned and sensitive Joey and his mother were to each other's reactions. Further, we observed the ways that the roles they adopted in their relationship impacted the mother's ability to set limits and Joey's ability to persist with challenging tasks.

Throughout the course of the assessment, we also learned how aspects of the mother's personality and her history impacted the way that she was able to process information obtained during the assessment. Although the loss of Joey's sibling had consumed the family and reinforced potentially maladaptive family dynamics, it was clear that the mother had a difficult time allowing herself or her family to truly feel and process the grief they were experiencing. In our consultation sessions with the mother, we noticed that she didn't hesitate to use the opportunity and was eager to share all of her ideas and thoughts, especially those that were consistent with her view of Joey as being sick or fragile. Her strongly held story limited the possibility of exploring alternative explanations about Joey's difficulties or to help the mother identify sources of support.

In order to make sense of what was beginning to emerge in the testing data as well as our observations, we consulted with each other and Dr. Finn about family dynamics and roles that might be reinforcing the client's behavioral challenges and limitations. We came to understand that Joey's mother was fearful of pushing him too much and had created a story of Joey as a fragile, somewhat incompetent boy. Joey's mother saw herself as his sole caretaker who was alone in that task. We began to wonder what might happen if Joey was more competent or not as fragile. How would that change the mother's view of his need for her? We also began to hypothesize that Joey was fulfilling the role of the "sick child" with his mother and that he might be capable of doing more. Dr. Haydel, who had the opportunity to test and interact with Joey alone, reported that in their one-on-one interactions, he seemed more like a 6-year-old boy and was not as meek. In fact, she indicated that he opened up, became playful, energetic, and even assertive.

Impressions of Joey with Mother in the Room

The opportunity to observe Joey with and without his mother allowed us to see an emergence of significant differences in his presentation. When his mother was in the room with him, Joey often appeared sad, quiet, insecure, and constricted, as though the weight of the world rested on his shoulders. During the first activity in the initial session, Dr. Haydel asked Joey to draw a picture of a house (Buck, 1973). Joey repeatedly expressed self-doubt, stating, "I'm not good at drawing a house," "I'm not good at drawing doors," and, "This doesn't look like a house to me." While completing a Kinetic Family Drawing (KFD; Burns & Kaufman, 1987), Joey became anxious, periodically looked at his mother, and said, "I don't know how to draw anymore." When Dr. Haydel asked him to tell stories using the Roberts Apperception Test (McArthur & Roberts, 1982) and Children's Apperception Test (CAT; Bellak & Bellak, 1949) cards, he again said, "I can't tell stories." We administered a series of incomplete sentences constructed by the assessment team, based on the presenting issues. Joey's responses helped reveal the extent of his grief and sadness over the death of his sister, Lily; for example, "When I think about my family … I think about Lily"; "My best friend is … Lily"; "I miss … Lily"; and "I get sad when … we go to the grave." During the Rorschach (Exner, 1993), Joey appeared anxious, fearful, and overwhelmed. His responses contained shadows, skeletons, and bones, which suggested a sense of fragility and vulnerability. We also hypothesized that the responses were related to the impact of his sister's long illness and eventual death.

Thus, while in his mother's presence, Joey's presentation appeared to be consistent with her image of him: a fragile, sensitive, caring boy, who had a restricted range of emotional expression. This was exemplified during the sentence completion test, in which he had difficulty expressing any emotion other than sadness and happiness; for example, "I get mad when … I don't get mad" and, "Most people don't know it, but I'm afraid of … I don't know." During a drawing activity, in which Joey drew a picture of a dinosaur with his mouth turned down, when Dr. Haydel asked him how the dinosaur was feeling, Joey said that he was mad and that he chases people. His mother disagreed, commenting that the dinosaur looked sad rather than mad, and that Joey never gets mad. This activity revealed that Joey's mother was discouraging Joey from expressing anger. We began to hypothesize that she had difficulty tolerating the expression of any feelings other than sadness and happiness.

We observed that Joey was preoccupied by his mother's sadness and that he appeared to monitor his responses in an effort to keep her from crying. During Joey's stories on the Roberts Apperception Test and Children's Apperception Test, he initially worked hard to try to make the characters in the stories happy, but eventually more painful emotions emerged. The stories further revealed Joey's experience of feeling constrained. Throughout the stories, there was a sense that if the characters expressed themselves or did what they really wanted to do, there was always a negative consequence. For example, if the child played outside, painted on the wall, or held his baby sister, he would inevitably either get into trouble or end up doing something bad, such as drop the baby.

An Alternative View of Joey

When Joey and Dr. Haydel had one-on-one interactions in another room, he became more spontaneous, creative, and even assertive at times. He was more verbally expressive, appeared relaxed and playful, and he began to discuss a wider range of emotions. His caretaking tendencies, however, remained strong. On the first day of testing, as soon as he and Dr. Haydel left the room to get a snack, Joey explained that he stopped drawing because he didn't want to draw his sister, which was certain to make everyone sad. He then went on to explain that they had all stopped telling stories when she died. Through play and direct discussion, he talked about feelings of sadness, anger, and worry. He refused to beat Dr. Haydel in a card game of UNO®, and apologized for giving her too many *draw two* cards, explaining that if she lost, it might make her sad.

As the discrepancies began to emerge, we consulted with one another, and began to formulate hypotheses about the dynamics between Joey and his mother, and the impact that that they might be having on his emotions and on his ability to effectively think. We decided to test our initial hypotheses during the cognitive testing, by administering some of the measures without his mother present.

Dr. Haydel administered the Differential Abilities Scale, second edition (DAS-II; Elliot, 2007), while his mother was in the room, and Joey's General Cognitive Abilities score of 88 fell into the below average range. He earned scores of 97 on Verbal composite and 96 on the Spatial composite, both of which were in the average range. His Nonverbal Reasoning composite score of 79, however, fell into the low range. His lowest score (34) was on the Matrices subtest, which fell into the fifth percentile. We decided to explore our hypothesis that Joey might perform differently without his mother in the room. The tests that Dr. Haydel administered without his mother present included the Matrix Reasoning subtest of the Wechsler Intelligence Scale for Children, fourth edition (WISC-IV; Wechsler, 2003), and the Children's Category Test (CCT; Boll, 1993). On the WISC-IV, Joey earned a score of 11, which fell in the 63rd percentile. His score of 61 (mean = 50) on the Children's Category Test (CCT; Boll, 1993), which fell into the 84th percentile, was his best performance on any of the cognitive measures.

During our final testing session, just before giving him the Children's Category Test, Joey began to get squirmy and started to lose his focus and concentration. Dr. Haydel encouraged him to put on his "thinking cap" and to listen "with both his ears." Afterwards, the following discussion ensued:

Joey: I don't need a thinking cap. I don't trust it.
Dr. H: You don't trust it?
Joey: I'm tricking you! I don't have a thinking cap. My mom didn't put one on me.
Dr. H: You mean, when you were born?
Joey: Yeah, when I was born.
Dr. H: Well, maybe we could make our own thinking cap, and you can put it on whenever you need to think hard.
Joey: No way! My mom said I can't do that anymore. She doesn't let me.
Dr. H: Well, what do you do when you have to think hard?
Joey: I don't need a thinking cap.
Dr. H: You mean you can think just fine without it?
Joey: Yeah ... you have one, huh?
Dr. H: Sometimes, I have to put one on if I want to think really hard.
Joey: I used to have one, I think, but my mom took it out. It makes it really hard to think.

Dr. H: Maybe all of us together with you and your mom could come up with a way to make a new thinking cap.

Joey: No way; she won't make another one. The first one was too hard to make.

Dr. H: You're right, thinking caps are hard to make. But, I think we might be able to make one if we did it together. Could we ask her?

Joey: No way. Well, maybe, if I could sit in the egg chair and put the top down.

Dr. H: OK, that's a deal.

Our use of the TA model and ongoing consultation with one another enabled us to more accurately understand the many factors that had led to the destruction or disappearance of Joey's thinking cap. Such factors included the family's ongoing profound grief and sadness over the death of his 7-year-old sister, his hyper-awareness of other people's needs and emotional states, his own self-doubt and expectations of failure, his mother's belief that he could not do more, and that he would fall apart if she pushed him harder. These were among the many obstacles getting in his way. We also understood that although the loss of Joey's thinking cap was limiting him in many ways, it was also adaptive, in that it preserved a core dynamic of dependence between Joey and his mother and communicated to her that he needed her. Throughout the course of the assessment, it seemed that Joey was communicating to us that, in fact, he *was* capable of more, and that he was stronger than his mom gave him credit for. In fact, during the assessment, it became clear that he was quite clever, had strong flexible thinking skills, and could change strategies when the old ones were no longer working.

Revising the Family Story and Dilemmas of Change

The TA model includes several important underlying principles that contribute to the creation of lasting, positive change in the family system. One important principle involves helping children and families to revise their *story*, which is their own attempt to conceptualize and understand a child's behaviors, presenting problems, and ways of relating to others (Finn, 2007). Another principle entails identifying the family's *dilemmas of change*, which are the parts of the story that are both problematic and beneficial for the family in some ways (Finn, 2007). Our assessment team understood that our task of assisting in *revising the story* that Joey and his mother held for him was complicated and multi-layered. The opportunity for Dr. Rosenblatt and Dr. Mercer to collaborate with Joey's mother before and after each testing session allowed us all to get a clearer understanding of the family dynamics.

We identified a significant dilemma of change in the family system: Joey's mother was reluctant to shift the way that she viewed him. She had been a caretaker all of her life, and needed to see him as fragile as a way of ensuring that he would always need her. In addition, after experiencing the illness and death of her daughter, she was terrified of losing Joey, too. We hoped to shift her image of him, without ignoring her needs, by helping her to see him as sensitive and competent, but not as overly fragile, and as a boy who greatly needed her, but not in the same way that his frail and dying sister had in the past. We hoped to help her to understand and expect that he was capable of more. He needed her to refuse to give up on him and to push him, even when it was painful for her to do so.

Family Intervention Session

With our hypotheses regarding the family dynamics more fully developed, the treatment team consulted and began to plan the family intervention session. In our planning, we selected a combination of two methods described by Tharinger et al. (2008): (a) parent coaching and skill development, and (b) semi-structured play. By choosing these methods, we hoped to further test our hypotheses about the dynamic between mother and son as a contributing factor to his "lack of academic progress." We also hoped to give the mother the experience of supporting and encouraging him to set and achieve goals for himself, both in his play and in his schoolwork, and to stand her ground when he attempted to give up. In order to address and more fully understand one of his mother's chief concerns, Joey's inability to do more than five minutes of homework per night, we incorporated a homework activity into our family intervention session and planned to coach Joey's mother along the way.

The session began with the semi-structured play activity, in which Joey created and improvised upon a game requiring him to throw a ball into a basket, which he made progressively harder for himself as he went along. Initially, Joey's mom appeared somewhat indifferent and uninvolved during the task. The assessment team mirrored his excitement, and encouraged him through cheers for his success and for his effort. Joey's mother quickly joined in, began clapping for his accomplishments, and gave him recognition when he came close to making difficult shots. It was the happiest and most energized that we had seen either of them all week long. In those moments, Joey appeared determined, fearless, carefree, and proud of himself.

Next, we began the parent-coaching portion of the session. As planned, Joey sat in the egg chair, as we explained to his mom that he thought he had lost his thinking cap. We discussed how difficult it was to think hard, to pay attention, and to do homework without a thinking cap to help him. We also acknowledged that they were difficult to make, and that he would need all of our help in making a new one. She agreed to help, and they began their second task of the intervention session: working on Joey's homework. Joey initially worked hard and challenged himself to write every letter on the page, even when his mom told him that he did not have to. "Looks like the thinking cap is working!" Dr. Mercer said. After 20 minutes of hard work, he suddenly became more defiant, pushing the paper back to his mother, and asserted that he was finished doing homework. With the support of the team behind her, Joey's mother did not give in, was able to set limits, and compromised with him to write a few more letters. During the session, Joey completed 35 minutes of homework, and in the process, he had successfully begun to create a new thinking cap! At the end of the session, Joey's mother appeared surprised about her and her son's accomplishment. "We've never done more than five minutes of homework before!" We acknowledged that they had both worked hard to get there.

Feedback Story

In our final session with Joey, we read the story that we had created for him, incorporating some of what we had learned over the course of the intensive weeklong assessment. We read him the story about a young puppy named Naji who was having trouble with his schoolwork, despite being smart and capable. We read about three frogs that appeared out of a pond to help the young puppy better understand why he had a hard time thinking:

> The frogs asked Naji why he was so sad. Naji wasn't sure he wanted to tell these frogs anything at all. But he told them that he felt sad because he just couldn't think sometimes. The frogs talked to each other and asked him questions, had him count lily pads, and asked him to write his letters. After a while the frogs said, "Maybe you just lost your thinking cap. We think we can help you make a new thinking cap … . You'll need your mom's help—go and get her and together we can figure out how to make a new thinking cap." … The frogs told his mom that even though Naji thinks he can't do a lot of things, and that he might try to run away when he thinks he can't do things, he is smart and he really can do a lot of things. The frogs told his mom, "Don't let him run away, help him keep trying until he gets it, because we know he can! That's how he'll start to make a new thinking cap!"

Assessment Conclusions

The opportunity to utilize the TA model and to work as part of a team that consulted with one another each step of the way enabled us to gain a more complete understanding of Joey's emotional, cognitive, and behavioral functioning. As a team, each member was afforded the opportunity to be attentive to different aspects of the family and of the dynamics between Joey and his mother. In our team, one member focused on Joey's role as the "sick child," and the ways in which the role was both creating and maintaining many of his symptoms. Another member focused on the family culture and history of loss, and the ways that these contributed to Joey's prescribed role in the family. The third member was attuned to the mother's own history of loss, abuse, and trauma, and reflected on the ways that she had become entrenched in her identity as the family caretaker from a very young age. As the team members met together, we were able to more clearly grasp the underlying impact of the family dynamics in order to help shift Joey's mother's own faulty conceptualizations of her son. During the planning of the intervention sessions, Dr. Finn's experiences working with similar types of families helped to remind us that we could focus on smaller changes between Joey and his mother. These changes involved encouraging the mother to support her son's ability, while increasing their tolerance for frustration. As a team we came to understand the importance of helping the family experience these interactive changes as successful, in order to have a better chance of creating lasting positive change in the family system.

Countertransference in Psychological Assessment

Listening to the stories from traumatized children is to participate in a kind of truth commission—hearing tales of cultural war, family violence, and personal loss. We have the task of not forgetting this traumatic material, of doing what Alvarez (1992) called *brave listening*; but to succumb to it risks our own despair and creates the possibility of losing sight of the task of helping children to get closer to the developmental path ahead. We have to stare into the dark heart of this data, grind it up, and transform it into something palatable and useful. We have to do Bion's (1962) work of taking the noxious *beta* elements and making them into more bearable and hopeful *alpha* ones: "Despair must be transformed into contact with emotional life rather than disowning it" (Gin, 2008, p. 83).

In Joey's case, we plummeted unexpectedly into a family who had recently lost a member through cancer. The entire family had gone to the hospice and stayed with Lily at the time of her death. She was only 7 years old. In these assessments, whether through the clinical interview prior to testing or through revelation of traumatic material in the Rorschach and projective stories and drawings, we must risk being susceptible to this material, but combine this susceptibility with sufficient detachment to provide language, thought, and boundaries. Without this apparent dichotomy of emotional openness and distance, the therapist and/or assessor will either have to repress countertransference or drown in it (Racker, 1968).

The loss of his sister was acutely on the mind of Joey's mother, and absorbed by Joey for his own reasons and because of his mother. At age 6, he was just beginning to develop a concept of death and loss. Yet he was also at the stage where mastery, self-control, and identity development are central. Joey's mother had experienced trauma and loss her entire life and felt she carried this alone, but Joey was acutely sensitive to his mother's sadness and fears. Linked with this, Joey's testing revealed that when he was with his mother he regressed, was inhibited, and performed poorly on psychological tests. Joey wanted to develop as a normal 6-year-old. He performed at a higher level when he was tested on his own and was more communicative in his responses. In addition, he was both expressive and responsive to limits when his mother was helped to respond to him in more age appropriate ways.

Finn's training emphasized the importance of assessors monitoring their own anxieties and reactions by checking in with themselves and each other to monitor countertransference (Finn, 2007). When we reflected on our first session with Joey's mother, we each identified our responses to the family's dilemma. Dr. Mercer shared the following: "I felt overwhelmed by grief and cried. I tried to imagine what it was like to lose a daughter." We all discussed how the mother was invested in seeing Joey as a sick child, how she was focused on his sensitivity and lack of self-confidence, how she saw every feeling in him as being related to the loss of his sister. Drs. Rosenblatt and Haydel noticed the mother's repetitive pattern of underestimating his performance, and they felt a certain exasperation of her difficulty with seeing Joey as competent. At different times, we each felt hopeless about his progress and her ability to hear the results of the testing. These three countertransference reactions shadowed us through the week. Each of our individual reactions added a piece to the whole picture of Joey's family. We noticed that even the mother's reports of absent family members paralleled our own reactions. For example, the mother's boyfriend reportedly thought the mother babied Joey. The older sister would become exasperated with Joey and admonish him. At the end of our assessment, we presented the case to our colleagues in the agency, and many of our staff highlighted how intensely the loss of the sister must be affecting family dynamics. All of these countertransference reactions reflected different aspects of the truth about Joey and his family.

We incorporated our countertransference reactions and transformed them into feedback and interventions: We gave ongoing feedback to Joey's mother about how the loss might make it hard for her to believe in Joey's strengths; we pondered if reading to him might assist him with addressing difficulties with letters and beginning words. She countered that she had given up reading completely since Lily's death because they had read to *her* constantly. We looked for ways to invite her boyfriend to the sessions (he refused), and ways that she might see she could get help. We developed ways to encourage the mother to be less invested in carrying the family burden alone. We planned an intervention, described above, that would encourage her to believe that Joey could be competent and not forever sad.

When we presented the case to our staff in a Grand Rounds/consultation format, the staff confirmed our feeling that in addition to the psychological dynamics, the family's loss was profound and very recent. With Dr. Finn guiding the questions and discussion, our own staff served as our consultants, and we experienced them as both holding the difficult material and answering our questions. They were able to discuss the mother's traumatic history and object loss in light of the presenting problem, the complexity of family dynamics, and the reality of grief for all the family members. Their validation of these issues enabled us to diminish our feelings of hopelessness and to think more clearly how to present the test findings to Joey's mother.

In the summary/discussion session with the mother, we began with Joey's learning issues, telling her about his competent intelligence, but also about his problems with learning that required school intervention. We assured her we were willing to help her advocate for extra services. We went on to talk about Joey's sensitivities and answered her question about how he had been affected by the death of his sister. We allowed space to acknowledge that the family had suffered a terrible loss, that little time had passed, and that they were still in a process of grieving. Instead of pushing onward with additional feedback, we made room for the mother's response. She cried, and said she hadn't had time to grieve herself. After a few moments, we were able to continue, and talked about his competence when she set limits or encouraged his abilities, about his developmental need for friends, and his desire to pursue happy play and not have to be sad all the time. At this final session, Joey's mother revealed that the day before, she had gone to the store and bought age-appropriate books for all the children. She also confided the thought that her boyfriend has been resistant to working with Joey because he did not want to endure another loss. Although this did not confirm a shift in the boyfriend's attitude, it did suggest that the mother was thinking more psychologically about family dynamics. We took these as signs the sessions had made some impact and that there was some potential for the mother to diverge from her habitual role in the family.

At the end of our sessions we again discussed our reactions. Dr Mercer felt relieved and not so bogged down with sadness. Both Dr. Haydel and Dr. Rosenblatt stated that they felt more connected to Joey's mother, empathic, and for the first time, genuinely sad. Conducting psychological assessments in a collaborative, therapeutic way pushes the assessor to manage these emotional reactions. In the course of our assessments, Pandora's box is opened for both the client and assessors. Without this level of involvement, however, it is hard to imagine the benefits of offering a 10-page report to a parent about the impact of trauma on her child, and his *distortion of social cues* or impulsivity. It is essential to titrate this information, within a holding environment, in a way that the parent, foster parent, or social worker can use for the child's progress. We want to provide the data in a manner they can make it their own. We want to bring it alive in answering their questions. But we want to do this without knocking them out. In conducting our therapeutic assessments, we need to bring with us the role of scientist/ assessor and clinician/therapist, where in the traditional psychological assessment process, the clinician/therapist usually is not present. We need to keep a structure, yet allow the processing of emotional material; to adapt to regressions, but stick to the data as it is useful to the client; and to decide whether to restrict information or allow more material to emerge.

Not all of our assessments are done in this comprehensive manner, although in every assessment we generate questions from social workers, foster parents, children, and adolescents, and we provide feedback in a letter and story as well as a report. We often encourage meetings during which social workers, caretakers, and therapists are present to listen and brainstorm about recommendations, ensuring all the information is on the table. We have repeatedly experienced how a community assessment, in its emphasis on a jointly shared dilemma, helps develop a container for these difficult life experiences and for creating a sense of being understood. Bion (1962) spoke about developing an inner reflective space, a need to create minds to think about meaning and solution. In therapeutic assessment training, we develop a community mind—the mind of therapists, consultant, and staff. We take our thoughts and translate them to our clients during the assessment process in an effort to create a constructive view of the presenting problem. As a consequence, we the clinicians are checking our own knowledge, feelings, and biases as assessors and finding new ways of listening and being therapeutic with our clients.

References

Alvarez, A. (1992). *Live company.* London: Routledge.

Bellak, L. & Bellak, S. S. (1949). *The Children's Apperception Test.* Larchmont, NY: CPS.

Berant, E., Saroff, A., Reicher-Atir, R., & Zim, S. (2005). Supervising personality assessment: The integration of intersubjective and psychodynamic elements in the supervisory process. *Journal of Personality Assessment, 84*(2), 205–212.

Bion, W. R. (1962). *Learning from experience.* London: Marsfield.

Boll, T. (1993). *Children's category test.* San Antonio, TX: Psychological Corporation.

Buck, J. N. (1973). The H-T-P technique: A qualitative and quantitative method. *Journal of Clinical Psychology, 4,* 317–396.

Burns, R. C. and Kaufman, S. H. (1987). *Kinetic family drawings (K-F-D): An introduction to understanding children through kinetic drawings.* New York: Brunner/Mazel.

Elliot, C. D. (2007). *Differential abilities scale II (DAS-II®).* San Antonio, TX: Pearson Education, Inc.

Exner, J. E., Jr. (1993). *The Rorschach: A comprehensive system: Vol. 1. Basic Foundations* (3rd ed.). New York: Wiley.

Finn, S. E. (2007). *In our client's shoes: Theory and techniques of therapeutic assessment.* Mahwah, NJ: Lawrence Erlbaum Associates.

Finn, S. E., & Tonsager, M. E. (1997). Information-gathering and therapeutic models of assessment: Complementary paradigms. *Psychological Assessment, 9,* 374–385.

Fowler, J. C. (1998). The trouble with learning personality assessment. In H. Handler & M. J. Hilsenroth (Eds.), *Teaching and learning personality assessment* (pp. 31–41). Mahwah, NJ: Lawrence Erlbaum Associates.

Gin, K. B. (2008). Demands upon the mind for work: Fostering agency within an organization. *Journal of Infant, Child, and Adolescent Psychotherapy, 7,* 79–87.

Hamilton, A., Fowler, J., Hersh, B., Austin, C., Finn, S. Tharinger, D., et al. (2009). Why won't my parents help me?: Therapeutic assessment of a child and her family. *Journal of Personality Assessment, 91*(2), 108–120.

Handler, L., Hess, A., Hess, K., & Hess, T. (Eds.) (2008). Supervision in collaborative and Therapeutic Assessment. In Allen K. Hess (Ed.), *Psychotherapy Supervision: Theory, research, and practice* (pp. 200–222). New York: Wiley.

McArthur, D. S. & Roberts, G. E. (1982). *Roberts Apperception Test for Children: Manual.* Los Angeles: Western Psychological Services.

Potash, H. M. (1998). Assessing the social subject. In H. Handler & M. J. Hilsenroth (Eds.), *Teaching and learning personality assessment* (pp. 137–146). Mahwah, NJ: Lawrence Erlbaum Associates.

Racker, H. (1968) *Transference and countertransference.* New York: International University Press.

Tharinger, D. J., Finn, S. E., Austin C. A., Gentry, L. B., Bailey, K. E., Parton, V. T. et al. (2008). Family sessions as part of child psychological assessment: Goals, techniques, clinical   utility, and therapeutic value. *Journal of Personality Assessment, 90,* 547–558.

Tharinger, D. J., Finn, S. E., Wilkinson, A. D., & Schaber, P. M. (2007). Therapeutic assessment with a child as a family intervention: A clinical protocol and research case study. *Psychology in the Schools, 44,* 293–309.

Wechsler, D. (2003). *Wechsler Intelligence scale for children: 4th Edition (WISC-IV®).* San Antonio, TX: Harcourt Assessment.

12 Surface Ripples or Deep Water?

Finding the Level for Children's Feedback Stories

Caroline Purves

Anna Freud and Melanie Klein held strongly different views on how a therapist should speak to children about themselves. Melanie Klein (1955) believed that children felt understood if their primal anxieties were named and addressed. Anna Freud (1944) took a more protective view that children's defenses need to be supported in order for them to tolerate hearing about their unconscious processes. I have been noticing both with my own feedback stories and those of interns and staff therapists that different stories illustrate these two styles of relating to children. For example, a story can reflect behavioral difficulties that the child knows is making her life a struggle, with suggestions for change. Conversely, the story can address painful, pervasive anxieties that are unarticulated but that underlie the behavior problems.

Here are excerpts from three stories that illustrate the differences. (Incidentally, I am deliberately refraining from calling them fables, as a story seems more individualized. Even "stories" isn't always the correct name, as in one of the following examples, a letter was sent to the child, which answered her questions directly.)

The first story is for 9-year-old Ralphie. It's called *Ralphie learns a new skill*. A few paragraphs will give you the idea of the main message:

> Ralphie was a boy who loved playing sports. He loved all kinds of games; even physical activities that you do by yourself. Ball games, running, riding a super fast bicycle—these were all things that he really, really enjoyed. And he was good at them—some, of course, better than others. Whatever Ralphie played, he played with all his might. You might say he put his heart and soul into his play.
>
> Sometimes he played so hard, he forgot about the other kids on the team. He just wanted to win. If a boy got in his way, for example, Ralphie might shove him aside in his eagerness to score a goal. Or he might throw the ball super hard in Dodgeball and actually hurt someone. Naturally, that someone would be very mad … might yell at Ralphie or complain to the coach. This made no sense to Ralphie. Didn't everyone want to win?
>
> After the playing was finished, Ralphie would want to hang out with the other boys and girls. Often they would turn their backs and go off without him. He hated this. It made him feel lonely and left out. He had no idea that his eagerness to win at games made the other children want to avoid him. He just felt a big lump in his chest.
>
> To make himself feel better, he would help his teacher—something he was just great at. If the teacher wanted someone to pass out the books, or hold the door open, Ralphie was always there. He was the first one to jump up and help. As he passed out

papers for his teacher, or helped arrange the line-up for lunch recess, he felt proud. The smile on his teacher's face told Ralphie that she was pleased with him.

The story goes on to describe how much the other children didn't like him and how lonely he was. He goes to a clever doctor who teaches him how to play with other children:

"Yeah," said Ralphie eagerly, "That's me. I'm really great at math. It's easy for me." "Yup," said Dr. W (which is what Ralphie was starting to call him in his head), "and it probably surprises you when other boys and girls can't do simple arithmetic." "Yessir, when it's so obvious and easy." "Uh huh," agreed Dr. W. "But just the opposite is true for you when it comes to understanding feelings, and especially other people's feelings."
"Wait a minute," Ralphie felt himself go red in the face as he raised his voice …
"Hold on there, young man," said Dr. W calmly. "It's not your fault and it doesn't mean you're a bad boy. And, it's something that you can learn. And believe me, it will pay off for you … you'll see."

And Ralphie does learn how to be more collaborative. This story operates at a fairly surface level. Ralphie was quite aware that he had difficulties with friends, but had no idea why he wasn't liked. The story addresses his conscious worry directly, his angry defense in the initial resistance to the doctor, and helpful ways to think about new behaviors.

What is not being addressed is a far deeper anxiety. To his TAT cards (Murray, 1943), he unexpectedly told stories about being an orphan or losing a parent, in spite of coming from a professional and intact family. For example, to card 3BM, which depicts a figure in a dejected posture slumped over a sofa, Ralphie told this story:

This is a kid crying because she lost her family in the war or something like that. And at the end of the story she gets adopted. (What happens?) And then she has a better life and wish she already knew this family in the beginning.

The next card, 13B, is a picture of a young barefoot boy sitting in the doorway of a log cabin. Here is Ralphie's story:

This is a little kid. He lives in an old house and he doesn't have any parents, and he has only a set of clothes. And he lives in this house and someone's gonna find him sooner or later and put him up for adoption. (What happened to his parents?) They died in a car crash. He doesn't want to be adopted because he wants his own family and he wants to see if he could survive on his own.

And finally, to card 8BM, which shows an adolescent boy in the foreground of what appears to be an operation of an adult male occurring behind him, Ralphie told this story:

He's a kid and he's looking at his dad having surgery and he's figuring, "Is my dad going to be okay or is he going to die?" He's figuring out that he might die so he's planning to see how he's going to live on his own.

(So what does he come up with?) Selling his dad's car ... making a lot of money. Buying his own house, buying his own car; growing up to be a success ... I don't know how to say it. Successful adult.

The themes running through here are of adoption, abandonment, and not really knowing one's origins. In other words, Ralphie demonstrates confusion about where he comes from and what is going to become of him, though there is no demonstrable evidence that his family is in any way problematic. These themes often occur in the responses of children who, in fact, come from broken families or who are in an adoptive home.

What I did not feel I could share with him was that his conception was the result of a sperm donor, which his parents had not so far revealed to him. The father felt such shame that in nine years he had not been able to talk to Ralphie about his conception, that Ralphie knew at an unconscious level—the unthought known, described by Christopher Bollas (1987).

It was their challenge, I felt, to find a way to tell their son, and my task to help them. At that point his therapist could address the anxieties about belonging and alienation that underlaid his difficulties with the other children. Where did he come from, who did he belong to? But to address it in Ralphie's story at the time we met would have been, in my opinion, premature and unhelpful. Furthermore, and more importantly, it was not my story to tell. This information had to come from his parents, supported by their therapist, if they so desired.

Daniella, an 11-year-old Caucasian girl, was in an adoptive home. She had witnessed her mother, whilst riding on her bicycle to meet Daniella after school, get hit and killed by a train. Even before this tragedy, Daniella's life with her mother had been less than satisfactory, with occasional reports to Child Protective Services for neglect. Daniella's presentation was mature and poised; in fact, given her life experience, eerily contained. Her questions, however, revealed her real anxieties.

She posed two questions: "Am I dumb?" and "Am I crazy?" She pulled back the "Am I dumb?" question, but in her letter I addressed them both, explaining how we psychologists understood slips of the tongue. Both of her questions truly spoke to her deepest fears which I addressed by giving examples from her test scores and Rorschach (1923/1994) responses. For the first, I explained directly how children who are verbally adept often don't realize that they have to work hard at other kinds of learning:

"When you have to work at learning new material or when the subject matter is not about words, then it can be quite hard for you. You have to struggle to understand what the pictures, maps, graphs, and so on mean. For instance, remember the task when you had to fill in those little boxes with the shape that matched the number? That was a real challenge. You worked carefully and didn't make mistakes, but it took you longer than most kids."

The letter explains clearly that she is anything but stupid, but her worries about it make sense.

When it came to the second question, "Am I crazy?" the side red details on card 3 of the Rorschach were particularly helpful as she saw them as two birds dancing in the sky, then spinning round and round. I wrote about the "outside girl" who worked incredibly hard to be mature and seem happy, and the "inside girl" who was often scared and confused, spinning round and round. She often felt that she was, indeed, going crazy.

Trying to soften her worry would be avoiding her pain. By asking the question, she was opening up, allowing me to see what she worked so hard to control. To not share these findings, at an 11-year-old level, would be to let her down.

When we have our weekly case conference check-in at WestCoast, as the conference leader, I usually don't join in, but this time I did, asking their thoughts about the topic. Among the more obvious ideas, such as using the child's words and images, two stood out particularly. One staffer said how she developed from writing very surface, even Pollyanna stories, to addressing the real anxieties. She called it "disturbing the system, not upsetting it." Another clinician said that she felt the best stories gave both the problematic behaviors, then the underlying anxieties that were contributing to it, to make the behaviors understandable. This quite naturally led into exploring who were the stories written for. Sometimes the parents learn more about their child from the metaphors and examples in the stories than they do from the direct explanation of the results. Just as the stories short-circuit defenses for the children, they do so for the parents who thus come to understand their child's behaviors in a different way. The parents find themselves more empathic, not as overwhelmed by all the details of the results.

The following story is, hopefully, the blending of the behavior and the underlying anxieties, just as the person in the case conference suggested.

The story for Edward, even though he was much younger—five at the time of testing— really did speak to his fears along with his problematic behaviors. Edward, an African American child, had been shuttled back and forth between his biological parents and foster homes. When he came for his assessment he was in a foster-adopt home. The excellent mother told me not to end his story with a guaranteed forever family as she had not yet signed the final adoption papers. Here are some parts of his story (the protagonist is called Frankie):

> When it was time to go back to class (you see, Frankie was in kindergarten), he pushed his way to the front of the line. He sat at his desk, while his teacher, Mrs. Snodgrass, told them all about what they were going to do next. At first he really listened, but in a few minutes he couldn't hear her words anymore. It all sounded like a big buzz, like a fly buzzing in the sunlight. He decided to go over to the book table and try to find a book he might like. Suddenly he heard Mrs. Snodgrass loud and clear: "Frankie, go back to your seat this minute!!"
>
> Oh, no. Was he in trouble again? What did he do wrong this time? Didn't Mrs. Snodgrass like him? He felt so sad, that he started to cry, just a little. He really, really wanted his teacher to like him, but she seemed to be mad at him a lot. He really didn't know why she was always mad at him. Well, sometimes he knew why … that he wasn't sitting on the carpet with the other kids, or that he just wandered away from his seat. But, he didn't do those things to be bad.

This is a description of his behavior and confusion: surface ripples. But the plot thickens. As the story plunges deeper into demonstrating his strengths and weaknesses, the primal anxieties surface. He goes to see the psychologist:

> She asked him to do a bunch of stuff, like draw and tell stories, even what his first memories were. Sometimes he liked it, and sometimes, he wasn't sure. At first, he

thought it was going to be too hard, and that he couldn't do it. But that lady said he could do it. And guess what? He *could* do it. He told interesting stories and made a lot of drawings. And he could spell his name just right!

Actually, this happened to Frankie quite a lot. At first he would be a bit nervous. He didn't know why he got so nervous and would say NO. But most of the time, once he settled down, he could do most things and a lot of them just fine.

After he left, the lady looked at all the things he had done, and went over all the things that he said, and read about his life before he came to see her. She found out that he had another mom and dad before these, and that he had to live in some different places with people he didn't even know. One time when he went back to live with his first mom and dad again, he was very mixed-up. He could not figure out what was happening. He could not understand why he kept moving. All he knew was that there was a lot of noise and confusion, and sometimes the grown-ups weren't very nice to each other. And sometimes his first mother just didn't seem to notice him.

The story then brings him to the crux of his current dilemma

One day he went to live with another family. They seemed nice but Frankie felt very, very nervous. Here we go again, he thought to himself. Now I have to learn all about this new family. I wonder how long I will stay this time ... and so on. Then the current fear is broached: "He wasn't sure that he wanted to get too friendly with them, because he probably would have to leave anyway."

It continues with descriptions of the warmth of the parents and the enjoyable activities they do together.

The ending is hopeful, but without false promises, because the situation *was* hopeful, though still unresolved.

How then, is the decision made—at which level to pitch the story? I suggest that there are striking differences in how we all approach this challenge, related, of course, to our style of thinking, understanding, and writing. Some people are consciously thoughtful and organized, picking up themes and conflicts directly from the material and their interactions. They can state clearly that they, for example, used the child's words or images, and gauged the level of resistance.

Others, like myself, may fall into a dreamy state as they go over the responses, the history, and the interactions. Intuitive? Well, as John Scully, the former head of Pepsi said, "I was intuitive after 17 years of leading the company." Not so intuitive at Apple, hmm? It is as if we have been offered a pathway into the child's psyche, and our task is to help clear out some of the underbrush so the child can see and understand what we have learned about him. In addition, it is to help the parents see the problems in new and empathic ways. The stories are a means to help them face their own fears of the real pain their child is experiencing. Then, as in the story for Ralphie, to find the courage to deal with their own anxieties, which then will help them understand their child.

Is one better than the other? Klein or Freud? To reach a rather wobbly conclusion, I suggest that it depends both on what the child and her parents bring to the assessment, their capacity to manage difficult feelings, and the comfort level of the assessor in facing the level of pain the child is handling.

References

Bollas, C. (1987). *The shadow of the object*. New York: Columbia University Press.

Freud, A. (1944). *The psycho-analytic treatment of children*. New York: International Universities Press.

Klein, M. (1955). The psycho-analytic play technique: its history and significance. In M. Klein, P. Heimann & R. E. Money-Kyrle, *New Directions in Psycho-Analysis*. London: Tavistock.

Murray, H. (1943). *Thematic apperception Test*. Cambridge, MA: Harvard University Press.

Rorschach, H. (1923/1994). *Plates*. Berne, Switzerland: Verlag Hans Huber Hogrefe.

Section III
Case Studies in Community-Based Psychological Assessment

13 Why Did She Put Nail Polish in My Drink?

Applying the Therapeutic Assessment Model with an African-American Foster Child in a Community Mental Health Setting

Brooke Guerrero, Jessica Lipkind, and Audrey Rosenberg

Finn and colleagues have developed a semi-structured assessment approach, Therapeutic Assessment (TA), which brings together skills from assessment and psychotherapy models and from multiple theoretical frameworks. The resulting approach considers assessment to be a therapeutic intervention in and of itself (Finn, 2007; Finn & Tonsager, 1992, 1997). TA is a form of collaborative assessment that is related to the work of Fischer (1985/1994), Handler (2006), and Purves (1997). Much has been written regarding its effectiveness with adults (Finn, 2003; Finn & Kamphuis, 2006; Finn & Tonsanger, 1992, 1997; Newman & Greenway, 1997; Peters, 2008), as well as with children and families (Hamilton et al., 2009; Handler, 2006; Smith & Handler, 2009; Tharinger et al., 2009; Tharinger, Finn, Wilkinson, & Schaber, 2007). While much of this work has been done in private practice or university research settings, a few articles have encouraged the use of this model in school-based settings (Tharinger et al., 2007) and with foster children and their families (Purves, 2002). There has been little research regarding using this model in community mental health settings and within culturally and racially diverse communities. This article focuses on the application of TA in a community psychology setting with an African American child living in foster care.

Fischer (1985/1994) has illustrated the usefulness of therapeutic techniques in a variety of settings, and our clinic has been influenced by her work, as well as by the teachings and writings of Purves (1997, 2002). Consequently, our clinic has utilized collaborative therapeutic techniques, including gathering questions from caregivers and clients and writing fairy-tale feedback stories to children since the mid- to late-1990s. We have been fortunate enough to have Dr. Purves and Dr. Mercer on staff and have received multiple trainings from Dr. Finn.

This case presentation illustrates one of the first cases our clinicians completed utilizing Finn and colleagues' comprehensive TA model with children (Finn, 2007; Tharinger et al., 2009). The case we present was part of a week-long intensive training with Dr. Finn. The one-week time frame is unusual for TA assessments and was based on the training needs of the staff and scheduling factors. Dr. Finn served as the consultant on this case. Dr. Guerrero conducted the testing with the client, Lanice, and the testing sessions were viewed via live video feed in a separate room by Lanice's aunt and mother. Dr. Rosenberg supervised the case and worked on a team with Dr. Lipkind. They observed each assessment session with the aunt and mother. Despite some alterations in timeframe and clinician configuration, we followed Dr. Finn's suggestions regarding TA steps and procedures. We found it to be a highly effective method with our client and her family. This case illustrates how the TA model had a significant impact on our clients. However, the crisis that occurred during the assessment process and the clinicians' response to and use of this crisis underscores several important considerations and modifications in our application of this model. This case also highlights the necessity of integrating race and class in the application of TA. Additionally, this case emphasizes the need to extend the interventions beyond the family to larger systems and adopt Boyd-Franklin's (2003) approach to joining African American families around "real life" problems, such as engaging extended families and outside agencies in the process.

Background of Case

Reason for Referral

At the time of the assessment, Lanice[1] was an 11-year-old African American girl in the fifth grade. She was referred to our clinic by her aunt, with whom she lived, to evaluate her cognitive and emotional functioning, as well as to determine possible causes for her oppositional behaviors and angry outbursts. Lanice often refused to do schoolwork and exhibited acting-out behaviors with her teachers. She reportedly spaced out in class for extended lengths of time and had trouble paying attention. At home, Lanice was generally respectful to her aunt, but she displayed some concerning behaviors that left her aunt feeling confused and angry. On one occasion, Lanice poured nail polish into her older cousin's drink when she wasn't looking and sat quietly while she waited for her cousin to ingest it. Additionally, Lanice left shavings of wax from a candle in the carpet and on furniture in the home. Her aunt also reported that Lanice tore up pieces of paper and left them in random places around the house. Lanice did not verbalize why she had so frequently engaged in these behaviors. Her aunt also stated that Lanice was often disrespectful and physically aggressive toward her developmentally delayed mother.

Relevant History

Lanice lived with her aunt, Paula, and her aunt's adult daughter. Lanice's mother, Jakara, was diagnosed with Mild Mental Retardation and left Lanice with relatives when Lanice was a baby. Jakara continued to be a part of her life, as she visited with Lanice and occasionally had overnight visits, but her role was closer to that of a cousin than of a parent. Lanice never had a relationship with her biological father. Lanice lived with several different family members, but spent the majority of her life with her grandparents until they passed away in 2007. After their death, she moved in with Paula and Paula's daughter. Lanice attended her grandfather's funeral, as he passed away first, but Paula felt it would be too difficult for Lanice to attend her grandmother's funeral. Paula stated that Lanice had never spoken about her losses. Lanice's grandparents were elderly and reportedly in poor health, which left Lanice without close supervision and limit setting.

Paula stated that Lanice was "spoiled" during her time with her grandparents due to the lack of discipline and explained that she was permitted to do as she pleased without consequences.

For many years, Lanice struggled with her academic performance and behavior in school. Paula wondered if Lanice had a learning disability due to her difficulties with reading and completing homework. Her third and fourth grade teachers urged Paula to request testing for Lanice due to their suspicions of a learning disability. These teachers reported that, despite intensive tutoring and extra attention during class, Lanice was far behind the other students in her grade. Due to unknown reasons, a year and a half passed from the time Paula initially requested the Individualized Education Program (IEP) to the time an actual IEP meeting was held. The school asserted that Lanice did not qualify for services because no significant discrepancy between her cognitive and achievement scores was found. Regardless of their assertion, her reading achievement scores were assessed to be at the kindergarten level.

Participants in the Testing Process

Paula agreed to participate in the TA process and we asked if Jakara could also take part. We encouraged Paula to engage Jakara in the process and welcomed any other important people in Lanice's life to attend, including Paula's adult daughter. Paula's daughter declined the invitation; thus the individuals who participated in the TA were Paula, Jakara, and Lanice. We also engaged the school system, which included Lanice's teacher, her previous year's teacher, and the Resource Specialist in the Special Education Program.

We began the assessment by meeting with Paula and Jakara together, gathered background information, and developed their questions for the assessment. During this meeting, some of the obstacles to the TA model became apparent. Although Jakara was diagnosed with Mild Mental Retardation, we hypothesized that her functioning was somewhat lower. For example, we struggled with her tendency to derail the discussion by introducing off-topic facts and her difficulty understanding questions. In addition, although Paula wanted to know why Lanice had angry outbursts at school, she firmly stated that she did not see Lanice's anger and had virtually no problems with her at home, aside from the few previously mentioned behavioral incidents.

We quickly discovered that Paula's expectations were inconsistent regarding Lanice's ability to tolerate emotions, which resulted in her sending mixed messages. For example, Paula reported that Lanice avoided her painful feelings, but Paula did not take Lanice to her grandmother's funeral because she felt it would be too difficult for Lanice. It seemed that her aunt could objectively see that Lanice's denial of negative feelings was not healthy, yet there was no space for Lanice's negative affect to come out, other than at school. As a team, we wondered how to handle this issue during the discussion/summary session, as Paula seemed to have difficulty tolerating painful feelings.

Our team worked with Paula and Jakara to develop and refine their questions for the assessment and they identified six questions (see Table 13.1). Their primary questions regarded Lanice's reading difficulties and oppositional behavior.

Table 13.1 Paula and Jakara's Assessment Questions

1.	Does Lanice really not have a learning disability?
2.	Why is she so angry?
3.	Why does she space out? Does she have problems with attention?
4.	How can I get her more excited about reading?
5.	How can I get her to be more responsible about cleaning up after herself?
6.	Why does she push limits with people who are helpless or can't stand up for themselves?

Testing Process and Themes Revealed

Dr. Guerrero[2] met with Lanice to conduct the testing, while Drs. Rosenberg and Lipkind met with Paula and Jakara in another room where they observed the testing sessions via a live feed displayed on a flat-screen television. In the first testing session, Dr. Guerrero began with projective drawings to establish rapport, which included Draw-A-Person (D-A-P; Harris, 1963), House-Tree-Person (H-T-P; Buck, 1966), and Draw-A-Person-In-The-Rain (D-A-P-R; Verinis, Lichtenberg, & Henrich, 1974). Dr. Guerrero also administered the Conners' Continuous Performance Test (CPT-II; Conners & MHS Staff, 2000), the Childhood Depression Inventory (CDI; Kovacs & Beck, 1977), the Revised Children's Manifest Anxiety Scale (RCMAS; Reynolds & Richmond, 1979), and a series of incomplete sentence stems constructed by the assessment team based on the presenting issues. Dr. Guerrero also conducted a play interview with Lanice, where a nondirective approach was utilized and imaginative play was encouraged.

As the administration began, Lanice's tendency to minimize her feelings and deny negative affect immediately became apparent. For example, Lanice stated that she always felt happy. When tasks obviously frustrated her, Dr. Guerrero reflected her frustration, but Lanice actively denied feeling any negative emotions. Her projective drawings provided additional information. While her Person-in-the-Rain (Figure 13.1) was protected by an adequately sized umbrella, the rain was abundant and formed a puddle larger than the person just outside of the umbrella's reach. While protection such as an umbrella symbolized the presence of emotional defenses, the puddle represented Lanice's perceived external stress, which she narrowly escaped (Oster & Crone, 2004). Her tree was filled with apples, which represented high dependency needs (Ogden, 1975). We hypothesized that this could be related to emotional deprivation early in Lanice's childhood.

A play interview was conducted to better understand Lanice's inner world and observe the reported behaviors. During the play interview, Lanice engaged in symbolic dollhouse play and invited Dr. Guerrero to join her for a picnic, where they worked together to prepare and enjoy a meal. Lanice became frustrated at various points during the play, but when asked, she denied negative feelings. Soon after becoming frustrated, she engaged in oppositional behavior that necessitated limit setting. She intrusively held objects directly in Dr. Guerrero's face and intentionally knocked items onto the floor. During this initial session, Dr. Guerrero set few limits in order to test how far Lanice would push the boundaries. However, when Dr. Guerrero intervened, Lanice responded positively and quickly stopped the undesirable behavior. We decided as a team that it would be important to set more limits with Lanice in the subsequent testing sessions.

Figure 13.1 Lanice's Person-in-the-Rain

During the second testing session, Dr. Guerrero administered the Rorschach Inkblot Method (Exner & Weiner, 1995), Roberts Apperception Test (Roberts, 1994), Children's Apperception Test (CAT; Bellak & Bellak, 1949), and the Early Memories Procedure (EMP; Bruhn, 1992). In addition, two subtests of the Woodcock-Johnson III Test of Achievement (Woodcock, McGrew, & Mather, 2001) were given to supplement the testing obtained from Lanice's school. Specifically, the subtests *Auditory Attention* and *Understanding Directions* were administered to better understand Lanice's problems with attention. She performed well on these measures, but the data suggested that she learns better when visual cues are paired with auditory cues (*Auditory Attention standard score* = 81; *Understanding Directions standard score* = 102). The treatment team also reviewed the school's test results and found that Lanice scored in the Low Functioning and Borderline range on the cognitive measures and was achieving academically between the equivalent of a kindergartener and a second grader. The school argued that there was not a large enough discrepancy (1.5 standard deviations) between her cognitive and achievement scores, thus she did not qualify for special education services as a learning disabled student. However, her school did not address the findings that Lanice read at the kindergarten level and performed in math at the second-grade level. The school staff expected her to work at the fifth-grade level and complete fifth-grade homework. We could not find any justification as to why Lanice did not receive any assistance and support for her significantly below grade level reading.

With regard to emotional functioning, we learned that while Lanice had difficulty putting words to her own feelings and experiences, she could use projective materials to express herself quite well. We immediately saw her difficulties with school emerge on the projective measures. In her responses to the Roberts' Apperception Cards, Lanice creatively linked the cards to produce one entire story. This story depicted a young girl who struggled with her schoolwork and reading and became angry as a result. In her story, the young girl also missed out on opportunities for fun because of her poor academic performance.

Table 13.2 Lanice's Structural Summary

Comprehensive System 5th Edition Structural Summary

LOCATION FEATURES	DETERMINANTS	CONTENTS	APPROACH

LOCATION FEATURES	BLENDS	SINGLE		
			H = 2	I : DsS.DdS
Zf = 8	M.FC'	M = 2	(H) = 2	II :D.D.D
ZSum = 25.5	M.m	FM = 0	Hd = 3	III :D.D.D
ZEst = 24	M.CF	m = 0	(Hd) = 0	IV :W
		FC = 5	Hx = 0	V :W.D
W = 5		CF = 2	A = 7	VI :W
D = 10		C = 0	(A) = 0	VII :W
W+D = 15		Cn = 0	Ad = 3	VIII :W
Dd = 4		FC' = 0	(Ad) = 0	IX :Ds.D.D
S = 2		C'F = 0	An = 0	X :Dd.D
		C' = 0	Art = 0	
		FT = 0	Ay = 0	SPECIAL SCORES
DQ		TF = 0	Bl = 0	

DQ									
			T = 0	Bt = 0			Lvl		Lv2
+ = 5			FV = 0	Cg = 4		DV	= 0 x1		x2
o = 14			VF = 0	Cl = 0		INC	= 2 x2		x4
v/+ = 0			V = 0	Ex = 0		DR	= 1 x3		x6
v = 0			FY = 0	Fd = 2		FAB	= 0 x4		x7
			YF = 0	Fi = 0		ALOG	= 0 x5		
FORM QUALITY			Y = 0	Ge = 0		CON	= 0 x7		
			Fr = 0	Hh = 0		Raw Sum6 =		4	
	FQx MQual	W+D	rF = 0	Ls = 0		Wgtd Sum6 =		11	
+ = 0 = 0		= 0	FD = 0	Na = 0					
o = 6 = 2		= 6	F = 7	Sc = 0		AB	= 0 GHR = 1		
u = 8 = 2		= 6		Sx = 0		AG	= 1 PHR = 6		
- = 5 = 1		= 3		Sx = 0		COP	= 0 MOR = 2		
none = 0 = 0		= 0		Xy = 0		CP	= 0 PER = 0		
			(2) = 7	Id = 2			PSV = 0		

---------------------------------RATIOS, PERCENTAGES, AND DERIVATIONS---------------------------------

R = 19	L = 0.58		FC:CF+C = 5:3	COP = 0 AG = 0
			Pure C = 0	GHR:PHR = 1:6
EB = 5:5.5	EA = 10.5	EBPer = N/A	SmC':WSmC = 1:5.5	a:p = 5:1
eb = 1:1	es = 2	D = +3	Afr = 0.46	Food = 2
	Adj = 2	Adj D = +3	S = 2	SumT = 0
	es			
			Blends/R = 3:19	Human Cont = 7
FM = 0	SumC' = 1	SumT = 0	CP = 0	PureH = 2
m = 1	SumV = 0	SumY = 0		PER = 0
				Isol Indx = 0.00

a:p = 5:1	Sum6 = 4	XA% = 0.74	Zf =	3r+(2)/R = 0.37
Ma:Mp = 5:0	Lv2 = 1	WDA% = 0.80	W:D:Dd =5 :10 : 4	Fr+rF = 0
2AB+Art+Ay = 0	WSum6 = 11	X-% = 0.26	W:M = 5:5	SumV = 0
MOR = 2	M- = 1	S- = 1	Zd = +1.5	FD = 0
	Mnone = 0	P = 4	PSV = 0	An+Xy = 0
		X+% = 0.32	DQ+ = 5	MOR = 2
		Xu% = 0.42	DQv = 0	H:(H)+Hd+(Hd) = 2:5
PTI = 0	DEPI = 3	CDI = 3	S-CON = N/A	HVI = No OBS = No

Copyright 2001 by Rorschach workshops. Reprinted with permission.

The last part of the story described the girl at home and painting on the wall because she continued to feel angry about what happened at school. It was as if Lanice had directly answered the question about her strange behaviors at home and showed the assessment team, as well as Paula and Jakara, who watched, what led her to rip up pieces of paper, pour nail polish in drinks, and destroy candles. Fortunately, because Paula and Jakara had the opportunity to observe the testing throughout the administration with Drs. Lipkind and Rosenberg, they more readily understood what this sequence of stories represented. We observed a story about a girl who felt incompetent, missed out on activities with her peers, and tried to remain hopeful, but became disappointed. Such experiences resulted in her feeling angry and displaying strange behaviors. Paula appeared to feel relief from understanding Lanice's struggles and she began to cry as she heard the story.

Lanice's Rorschach responses (Exner, 2001) (Table 13.2) revealed low self esteem (Egocentricity Ratio $(3r+2/R)= .37$; $MOR = 2$), minimization of needs ($FM = 0$), and constricted affect ($Afr = 46$). Her minimization of affect was also evident on the Early Memories Procedure. For example, when prompted to identify a time when she felt angry, Lanice responded, "I never got angry." However, her responses on the Rorschach had an elevated Aggressive Content score ($AgC = 5$) (Gacono & Meloy, 1994). Lanice's early memories were somewhat superficial and, while she observed, Paula commented that these memories appeared to be from photographs in the home, rather than actual experiences. Our team wondered about the possible paucity of early meaningful experiences, but were concerned that Paula would have difficulty accepting this, as it was her parents who cared for Lanice when she was young. During the session where projective material was administered, Lanice engaged in behavior that pulled for limit-setting as she spun the Rorschach cards on her finger like a basketball, laid the top half of her body across the table, and put her feet on the table. In this session, however, Dr. Guerrero set firm limits throughout the testing and these behaviors vanished by the end of the session.

Family Intervention and Crisis

This section focuses on the family intervention session and the crisis that unfolded during the check-in before the session. Additionally, we discuss how the assessment team and family used the crisis to become more reflective and to understand the impact of class and cultural issues.

Family intervention sessions play an important role in TA with children. Family intervention sessions have been used to highlight systemic issues which impact the child's functioning and to help the assessment team better understand what the family can and cannot tolerate (Tharinger et al., 2008). We utilized Finn's system of categorizing information based on how readily a family can hear the feedback (Finn, 2007; Tharinger, Finn, Hersch, et al., 2008). For instance, *Level 1* findings are those that the clients can easily accept and verify themselves. *Level 2* findings tend to modify a client's way of thinking or "amplify" the ways that they think about themselves. *Level 3* information is quite difficult for clients to tolerate and they may reject or deny the information.

The family intervention session occurred the day after the testing session described above. The assessment team had decided to meet with the family prior to the intervention session to address any questions they had thus far. Subsequently, we asked the family to engage in a consensus story-telling task. Tharinger et al. (2008) reported:

Using this technique, family members are asked to craft stories together to TAT or other picture story cards. The assessor may choose cards for the family that pull for different affective states, creating the opportunity for family to see how they respond under these different conditions. (p. 556)

We hoped that using this task in the family intervention session would elicit family dynamics, highlight themes that addressed the family's assessment questions, and bring the family together. The assessment team was surprised by what happened when the family arrived for the session. Paula was visibly upset. She stated that Lanice had gotten into serious trouble at school after the previous day's testing session. Paula was so distressed that she had considered withdrawing from the assessment altogether. On the previous day, Lanice had missed most of her classes because of the testing and, upon her return to school, went directly to the after-school program. Lanice thought that she did not have any homework, but shortly after arriving at the after-school program, her teacher brought her a packet of homework. Lanice became angry and would not do her work. She pulled herself away from the after-school teacher, refused to do what he had asked, and would not comply with the program rules. The teacher was rather upset and, when Paula went to the school to pick up Lanice, she was met by a young student who informed her that the teacher wanted to speak to her and that Lanice had "acted up." Paula reported feeling caught off guard, as she reasoned that everything had been fine after the assessment session and the family had been laughing together when she dropped Lanice off at school.

Paula was rather frustrated and flustered, and linked Lanice's disrespectful behavior to the testing and, particularly, to having "too much freedom" in the sessions. She brought up two prior incidents in the assessment where she felt limits were not appropriately set on Lanice's behavior. The first happened several days prior during a time of free play when Lanice tried to make Dr. Guerrero drink some pretend "dirty milk." Dr. Guerrero refused, but let the play continue to observe some of Lanice's behaviors and feelings. The second incident occurred the next day during the administration of the Rorschach test. Lanice appeared somewhat agitated during this task and frequently squirmed in her seat. At one time, she had the top half of her body lying on the table. Paula firmly believed that Lanice had been given too much latitude and, as a consequence, she no longer understood that she needed to behave with adults and had, in essence, said, "I don't have to listen to you."

Paula's response elicited great surprise in the team. As a group, we tried to validate her experience by acknowledging how worried and upset she was and how serious her concerns appeared. We attempted to reframe some of her perceptions and explained that Dr. Guerrero made a conscious decision to let Lanice test limits to see what was causing her behaviors, since it was these same behaviors which got her in trouble. Dr. Guerrero also explained that she had set more limits throughout the previous day's testing session. In addition, we tried to make a link between her behavior at school after the session and the material that emerged from the testing. There was an uncanny parallel between her extended story on the previous afternoon's Roberts Apperception Test and her reaction later that day when she returned to school and discovered that, even after a hard day of testing, she still had to complete homework.

The following are two consecutive responses to Roberts' Female Card 16, followed by Card 13:

Roberts Card 16 (in the version we used, this card shows a middle-aged African American man sitting in a chair reviewing papers and a young African American girl standing expectantly as he reads the papers):

> That's her teacher, sitting in the chair reading her homework. She stands up with her hands behind her back. He's looking at the homework, deciding if she can go to recess. The girl is feeling a little bit happy. She's happy he's reading her paper. Thinking he is gonna say "yeah." He's thinking maybe she's going to go outside.

Roberts Card 13 (this card depicts a young African American girl holding a chair over her head):

> She's angry. She got to go home. She threw the chair. She has Nike shoes, pants, sweatshirt, black. She's mad because he said no. She throws him out of the chair. She threw the chair to the floor. I'm going to kill him! She gets mad and leaves.

These responses provided a glimpse into the reasons for Lanice's defiance later that day in school. We tried to make this link with Paula and Jakara and to convey that her behavior was a form of communication. We also suggested to Paula that she was not alone in this struggle and that we would talk to the after-school teacher to explain our understanding of the situation and Lanice's behaviors. We acknowledged that the previous day's session was rather intense and that we would do more to plan for Lanice's transition from the testing session to school. We made a plan to help contain and process any feelings that were generated so the family would be more prepared for behaviors that might erupt. By the end of our discussion, Paula appeared more relaxed, made frequent eye contact, and the family was ready to engage in the rest of the day's session.

Finn (personal communication, September 9, 2008) had spoken to us earlier about the crisis that might occur during the course of the assessment. Despite this previous consultation, the crisis felt like a surprise and, in the moment, was challenging to navigate. Luckily, we were able to work through this crisis and use it to highlight many of Lanice's struggles that were revealed throughout the testing. It once again showed us how challenging schoolwork and the school environment were for Lanice and how her defiance was one way she reacted to feeling barraged by expectations she felt unable to meet. Furthermore, while she was able to articulate her experience on the Roberts cards, Lanice was not able to articulate what had happened to her in the moment or later that day. This coincided with test findings that Lanice had few words for her feelings, that she often reacted unexpectedly, and when asked to explain her actions, she had difficulty linking her behaviors to her feelings.

After the resolution of the crisis, we went forward with our plan for the family intervention session. The session had three parts: the consensus story telling task, reflection on the task, and a game of UNO®. We chose several story cards from the TAT and the Roberts. It took some time for everyone to agree to a story, but by the third card, the family was actively engaged. During the game of UNO®, the assessment team and Lanice's family became animated and genuinely enjoyed the game. However, it was noteworthy that Jakara became highly stimulated by the game, as evidenced by her squealing, clapping her hands repeatedly, and rocking back and forth.

Several themes emerged during the consensus story telling task. First, both Lanice and Paula were well aware of Jakara's limitations. This was evidenced by Paula's continued reference to Jakara as a "Re-Re" (a slang term for mentally retarded). Likewise, Lanice frequently became dismissive of her mother's responses and behaviors. Secondly, Lanice was very uncomfortable with Jakara's behavior. Finally, Lanice tried to talk about deprivation by alluding to the neglect she had experienced early in life, while Paula denied the neglect or lack of resources. This was evident in the Consensus Story Telling Task on Card 13B of the Thematic Apperception Test (Murray, 1943; the card depicts a young boy sitting outside a wooden framed house). Lanice spoke of a little boy with no shoes who could not go outside because he might injure his feet. Paula, however, had a different interpretation and responded that the little boy chose not to wear his shoes. Paula denied that the boy had any negative feelings regarding the lack of shoes, while Lanice stated that the boy was angry about it. In turn, Paula countered that he was not mad, but was rather "deep in thought." The following is the story the family agreed on:

> A little boy lived in a wooden house with a wooden doorway and a wooden TV. Pants are dirty and he has no socks or shoes. He's thinking about going inside the house to play old-school video games.

At this time, however, Paula readily linked Lanice's anger and defiance to school failure on the next card. The family agreed to the following story on Roberts Card 13 (girl depicted with chair over her head):

> There was a girl who had to do homework, she thought she was done with it. And her dad asked to look at it and it wasn't done. She was sad that she couldn't go out to play outside to skate. So she got very angry and picked up a chair and was going to throw it. But didn't, the end.

This powerful story was a conglomeration of three of Lanice's earlier stories from the previous day. In addition, the family began to listen, tolerate, and identify Lanice's anger and frustration.

As Tharinger et al. (2008) suggested, the themes that emerged during the family intervention session helped us answer the family's questions. The session clarified what would be most useful to the family at this point in time. We observed Paula's difficulty acknowledging her own parents' limitations and how their challenges may have impacted Lanice's attachment and early development. She was, however, able to acknowledge Jakara's limitations. Both she and Jakara voiced their concern that Jakara's earlier abandonment of Lanice continued to impact her daughter. In addition to focusing on school problems and Lanice's difficulties putting feelings into words, we also addressed the family's questions: "Why does Lanice push limits with people who are helpless or can't stand up for themselves?" and "Why is Lanice so angry?" The following are excerpts from the discussion letter written to Paula. In regard to pushing limits, we wrote, "Lanice needs more structure to feel contained and that she actually can get angry and frustrated when there is less structure in her environment because, in these cases, she doesn't feel safe." We continued to link Jakara's limitations by writing:

> It is very common for kids Lanice's age to be embarrassed by their parents, and that Lanice's feelings of embarrassment about her mother are stronger than others her age. Lanice is struggling with how to understand and deal with her mother's limitations and she tends to be disrespectful and angry in response to her mother's behavior. This may be compounded by feelings of rejection and abandonment from her mother leaving her so many years ago.

The family was also able to acknowledge Lanice's school problems and difficulty putting feelings into words. We integrated this understanding into their school-related questions, "Does she have a learning disability?" and "How can I get her more excited about reading?" We were also able to link these difficulties to her anger.

The crisis created by Lanice's disruptive behaviors offered an opportunity for us to reflect on the assessment process and its implications in Lanice's life. We were struck by some of the cultural and socioeconomics implications of the TA process. Altman (1995) suggested that issues of class, race, and culture permeate our interactions in clinical work. Thus, integration of these issues into our work are paramount. We were three highly educated, White women who suggested to a young African American girl, her aunt, and her mentally challenged African American mother, that reflecting together on feelings and behavior was the best approach. We also realized that the exploration of feelings placed our clients at risk. When Paula allowed herself to believe that such reflection and focus on feelings was possible, or even helpful, the reality of her life did not support this. She was told that if Lanice misbehaved, she would be expelled from her after-school program. When Paula tried to reflect with the after-school program director about the impact of the testing on Lanice's behavior, she was told that this did not matter and that, despite Lanice's emotional state, she needed to respect her. Paula's concern over Lanice's behavior reflected the very real concerns she had for her niece; a young African American girl who, in many settings, did not have the privilege to express her feelings. We reflected on our cultural and socioeconomic expectations and the emphasis so many of our clients' families put on respect and behavior. We wondered why they couldn't see the grief, disrupted attachment, or feelings behind these behaviors. The team came to understand that, in Lanice's world, there was no room for negative feelings and that her actions had real and immediate consequences.

Summary/Discussion

The assessment with Lanice and her family was conducted over a one-week training with Dr. Finn at WestCoast Children's Clinic. Through the initial interviews, testing sessions, family intervention session, and summary/discussion session, we developed a coherent understanding of the issues that contributed to Lanice's behavioral problems and poor management of affect. Our theories were reinforced by the crisis we endured with the family, which highlighted Lanice's struggle to express her emotions and how that directly resulted in her outbursts. We ascertained that the Level 1 information included Lanice's reading deficits, which severely impacted her ability to function at the same level as her peers. In addition, the behavioral problems she displayed in school and with Jakara, also Level 1 information, needed to be addressed to allow her to continue to interact with and be supported by her varying systems. The Level 2 information was determined to be Lanice's denial of painful feelings, particularly sadness and anger, and how this contributed to her sense of incompetence in her daily life. Finally, the Level 3 information was centered around the emotional neglect Lanice experienced early in her life due to her mother and grandparent's limitations.

In our discussion session with Paula and Jakara, we explained that not only was there a clear learning disability present but that we would work as a team to advocate for services within the school district. The crux of our intervention was to help Lanice's aunt recognize that she was not alone with this task, but that we were a team and that, in this way, we could get the school to acquiesce. Paula tried to obtain services for Lanice on multiple occasions and was told, in essence, that her hunch about Lanice's needs was incorrect and no services were available for her. We had the conviction, assuredness, and experience of advocating for our underserved clients within a variety of school districts and succeeding. We were sure that we would prevail in this case, as well. However, following the discussion/summary session, Dr. Guerrero attempted to contact the school multiple times to discuss the test results and to make a case for a meeting to occur. Phone calls were not returned, emails were ignored, and we began to get a glimpse into Paula's experience. As this continued over a few weeks, we felt helpless, ignored, enraged, and disheartened about our inability to exact change for Lanice. It became apparent to us that we were operating on assumptions of privilege, even though this was out of our awareness at the time. We believed that our White faces and advanced degrees would be more powerful than Paula's words and concern. At this point, we were pushed to reflect on how the issue of privilege, particularly White privilege, arose in this case.

White privilege is defined by McIntosh as, "an invisible package of unearned assets that I can count on cashing in on each day, but about which I was 'meant' to remain oblivious" (McIntosh, 1990, p. 1). As three White, well-educated women of middle-class status, we believed there were certain truisms about our roles and the power connected to these roles. Once we realized how we utilized our privilege, we had to step back and reevaluate the process, as well as our assumptions. We realized that we intended to empower Lanice's aunt by-proxy; giving her power as an extension of ours. We understood that "power from unearned privilege can look like strength when it is in fact permission to escape or dominate" (Wildman & Davis, 2002, p. 100). The team agreed that we needed to find more appropriate ways to empower Paula for who she was, what she had done, and what she could do for Lanice. Unfortunately, the reality of the situation was that we were unable to make changes within the school system, despite our attempts to do so. Thus, we fell back on our privilege once more (the privilege of having connections in high places) and contacted an attorney to work with Lanice's family on a pro bono basis to advocate for learning disability services. Although none of us regret this last step, it is crucial that we stay aware of what we represent to our clients, as well as how we see ourselves. The therapist's power in the relationship is not a new idea, nor is it a new concept that we should be aware of how we use that power. However, with our underserved, underrepresented, and oppressed clients, it is imperative that we are attuned to how we use ourselves and extend our power, sometimes replicating years of oppression and racism in the process (Ridley, 1995).

In Lanice's case, we walked the line of abusing our privilege, but by supporting each other in the treatment team, we were able to identify our motivations, their impact, and the source of our perceived power. Our interventions were reevaluated and we proceeded with the plan we felt would be most beneficial. This plan focused on assisting Lanice with obtaining services, empowering Paula, and fostering a positive relationship between Paula and Dr. Guerrero, who became Lanice's individual therapist. In their ongoing work together, Dr. Guerero has continued to advocate for Lanice's needs within the school district by engaging an alternate system to the one we originally approached. By teaming up with Lanice's aunt, teacher, and special education caseworker, instead of the special education administrators, a new plan was developed to access services. This team was ultimately successful, thus reinforcing Dr. Guerrero's relationship with Paula and allowing her to deepen Lanice's treatment. For instance, their successes together brought Dr. Guerrero and Paula closer, allowing Dr. Guerrero to slowly introduce Level 3 information. For example, Paula was able to think about the idea that Lanice was "not watched enough" when she was young and that some things "fell through the cracks" in her early years.

One of the most significant differences for us in using TA, compared to our usual way of doing assessments, was the presence of a treatment team. In Lanice's case, her presenting problems and history were not as severe and intense as many of the children we have evaluated. However, each day the three of us were amazed by how tired and overwhelmed we felt by the day's work. We realized that these feelings were not only due to the clinical issues and the compressed time frame in which we completed the assessment, but also to the level of direct and intimate involvement with the family. Although we are very invested and committed to our clients, our work with Lanice and her family occurred on an additional level and we were drawn into family dynamics and defenses. In addition, through our work with Lanice's family, we were able to support one another to hold the pain and loss that arose in the case. At different points in the work, we experienced periods of helplessness, anxiety, sadness, exhaustion, and anger. Sometimes, the three of us felt these emotions simultaneously and we could sit together and theorize about why such feelings were affecting us all. We could also relate to each person's experience—occasionally this even occurred on a nonverbal level. At other times, our differing feelings arose concurrently, allowing us to each push our team members to explore their feelings and recognize which part of the case each of us was holding and with whom we were identifying. This team provided a holding environment for us as clinicians to delve into Lanice and her family's more painful affect. The support of the team allowed us to do so in a profound manner, which we rarely have the luxury to explore in such depth. The team approach also allowed for this necessary parallel process, as we went on a journey of exploring distressing feelings and creating a story around their presence, just as Lanice's family did in the assessment process.

At the conclusion of the assesment, we had the opportunity to reflect on the overall process. All three of us were struck deeply by the innumerable ways this assessment differed from our other experiences conducting assessments at WestCoast Children's Clinic. Typically, our population of children present for assessments with histories of complex trauma, intergenerational abuse, community violence, and multiple losses and attachment disruptions. Moreover, our work is conducted in the realm of multiple systems, often involving the child, their biological family, foster family, dependency court, juvenile justice system, and school. Integrating questions from all these providers and caretakers, as well as their varying levels of clinical understanding and participation in the process, can result in the presence of additional and complex dynamics. Often, each adult involved in the case has a distinct role in the child's life and their own unique goal for the assessment. Moreover, because many of our clients are in foster care or move, sometimes unexpectedly, from placement to placement, they may have very little support from caregivers to modulate their experience of the assessment, or even to develop their questions. Since our clients are affected by long histories of trauma, loss, and abandonment, our clinicians are faced daily with the task of titrating the trauma and painful feedback in discussion/summary sessions. In addition, clinicians must be highly alert to what may be Level 1, Level 2, or Level 3 information. In many cases, significant portions of the feedback must be withheld or discussed in very small doses over multiple sessions to allow the child's caregiver to remain empathetic and available, as well as to avoid flooding them with the child's emotional experiences and needs. This, of course, leaves the clinicians holding heavy loads of painful affect, traumatic memories, and feelings of worry and helplessness for many of our clients.

As evidenced in the above discussion, the assessments conducted at our clinic entail challenges that are not faced in all treatment settings. At the start of the TA training, we presumed that we would become better assessors. We also presumed that, at the conclusion, we would feel more competent at conducting evaluations using TA. But our team had little insight into how deeply this training pushed us to stay on the path of evaluating our roles as White clinicians working within multiple systems with severely traumatized youth, many of whom are youth of color. The training with Dr. Finn reinvigorated the team's commitment to being acutely aware of these powerful issues. Although we set out to help this family change their story about who they were and why they behaved as they did, we left the process continuing to change our own story about ourselves in relation to our clients and the systems in which they are engaged.

Notes

1   Pseudonyms are used to protect confidentiality.
2   While we refer to ourselves in this article with the use of "Dr." attached, note that in order to join with the family, only first names were used with our clients.

References

Altman, N. (1995). Race, culture and social class. In S. A. Mitchell & L. Aron (Eds.), *The analyst in the inner city: Race, class and culture through a psychoanalytic lens* (pp. 74–118). Hillsdale, NJ: Analytic Press.

Bellak, L. & Bellak, S. S. (1949). *The Children's Apperception Test*. Larchmont, NY: CPS.

Boyd-Franklin, N. (2003). *Black families in therapy: Understanding the African American experience*. New York, NY: The Guilford Press.

Bruhn, A. R. (1992). The Early Memories Procedure: A projective test of autobiographical memory, parts 1 & 2. *Journal of Personality Assessment, 58*(1), 1–15 and *58*(2), 326–346.

Buck, J. N. (1966). *The House-Tree-Person Technique, revised manual*. Los Angeles: Western Psychological Services.

Conners, C. K. & MHS Staff. (Eds.). (2000). *Conners' Continuous Performance Test II: Computer Program for Windows Technical Guide and Software Manual.* North Tonwanda, NY: Mutli-Health Systems.

Exner, J. E., Jr. (2001). *The Rorschach workbook for the comprehensive system* (5th ed.). Asheville, NC: Rorschach Workshops.

Exner, J. E., Jr., & Weiner, I. B. (1995). *The Rorschach: a comprehensive system. Vol.3: Assessment of children and adolescents* (2nd ed.). New York: Wiley.

Finn, S. E. (2007). *In our client's shoes: Theory and techniques of Therapeutic Assessment.* Mahwah, NJ: Lawrence Erlbaum Associates.

Finn, S. E. (2008). Personal communication, September 9.

Finn, S. E. (2003). Therapuetic Assessment of a man with "ADD." *Journal of Personality Assessment, 80*(2), 115–129.

Finn, S. E., & Kamphuis, J. H. (2006). Therapeutic Assessment with the MMPI-2. In J. N. Butcher (Ed.), *MMPI-2: A practicioners guide* (pp. 165–191). Washington, DC: APA Books.

Finn, S. E., & Tonsager, M. E. (1992). The therapeutic effects of providing MMPI-2 test feedback to college students awaiting psychotherapy. *Psychological Assessment, 4*, 278–287.

Finn, S. E., & Tonsager, M. E. (1997). Information-gathering and therapeutic models of assessment: complementary paradigms. *Psychological Assessment, 9*, 374–385.

Fischer, C. T. (1985/1994). *Individualizing psychological assessment.* Mahwah, NJ: Lawrence Erlbaum Associates.

Gacono, C. B., & Meloy, J. R. (1994). *The Rorschach assessment of aggressive and psychopathic personalities.* Hillsdale, NJ: Lawrence Erlbaum Associates, Inc.

Handler, L. (2006). The use of therapeutic assessment with children and adolescents. In S. R. Smith & L. Handler (Eds.), *Clinical assessment of children and adolescents: A practitioner's guide* (pp. 53–72). Mahwah, NJ: Lawrence Earlbaum Associates, Inc.

Hamilton, A., Fowler, J., Hersh, B., Austin, C., Finn, S. Tharinger, D., et al. (2009). Why won't my parents help me?: Therapeutic Assessment of a child and her family. *Journal of Personality Assessment, 91*(2), 108–120.

Harris, D. B. (1963). *Children's drawings as measures of intellectual maturity.* New York: Harcourt, Brace & World, Inc.

Kovacs, M., & Beck, A. T. (1977). An empirical-clinical approach toward a definition of childhood depression. In J. G. Schulterbrandt & A. Raskin (Eds.), *Depression in childhood: Diagnosis, treatment, and conceptual models* (pp. 1–25). New York: Raven Press.

McIntosh, P. (1990). White Privilege: Unpacking the invisible knapsack. *Independent School, 49*(2), 31–36.

Murray, H. A. (1943). *Thematic apperception test manual.* Cambridge, MA: Harvard University Press.

Newman, M. L., & Greenway, P. (1997). Therapeutic effects of providing MMPI-2 test feedback to clients at a university counseling service: A collaborative approach. *Psychological Assessment, 9*, 122–131.

Ogden, D. P. (1975). *Psychodiagnostics in personality assessment* (2nd ed.). Los Angeles: Western Psychological Services.

Oster, G. D. & Crone, P. G. (2004). *Using drawings in assessment and therapy: A guide for mental health professionals* (2nd ed.). New York: Routledge.

Peters, E. J. (2008). Am I going crazy, doc?: A self psychology approach to Therapeutic Assessment. *Journal of Personality Assessment, 90*(5), 421–434.

Purves, C. (1997, March). Therapeutic assessment in juvenile hall: Can it be done? In S. E. Finn (Chair), *Collaborative assessment of children and families.* Symposium conducted at the annual meeting of the Society for Personality Assessment, San Diego, CA.

Purves, C. (2002). Collaborative assessment with involuntary populations: Foster children and their mothers. *The Humanistic Psychologist, 30*, 164–174.

Reynolds, C. R., & Richmond, B. O. (1979). What I think and feel: A revised measure of children's manifest anxiety. *Journal of Abnormal Child Psychology, 6,* 271–280.

Ridley, C. (1995). *Overcoming unintentional racism in counseling and therapy: A practitioner's guide to intentional intervention.* Thousand Oaks, CA: Sage Publications.

Roberts, G. E. (1994). *Interpretive handbook for the Roberts Apperception Test for Children.* Los Angeles: Western Psychological Services.

Smith, J. D., & Handler, L. (2009). Why do I get in so much trouble?: A family therapeutic case study. *Journal of Personality Assessment, 91*(3), 197–210.

Tharinger, D. J., Finn, S. E., Gentry, L., Hamilton, A., Fowler, J., Matson, M., et al. (2009). Therapeutic Assessment with children: A pilot study of treatment acceptability and outcome. *Journal of Personality Assessment, 91*(3), 238–244.

Tharinger, D. J., Finn, S. E., Austin C. A., Gentry, L. B., Bailey, K. E., Parton, V. T., et al. (2008). Family sessions as part of child psychological assessment: Goals, techniques, clinical utility, and therapeutic value. *Journal of Personality Assessment, 90,* 547–558.

Tharinger, D. J., Finn, S. E., Hersh, B., Wilkinson, A., Christopher, G. and Tran, A. (2008). Assessment feedback with parents and pre-adolescent children: A collaborative approach. *Professional Psychology: Research and Practice, 39,* 600–609.

Tharinger, D. J., Finn, S. E., Wilkinson, A. D., & Schaber, P. M. (2007). Therapeutic Assessment with a child as a family intervention: A clinical and research case study. *Psychology in the Schools, 44,* 293–309.

Verinis, J. S., Lichtenberg, E. F., & Henrich, L. (1974). The Draw-A-Person-in-the-Rain technique: It's relationship to diagnostic category and other personality indicators. *Journal of Clinical Psychology, 30,* 407–414.

Wildman, S. M., & Davis, A. D. (2002). Making systems of privilege visible. In P. S. Rothenberg (Eds.), *White privilege: Essential readings on the other side of racism* (2nd ed.) (pp. 95–101). New York, NY: Worth Publishers.

Woodcock, R. W., McGrew, K. S., & Mather, N. (2001). *The Woodcock-Johnson III**. Itasca, IL: Riverside.

14 Getting to the Heart of the Matter

Elisa Gomez and Brooke Guerrero

The following is an account of two assessors reflecting on an assessment where one assessor tested the child, and the second clinician worked with the mother. It is presented as a dialogue, as both the process and the determination about the problem and the solution come out of a back-and-forth among the assessors and the parent and the child.

Elisa

Clients come to us for assessment with questions. They ask us things like:

- What is Malik's diagnosis?
- Why can't Daija sit still?
- Why does Joseph get so angry?
- Why is Brianna failing all her classes?

In addition to these stated referral questions, we have discovered that there are often unstated questions that have to do with our clients' deepest fears, worries, or perceptions of themselves or their families. These unstated questions are often unrecognized—at times even unknowable—and we tend to think of them as the thing that can't be stated or spoken about. Thus, there are the "presented" referral questions, and what we think of as the "real" referral questions.

In a traditional assessment, we may only have access to the presented referral questions, and the real referral questions may remain hidden from view. One advantage of using a therapeutic collaborative model is that these real referral questions can be assessed for, detected, and addressed more readily. The collaborative model allows us to use countertransference reactions and collaboration with caregivers and therapists to create a therapeutic thinking space. The opportunity to view the assessment and watch the data unfold ignites curiosity in caregivers, and the experience of feeling held by assessors as they do this allows both parties to recognize, access, and speak about the thing that was previously too sensitive to acknowledge.

To illustrate the use of collaborative assessment techniques in getting to the real referral questions, we will present the case of James, a 10-year-old Caucasian boy who was referred to our clinic by both his adoptive mother and his therapist. The presented referral questions included: Does James have ADHD? Is there something wrong with his brain? Does he need medication? Why doesn't he show empathy or remorse? Is James going to develop more antisocial traits and become dangerous? What type of therapy does he need?

Armed with these referral questions in mind, I set out to begin the assessment process by observing James at his school. Normally when I walk into a classroom to observe an assessment client, it is obvious within a few minutes which child is the one I'm supposed to be observing. With James, I expected to be able to pick him out of the crowd of students based on his mother's reports to me of his aggression, hyperactivity, and defiance. She described him as the kid who gets easily upset and dysregulated, and who acts out by tantruming and running out of the classroom. But when I showed up, I was stumped as to who James was. In a small classroom of well-behaved children, he did not stand out at all. Keeping in mind that his behavior that day might have been an anomaly, I nevertheless began to wonder whether this was my first clue that there was more to the story than was being talked about.

My next clue that there was more to the story came when talking with James's therapist, Diane. Diane, who had been seeing James in individual therapy for the past two years, reported that he was one of her most confusing clients. She had a hard time reconciling his mom's reports of his troubling behaviors at home and school with the sweet boy she saw in her office each week. She often wondered about whether he really needed therapy, and worried that she was not being an effective therapist. Finally, Diane reported that a colleague of hers who had been seeing James's brother in individual therapy for about the same length of time was planning on terminating the therapy after having the same questions about the necessity and usefulness of the treatment. Although Diane and her colleague had both tried on different occasions to engage James's parents in collateral sessions and family therapy sessions to try to better understand the discrepancies in James's presentation, these interventions often fell flat and left Diane confused about how to proceed with treatment.

The final and perhaps most powerful clue came when talking at length with James's adoptive mother. As she told me the story of James's life and how she came to adopt him, it became clear that there were layers of family history, complex and difficult relationships, and deeply embedded fears that were being constellated in James and his presenting problems. She told me that James spent the first four years of his life with his substance-abusing biological parents, witnessing severe domestic violence between them, and experiencing profound neglect as a result of their substance abuse. She told me that James was physically abused by his mother during this time, and that during his toddler years he was somehow responsible for taking care of his younger siblings. She also told me that James's biological father was her own brother, that she had been essentially responsible for raising him from a young age, and that she was worried that James would turn out to be just like his dad: a substance-abusing, violent, and angry young man with mental health needs that were never properly addressed. It was at this point that my hunch that there was more to the story became a solid hypothesis, and I pulled Dr. Guerrero on board to transition to using the therapeutic collaborative assessment model with this family.

Brooke

At WestCoast Children's Clinic, we typically set up our collaborative assessments in the following way: in one room, an assessor administers the tests with the child, while in another room, the co-assessor works with the caregivers while watching a live feed of the test administration. We decided that I would work with Pamela, James's adoptive mother, and Dr. Gomez would conduct the test administration. Once in the room with Pamela, I quickly discovered how challenging the work would be. She had a deeply held belief, which we conceptualize as her "story," that was rooted in pathology. This story began with James's father, who Pamela viewed as very ill. Pamela had spent her life trying to help her brother and ultimately felt like she failed to save him because she had lost him to drugs and alcohol and he had ended up in and out of jail most of his life. It became apparent that James had inherited this story, as Pamela viewed him as ill and in need of rescuing. Dr. Gomez and I met in between sessions and discussed the story as it was being revealed to me while viewing the administration. We became concerned that simply answering the referral questions about whether or not James had ADHD, a problem with his brain, or was going to become a sociopath would not even begin to shift this entrenched family narrative. It seemed like the real question was: *Is James going to be like his father?* We worried that providing her with simple yes or no answers to her stated referral questions would leave her feeling unsatisfied and would gloss over the depth of her fear, leaving the real question untouched. It felt akin to putting a Band-Aid on a gaping wound.

Before pursuing this direction in the assessment, Dr. Gomez and I weighed the pros and cons of addressing such intense material with her. Based on our interactions and observations of Pamela, we felt that she could handle this more intensive intervention and perhaps was even asking for it. Pamela was naturally insight-oriented and analytical, was not a stranger to the therapeutic process, and had enough ego-strength and social resources to tolerate the pressure that would come from addressing the family story. With this in mind, I set about listening for the real referral questions, trying to pinpoint Pamela's deepest concerns and looking for points of entry in shifting her narrative. Two other questions that became apparent to me related to Pamela's own insecurities. It seemed she wanted to know, *Am I a good enough mother to James?* and wondered, *Does James love me?* It seemed that she was in need of reassurance that James was not another hopeless case like her brother and that she was not doomed to repeat what she perceived as parental failure on her part.

In looking for points of entry, I encountered many challenges, the biggest being that Pamela routinely rejected my attempts to communicate empathy about how difficult it could be to parent a child like James, who often pushed her away and could be emotionally distant. I did observe, however, that when I floated an idea or curiosity by Pamela, she would initially reject, ignore, or interrupt me but then later come back to the idea and express it as her own. Once I observed the pattern, experiencing the repeated rejection by Pamela became easier. I understood her need and defenses around protecting herself and needing time to process and integrate these new ideas into her existing narrative.

Dr. Gomez and I discussed this pattern of rejection and came to the conclusion that there might be two issues at hand. One was that Pamela exhibited her own dismissive attachment tendencies, as she needed to be self-reliant and expressions of empathy left her feeling vulnerable. The other issue was that Pamela felt insecure in her parenting abilities, but had difficulty acknowledging or expressing this, as she viewed it as a weakness. This made the work tricky because empathy and putting ourselves in our client's shoes is typically the most effective way at shifting a family's story; it was like having our biggest tool as therapeutic assessors stripped from us.

Elisa

In consulting with Dr. Guerrero, we realized that there was a parallel process going on, with these same issues popping up in the assessment room with James. Although James was, by our standards at WestCoast, a remarkably compliant and "easy" child to test, he was also incredibly difficult to connect with on an emotional level. Simple and typically engaging questions like "What's your favorite video game?" fell flat with James. He responded with "I don't know" to most questions, and seemed to have no interest in having a conversation with me. It is important to note that he was not being resistant; it seemed instead that his relational capacity was collapsed. One shining example of this was during our second testing session, when all of James's nonverbal cues pointed to him being exhausted: he yawned constantly, his eyelids were heavy, and he was disengaged. I suggested that we take a break, and joked that maybe we should both take a nap. In an attempt to join with him, I stretched my arms out wide, yawned dramatically, and put my head down on the table, pretending to nap and hoping that he would follow suit. After a few awkward seconds, I realized that James was still sitting in his chair, not napping, not smiling at my antics, not reacting *at all*. It was at moments like these that I was acutely aware of the cameras in the room, recording my every move and documenting for all to see just how ineffective I was at connecting with this little boy. It seemed that while Dr. Guerrero was busy being rejected by Pamela, I was experiencing the same thing with James.

Dr. Guerrero and I began to think about how to use my experience in the room as a point of entry. I felt like I had a very vivid experience of what it might feel like to parent James. The real referral questions ("Does James love me?" and "Am I a good enough mother?") made even more sense. It was clear that these worries were based in Pamela's reality of parenting James, and that they only heightened her preexisting insecurities around relationships and parenting. We realized that I could speak to my own experience of feeling rejected and incompetent in order to empathize with Pamela in a way that she might be able to hear. It doesn't get more "in her shoes" than that.

We decided to meet with Pamela to talk about what we termed "miscuing" on James's part. We wanted to operationalize the relational process in which James pulled for mirroring from others, only to reject, ignore, or not notice the response he got. We also wanted to plant the seed for what would be our likely recommendation for family therapy, and prepare her for the upcoming family intervention session. In sharing with Pamela the nap example that I spoke about earlier, I was able to speak directly to my overall experience of James in the room. I also realized that I had to walk a very fine line between maintaining my professional credibility and exposing my own vulnerabilities and feelings of incompetency. I presented my experience and enlisted her as a collaborator, helping me to understand if this was something that happened routinely or whether it was unique to the testing situation. I shared that I felt rejected and confused when James miscued me, and that I wondered whether he liked me, whether I was being a good enough assessor, or whether I was doing something wrong. One look at Pamela's face and we knew right away that this was the key to addressing the real referral questions. In validating *my* experience, Pamela received her own validation and talked openly for the first time about how emotionally difficult it was to parent James, how she wondered whether she was the right mother for him, and how insecure she felt about his feelings toward her.

And, almost as if on cue, James's test data in the next session spoke to some of these fears that Pamela had, and provided her with a reassurance that we as assessors would never have been able to give so poignantly. James's responses on the Early Memory Procedure (Bruhn, 1992) communicated his perceptions of how he came to be adopted by Pamela. His first early memory described the event that led to his removal from his biological mother, involving a violent fight he witnessed between his mother and another adult. While this first early memory helped Pamela to empathize with James and how horrific some of his early experiences were, it was the second memory that really shed light on James's internal, unspoken experience of being taken in by Pamela. James told in great detail his story of anxiously waiting to see what was going to happen to him after being taken from his biological mom, and clearly communicated his relief when Pamela arrived to pick him up from social services. Pamela was left speechless, with tears in her eyes, as she watched and listened to James tell this story so vividly. Hearing James talk about this experience seemed to provide Pamela with some of the reassurance that she had been looking for, alleviating some of her fears about how James felt about her role in his life.

And then we noticed that something else was happening too. It was almost as if, in the telling of this story, James had communicated to Pamela: "You *are* my mom. I *do* love you." This seemed to allow Pamela to connect with the maternal parts of herself, creating greater empathy for James's experiences and allowing her to become curious about whether there were emotional factors causing some of his behaviors. With our help, she began to wonder why James was able to sit still for some of the testing procedures (such as the WISC-IV) (Wechsler, 2003), but not for others (such as the Rorschach, when he was literally trying to do backflips out of his chair). We reviewed relevant findings from the test data, which included a Lambda of 20 and an X-% of 0.38 on the Rorschach (primarily occurring on responses with human content), and a CPT (Conners, 2000) profile that better matched a nonclinical than a clinical profile. Together, we came to the conclusion that anxiety related to his past experiences of trauma, and not ADHD, was the root cause of most of his distractibility and hyperactivity.

Brooke

As we moved toward completion of the assessment process, Pamela began to tell us stories about things that had happened in between sessions that reflected her increasing maternal connection to James, and communicated to us that a shift was taking place in the family story. We explained to Pamela that in therapeutic collaborative assessments, we often incorporate a family session to test out some of our hypotheses about what might be going on with a child. What we didn't say was that we also often use family intervention sessions to highlight the problem, to begin to shift the family's story in an experiential way, or to use it as a prelude to family therapy. In our case we were using the family intervention in all of these ways. We wanted to emphasize the shift that was already taking place in the family story, and to demystify the experience of family therapy, as Dr. Gomez and I had realized that this would be one of the primary recommendations to come out of the assessment. During the family session, we delivered interventions that created opportunities for mutually satisfying experiences, as well as some corrective experiences around the miscuing that happened within the family.

Our observations from the family intervention session provided us with a natural segue to an initial feedback session with Pamela. Without explicitly stating what we had conceptualized as the real referral questions, we provided her with our observations and feedback related to James's attachment, Pamela's strengths as a mother, and the incredible growth that James has demonstrated since being in her care. This was essentially a strengths-based intervention that provided her with reassurance that yes, he loves you, yes, you're a good enough mother, and no, he does not seem to be on the same trajectory as his father. Because we had been planting these seeds throughout the entire assessment, Pamela was able to engage in this discussion session and discuss her previous concerns at length, eliciting even more reassurance from us. By the time we met again to answer her stated referral questions, she seemed to already have the answers to her questions and seemed to have what she needed from the assessment.

Without having addressed the real referral questions, we might have sent Pamela off with easy answers to her questions but no real satisfaction or sense of being understood and seen. While the concrete test data provided us with answers to her stated referral questions, the collaborative model allowed us to listen for and address the real referral questions. It allowed us to make use of the less tangible data, which came in the form of countertransference reactions, parallel processes, styles of relating, and observations. And perhaps most importantly, it allowed us to put ourselves in her shoes, recognize her fears around not being a good enough mother, and provide her with hope for James's future. We recognize that there was a very good reason why these real referral questions were hidden from view; as assessors we need to be aware of the intensity that surrounds these questions and acutely aware of our responsibility to be respectful, cautious, and thoughtful about if, when, and how we address them over the course of an assessment.

References

Bruhn, A. R. (1992). The Early Memories Procedure: A projective test of autobiographical memory, parts 1 & 2. *Journal of Personality Assessment*, 58(1), 1–15 and 58(2), 326–346.

Conners, C. K. & MHS Staff. (Eds.). (2000). *Conners' Continuous Performance Test II: Computer program for Windows technical guide and software manual*. North Tonawanda, NY: Multi-Health Systems.

Wechsler, D. (2003). *Wechsler Intelligence Scale for Children*: 4th Edition (WISC-IV*). San Antonio, TX: Harcourt Assessment.

15 The Topsy-Turvy Tearmeter

Clinical Crisis and Assessment Intervention

Tricia Fong and Erin Rosenblatt

Maternal mental illness poses several challenges for children, particularly if combined with psychosocial stressors such as poverty, marital stress or family conflict, and single parenthood (Goodman et al., 2011; Oyserman, Mowbray, Meares, & Firminger, 2000). While children whose mothers struggle with mental illness may be more likely to struggle with emotional difficulties, research also suggests that these challenges may be tempered by protective factors that contribute to their resilience (Cummings & Davies, 1999; Mowbray, Bybee, Oyserman, Allen-Meares, MacFarlane, & Hart-Johnson, 2004). These protective factors include resources and social supports, as well as the quality of the mother–child interaction. Mowbray and colleagues (1995) further suggest that parenting may have a motivating effect for mothers with mental illness to remain in treatment, as the role of motherhood itself may serve as primary outlet for care and concern, and affirm a valued and normative social role.

This chapter will discuss how extreme turmoil, spurred by a parental mental health crisis did not prevent the family's participation or make the interventions of Therapeutic Collaborative Assessment less useful, but unexpectedly opened up the case in a way that provided a holding space for the family's pain, a voice for the child's distress and fears, and a concerted effort towards family change. We also discuss the ways that we adapted the assessment course in order to respond to the family's motivation while ensuring their participation given the reality of their circumstances and the unpredictability inherent in a mental health crisis. In this case, the assessment intervention was upheld, but adapted by incorporating the family's support system, or its village, and relying on its members during critical moments of the assessment process.

The Assessment Referral

Sara was a 9-year-old female who was referred for a psychological evaluation by her individual therapist from a local community mental health organization. This therapist, an astute and insightful clinician, was curious about Sara's mood symptoms and lack of peer relationships. Her attunement and compassion moved her from collegial referrant to collaborative partner whose steady presence would be relied upon as the assessment process unfolded (Table 15.1).

At the time of the referral, Sara struggled with sadness, irritability, and problems with her elementary school classmates. Moreover, she struggled with misappropriated and perseverative self-blame brought about by memories of a traumatic event that had occurred within her already difficult life. At age 6 her father, while intoxicated, beat

Table 15.1 Therapist's Assessment Questions

1. How have the effects of trauma impacted Sara's overall functioning and academic performance?
2, How can we help her heal from internalizing responsibility and self-blame?
3, How can we help her feel safe in the classroom?
4, How can we help Sara build positive relationships with her friends and her classmates?
5, How can we support Sara's mother in helping Sara feel accepted?

her as a consequence for a minor infraction that had occurred in school. This event had become sentinel in her young life, and the lens through which all other events and interchanges were filtered. While a dispositionally sensitive child, Sara's depressive symptoms culminated in an incident where she threatened to kill herself with a knife in the presence of her younger brother. Although a bright student, Sara also had frequent emotional outbursts in her classroom. According to her teacher, Sara would "fall out" in response to innocuous events, and would hide under her desk or sob uncontrollably. As a result, Sara was often excused from the classroom and had difficulty making friends. She often sought refuge in the vice principal's office on an almost daily basis. Both the teacher and Sara's mother, Annie, were concerned about the amount of academic instruction she had missed.

Sara's Family History

As is often the case in our work, Sara's family and psychosocial history was multi-layered. At the start of the assessment, we had a brief sketch of the family history marked with some markers of the more profound moments in their family story. Sara was born to the care of her biological parents in an inner-city neighborhood. Sara's father struggled with alcohol and substance abuse throughout his life, and vacillated between periods of intense use, brief sobriety, and relapse. Sara's mother met and married Sara's father during her teenage years. Their relationship was marked by chronic and severe domestic violence that spanned the length of their 10-year union. Explosive incidents were witnessed by Sara and her younger brother, and often resulted in injury to Annie or temporary periods during which Annie and the children would leave their home and take refuge with either her sister or a member of their spiritual community.

When Sara was 6 years old, she endured a severe beating by her father for fiddling with her belt. When Annie arrived home that afternoon and while her father was asleep, Sara showed her the severe bruises on her bottom and legs. Annie gathered Sara and her brother and sought help, first from a member of her community and later from the local police department. Annie filed a criminal restraining order that was granted for a period of three years, and her father's whereabouts were unknown at the time of the assessment.

During these initial parent meetings, Annie carefully selected the fragments of her life that she would consciously and intentionally entrust to us. The complexity of the family history evidenced as the assessment unfolded, not through narrative or self-report, but through the opportunity to witness the emotional enormity of the family's lived experiences and the unspoken impact of mental health issues and substance

Table 15.2 Mother's Assessment Questions

1. Why does Sara feel so unloved and rejected when she emotionally breaks down?
2. How can I, or the people in Sara's life, help her make peer-level friendships?
3. How can I support Sara in being herself and feeling comfortable with who she is?
4. How can I provide a means of comfort when Sara has issues at home or at school?

use. During the initial parent meeting, Annie calibrated her risk to be fully known or seen. She was kind and amiable, and her genuine desire to help her child was palpable. Consistent with the therapeutic collaborative assessment model, Annie's questions about Sara were gathered and identified (Table 15.2). Given Annie's avid interest to better understand Sara's struggles, the model in which the parent viewed the assessment live was determined to be an appropriate intervention. Dr. Fong met with Sara to begin the psychological testing. Dr. Rosenblatt came onto the case as the co-assessor to support Annie by exploring possible responses to her questions while she observed Sara's testing sessions through a live video feed that connected the clinic's assessment and consultation rooms.

Getting to Know Sara

As part of the assessment process, Dr. Fong observed Sara in the school setting prior to the first meeting. Sara attended a local public school in her inner-city neighborhood. On that day, Sara had a substitute teacher who complained to the assessor that she had had a "crying fit" after being teased by other students earlier that morning. During the observation, Sara appeared withdrawn and distracted, often staring off into the distance. While she was redirected, she seemed agitated by the presence and direction of the substitute teacher. Uncertain of and anxious about her teacher's authority, Sara frequently raised her hand to ask simple questions. Her repeated, unsophisticated, and simplistic requests exasperated the teacher, and this response appeared to increase Sara's anxiety. During the class transition, Sara became frustrated and agitated when she encountered difficulty zipping up her jacket. "I need someone to help me!" she demanded several times to the dismay and eventual rejection of her classmates.

During the first testing sessions, Dr. Fong struggled to build rapport with Sara. Sara vacillated between seeming inattentive and distracted, and lethargic and disengaged. She presented with a restricted range of emotions, and often spoke immediately and without pause. The assessor quickly exhausted efforts at empathy, positive regard, and talk of learning about herself through the testing. Sara's stoicism forced the almost immediate emergence of the assessor's play supplies. However, Sara would neither be wooed by board games or puppets nor enticed by stickers or prizes. She remained avoidant and evasive. When asked directly about her emotions, she became anxious, sat at the edge of the chair, and spoke tangentially and excessively in a stilted and pseudo-mature manner. Occasionally, Sara became teary-eyed. However, when the assessor noticed, Sara quickly stated, "Oh, there's dust in my eyes, dust in my eyes." Sara's lone question for the assessment was, "Why do I keep thinking about my friend who moved away?"

The Crisis

After the first testing session, Annie and Sara did not show up for their scheduled appointment. After multiple unreturned messages, Annie reported, through voicemail, that she had been hospitalized but said nothing further. The ambiguity of the call and the weight of its emotional tenor gave rise to concerns about the family's safety. The clinicians had fantasies of Annie and Sara being in danger or being somehow prevented from participating. Annie confirmed her appointment for the following week. While the therapeutic collaborative assessment model encourages parent observation of each testing session, it also allows for flexibility and values the collateral support of the parent. Given the mystery of their missed appointment the previous week, we decided to turn the camera off. Dr. Rosenblatt would check in with Annie as to allow her the privacy to talk about what happened while Dr. Fong would continue to facilitate the assessment with Sara. During the collateral meeting, Annie revealed that she had been hospitalized for a manic episode and suicidal gestures. She disclosed that she had heard harmful voices as she walked around campus with a knife and a bottle of alcohol in her backpack.

During this meeting, Annie revealed more of what was truly happening in her life during the last several months. Annie described a long history of minimizing and fighting her symptoms in the hope of keeping her family together. She explained that she sometimes drank alcohol to quiet the voices that had become increasingly louder over the years. She described the central role of her sister, Mary, who would step in for her when she was not able to care for her children.

After this session, the assessors began to wonder if this family was a good candidate for a therapeutic collaborative assessment. In other mental health settings, the impulse or the directive would be to stop the assessment and assume that the crisis itself signaled a lack of readiness or ability. The assessors relied on consultation with their "village," their supervisors, and colleagues, to better understand the factors that would determine whether they should move forward. Could this mother participate and benefit from this type of assessment? Would it be too intense for her to handle given the crisis that they were in?

Given Annie's investment and motivation, the assessors spoke directly with her about our concerns and offered modifications if necessary. Annie appeared thoughtful and engaged during this meeting and intent on understanding the struggle of her daughter. As Annie described the circumstances that lead to her hospitalization, she recalled intense worry about the safety and well-being of her children. In the haze of her mental state, she described mobilizing herself to ensure that her children were cared for. Annie had retained, to the best of her ability, her parenting agency and her sense of self as a mother appeared to ground her. In the aftermath of her hospitalization, she remained committed to continue to the best of her ability. Annie's ability to hold her children in the forefront of her mind despite her own instability was remarkable and became a driving force with which to continue.

Bringing in the Village

As clinicians in an assessment role, the assessors needed to ensure that Annie had support, and we actively outreached to the other treatment providers who were working with the family. In doing so, we learned that Annie had a mental health team with whom she met occasionally. Sara's therapist had not been informed of the family's crisis. While the assessors felt strongly that she needed to be made aware, they faced the dilemma of respecting Annie's confidentiality. Dr. Rosenblatt gently encouraged Annie to share with Sara's therapist her mental health struggles. Annie was hesitant in her immediate response to our request, but she reached out to the therapist in an urgent and intimate way shortly after our meeting. Annie encountered another mental health crisis and contacted Sara's therapist who initiated another hospitalization. Following this incident, Sara's therapist became an intricate part of the team and was pivotal in carrying forward the feedback into her long-term work with the family.

Despite her earnest desire to continue with Sara's assessment, the next few sessions with Annie were unpredictable because of her instability. Annie's appearance had drastically changed, she giggled, and she acknowledged feeling slightly manic. However, she continued to participate to the best of her ability, making it clear that she was making every effort to help her daughter. During these weeks the assessors quickly and carefully identified ways to modify the collaborative assessment process according to what was most needed in the moment. When feasible, Annie viewed portions of Sara's testing sessions from the consultation room with the support of Dr. Rosenblatt. Other times, the cameras remained off and Dr. Rosenblatt supported Annie for the entirety of the meeting while Dr. Fong worked with Sara.

Another day, Sara was transported to the clinic by her Aunt Mary, Annie's older sister. The extent, involvement, and investment of her extended family became woven into the fabric of the assessment as the necessity of their support heightened in response to the multiple crises that we continued to encounter. While Annie had spoken about her sister, the team did not anticipate that they would meet her. However, Mary held a pivotal role in this family system. She served as the primary caregiver for Annie's children when she was hospitalized, an event that would occur a total of four times for varying periods of time during the course of the assessment. Although the assessors had Annie's permission to speak to Mary, they hadn't explicitly discussed her participation in the therapeutic collaborative assessment. Doing so would pose several dilemmas, including replacing Annie's parenting role with that of a kin caregiver. The team had witnessed Annie's life story through her verbal narrative and through the in vivo unfolding of her mental illness. While her health posed the immediate concern, they wanted to preserve her place as mother and honor the mindfulness about her children that she fought to retain despite her physical absence. The assessors decided to wait for Annie's explicit permission to allow Mary to observe the assessment. Dr. Fong would continue the assessment with Sara, and Dr. Rosenblatt would meet with Mary to gather her perspective on the family since she was so involved in caring for the children.

The collateral meetings with Mary were overwhelming. It became clear that Mary saw herself as the most functional adult, the family caretaker, and the sturdy survivor. She unlocked additional secrets about the family history, including multiple abuses that she and Annie had endured from their mother who had also suffered from substance abuse and serious mental health issues. While describing these moments of horror, Mary also narrated the legacy of the village. She described moments when they, as children, would escape from the home and seek safety at a neighbor's home.

Psychological Assessment as Family Intervention

While Mary did not view the assessment, welcoming and acknowledging her important role in the family allowed her to be an active participant in the intervention. Mary was direct in voicing her concerns and beliefs that Annie was heading down the same road as their mother's ill-fated journey. Furthermore, she believed that Sara was beginning to show signs of serious mental illness, and interpreted Sara's "odd" behaviors as premorbid signs of psychosis. Although these sessions were difficult to tolerate, it became clear that the family's story about young Sara was that she was "sick" and on the trajectory of longstanding mental illness. It was a legacy that was passed down from grandmother to mother, and mother to daughter. Although Mary was rigid in her belief that this was happening, she also looked for ways to lessen the impact. Mary utilized these collateral sessions to entertain the possibility of an alternate narrative for her niece, and by extension, her family.

When Annie eventually returned to the assessment, the pieces began to fit together more easily. While Annie was interested in the questions that she had initially posed, the more pressing question was whether or not Sara suffered from Bipolar Disorder. Her question had become, "Is Sara going to end up like me?" When Annie viewed Sara over the live video feed, she saw both her daughter and herself as a young girl. Annie's own mental health impasse allowed for the family secrets to be revealed, and the assessment allowed for her to share her deeply rooted fears about her daughter. The therapeutic collaborative assessment became an unexpected opportunity for Annie to question the family legacy and provided an attempt to shift the narrative.

Assessment Data as a Therapeutic Porthole

As the family crisis unfolded around her, Sara sought emotional safety within the confines of the assessment space. The tenants of the Therapeutic Assessment model allowed her to better tolerate a verbal dialogue of her family traumas and the difficult and complex emotions associated with them. In some way, her standing assessment appointment was an unexpected touchstone. In the midst of her family's crisis, Sara seemed intent on telling her story. At times, she intensely focused on the camera so as to garner the attention of the family member on the other side. Sara utilized projective measures to communicate her distress about her experiences of family violence, her mother's illness, and the fleeting physical and emotional presence of her parents. During a projective drawing task (Buck, 1960), Sara drew a bird's nest and stated,

> The baby birds will hatch soon. The babies are gonna hatch any time. The mommy and daddy make it too late ... all of them hatched ... Except I hatched but I fell to the ground and died cause I wanted to look for my mommy and daddy.

In response to a projective storytelling card that typically addresses parental affection, Sara's response contained themes of uncertainty about the capability of caregiving figures. She stated, "One day, the father walked home with his new girlfriend. The daughter said, 'Where have you been? The babysitter didn't feed me. Who is that? Is that my real mommy?'"

During subsequent sessions, Sara spoke of her father's alcohol abuse and violence. She whispered her memories to her mother through the camera in a way that demanded her mother's attention while simultaneously asking her mother's permission to give voice to the family's longstanding secrets. She stated in a hushed voice, "I want to tell about the alcoholism and about when he hit me." She later stared directly at the camera and whispered, "Whenever they had an argument, I would peek into the hallway and I would come out crying cause I wanted them to stop. I would cover my ears because daddy was a drinker." Sara remained unaware that her mother was struggling to maintain a calm and coherent state on the other side of the camera. However, the therapeutic collaborative assessment model allowed the camera to hold the concept of dialogue, the possibility of being heard, and provided the containment and safety for her to do so.

As her family environment became increasingly unstable and unpredictable, Sara became actively engaged in the therapeutic collaborative assessment process. She continued to utilize emotional measures and projective tasks to express her fears about the unfolding crisis that her family faced. Themes from her projective stories (McArthur & Roberts, 1982) centered on "getting sick" and worry about the availability, health, and permanency of parental figures. She began one projective story with "One day, the mother bird got really sick and then the mother bird died." In response to another projective card, she stated,

> One day there was four birdies. They had a secret recipe but only the mother knew it … One day the mother bird got really sick and then the mother bird died. So, the sister bird wasn't old enough to cook … So, she decided she could take lessons to know how many degrees to make the broth just right.

As the assessment moved forward, Sara became better able to directly discuss the complexity of her mother's illness, using the first person rather than projecting her fears onto animal stories. While constructing a picture of a person, Sara wondered aloud, "Why is my mom different one week and okay the next week?" Her drawing became a rendering of her mother, and she shared fears of her mother being hurt, forever gone, or otherwise unable to recover either because of her father's violence or because of Annie's own obstacles. Sara spontaneously recalled a memory of her mother getting into a car accident when she was five years old. She stated, "After I went to bed, I had a nightmare that my mommy would stay in the hospital forever." Consistent with her family's evolving narrative, Sara's data responses began to demonstrate her struggle to understand her identity in the context of the story that the family had created. Consistent with the family legacy, she expressed fears for her own well-being. However, she also explored the possibility that her mother's mental health was independent from her own. During the testing, Sara expressed fears of "catching" the family illness. When asked about her first early memory (Bruhn, 1992), she stated, "I remember when grandpa died. I visited the morning he died and he died a couple of hours later. I was too scared that his sickness would rub off on me and that I would die." As the testing meetings came to a close, Sara openly expressed her distress over the family legacy of debilitating and destructive illness.

The Feedback Meetings

Feedback in Therapeutic Collaborative Assessment requires that assessors present their results in everyday language (Tharinger et al., 2008). For children it also aims to instill a sense of self-worth and respect while facilitating trust in those central to the child's life. The task of the assessors and the family is to aid in the self-verification of the child while creating the opportunity for a new story. During the assessment, Sara had projected deep emotional conflict onto animal stories, whether elicited by storytelling cards or her own projective drawings. The assessors followed her lead using her narrative of a family of birds, but shifting their fatalistic outcome. "The Topsy-Turvey Tearmeter," Sara's story or fable created by the assessors, acknowledged the family legacy while tempering it with the family's strengths. It offered an alternative explanation for the complexity of Sara's feelings rather than confirming the family's worst fear of the inevitable outcome of severe mental illness. The assessors also wanted to honor the family secrets that came to light during the course of the assessment. Sara's fable alluded to the sentinel family events they shared, namely Annie's illness and Sara's experience of abuse. By weaving these events into the fable, the assessors offered an alternative explanation to the intensity of Sara's emotional experience, integrating the emotional impact of these adversities as contributing factors to her stress.

The assessors decided that given the family's level of stress, the focus would turn to facilitating a meaningful summary and discussion meeting. The assessors would utilize the feedback session as a bridge to begin family therapy. The central activity would be sharing the fable that the assessors had created for her. Sara was given the task of inviting whomever she wanted to this meeting. In doing so, she identified her village and requested the presence of her mother, Aunt Mary, brother, individual therapist, and two cousins at the feedback meeting. Sara chose to read the story herself, and her family listened attentively while she did so. Sara's newly assigned WestCoast family therapist also made an introduction.

Concluding Remarks

In his comprehensive work, Finn (2007) discusses the humanistic components and qualities of Therapeutic Assessment. These components include: enlisting clients as co-collaborators in setting goals or identifying questions for the assessment, using psychological tests as "empathy magnifiers" that allow assessors to walk alongside clients rather than independently discover some objective truth about their person, sharing authentic observations and interchanges with the client, and recognizing the clients' intrinsic healing potential. This chapter attempted to highlight and discuss these foundational components through a case of a young girl and her mother as they struggled through parental mental health crises in the midst of a therapeutic collaborative assessment. While neither linear nor explicitly intentional, the assessment became a place for the child, mother, and kin caregiver to explore the humanity of their experiences, both past and present. The therapeutic collaborative assessment was modified to accommodate the intensity of the mother's crisis and involved additional caregivers when she was unable to attend the meetings. Despite the tenacity of Annie's mental health struggles, the assessors aimed to uphold the strength of her parenting mind and the compassion she held for her child. In doing so, the assessment attempted to shift the longstanding family narrative of the child that had been intertwined in a legacy of mental illness. Through feedback and fables, an alternative explanation was co-created with the child and family, in which Sara's problems were understood as a consequence to her adverse and traumatic experiences rather than as signals of an inevitable mental disorder. While psychological assessment tools brought Sara's inner conflicts to the forefront as she moved from projective stories to conscious disclosure, the humanistic qualities offered by Therapeutic Assessment provide a sustainable frame for family intervention.

References

Bruhn, A. R. (1992). The Early Memories Procedure: A projective test of autobiographical memory, parts 1 & 2. *Journal of Personality Assessment, 58*(1), 1–15 and 58(2), 326–346.

Buck, J. N. (1960). *The House-Tree-Person Technique,* revised manual. Los Angeles: Western Psychological Services.

Cummings, E. & Davies, P. T. (1999). Depressed parents and family functioning: Interpersonal effects and children's functioning and development. In T. Joiner & C. James (Eds.), *The interactional nature of depression: Advances in interpersonal approaches* (pp. 299–327). Washington, DC: American Psychological Association.

Finn, S. E. (2007). *In our client's shoes: Theory and techniques of therapeutic assessment.* New York: Psychology Press.

Goodman, S. H., Rouse, M. H., Connell, A. M., Broth, M. R., Hall, C. M., & Heyward, D. (2011). Maternal depression and child psychopathology: A meta-analytic review. *Clinical Child and Family Psychology Review, 14,* 1–27. doi:10.1007/s10567-010-0080-1.

McArthur, D. S. & Roberts, G. E. (1982). *Roberts Apperception Test for children: Manual.* Los Angeles: Western Psychological Services.

Mowbray, C. T., Bybee, D., Oyserman, D., Allen-Meares, P., MacFarlane, P., & Hart-Johnson, T. (2004). Diversity of outcomes among adolescent children of mothers with mental illness. *Journal of Emotional and Behavioral Disorders, 12*(4), 206–221.

Mowbray, C T., Oyserman, D. & Ross, S. (1995). Parenting and the significance of children for women with serious mental illness. *Journal of Mental Health Administration, 22,* 189–200.

Oyserman, D., Mowbray, C. T., Allen Meares, P., & Firminger, K. B. (2000). Parenting among mothers with a serious mental illness. *American Journal of Orthopsychiatry, 70*(3), 296–315.

Tharinger, D. J., Finn, S. E., Hersh, B., Wilkinson, A., Christopher, G. B., & Tran, A. (2008). Assessment feedback with parents and preadolescent children: A collaborative approach. *Professional Psychology: Research and Practice, 39*(6), 600–609.

16 How Can I Stay Safe?

Assessment with a Sexually Exploited Minor

Brooke Guerrero

One of society's dirty secrets is slowly being unveiled. In recent years, the sexual exploitation of children has gained increased attention in the field of mental health, the legal system, and the media. This multi-billion dollar commercial industry that involves the sexual abuse of children and adolescents via the exchange of sexual favors for payment (e.g., money, material goods, drugs, food, shelter) or pornography is referred to as the Commercial Sexual Exploitation of Children (CSEC). The CSEC population has a unique and complicated set of needs, often misunderstood by society and law enforcement, as they are frequently seen as willing participants and arrested when found engaging in prostitution.

Girls can enter "the life" through a number of ways. Some are kidnapped and isolated, drugged, or beaten until they willingly engage, while others live on the streets and sell themselves as a means of survival. Others have family members who have been involved in exploitation and have either grown up around it or even encouraged by family to enter the life. Many are romanced into the life by charismatic "boyfriends" who alternate between loving and punishing, a cycle akin to intimate partner violence, where eventually a trauma bond is formed with the boyfriend/exploiter (Walker, 2013). A range of factors put youth at risk for sexual exploitation. Risk factors include age (vulnerability increases with younger age); history of emotional, physical, or sexual abuse; poor school achievement or learning disabilities; poor family functioning; and parental substance abuse (Twill, Green, & Traylor, 2010). CSEC youth often come from minority populations and have experienced poverty, with a disproportionate number of African American youth represented in the CSEC population in California (Walker, 2013). A major risk factor for CSEC youth is a history of involvement in the child welfare system. According to the Child Welfare's Council Report, studies estimate that anywhere between 50 to 80 percent of CSEC are or were formerly involved in the child welfare system (Walker, 2013). In a study conducted by our agency, WestCoast Children's Clinic, over 75 percent of the 113 CSEC youth had a history of child abuse or neglect prior to exploitation (WestCoast Children's Clinic, 2012). In a demographic study of sexually exploited foster care minors, Rorschach data of girls involved in prostitution revealed high Trauma Content Scores (Armstrong & Lowenstein, 1990). This population has a complicated set of treatment needs involving a significant trauma history coupled with the ongoing, sometimes daily, trauma involved with being trafficked and/or exploited.

While the Bay Area as a whole has a high density of sexually exploited minors, WestCoast Children's Clinic is located in Oakland, where a thriving underage sex market exists. In response to the need for comprehensive treatment, WestCoast Children's

Clinic developed the C-Change program, which serves girls ages 11 to 21 who are at-risk for, have a history of, or are currently being sexually exploited. The model of treatment involves a combination of trauma-informed care, case management, and a multi-systemic approach to engaging the many systems in which the girls live (e.g., child welfare, probation, school). In this model, sexual exploitation is not seen as the young girl's defining characteristic, but rather as a symptom of complex trauma and a multi-systemic failure to protect the youth.

This chapter will present the case of Diane, who found herself "in the life" of sexual exploitation the way many girls enter—through a "romeo pimp." In this cycle of exploitation, a girl finds herself wooed by a charismatic, often older, male who communicates his desire to be her boyfriend. The girl is showered with love, affection, gifts, and promises of security. Then the romance deteriorates, a financial "need" arises, and the boyfriend asks the young girl to do him a "favor" in order to provide for the union. Sometimes the girls are initially asked to engage in sex acts with the boyfriend's friends or acquaintances, which gives way to sex acts with anyone willing to pay. Soon, the youth is working for her boyfriend/exploiter and remains loyal and hopeful that one day the loving relationship will return (Walker, 2013).

The Case

Diane was 17 at the time of referral for psychological assessment. Diane was receiving individual therapy services from our clinic's C-Change program. She had been receiving services for two months prior to the assessment referral. While her therapist initiated the referral, Diane's parents had requested the evaluation due to their concerns about Diane's "out of control" behavior. They knew she routinely put herself in risky situations and, knowing she had a history of exploitation, they feared that she was once again "in the life." They noted that Diane frequently took public transportation to a neighboring city where her ex-boyfriend/former exploiter lived and noticed she frequently came home with money or new items such as boots or purses. When asked where she got the money or items, Diane would say her boyfriend bought them for her. Diane's parents expressed significant concern about Diane's future, as she would soon be 18 and was beginning to transition into adulthood. It was clear they loved and cared about her very much, but felt helpless in knowing what to do to help her. Their questions reflected both their insight about their daughter, as well as their concern, sense of urgency, and overwhelm.

1   Why does Diane keep seeking out older men?
2   How do we keep Diane safe as she transitions to adulthood?
3   Why is she so easily taken advantage of and why is she so trusting?
4   Why is she drawn to negative and unsafe situations?
5   Why is everything so intense with Diane?

In addition to Diane's risk and involvement in sexual exploitation, she also struggled to control her anger, could be oppositional, argumentative, aggressive, easily upset, and she had run away on several occasions. Diane and her father frequently engaged in heated arguments that, at times, escalated to physical altercations. She had difficult peer relationships and did not have any friends. Diane's parents did not report symptoms of depression, but both Diane and her therapist communicated Diane's ongoing struggles with depressive symptoms since age 14—decreased or increased appetite, feeling down, frequently upset, sad mood, irritability, feelings of overwhelm, difficulty sleeping, and some suicidal ideation.

Diane lived with her mother, father, and severely physically disabled younger brother (16) in a low-income housing project. Her parents had been married for over 30 years. Her parents were older, in their early 60s, both African American, and from the Deep South. The family maintained many of their cultural practices, beliefs, and Southern accents. Diane and her parents both reported that she generally had a happy childhood and they all experienced close and loving relationships. Diane was born prematurely and had to spend her first three months in the Neonatal Intensive Care Unit. By age 3, Diane had identified developmental delays in language, fine motor skills, and adaptive self-help skills. She was found to have severe receptive language impairment and a moderate to severe expressive language impairment. She received services to increase her skills in the areas of cognitive, expressive/receptive language, fine/gross motor, self-help, and social/emotional skills. While she made improvements in all areas, when Diane was in kindergarten, she was evaluated by her school and identified as having Mild Mental Retardation. She was transferred to a Special Day Class, where she remained throughout elementary school. She was also referred to the Regional Center and was still receiving case management services at the time of the assessment.

When Diane was 11, the family experienced a significant loss when her paternal uncle unexpectedly passed away. The next year, after spending her elementary years in a Special Day Class, Diane was mainstreamed in middle school. Around this time, Diane and her parents both reported a shift in Diane's mood and behavior. Her parents reported she began lying, stealing, and defying rules, and she became increasingly impulsive. In the years that followed, Diane demonstrated aggressive behaviors and became increasingly argumentative. Her peers had begun taking advantage of her early on and, at the age of 13, she became sexually involved with a man who was 25 years old. At age 14, Diane had a sexual relationship with a 30-year-old man. She had met both of these men online and had snuck out to meet them. Her parents pressed charges against each of them for statutory rape and both men spent time in jail as a result. When Diane was 14, she began dating a 16-year-old boy. This relationship lasted, on and off, for three years. She ran away several times during these years to be with this boyfriend. On at least one of these occasions, he sexually exploited Diane, convincing her to solicit for him on the streets. He also had sex with other women in front of Diane. She was on the streets with him for nearly five days before contacting her parents to help her escape the situation. Following these experiences of exploitation, Diane experienced feelings of sadness, anxiety, and fear, with flashbacks of the encounters. She reported feeling upset all of the time, feeling like she was never happy, was easily overwhelmed, angry, irritable, and on edge. She began fighting with others. By age 15, Diane also began abusing alcohol and pain medication, using daily to the point of blackout until entering an outpatient drug treatment program at age 17. At the time of assessment, Diane had been sober for six months. She had not been in any fights with peers, was on track at school, and was more stable than she had been in years.

Diane was a senior in high school on independent study, which she had been on since eighth grade. She had brief periods of school refusal between the ages of 15 to 16, but received average grades (As to Cs) when putting forth effort. She was on track to graduate.

The Assessment

Administration

The assessment administration took place at the office, while the collateral work with Diane's parents took place in their home. Diane was attractive, wore stylish outfits, and frequently wore a big smile on her face. She was pleasant, friendly, and very easy to engage with and build rapport. She spoke openly about her experiences and presented with higher intellectual functioning than her scores would later reflect. She expressed a real desire to make changes in her life and put her past behind her. She had started dating a new boyfriend just prior to beginning the assessment and reported that this was a healthy relationship; he was different than past boyfriends. She was giddy about this relationship and communicated that she felt like he had completely changed how she felt about herself. In spite of this, she did report ongoing struggles with feeling vulnerable and depressed, and she expressed a desire to better understand why she continually finds herself in unsafe situations. Her relationship with her father was her biggest source of struggle and pain. She explained that her father began gambling and drinking heavily when she was around 12, after her paternal uncle's death. While he never physically left the family, she felt like she had lost her father at that time. She was now resentful that he had been emotionally absent for so long and then, in the past year, recently reengaged in her life.

Due to Diane's slower processing speed, the assessment process was lengthy, taking five sessions to complete the administration. The full battery included the Differential Abilities Test, second edition (DAS-2; Elliot, 2007), Vineland–II (Sparrow, Balla, & Cicchetti, 1984), Beery VMI (Beery, Buktenica, & Beery, 2010), Millon Adolescent Clinical Inventory (MACI; Millon, 1993), Behavior Assessment System for Children, Second Edition (BASC-2) Parent Rating Scales (Reynolds & Kamphaus, 2004), Trauma Symptom Checklist for Children (TSCC; Briere, 2011), Rorschach (Exner, 1993), Roberts Apperception Test (McArthur & Roberts, 1982), Projective Drawings (Buck, 1977), Life Timeline (Perryman, Personal Communication, 1992), and the Rotter Sentence Completion (Rotter & Rafferty, 1950). It became quickly apparent that Diane had the tendency to minimize or deny negative affect and symptoms. While completing the MACI and TSCC self-report measures, she commented on how different her responses would have been a year ago when she was having a harder time.

During the course of the administration, Diane's father frequently called expressing his concern for his daughter, his overwhelm, and his feelings of helplessness as a parent. Diane's father was outraged about her exploitation and acting out behaviors. In response to his outrage and desire to protect her, he alternated between trying to control her and shaming her. It became clear that incorporating Diane's parents into the assessment was needed. A modified Therapeutic Collaborative Assessment was planned, which involved using test data to help them understand their daughter's functioning, with family support and interventions delivered along the way. Diane welcomed her parents' involvement, as she felt misunderstood and frustrated.

Findings

As previously stated, although Diane had been designated at a young age with an intellectual disability, she did not present with obvious lower intellectual functioning. Testing from the DAS-2 confirmed, however, that Diane's overall cognitive ability was in the 1st percentile, ranging from Low to Very Low (*General Conceptual Ability* = 63). Her overall adaptive functioning, as measured by the Vineland-II, was also in the 1st percentile and in the Low range of functioning (*Adaptive Behavior Composite standard score* = 63). While her Verbal Ability was in the Very Low range (56), she was rather emotionally astute and street savvy and therefore presented as more capable. Nevertheless, this was a young woman with significant cognitive impairments.

With regard to emotional testing, as expected from observations during the test administration, Diane's self-report measures returned nearly flat profiles for both the MACI and TSCC due to her underreporting and minimization of negative affect. During the TSCC, she verbally communicated her high-trauma symptoms as she went through the items, stating, "But they went away about a month ago when I got my new boyfriend and my whole life changed." She verbally communicated that after being sexually exploited she experienced feelings of sadness, anxiety, and fear, and she had flashbacks of the encounters. She reported having felt upset all of the time, like she was never happy, and felt easily overwhelmed, angry, irritable, and on edge. She also experienced passive suicidal ideation, where she used to wish she would fall asleep and not wake up. She began getting in fights more frequently and began abusing substances. In spite of her verbal report, she primarily endorsed trauma symptoms as occurring only "sometimes," which produced the flat profile. Her only elevations on the MACI related to family discord and difficulty controlling anger.

Diane's projective drawings and stories were concrete with superficial resolutions and unrealistic positive endings. The Rorschach, on the other hand, revealed more about her psychological state. Diane's Rorschach profile (Table 16.1) indicated that she was experiencing painful emotion, chronic overwhelm, and helplessness, and she had high needs for closeness and intimacy that were going unmet. It also revealed, however, that Diane expected positive, collaborative, and mutually supportive relationships. With sexual exploitation in mind, Diane's trusting nature in relationships combined with emotional neediness and interpersonal passivity made her much more vulnerable to being exploited and manipulated. Moreover, while her profile indicated good reality testing, the ability to think and consider different points of view, and the tendency to form accurate impressions of others and their intentions, when her neediness was activated, it likely transcended her better judgment. In terms of thematic content, it is notable that in her 22-response record, four responses contained images of butterflies. In her sign off response to Card X, she stated, "This is a type of butterfly, you know how they have a caterpillar in the middle? Has wings that are longer. It's a butterfly person with wings." In the inquiry she explained, "It got the wings and looks like a person who got hands they are holding up here above their head. If you look close, you see two eyes and a nose. That darker part. The wings are long, longer than butterfly wings. It's a butterfly person." The image of a young woman with high aspirations trying to spread her long beautiful wings is conjured, but with the reality that this young woman has significant emotional pain and with that comes some unraveling.

Table 16.1 Diane's Structural Summary

Comprehensive System 5th Edition Structural Summary

Location Features	Determinants Blends	Determinants Single		Contents		Approach	
				H = 1		I : DsS.DdS	
Zf = 8	FM.FC	M = 0		(H) = 1		II :D.D.D	
ZSum = 22.0	FM.FY	FM = 4		Hd = 0		III :D.D.D	
ZEst = 24	FM.FC	m = 1		(Hd) = 0		IV :W	
	FY.V	FC = 1		IIx = 1		V :W.D	
W = 5	CF.FT	CF = 0		A = 14		VI :W	
D = 15	FY.M	C = 0		(A) = 0		VII :W	
W+D = 20		Cn = 0		Ad = 3		VIII :W	
Dd = 2		FC' = 1		(Ad) = 0		IX :Ds.D.D	
S = 0		C'F = 0		An = 0		X :Dd.D	
		C' = 0		Art = 2			
		FT = 1		Ay = 0		Special Scores	
DQ		TF = 0		Bl = 0		Lv1 Lv2	
+ = 5		T = 0		Bt = 0		DV = 2 x1 0 x2	
o = 17		FV = 0		Cg = 0		INC = 1 x2 2x4	
v/+ = 0		VF = 0		Cl = 0		DR = 2 x3 0x6	
v = 0		V = 0		Ex = 0		FAB = 0 x4 0x7	
		FY = 2		Fd = 0		ALOG = 0 x5	
		YF = 0		Fi = 1		CON = 0 x7	
		Y = 0		Ge = 0		Raw Sum6 = 7	
Form Quality		Fr = 0		Hh = 0		Wgtd Sum6 = 18	
		rF = 0		Ls = 3			
FQx MQual W+D		FD = 0		Na = 0		AB = 0 GHR = 2	
+ = 0 = 0 = 0		F = 6		Sc = 1		AG = 0 PHR = 1	
o = 11 = 0 = 11				Sx = 0		COP = 2 MOR = 0	
u = 6 = 1 = 5				Xy = 0		CP = 0 PER = 0	
- = 4 = 0 = 3				Id = 0		PSV = 0	
none = 1 = 0 = 1		(2) = 4					

-----------------------------------Ratios, Percentages, and Derivations-----------------------------------

R = 22	L = 0.38			FC:CF+C = 3:1	COP = 2	AG = 0
				Pure C = 0	GHR:PHR = 2:1	
EB = 1:2.5	EA = 3.5	EBPer = N/A		SmC':WSmC = 1:2.5	a:p = 3:6	
eb = 8:9	es = 17	D = -5		Afr = 0.57	Food = 0	
	Adj = 13	Adj D = -3		S = 0	SumT = 2	
	es					
				Blends/R = 6:22	Human Cont = 2	
FM = 7	SumC' = 1	SumT = 2		CP = 0	PureH = 1	
m = 1	SumV = 1	SumY = 5			PER = 0	
					Isol Indx = 0.14	

a:p = 3:6	Sum6 = 7	XA% = 0.77	Zf = 8	3r+(2)/R = 0.18
Ma:Mp = 0:1	Lv2 = 2	WDA% = 0.80	W:D:Dd =5 15 : 2	Fr+rF = 0
2AB+Art+Ay = 2	WSum6 = 18	X-% = 0.18	W:M = 5:1	SumV = 1
MOR = 0	M- = 0	S- = 0	Zd = -2.0	FD = 0
	Mnone = 0	P = 4	PSV = 0	An+Xy = 0
		X+% = 0.50	DQ+ = 5	MOR = 2
		Xu% = 0.27	DQv = 0	H:(H)+Hd+(Hd) = 1:1

PTI = 1	DEPI = 4	CDI = 3	S-CON = 5	HVI = No	OBS = No

Copyright 2001 by Rorschach Workshops. Reprinted with permission.

Feedback and Family Intervention

As previously mentioned, Diane's parents became highly involved in the assessment. Diane's therapist had communicated that working with the family, and dad in particular, had been difficult for her due to his reactivity and shaming of her client. Diane's father was deeply troubled by Diane's exploitative relationships. Out of desperation, he tried to control Diane and attempted to set restrictions and limitations on her as though she was much younger. When she resisted his control and defied his rules, he said derogatory and inappropriate things to her such as calling her a "ho," saying her sexual assaults had been her fault, and shaming her for her exploitation. In reality, Diane was a victim of exploitation and sexual abuse, which was the paradigm from which her therapist was working. Diane's therapist and father had difficulty working together due to an inability to find a common ground and language around exploitation.

Concerned about creating a split and greater distance between therapist and parents, I frequently met with Diane's therapist and invited her to all meetings with Diane's parents. One of these meetings took place just two weeks into the assessment. The purpose of the meeting was essentially to come together to hear Diane's parents' concerns, continue to build rapport, offer some preliminary observations from the testing, and come together as a team that included Diane's therapist. My hope was to utilize test data and observations to help them begin creating common language and understanding around Diane's difficulties. Sitting across from Diane's parents at their kitchen table, I was acutely aware of the significant cultural and generational differences between providers and parents. We had two older African American parents from the Deep South and two significantly younger providers, one White and one Latina, sitting around a table together trying to discuss Diane's difficulties in a way that was supportive and helpful. It was important to understand her parents' expectations, perceptions, and thinking as well as recognize their authority in parenting and as elders. Much of this time was spent joining with the family, acknowledging their love and concern for their daughter, and recognizing their efforts.

I was able to take advantage of my position as the new person to the table and asked them to tell me about their concerns, fears, and hopes for their daughter. They saw her as vulnerable and sweet natured, but Diane's desperation for love and affection was painful to her parents, especially her father. In response to this frustration, they began to blame Diane for her neediness and even partially blamed her for her sexual assaults and sexual exploitation, as she should have known better and not had such high needs for love and affection. As this conversation occurred, an organic shift took place and Diane's father began to open up about his concerns about his parental shortcomings, confusion about how to parent Diane, and an opening was created to become more curious about Diane and her experience, rather than blaming her for her behaviors and choices. Diane's therapist was also able to develop more empathy for Diane's parents, as she could clearly see where the shame and blame were originating. Another meeting a few weeks later built on this conversation and I began to present findings from the assessment, communicating that Diane may appear more capable than she really is. Diane's lower cognitive functioning was discussed and how this impacts her judgment, ability to problem solve, and risk of being taken advantage of. Diane's father became emotional as he revealed that he himself had been diagnosed as "slow" and knew how this had made life more difficult for him and worried for his daughter's future. At the conclusion of this meeting, I began to integrate the conversations between our past two meetings and named their love for Diane, their feelings of helplessness, and their response to this helplessness (i.e., control and shame Diane). I also named how the challenges presented to them due to Diane's cognitive difficulties and emotional struggles are incredibly difficult, especially if they trigger their own personal struggles. I recommended family therapy to help them sort through all of these issues and gain parenting support. They accepted the recommendation and the referral for family therapy was made at this point in the assessment.

After these meetings, the family reported that their relationship with Diane began to slightly improve, as they were more understanding and less critical of her. Diane, in turn, had become more open with her parents and they began discussing their hopes for her future in a more collaborative way. The family's shift was also apparent in the sudden decrease in crisis phone calls to this writer. The final feedback sessions included one meeting with Diane, one with her parents, and one altogether. Diane's therapist was present at all meetings and becoming increasingly involved in working with the family.

For an adolescent, a letter answering Diane's questions would typically be provided to her at the feedback session. Due to Diane's lower cognitive functioning, this writer opted to provide a feedback story instead, which is usually how younger children receive information about their assessment. While these stories range from metaphorical to fairy tale-like to more obviously biographical, a central commonality is that the client is the main character in the story and their struggle and recommendations are embedded within the storyline. With Diane's Rorschach responses in mind, I chose a butterfly as her main character. In Diane's story, Kimimi the happy but naïve caterpillar who likes her simple life goes on a more challenging journey when she becomes a beautiful butterfly ready to spread her wings and leave the garden. Kimimi's parents explain to her that her wings are fragile and can easily tear, thus the need for her to keep herself safe was imperative. In the story, Kimimi enjoys her newfound freedom and begins to push limits, meeting a charismatic character along the way that convinces her to do things that put her in harm's way. When her wings tear, Kimimi's parents bring in a helper (i.e., therapist) to help her discern safe from unsafe. Kimimi's high needs for love and affection are also named, as well as how these needs cloud her judgment. In their therapeutic work, Kimimi's trust of the world is valued and seen as a strength, yet the ways that her trust put her at risk are also discussed.

At the feedback session, Diane laughed with delight as she read her story. She quickly identified herself as the butterfly. A rich discussion ensued, keeping with the metaphor of the butterfly while directly addressing her vulnerability related to getting taken advantage of and the importance of recognizing safety issues. Diane then applied it to her current relationship and revealed that her once loving boyfriend had recently began asking her to do things for him that she felt uncomfortable with, but that she feared losing the relationship. Support was provided to her around this and recommendations were made around working on identifying warning signs within relationships and how to set limits and assert her needs when these arise. Diane requested for her story to be shared with her parents at the final feedback session, as she felt like it named her experience, as it recognized her strengths as well as her struggles.

The feedback session with Diane's parents took place after Diane's session. Because so much of the work had already been done around increasing parents' understanding of

Diane and her needs, their feedback session focused on reviewing and consolidating the discussions. The conversation began with focusing on recognizing parental efforts, the good job they had done with her to have raised a young woman who was so trusting in relationships and optimistic. Diane's high needs for love and affection, ongoing struggles with depression, and cognitive difficulties were also reviewed and the link to how these put her at risk for poor judgment, substance use, and exploitation was made. Diane's parents could take this in and engage in the conversation in a collaborative and more hopeful way. When Diane joined the next feedback session, her story was read and the family and providers again reviewed the findings and recommendations, but this time through the use of the metaphor of the trusting butterfly leaving the garden.

Approximately three months after the assessment was complete, Diane's father and therapist reached out and requested a follow-up feedback session to revisit the findings of the assessment. While Diane's relationship with her parents had generally improved in the months following the assessment, Diane had recently begun to once again engage in high-risk behaviors and was taking public transportation to a nearby city known for high rates of sexual exploitation. Parents and providers met, while Diane refused to participate in the meeting. It seemed that the family had not followed through with the family therapy referral made during the course of the assessment. They were understandably frustrated with Diane's behaviors and felt helpless. As a result, they had trouble holding onto their empathic view of Diane and had begun to blame and criticize her once again for getting taken advantage of. The findings from the assessment were revisited and the recommendation for family therapy was once again made. Diane's parents were receptive and agreed to follow through with the referral to obtain the parental support they needed.

Discussion

Diane's case highlights some of the vulnerabilities that exist for CSEC youth and how these vulnerabilities can put a youth at risk. A young African American girl of low socioeconomic status, Diane was 13 at the time of initial exploitation; a time when her father was abusing alcohol, gambling, and was absent in her life. Her reasonably solid childhood and lower cognitive functioning lead her to be more trusting in relationships, and she then chased her needs for love and affection. Her experience of being exploited resulted in trauma and depressive symptoms and she began using drugs and alcohol as a means of coping with her intensely negative affect and overwhelm. She also continued to look for love to ease her pain, but this lead to a vicious cycle of exploitation and further pain. Her neediness transcended her better judgment and she found herself in the same position over and over again.

Due to Diane's cognitive difficulties and low adaptive living skills, she will likely live with her parents well past her 18th birthday and into young adulthood. We were able to reconnect Diane with the Regional Center following the assessment to get her case management services for extra support. It was later learned that the family did not follow through with the family therapy referral, but Diane's individual therapist continually referred the parents and Diane back to the assessment results and recommendations to help them work through crises as they arose.

This case illuminates the harsh realities that are inherent to working with the CSEC population. While the hope is to help girls escape the life of exploitation, we recognize that this is a long-term process that often involves a cycle of getting out of the life and going back in. Like any process of rehabilitation, there are often setbacks and relapses. When working with the CSEC population, progress is measured incrementally. Progress in this case was observed in Diane and her family's increased awareness. While Diane and her family experienced regression in the months after the assessment, they had a story they could refer to that involved a different view of Diane's struggles: a story that recognized her strengths, but named her vulnerabilities and risk factors. They would forever have a reference point and an awareness with which they could reconnect if given some support in doing so.

References

Armstrong, J. G. & Lowenstein, R. J. (1990). Characteristics of patients with multiple personality and dissociative disorders on psychological testing. *Journal of Nervous and Mental Disorders, 178*, 448–454.

Beery, K. E., Buktenica, N. A., & Beery, N. A. (2010). *Beery-Buktenica Developmental Test of Visual-Motor Integration: Administration, scoring & teaching manual* (6th ed.). Minneapolis, MN: NSC Pearson.

Briere, J. (1996). *Trauma Symptom Checklist for Children (TSCC) Professional Manual*. Odessa, FL: Psychological Assessment Resources.

Buck, J. N. (1977). *The House-Tree-Person Technique, Revised Manual*. Los Angeles: Western Psychological Services.

Elliot, C. (2007). *Differential Ability Scales-II (DAS-II)*. San Antonio, TX: Pearson.

Exner, J. E., Jr. (1993). *The Rorschach: A comprehensive system, vol. I: Basic foundations* (3rd ed). New York: John Wiley & Sons, Inc.

McArthur, D. S. & Roberts, G. E. (1982). *Roberts Apperception Test for Children: Manual*. Los Angeles, Western Psychological Services.

Millon, T. (1993). *Millon Adolescent Clinical Inventory: Manual*. Minneapolis, MN: National Computer System.

Perryman, H. (1992). *Life Timeline*. Personal Communication.

Reynolds, C. R., & Kamphaus, R. W. (2004). *Behavior Assessment System for Children* (2nd ed.). Circle Pines, MN: American Guidance Service.

Rotter, J. B. & Rafferty, J. E. (1950). *Manual: The Rotter Incomplete Sentences Blank*. New York: Psychological Corp.

Sparrow, S., Balla, D. A. & Cicchetti, D. V. (1984). *Vineland Adaptive Behavior Scales, Second Edition*. New York: American Guidance Service.

Twill, S. E., Green, D. M., & Traylor, A. (2010). A descriptive study of sexually exploited children in residential treatment. *Child & Youth Care Forum: Journal of Research and Practice in Children's Services, 39*(3), 187–199.

Walker, K. (2013). Ending the commercial sexual exploitation of children: A call for multi-system collaboration in California. California Child Welfare Council. Retrieved from www.chhs.ca.gov/CWCDOC/Ending%20CSEC%20-%20A%20Call%20for%20Multi-System%20Collaboration%20in%20CA%20-%20February%202013.pdf.

WestCoast Children's Clinic. (2012). *Research to action: Sexually exploited minors (SEM) needs and strengths*. Oakland, CA: WestCoast Children's Clinic.

17 The Case of the Bullet-Proof Vest

Complex PTSD, Racial Wounds, and Taking Matters into Your Own Hands

Christopher Arrillaga

While the San Francisco Bay Area attracts much media attention for its Internet giants, famous entrepreneurs, high cost of living, and beautiful natural landscapes, the region also has its fair share of social and economic woes. Like other urban areas across the United States, pockets of the Bay Area are riddled with community violence that occasionally garner national attention because of fatal shootings and gang warfare in cities such as Oakland and Richmond. While local news channels highlight the frequent shooting deaths of largely African American and Latino teenage young men and boys, the full story of the survivors is rarely highlighted. Many survivors frequently battle what Bessel van der Kolk helped term *developmental trauma disorder*, a form of complex post-traumatic disorder (Luxenberg, Spinazzola, & Van Der Kolk, 2001).

Most individuals think of PTSD as the terrible traumas faced by war veterans or a cluster of enduring symptoms related to one discrete traumatic event (i.e., being assaulted during a mugging or failing to rescue a loved one from a burning building). However, many people suffer from post-trauma stress due to an accumulation of traumatic incidents. This accumulation occurs when an individual (or someone close to them) is physically and/or emotionally harmed, and the threat continues to persist daily. One common example that can be found in numerous economically disenfranchised neighborhoods is the omnipresent threat of becoming the victim of gun violence. Many youth of color from the poverty stricken neighborhoods of Oakland have been either the innocent bystander or intended target of community violence. Following an incident in which they or someone they care about has been shot, many individuals develop an ongoing fear of being harmed by surrounding neighborhood violence perpetuated by community members and police officers.

The psychological wounds inflicted by violence or the threat of lethal force by one's neighbors or the police frequently cross racial lines. Brown and Black adolescents are frequently racially profiled and suspected of being criminals as they simply walk down the street. In addition to the real threat of violence, these youth have to navigate the additional stress of being perceived as a "gangsta" and assumed they are going to amount to nothing more than a criminal. This in turn can lead to what Dr. Ken Hardy coins the "internal wounds of racial oppression and a cycle of racial self-denigration" (Hardy, 2013, p. 28). These youth frequently have accumulated both a wealth of traumatic experiences in their neighborhood as well as being persistently devalued and assumed to be delinquents. Many urban male youth of color develop chronic PTSD mixed with symptoms of self-devaluation and depression as well as a sense of a foreshortened future.

For many youth of color, particularly those in poor Bay Area neighborhoods, they find themselves in an ongoing war zone. They may be sitting on the sofa watching T.V. and apprehensive of the stray bullet that may fly through their front window. The moment they step foot on the sidewalk outside their home, they may confront the real possibility of police racial profiling and the excessive use of force. Once a youth has become the victim of these forms of community violence, they are frequently at increased risk for developing complex PTSD. Additionally, they can find themselves at risk of internalizing the negative assumptions others have of them as young men of color and displaying a wide array of symptoms of depression. As a result of violent traumas and racial oppression, this mixture of PTSD with mood disturbances can be an all-too-common reality for youth in a multitude of economically disenfranchised neighborhoods in Oakland and Richmond, California.

The following case tells the story of one such youth, Julian, an 18-year-old innocent victim of community violence. This chapter details the therapeutic journey Julian embarked on when he reached out to me, a local clinical psychologist, nine months after a traumatic incident to find out how he could "live in peace, succeed in college and help his mom out." This chapter illustrates the therapeutic utility of incorporating tenants of the assessment model founded by Dr. Stephen Finn and emphasizes that this model can be adapted to work effectively in multiple contexts. This case example also helps to elucidate how conducting collaborative therapeutic assessment with a resilient, young Latino man can offer the opportunity for accurate diagnosis, legal and educational advocacy, and a sense of hope in the future for both client and assessor.

The Case of Julian

On a hot, July day, Julian had been casually driving through his West Oakland neighborhood with his buddy. Suddenly, out of nowhere, bullets were flying through the windshield of their car. Julian ducked, but it was too late. He looked down and saw blood pouring out of his hip and holes in his left hand. According to Julian, the rest of that day was a blur.

Almost a year had passed since the shooting, and Julian did not know if he or his friend were the intentional targets of this violence. Since Julian was not actively involved in a gang, I did not understand why he would be a target, but often even distant connections can lead to being threatened. However, one thing was for certain. Since partially recovering from his injuries, Julian had changed almost every facet of his daily life to avoid being violently attacked again.

Meeting Julian

Almost a year after the shooting, Julian was struggling academically and socially. So, at the encouragement of his mother and therapist, he was referred to me for a psychological assessment. Julian's mother was Guatemalan, with Spanish as a first language. As a first step, I completed the intake process in Spanish with her and Julian. I met with both Julian and his mom for the initial intake interview at our community psychological clinic near his neighborhood. To my surprise, Julian greeted me with a big smile, firm handshake and sustained eye contact. He almost immediately pulled out various printouts from the

Internet regarding dyslexia. Julian had highlighted all of the symptom descriptors that he currently experienced with many handwritten notes in the margins. Julian explained, "I thought that these may help you as you try to figure out why I struggle so much in school."

During this first meeting, Julian's mother discussed her concerns regarding Julian's social isolation and academic failure. She described how he would learn things in school and then forget them the following day. He regularly had to be retaught various academic concepts. She also informed me that since being shot last year, he had increasingly shut himself off to the outside world. However, she also explained that since he was a toddler, he had a long history of indifference toward social relationships, and she wondered if he was autistic. She explained how Julian's uncle had recently watched a daytime talk show on Univision that explained the symptoms of mild autism. His uncle then exclaimed, "That is just like Julian!" Julian's mom felt compelled to seek help and get answers to her questions about what could help Julian succeed academically and engage more with the world around him.

His mother also mentioned the most extreme measures Julian took to protect himself from being shot again. Julian's mother informed me that several months earlier, he had come home and excitedly announced, "Look what I bought mom! I got a real bullet-proof vest." Julian had reportedly done research online and discovered a vendor that sold authentic, professional grade bullet-proof vests. She told me that in the last several months since the purchase, Julian had not left the house without putting on his protective vest underneath his baggy sweatshirt. Julian had taken matters into his own hands and decided that he would feel safer outside his home if his torso were shielded from any future bullet that could rip through his body. I was stunned by both how resourceful and determined Julian was to keep himself safe and yet how symbolic this decision was in exemplifying his severe PTSD.

Julian's mom informed me that Julian's father had been in a county jail for the past four years awaiting his trial to determine if he was guilty of killing several individuals in a drug deal gone badly. Julian reported that he had not visited his father in prison the past several months, but used to see him behind the Plexiglas in shackles each weekend over the last many years. It became clear that Julian had strong feelings about his father being locked up and was ambivalent about his jail visits.

During this first meeting, I quickly became overwhelmed with the numerous domains of Julian's life that I would need to investigate to deeply understand his current psychological realities. Between the complicated relationship with an imprisoned father, being the victim of neighborhood gun violence, and questions surrounding his longstanding social and academic difficulties, I was at a loss as to where to start. I reminded myself of one of the initial guiding principles of therapeutic assessment: the value in helping our clients get curious about their presenting problems. My task was to help Julian formulate questions and then invite him to step back with me and look at his life, struggles, and strengths for answers.

After gathering the developmental and family history of Julian from the intake meeting with them both and an individual meeting with his mother, I scheduled a private meeting with Julian. During that meeting, I wanted to begin building a bridge of trust between us by hearing about his interests, concerns, hopes, and dreams. As a man who identifies as White, I knew that I likely would have to demonstrate my trustworthiness to Julian. Sure enough, in our first meeting Julian brought up our differences by stating, "It is not fair that Black and Brown guys have to worry about getting shot or robbed and you do not." This led to a conversation about the reality that his brown skin color puts him at risk of being the target of discrimination and violence and the injustice of these daily forms of racism. I wondered aloud with him if he may feel anger or rage at times, as this would be a natural response to the racial injustice that he sees surrounding him in his neighborhood.

Julian shared that he dreamed of leaving Oakland one day to live in the countryside and work on a farm. He explained how he enjoys taking care of animals and how living on a farm outside of Oakland would mean that he would no longer have to worry about being shot or mistreated. However, Julian explained that he could not afford to focus on this dream because he needed to find a job and help take care of his mother by helping pay for some of the household expenses. He then mentioned that he knew he had some type of learning difficulties. He asked for my help in determining whether he had dyslexia and what would be helpful in allowing him to do better in school. Julian explained that he had verbal memory problems and had to reread text many times in order to remember it. He went on to describe how he was very disorganized and had trouble planning what he wanted to say in his final research paper. This paper would fulfill his final graduation requirement from his continuation high school.

Administering the First Tests

After receiving this information from Julian and his mother, I administered the Wechsler Adult Intelligence Test-III (WAIS-IV; Wechsler, 2008) test to determine his current cognitive functioning. His results revealed that his abilities were quite unevenly developed. Therefore, it was not possible to determine an overall score to capture his cognitive functioning. Julian displayed a range from average to extremely low nonverbal reasoning abilities (Block Design = Scaled Score of 9 and Matrix Reasoning = Scaled Score of 3). He appeared to reason better with hands-on visual information like putting patterns of blocks together. However, he struggled profoundly when the visual information became increasingly abstract and he was required to identify patterns by holding the pattern in his head. Julian's verbal reasoning was evenly developed and below average across the board. It should be noted that given Julian's historic enrollment in extremely low achieving Oakland public schools and his parents low educational attainment as first generation, undocumented immigrants from Guatemala, Julian has not been afforded many of the English verbal learning opportunities that US children from middle- and upper-income homes have. Therefore, I knew that I needed to interpret Julian's sub-par verbal reasoning with caution as Julian was not formally exposed to English until age 5. His cognitive scores likely did not reflect his potential if given access to high quality academic enrichment opportunities and the same level of exposure to English as his White counterparts.

However, what did stand out was the fact that Julian's working memory and processing speed were evenly developed and in the borderline range. Julian demonstrated great difficulty recalling basic verbal information and struggled to quickly make sense of visual information. Immediately, I was given clues as to what may be contributing to his reported great difficulties with reading comprehension. He worked slowly, but also had trouble holding on to what he was reading. I subsequently gave Julian the Wechsler Individual Achievement Test-III (WIAT-III; Wechsler, 2009) achievement battery to reveal his current level of academic skills. Julian's scores indicated that his comprehension of text and reading speed were at the seventh grade level despite being 17 years old. Julian's reading accuracy when asked to read out loud was at the sixth grade level. Julian's ability to sound out made-up words with a variety of sound blends was also at the seventh grade level. Given this weakness in phonological processing, I decided to administer the SCAN-3 Test of Auditory Processing (Keith, 2009), as children that struggle to phonetically decode frequently have related challenges with accurately processing auditory information. Not surprisingly, Julian failed two subtests. He distorted the sounds within words, and he made numerous errors when asked to repeat words when distracting background noise was present or different words were presented to each ear simultaneously.

Julian's Continuous Performance Test-2 (CPT-2; Conners & MHS Staff, 2000), a test of sustained visual attention, did reveal a tendency to respond too quickly and impulsively, which warranted a deeper look at his executive functions. This was especially true given that Julian had also reported struggles with planning and organization. Julian's Wisconsin Card Sort Test (WCST; Heaton, Chelune, & Talley, 1993) revealed a low-average ability to adapt his strategy on a nonverbal reasoning task, which had rules that kept changing. Julian needed 52 trials to complete the first category due to his perseverative style of repeatedly trying the wrong strategy. While the average number of trials needed for a 17-year-old is only around 20, it was important for me to note that these neuropsychological test findings needed to be interpreted with great caution. An increasing body of research suggests that Latino adult patients from lower socioeconomic status and with a low level of acculturation generally score significantly lower on nonverbal neuropsychological measures (Saez et al., 2013).

Julian's family was living far below the poverty line, and on the Short Acculturation Scale for Hispanic Youth (SASH-Y; Barona & Miller, 1994) measure of acculturation, Julian's results placed him in the moderate level of acculturation. This level of acculturation suggested that Julian maintained a significant amount of traditional Guatemalan cultural practices. Given these aspects of Julian's demographic background and his fluency in Spanish, it was important not to put too much stock in his poor performance on particular WCST and CPT-II scales. At the same time, his results were quite extreme and suggestive of impaired executive functioning that went beyond cultural norms. Julian's difficulty shifting out his rigid approach to solving the WCST task despite ongoing feedback that his strategy was not working appeared to occur in activities of daily living as well. Julian described spending hours copying down the words almost verbatim after he reads a passage as a means of trying to remember it. He did so despite knowing for years that this process did not seem to help him comprehend and retain the written material.

Although Julian did not display any major attention deficits, he did endorse numerous symptoms of post-traumatic stress on the Trauma Symptom Checklist for Children (TSCC; Briere, 2011). Although eight months had passed since the shooting, Julian continued to display the following symptoms: hyperarousal, intense anxiety, intrusive thoughts, defensive avoidance, and somatic complaints. When asked about the symptoms he endorsed, Julian explained that since he was shot, he was afraid to go outside. He also obsessively closed the blinds in the front of the house and was nervous that he was being followed. Julian experienced intense distress when he had to drive fast on the freeway, when he walked outside, and when he was around peers at school. Julian stated that he avoided getting to know his peers in class or on campus as he was afraid that they may be associated with or know the individuals that shot him. Julian emphatically explained, "I don't want to make friends as you never know who they may know," suggesting that a new connection could ultimately put his life at risk, as a new acquaintance might be associated with the faceless enemy that Julian suspected may have intentionally shot him.

Given Julian's profound apprehension of being revictimized, I decided to administer the Rorschach (Exner, 1993) to better understand Julian's inner world of thoughts, feelings, and perceptions. Julian's mom had endorsed 20 items on the Social Communication Questionnaire (Rutter & Bailey et al., 2003). These results suggested that Julian might be mildly on the autististm spectrum. However, Julian's Rorschach protocol provided evidence that he was drawn to the interpersonal world of human connections, but was extremely pessimistic as to whether his needs could be met within relationships. Julian had experienced ongoing critical feedback from his largely absent, incarcerated father, and he had learned over many years that his severely traumatized mother was not always emotionally attuned to his feelings and needs. She had been in survival mode for years when Julian's father had chronically beaten her. Then she was left to support the family on her own once he was locked up.

As I continued with testing Julian, it became more apparent to me that he was not on the autism spectrum. He was more like a terrified boy who had been chronically, psychically, and physically harmed by people around him. He had constructed a huge wall around him to protect himself from the perils and risks of interpersonal relationships. To the casual outside observer, this wall could make it seem that he was indifferent toward relationships. But a deeper look at Julian revealed that he had largely given up on getting his needs met through human relationships (i.e., no Rorschach texture responses).

Julian's sense of threat was apparent in his Rorschach responses. He saw first "an aggressive mask," "someone staring," and "a heart that something went through to make it deformed," "hate," and "a shadow getting bigger," and finally, "gang signs." This speaks to the actual environment of street violence and hints at shootings, and the events that happened to him. These unusual responses were contrasted with images of vulnerability, need for others, and the desire to escape. He saw "something trying to grasp on to affection but there is nothing," "a big blur that wants to express something," "something that spills out what he sees and hears," and "eyes that look vulnerable." The structural data on the Rorschach confirmed that Julian retreats into his own distressed thoughts to manage fear and revealed a tendency to get flooded even as he made great effort to armor himself by putting a lid on his feelings. Julian appeared to seek out my guidance and validation throughout the testing process. His responses on the Rorschach also showed a yearning for support and growth. Julian appeared to seek out my guidance and validation throughout the testing process. Repeatedly, Julian asked throughout the assessment process if I thought he could succeed in college and if I could explain to community college personnel his strengths and learning challenges.

The moment I confidently knew Julian was not autistic was during our fourth testing session, when I qualitatively introduced several items from the Autism Diagnostic

Observation Schedule, Second Edition (ADOS-2: Lord & Rutter et al., 2012) and asked him about his understanding of loneliness, love, and his future dreams. Julian went on to describe in great depth his emotions and his yearning for love and closeness, as well as an elaborate picture of a future that entailed escaping the violence of Oakland and being at peace, working on a countryside farm tending to the livestock. Julian had the capacity to engage deeply with the world around him, but too many experiences told him it was safer to retreat inside himself and keep his distance from people that could harm him.

One of Julian's Rorschach responses seemed to sum up how Julian's acute trauma continued to haunt him, yet also illuminated his desperate hope for a better future. Julian described his perception to card number five as "a butterfly trying to open its wings and go forward; trying to fly and trying to get out of whatever it is in. Butterflies have sensors and it looks like it is going to something it wants. It wants to escape and get something better." This description seemed to parallel Julian's own awareness and desire to leave behind the danger, community violence, and suffering he has experienced in Oakland. Julian's goal of living and working in the countryside, and his formulation of key steps to reach this dream, served to help him endure his current psychological pain as he held onto the hope that life could be better.

Digging Deeper to Determine Other Complicating Factors

Julian's psychological experience was even more layered with preoccupying thoughts and very mixed feelings that Julian had about his incarcerated father. Julian had become increasingly reluctant to visit his father in jail, yet he encouraged me to include his father in the testing process by interviewing him in prison. Julian's mother thought his resistance to continuing visits with his father was due to reports that his father thought he was "a sissy and a momma's boy." I wondered if Julian did not feel strong enough in the eyes of his father. He may have been harboring anger towards his father for not being seen as a self-reliant young man. Julian's Rorschach revealed a boy who is mad (3 Integrated Space responses), but makes effort to suppress his normal needs and feelings. Julian would not speak with me about his feelings toward his father or their relationship. Because my attempts at exploration of these themes appeared to touch a vulnerable spot in Julian, I decided not to push further, but instead I respected Julian's need to divert this loaded and distressing topic.

Despite the fact that Julian remained resistant to discussing his relationship with his father, he did support the idea of having me visit his father in jail. While his father might ultimately be convicted of multiple murders, I knew that he also had important potential insights regarding Julian. I believed that if I could engage Julian's father in this collaborative assessment process, some of my lingering questions about what could best support Julian's continued development into manhood with improved psychological well-being might be answered.

Upon meeting Julian's father, shackled behind thick glass, he initially appeared perplexed as to why I was visiting with him. After explaining the testing process his son was currently undergoing and the importance of getting his father's perspective on what his son needed, Julian's father became quite open and candid about his regrets. He described trying to "toughen up his son" and the mistakes he had made as a father in not paying enough attention many years before when Julian needed him most. He spoke of his fear that his son was vulnerable as a brown teenage boy in Oakland. I acknowledged that as a White man I will never know what it is like for Julian to stay clear of trouble. However, I was concerned that his ongoing fear of being shot again could stop him from reaching out to others and engaging in the world around him.

Julian's father explained that he was confused about why his son had become so shut down, but wondered if he may be nervous on the inside. He also explained that he "did not want his son on any psychiatric medication" and that boys of color were often over-medicated. He wanted reassurance that I was not going to make this suggestion. I informed Julian's dad that once Julian had finished with testing, I would write a report with recommendations of what could help Julian continue to mature and function better in the world. I explained that I would send him a copy of the report and give him time to review it while he remained locked up in solitary confinement 23 hours a day. Then I would return to discuss the results, and each of our ideas of what could help his son. He was appreciative and anxious to know how much longer the process would take before I sent him the findings for us to discuss. I left the prison feeling inspired and feeling a deep sense of responsibility to answer this father's questions who sat powerlessly behind bars, unable to readily influence his son's development and shape his future in the ways he so desperately wanted.

Discussing the Results with Julian and His Father

Taken together Julian's test findings supported diagnoses of chronic PTSD, Major Depression, and a Learning Disorder NOS (deficits in auditory processing, executive functioning, reading fluency, working memory, and processing speed of visual information). I had identified several treatment recommendations that I believed could help ameliorate Julian's sense of paralysis in being held hostage by his traumas, depression, and learning disability. Illuminating these diagnoses and related treatments felt like a simple task compared to what lay ahead. I was profoundly uncertain about how to provide feedback to Julian about his PTSD and learning issues in a way that would not lead to him feeling "weak" and overwhelmed with shame. I also wanted to be sure that I could help him see his strengths in ways that could help him feel optimism about his future, despite his major learning challenges and, at times, debilitating depression and traumatic stress. Also, I was concerned about how my including Julian's father in this therapeutic process would ultimately unfold. I wondered what would ultimately be helpful to Julian given his intense resistance toward connecting with his father during the course of the assessment. Finally, I was unsure of how Julian and his parents would respond to my findings. Would they become overwhelmed by the findings or have a hard time swallowing them?

One key component within the philosophy of the therapeutic model of psychological assessment is making sure your testing feedback is not too threatening or contradictory to the client's understanding of the issues addressed. This model is constructed using three levels. Level One feedback is easy to take in, as the client and/or family already has the same belief or understanding. Level Two feedback includes new information that can be somewhat distressing to hear, but close enough to an individual's own hypothesis of how to understand the issue that they are able to process and consolidate aspects of the feedback. However, Level Three feedback is often too novel, and the results and/

or recommendations can feel foreign, threatening, and ultimately too overwhelming to process. Sometimes this level of feedback can be initially rejected as incorrect or not useful and may need to be approached indirectly and gradually (Finn, 2007).

It would be crucial that I lead with Level One feedback about Julian's cognitive strengths, learning challenges, and resiliency to start the feedback sessions. I thought this approach would help put Julian and his family at ease and demonstrate that we see eye to eye on our understanding of him. From there, I planned to address findings and recommendations that were somewhat novel, yet not terribly surprising—for example, that he is not autistic and that he can be very guarded as a means of protecting himself from future harm. Finally, I would get a sense of how this level of feedback was received by the family. This would help me to determine if it was worth risking the introduction of Level Three material in the feedback session. In my previous work, I had always found it useful not to bombard the client with too much Level Three feedback. Level Three feedback could mean the individual forgets the less threatening Level One feedback because they may get lost in the sea of emotionally overwhelming results and explanations that Level Three feedback springs on them. With regard to Julian, this meant that I did not disclose to him that I was aware that he secretly wore a bullet-proof vest and that this decision, while important for survival, appeared to be a manifestation of his severe PTSD.

After being granted permission to enter the prison again as a visitor of Julian's father, I anxiously approached the thick, bullet-proof Plexiglas and sat down on the old, dilapidated folding chair. I made eye contact with Julian's father in his orange jumpsuit as he sat in shackles with an eager look in his eyes. I asked him if he had received the psychological report I had sent two weeks earlier. He explained that he had just received it, as the prison seemed to take their time in reviewing the contents of the envelope and enclosed document to ensure there was nothing deemed inappropriate that would need to be confiscated. However, Julian's father stated that he had read the report and had numerous questions for me. We discussed his son's anxiety, and I explained how the anxiety works like a soldier coming back from war with "shell shock" that continues to haunt Julian. His father expressed regret that he had been so hard on his son in years past for not being tough and for having teased him about being a "momma's boy." He seemed to grasp how his son, a young Latino man, was struggling to feel good about himself given the PTSD and difficulties with learning that were pulling him down into a dark depression. I attempted to normalize his attempts to toughen his son up to prepare him for a world that was not always supportive of or accommodating to a young Latino man in Oakland.

I reflected back to Julian's father that it was clear how much he cared about his son and hoped for his future. We also discussed his son's learning and mood challenges, and I described how Julian's past traumas were standing in the way of him graduating high school and having the necessary energy to take on the challenges of each day. Julian's father shared his resistance to the idea of medication and how he believed many boys of color were overmedicated in an attempt to just "get them to behave." I empathized with his concerns and acknowledged the historical legacy of generations of African Americans and other minority folks being experimented on with new medications and treatments, and how this had led to undue mental anguish because of profound adverse side effects. However, I stressed that an antidepressant could help give Julian a boost of energy and reduce some of his anxiety to help him reach his goals of succeeding in community college, and I reminded Julian's father that it would not be a prescription for the rest of his life.

After explaining the numerous treatment ideas and educational accommodations that his son deserved and qualified for, his father thanked me for including him in the process. As I departed I handed Julian's father a letter based on the test results and assessment process. The feedback letter highlighted his son's strengths and current needs and how this related to his hopes, dreams and fears for Julian. As the guard escorted me out to the exit of the prison it began to set in how much I appreciated Julian's father's presence in this assessment process. He now appeared to have a deeper level of empathy for his son and was holding the treatment recommendations in mind in hopes of following up with Julian and encouraging him to seek out the supports. When I had initially started this case, I did not think it would be possible to apply the collaborative model in a prison setting, but I had been greatly mistaken.

The feedback meeting in prison with Julian's father had led to a small yet significant shift in his deepening awareness of his son's needs and strengths. In contrast, presenting the results to Julian himself felt like a far less daunting task. In my meeting with Julian, it quickly became apparent that the sheer volume of feedback was emotionally and cognitively overwhelming. Given Julian's current depression, it was very difficult for him to focus on and process all of the findings. I attempted to present the key findings in very short, abbreviated phrases to not overwhelm his poor working memory. At a certain point, Julian appeared to have a glazed look come over his face as he continued to nod and intermittently respond with "okay, okay" as he listened to me describe his learning and emotional challenges. I explained how it made a lot of sense why school had been so difficult. Julian was slower to make sense of visual information, remember and organize new class information, and accurately hear all of what he heard around him in class. Cumulatively, these challenges led Julian to feel paralyzed and confused at times as he attempted to take in new learning.

I felt like I was on the verge of losing him, as my words went in one ear and right out the other. I imagined that Julian might have felt that I was taking a magnifying glass to his psychic wounds and putting them on full display. I sensed that Julian was grappling with profound shame, and that he may have even been questioning whether I was suggesting that he was weak, as I explained his diagnoses. Therefore, I stopped. I then turned to Julian and exclaimed, "You know, I think this is too much information right now. I am going to let you read it and write down any questions you have later on. But for right now, I just want you know how impressed I am with how strong you are." I went on to use a soldier analogy of returning from war, and I explained that in his neighborhood the war never really ends.

What I wanted more than anything was for Julian to see how determined and resilient he was. He was so driven to reach his career goals, despite his depression, traumas, and learning challenges. I told Julian that he inspired me, and that I believed he could live one day without being haunted by the fear of being attacked. We discussed finding him a therapist and how this professional could help him with becoming desensitized to real and perceived threats in his environments. I explained how Eye Movement Desensitization and Reprocessing (EMDR; van der Kolk, 2014) could be a treatment that decreases his PTSD and how we could find him a therapist through Victims of Crime, a

California state-funded mental health service for citizens victimized during a reported crime. We discussed all of the accommodations he qualified for while attending junior college that could help him reach his initial goal of getting an associate degree. These accommodations included:

1   A laptop with speech-to-text software as well as the use of other students' notes, given his deficits in auditory processing, working memory, and processing speed.
2   Access to the Fast ForWord neuroplasticity program to help improve his reading fluency and comprehension.
3   Seating at the front of the class close to the teacher when they are engaged in verbal instruction.
4   An academic counselor to help co-create mini-deadlines on large projects, given his difficulty with planning and organizing and help break complex problems into component parts.

At the end of our session, Julian smiled and gave me a firm handshake exclaiming, "Thank you so much for all your help." I, too, was extremely thankful to Julian for the opportunity to work together, as Julian had taught me more than he will ever know about the realities of Oakland and being a young man of color trying to navigate through the chaos and danger to reach one's dreams.

Closing Thoughts

Although Dr. Finn's model of therapeutic assessment was originally designed for application with largely White, middle, and upper class families in Texas, it can be adapted to work effectively with urban youth of color that come from extremely disadvantaged backgrounds and are surrounded daily by community violence. The process of methodically gathering the presenting concerns of Julian and his parents regardless of how difficult it was to gain access to meeting together proved invaluable. The spirit of collaboration seems even more essential when conducting psychological testing as a member of the dominant culture with economically disadvantaged families of color that experience countless forms of racial oppression.

Dr. Finn's model of psychological testing invites the participants to share their perspectives, hopes, and fears within the process. It beckons the psychologist to sit with families as human to human, and honor their insights and their questions for the assessment (Finn, 2007). This approach can help foster trust and begin to build rapport and investment in the process, especially when cultural mistrust often looms large from the outset of the testing process with a White assessor treating a family with a different cultural background. The application of therapeutic assessment to urban, underserved youth of color seems more than just applicable, but essential to help empower and give voice to the family's experience, insights, and cultural realities. This model can lead to a deeper level of cultural trust, family investment in the process, and integration of test findings that lead to lasting therapeutic change for the child and their family.

In environments like Oakland where vast disparities in the distribution of economic resources more often than not are divided along racial lines, it seems of paramount importance for community psychologists who come from different experiences and backgrounds to listen to the voices of our clients and collaborate with families of color during the testing process.

References

Barona, A. & Miller, J. A. (1994) The Short Acculturation Scale for Hispanic youth. *Hispanic Journal of Behavioral Sciences, 16*, 155–162.

Briere, J. (2011). *Trauma Symptom Inventory-2, professional manual.* Odessa, FL: Psychological Assessment Resources.

Conners, C. K. & MHS Staff. (Eds.). (2000). *Conners' Continuous Performance Test II: Computer program for Windows technical guide and software manual.* North Tonawanda, NY: Multi-Health Systems.

Exner, J. E., Jr. (1993). *The Rorschach: A comprehensive system, vol. 1: Basic foundations* (3rd ed.). New York, NY: John Wiley & Sons, Inc.

Finn, S. E. (2007). *In our clients' shoes: Theory and techniques of therapeutic assessment.* Mahwah, NJ: Erlbaum.

Hardy, K. V. (2013). Healing the hidden wounds of racial trauma. *Reclaiming Children and Youth, 22*(1), 24–28.

Heaton, R. K., Chelune, G. J., & Talley, J. L. (1993). *Wisconsin Card Sorting Test manual.* Odessa, FL: Psychological Assessment Resources, Inc.

Keith, R. W. (2009). *SCAN-3: A test for auditory processing disorders in adolescents and adults.* Upper Saddle River, NJ: Pearson Publications.

Lord, C., & Rutter, M. D., et al. (2012). *Autism Diagnostic Observation Schedule, Second Edition.* Torrence, CA: Western Psychological Association.

Luxenberg, T., Spinazzola, J., & van der Kolk. B. A. (2001). Complex trauma and disorders of extreme stress (DESNOS) diagnosis, part I: Assessment. *Directions in Psychiatry*, Vol. 21 (pp. 373–393). Long Island City, NY: The Hatherleigh Company, Ltd.

Saez, P. A., Bender, H. A., Barr, W. B., Rivera Mindt, M. K., Morrison, C. E., Hassenstab, J., Rodriguez, M., & Vasquez, B. (2013). The impact of education and acculturation on nonverbal neuropsychological test performance among Latino/a patients with epilepsy. *Applied Adult Neuropsychology,* 21(2), 108–119.

Rutter, M. & Bailey, A., et al. (2003) *Social Communication Questionnaire (SCQ).* Torrence, CA: Western Psychological Corporation.

van der Kolk, B. (2014). *The body keeps the score.* New York: Viking.

Wechsler, D. (2008). *Wechsler Adult Intelligence Scale–Fourth Edition* (WAIS-IV). San Antonio, TX: Psychological Corporation.

Wechsler, D. (2009). *Wechsler Individual Achievement Test–Third Edition* (WIAT-III). San Antonio, TX: Psychological Corporation.

18 Liberating the Butterfly Boy

Engaging the Family and System in the Therapeutic Assessment of a Traumatized and Gender-Nonconforming Child

Lisa A. Greenberg

> Your generation, your culture, views us transgenders as so different. My friends don't care, it's just not as big an issue as you think. I am who I am.
>
> A former M-to-F transgender client's response to
> questions about her gender-nonconforming identity

The therapeutic assessor's mandate varies with every assessment. In some assessments, the goal is to uncover the uniqueness in a child's developmental and/or emotional profile. In others, the emphasis might be on helping the parent come to terms with, or even recognize his or her impact on, the child. In others, the hope is to collaborate with and engage supports in the school or community. In most community mental health assessments, the true mandate involves a combination of *uncovering* and *communicating* the child's profile in order to *advocate* for his or her needs. To do so successfully, the therapeutic assessor must identify the true mandate of the assessment (not always evident from the referral questions) as well as the barriers to achieving this mandate. This chapter illustrates the power of therapeutic assessment as an advocacy tool that builds on an accurate understanding of the child's profile and collaboration with community and educational supports to promote an atmosphere of acceptance in the family system, and, thereby, set the stage for the child to return to a positive developmental path.

For "Jael,"[1] a 6-year-old boy of Latino descent, identifying the real questions and barriers for the therapeutic assessment was critical. Though Jael was referred in order to uncover the reasons for his poor school performance and the impact of recent traumas, the mandate for his therapeutic assessment was much broader. Jael was gender-different and living in a family that was critical of his gender identity. His family (mother, sister, maternal aunt, and aunt's husband) were recent immigrants from Guatemala, who spoke little to no English. Additionally, Jael's mother was intellectually disabled with a history of trauma, both of which undermined her parenting and raised questions as to her custodial capacity. Because of this, Jael, his sister, and mother, were required to live in the family of his aunt and uncle, who also rejected his gender presentation. Their concerns came through in their questions for the assessment: "Why is he scared of everything? Why does he not listen at school and home? And why does he walk on his toes, and how can we fix it?" Thus, the mandate for the assessment expanded from one of diagnosing the child's school problems to educating and shifting the perspective of the family so they could better understand, accept, and parent Jael.

Jael's history and test findings reveal a combination of factors not uncommon to community mental health and foster children of compromised early caregiving and greater exposure to violence. However, a few moments with him also highlights the resilience of this sweet and intelligent child. Jael was born a year after his mother, "Ms. Garcia," immigrated to the United States to live with her sister. He had no contact with his biological father, who returned to Central America before his birth. Jael, his mother, and later his younger sister by another father lived intermittently on their own or in the home of Ms. Garcia's sister. While on their own, Jael and his sister were exposed to periods of neglect and inadequate supervision. Several times, he and his sister, both under 4 years of age, were found wandering the streets on their own. They were exposed nightly to horror films (e.g., *Chuckie*, *Halloween*), and only attended school sporadically. Jael also experienced and witnessed physical and sexual abuse at the hands of his mother's boyfriend. Jael's teacher made a Child Protective Services (CPS) report when she observed cuts on his face, which led to deportation of the boyfriend, temporary placement of Jael and his sister in foster care, and reunification with their mother under the provisional condition that the family live with the maternal aunt's family. To facilitate successful reunification with his mother, Jael's CPS worker sought out this assessment, arranged for Jael to participate in weekly psychotherapy, and began exploring supports for his mother through Regional Center services.

Jael met early developmental milestones on time, though following his traumatization he experienced frequent bladder and bowel accidents through 6 years of age. He was afraid of many things (i.e., noises, insects, doctors, and strangers), had poor attention at home and school, and, according to his aunt and uncle, was not responsive to discipline.

I met with Jael, a small, slender child with straight dark hair and large brown eyes, at his public school, in a small electronics room tucked between several offices. He was notably on edge. We often heard heaters humming, doors slamming, or electrical systems rebooting, to which Jael responded wide-eyed, with gasps of surprise and wonderings as to what might have caused the sounds, or how could they be stopped. Disturbing thoughts and images frequently interrupted his thinking, such as when he drew birds "that like to eat bloody worms." He spontaneously described stories about ghosts, swords, or Bigfoot. He avoided any talk of unpleasant topics, which took the form of difficulty getting words out, blending fantasy with reality, an inability to sequence events, and physical agitation while talking. He rejected many of the projective tests, including some Rorschach cards, getting through them by standing and leaning his body against mine as he worked. He typically responded to triggering items by talking and moving quickly, or withdrawing, struggling to cope with the surge of feelings that arose in him. His history, behavior, and the family- and self-ratings on trauma symptom inventories confirmed the presence of all symptom clusters of active Post-Traumatic Stress Disorder (PTSD).

Jael sized me up pretty quickly, figuring I was a friend and confidante—a "BFF," as he referred to me in our second session—rather than foe to his gender-different interests. Early in our time together, he watched my response closely as he asked to draw his favorite animal, the butterfly. He observed me as he suggested putting ribbons in my hair, then in his. By the second visit, he asked me to adjust his sweatshirt so it hung like a skirt from his waist, then he twirled with his arms outstretched and exclaimed, "Now, I'm the lunch lady!" From that point forward, he would enter sessions, adjust his clothing, decorate his hair, and look at me to start the day's activities. He dutifully and poignantly undid this metamorphosis at the end of each visit, already attuned to the demands of the conventional world for his conformity.

Jael's sensitivity to others was not just a function of hypervigilance but also because of his caring and gentle soul. Both teachers and peers adored him, and his friends turned to him first when upset or needing help with a conflict. This thoughtfulness and warmth was immediately apparent in our sessions. When I happened to strike my leg on a child-sized desk in our little testing room, Jael responded by grabbing a napkin, running around the desk, and patting my knee. At such a young age, he was already well-versed in caring for an adult's wounds.

The testing, conducted in Spanish and English (Jael's English was stronger in both formal testing and conversation), identified cognitive abilities in the average range, a source of great relief to Ms. Garcia, but problems in attention and information processing (working memory, visual processing), and below grade-level academic skills. Confounding all of these information-processing challenges was the fact that Jael had a very difficult time engaging in and sustaining moments of learning. In another child with a different history, these cognitive findings could easily have been attributed to a diagnosis of Attention Deficit Hyperactivity Disorder (ADHD), Combined Type (DSM-IV TR at the time) and possibly a learning disorder. But for Jael, this would have ignored the considerable impact of neglect, recent trauma, and their sequelae on his cognitive and academic functioning.

Thus, the assessment drew out the ways in which the absence of safety and consistent early nurturance undermined Jael's ability to build joint attention and curiosity, self-soothe, or sustain effort in hard tasks. Furthermore, his recent trauma exposure, coupled with the ongoing experience of being punished for his gender differences, elicited persistent hypervigilance and fear, and took a toll on Jael's ability to concentrate and turn to the age-appropriate task of learning. His brain was still doing the work of ensuring safety, triggered by a cacophony of both real and unreal threats. Thus, the treatment focus for Jael, outlined in the first part of the treatment plan, was to put a stop to any ongoing traumatization, treat the symptoms of PTSD, and stabilize the parenting system; then, once his trauma symptoms subsided, take another look at his attention and learning profile.

While this clear formulation of Jael's profile was an essential first step in ensuring that the assessment was therapeutic, the critical therapeutic work involved helping Jael and his family understand his needs, demystify his gender nonconformity, and shift the parenting dynamics. In a sequence of feedback meetings, I was able to share the comprehensive report with the family, school staff, the CPS social worker, psychotherapist, and his mother's Regional Center case worker, conveying Jael's character and cognitive strengths in addition to the impact of trauma on his learning, behavior, persistent fears, and limited coping resources. The report and ensuing feedback also explored the many cultural and gender identity issues that strained the family's ability to establish a value system that embraced Jael's identity differences.

These collaborative feedback meetings were particularly effective in marshalling the team of school and service providers to better understand and address Jael's needs. For example, in sharing the findings to the mother's Regional Center caseworker, she was then able to shadow Ms. Garcia at home and teach her safe and appropriate parenting practices. Similarly, Jael's therapist incorporated more family work with Jael's mother and caseworker to strengthen intimacy, nurturing, as well as attunement to Jael's trauma symptoms. The school affirmed Jael's eligibility for counseling and individualized educational supports, and established a two-year plan in which he would remain with his current teacher—a talented and compassionate advocate for Jael. Thus, providing a comprehensive picture of Jael's profile and needs to school and service providers laid the foundation for long-term change, as this family would not have been able to absorb and transform the findings into new parenting practices on their own.

Because a full understanding of Jael's functioning was complex and emotionally difficult for a parent or caregiver to take in, I conveyed the findings to his family in a series of answers to *their* questions (summarized in Spanish), that is, sharing his cognitive and information processing profile in response to their concerns about learning, his fears and trauma symptoms in the context of his agitation at home, and his gender identity differences in answer to their worries about his toe-walking. And while these and other discussions helped the family to *understand* Jael and his behaviors, it was the moment of sharing Jael's feedback story about a many-colored butterfly boy that helped the family *feel* his subjective experience, which was most instrumental in shifting the family dynamics.

Feedback stories, composed by assessors, are a key part of the therapeutic assessment. They are written for the child, designed to share developmentally appropriate information that is most relevant to each child. Feedback stories honor the child's own investment in the assessment process, as well as his or her ability to grow with greater self-understanding. Feedback to younger children often builds on a metaphor, such as a favorite animal or mythical creature. It plays out the child's profile of strengths and weaknesses in the form of a story. The use of feedback stories can be preferable to a direct discussion of the child's cognitive or emotional difficulties, because a direct approach may trigger a young child and make it difficult to integrate the feedback into their self-understanding. Furthermore, sharing the findings in the form of a compelling plotline carries greater emotional valence and explores the child's subjective perspective. These latter features of the feedback story—describing the child's internal and emotional experiences—drew the strongest reactions from Jael's mother, aunt, and uncle.

Jael introduced his story metaphor—the butterfly—early on during testing, somehow intuiting his own similarities to the animal's gentleness, fragility, beauty, and ability to metamorphose. The story described the butterfly boy's strengths: his sweet nature, sociability, and bright mind. It then delved into the challenges he was facing: how abuse at the hands of a bad man caused him to have fears, including a fear of showing his real butterfly colors. As the story progressed, the butterfly boy eventually learned, with the support of his mother and other special "helpers" in his life, how to cope with his challenges by talking with safe people in his life and calming his body, rather than retreating into his cocoon. The story ended with the theme of acceptance of the butterfly boy—that "there were lots of ways and colors for a butterfly boy to be," inviting Jael and other readers to color a large white butterfly any way they'd like. For Jael, this theme of acceptance came up the moment he entered the testing room and was allowed to be as feminine or masculine as he wanted. Had the issue remained in the testing room, however, it could have reinforced the idea that such behavior should stay behind closed doors. Indeed, by sharing this story jointly with Jael, his mother and family, and key "helpers" in his life, Jael had the experience of feeling safe in showing his true colors to his loved ones.

The feedback story had a similarly liberating effect on Jael's mother, aunt, and uncle. Each family member used the story's theme of acceptance to share his or her greatest fears about Jael and his gender variance. For the first time in the assessment process, Jael's mother became tearful. She seemed to understand the impact of trauma on her son's persistent anxieties, recognizing in herself the feeling of perpetual readiness for danger. Her welling up of compassion seemed to trigger her nurturing instincts, as she reached out and put an arm around Jael as he shared his story.

The butterfly boy's relief in being able to be any color he wanted triggered old wounds for Jael's mother and her sister. For the first time in the assessment process, they revealed that they had a brother who, because he was gay, was cut off from their childhood family. They admitted that their brother's experience caused them to worry for Jael. I wondered with them whether they were in some way following their parents' lead in chastising Jael for his gender differences. Jael's uncle raised his suspicion that sexual abuse may have contributed to Jael's gender differences since, according to the uncle, Jael changed after his trauma. I explained that research did not support this claim and that most gender-varied children were never abused. The uncle raised the dilemma of being caught between an ethic of "Latino Machismo" and Jael's decidedly "un-macho" behavior; it was hard for him to accept Jael. We approached this from many perspectives—discussing what was hard about it for each of the adults, the impact of rejection on Jael's development and sense of self, and ultimately, that we all do "hard" things in our life, particularly when it is in the service of our children. The family was able to see that rejection and punishment actually fueled Jael's fears and agitation, and undermined his ability to develop a coherent sense of self. We discussed how punishment for such behaviors could cause Jael to "go underground" in his gender expression and further withdraw from his mother and relatives.

The uncle, ever the pragmatist, asked how the family should respond when Jael wanted to play "girl" games in the home or go out in public in dresses. Together with the Regional Center caseworker and Jael's therapist, we laid out different choices that parents make along a continuum from restrictive to permissive in how the child dresses and presents, with some families making a distinction between how the child can behave in public versus private settings. We applauded the family's open dialogue as to how to parent to Jael's gender differences. We arranged for his mother, accompanied by a full-time translator, to attend a weeklong transgender conference for children and parents, and to continue family discussion about parenting practices as she learned more.

The therapeutic assessment by no means solved all of this child's problems. He and his mother, had many, many hurdles before them. But their ability to learn and shift in response to the therapeutic assessment and feedback went far beyond what I had hoped. At the outset of the assessment, it was not clear that Ms. Garcia (or her relatives) had the parenting skills or nurturing instincts to care for her son. But as the supportive services around the family grew and provided needed scaffolding for the family, Jael and his family were better able to make use of the therapeutic assessment. Furthermore, the severity of Jael's traumatic stress together with his already subdued gender differences pointed to a much broader mandate for therapeutic intervention than the original referral question about school problems. Jael needed more than understanding, he needed an advocate to make the case for change so that he could find safety, acceptance, and love. Thus, the assessment incorporated an extensive and collaborative feedback process to ensure that systemic supports were in place to guide Jael and his family in the long-term and engage the family in new ways of parenting. In short, the assessment actively engaged the family, school, and broader community to help build a much stronger structure for Jael to feel safe and rest his beautiful butterfly wings.

Note

1   Androgynous names are extremely rare in Latino cultures; in fact, "Jael" is one of only a handful I could find.

19 Living with Danger

Complex Trauma, Attachment, and Repair in Oakland, California

Barbara L. Mercer and Kevin Bunch

The following narrative of a 15-year-old African American girl, Sasha, being raised in foster care from age 10 in Oakland, while extreme in some respects, typifies the lives of girls in a transitional age youth program working with sexually exploited minors. The trajectory of early neglect, rejection, foster care, and adoption are typical of many adolescent clients in an economically deprived urban area. Dr. Kevin Bunch saw Sasha in therapy for three years. During her therapy, she also met with a case manager for a program working with girls at risk for sexual exploitation. Following a referral from her therapist, I met with Sasha and her adoptive mother Miriam to complete a psychological assessment. Sasha's psychological profile reveals how her depression, behaviors, and attachments are a reflection of her early maternal abandonment and witness to domestic violence and substance abuse. These complex developmental traumas are expressed in Sasha's projective testing material: the Rorschach (Rorschach, 1942), the Roberts Apperception Test (McArthur & Roberts, 1982), projective drawings (H-T-P; Buck, 1966), the Early Memory Procedure (Bruhn, 1992), and the Attachment Projective Picture System (George, West & Pettem, 1997–2007); they show Sasha's challenging task of attaching to a new caretaking figure (herself a trauma survivor) while continuing to identify with her biological mother, along with her drive to master trauma and relationships as an acting out and sexually exploited minor. Her therapy relationship with Dr. Bunch demonstrates the tenuous nature of trust and the balance of tolerance, engagement, and confrontation it takes to allow therapy to happen. Her work with her case manager illuminates another side of Sasha's sexual life and behavior that she at times displays openly or alternately keeps hidden due to shame.

Sasha's psychological struggle is a paradigm of youth growing up in an urban neighborhood where crime, poverty, discrimination, lack of supports, intergenerational trauma, and caretaker neglect offer a child's primary growth environment. The concept of complex developmental trauma, or Developmental Trauma Disorder, is a recent construct in the literature (van der Kolk, 2005). Exposure to multiple traumas, according to the work of Cheryl Lanktree and John Briere (2012, 2013) is often associated with those experiencing social marginalization, homelessness, commercial sexual exploitation, and community violence. While our description of her therapy and the raw material of her psychological assessment force us to face the visceral details of her trauma, in the face of this trauma is a design of what it takes to work through some of these deeper issues and move forward in life.

Oakland, California is almost a country in itself. In 2012, Oakland was listed as the third most dangerous city in the US with 1683 violent crimes and 26 murders per 100 thousand people (Fisher, 2012). Oakland's high levels of poverty and proximity to drug corridors continue to generate these problems. East Oakland, where Sasha grew up, was "once a flourishing middle class community. Changing land-use policies caused an exodus of industry and commerce that residents relied on, leaving more liquor stores, check-cashing agencies, tattoo parlors, and fast food businesses. The realities of life for youth in East Oakland are sobering. More than 40 percent of local young people are not enrolled in school. The rate of teen pregnancies is three times that of the county, and the murder rate is seven times higher than the national average" (Youth Uprising 2011). The clinic where Sasha comes for therapy is adjacent to the BART train station, where a 22-year-old father Oscar Grant was killed by a BART policeman using a real gun instead of a Taser gun to arrest him. Children and mothers of children are frequently killed by random drive-by shootings, and several of our clients or their relatives have been accidentally (and often purposefully) gunned down in the wake of drug and gang attacks.

Youth Uprising, a multiservice program in health, education, culture, and arts for Oakland youth, report that even with decades of disinvestment in the community, an unemployment rate twice that of the city, and half of households earning less than $30,000, "East Oakland is a resilient community where residents are active in organized groups, multi-cultural programs, youth agencies, and faith organizations, and families who have lived for generations in the neighborhood" (Retrieved from http://www.youthuprising. org). The Boulevard near Sasha's home (and our clinic) is called International Boulevard and reflects Oakland's multiethnic, multicultural citizens with more than 90 ethnicities and more than 100 spoken languages (Kemet, 2010).

Oakland is frequently a featured story in the San Francisco newspaper. A series about African American boys in the *San Francisco Chronicle* (Tucker, 2013), noted that among 600 African American boys starting high school in 2009, 80 to 100 were expected to graduate college-ready for the University of California system, with another 200 expected to graduate without meeting UC college requirements. Against this backdrop, school officials became the first in the nation to create a department with the sole focus of helping African American males (the African American Male Achievement Office) while sponsoring a charter school specifically for black boys. (Tucker, 2013).

Caille Millner, a *San Francisco Chronicle*, columnist described Oakland as "stumbling between potholes of greatness and misery" (Millner, 2013). In a *Chronicle* article about Juneteenth in 2013, JB Westbrooks described his 1939 journey from Jasper County, Texas, to Oakland (Jones, 2013). Part of the great Southern diaspora, JB got a well-paying job with the railroad and he and his wife, Florida Vidalia, raised five kids in West Oakland. When JB's son Malcolm was a kid, Seventh Street had theatres and nice clothing stores, upscale restaurants and groceries. The creeks were clean and safe. Everyone knew each other:

> Everyone was Miss Somebody or Aunt Somebody, even if they weren't your blood, … We could leave home in the morning and be home by dusk, and it was totally safe. … These people pulled off stuff against almost insurmountable odds, … They were tough, and they were smart. We are descended from great people, and it's important we remember that.
>
> (Jones, 2013)

Sasha's Background

Sasha's foster mother, who became her adoptive mother, "Auntie" Miriam, herself a trauma survivor, ran a transitional recovery home for substance abusers. Sasha's mother, Amber, was admitted five months pregnant with Sasha. Sasha's father had probably been her mother's pimp. Miriam helped Amber clean up and get her life back together. Almost at full term, Amber left and got high. Sasha was born tox-positive for cocaine. For the next ten years, Miriam assisted Amber with money, support services, welfare-to-work program, college, and child care. Amber continued to struggle with drugs and domestic violence, including the subjection of Sasha's younger brother to severe sexual abuse by cousins. The two children witnessed many horrible domestic violence scenes, including sexual activity and beatings with the mother's boyfriend trying to throw Amber feet first out of a second story window. The children were terrorized, too, and at one point the boyfriend told them he was going to kill them all. The mother made the children "pinky swear" not to tell Miriam any of this, but when the children returned to Miriam's house, she interrogated them and they broke down crying in front of her. Even after this, it was five more years before the children were placed in Miriam's stable home. With the help of Child Protective Services, Miriam became a certified foster parent for both children. One year prior to this assessment, she adopted the two children and soon after brought them to therapy. The therapy will be narrated by Dr. Bunch. The assessment will be described by Dr. Mercer.

Sasha's Therapy: Kevin

The initial stages of therapy set the stage for how the relationship can grow, but it is in the later stages where the youth experiences more security and can express conflict, dissatisfaction, or anger. Traumatized youth have difficulties with attachment and regulation and do not anticipate that relationships are collaborative or supportive. Many "tests" or challenges were introduced into the relationship, some of which were passed while others were not. I noted, "At times I find myself thinking I have done a good job, at other times, I feel I don't know what I am doing". Those are the times that Sasha communicates to me in a more visceral manner (in the psychoanalytic literature known as projective identification) one in which I experience the emotions that Sasha is unable to hold herself. In these times I feel hopeless to help Sasha change her life. If we both end up stuck we will not be able to move forward. Even in later stages of our work, when I was exploring my continued hope for Sasha in her education, she explained to me that it was helpful for me to communicate the hope at the times she doesn't have it.

Despite differences, Sasha let me enter her world: a Caucasian male in his mid-thirties—who, despite difficulties in upbringing and identity, did not grow up in an impoverished community riddled with violence—engaging with an African American female teen who faced poverty, discrimination, community violence, and danger.

We began our work when Sasha was 12 years old. She was isolating herself, sitting in the dark ruminating about her life and crying. She wanted to run away from home despite being adopted by her aunt a year earlier. She had conflicting feelings about her aunt despite her happiness of being adopted, but feared the connection would destroy her relationship with her biological mother. She did not think she was worthy of being loved and expressed a deep feeling of internal damage and defectiveness. Sasha vacillated between being vulnerable in sessions to being guarded and defensive. The vacillation served a purpose to enable Sasha to keep herself from becoming too overwhelmed.

I introduced a discussion of our differences, particularly in race and gender. Sasha minimized the differences in race, but did speak to differences in gender that were awkward, particularly in discussing sexuality. Sasha's internal representations of herself were negatively impacted by her traumatic experiences. Sasha internalized the abandonment from her biological family as something she had done wrong. She stated, "I hate my mom. My mom is so black. I hate black people. Black people are so ghetto." I explored her thoughts around race and privilege. Her first therapy collage relating to being Black had themes of violence, drug use, conflicted relationships, absent male role models, and low self worth. Her collage of perceptions of "White" involved money, an intact family, and more power. In therapy, we discussed issues of body image and music through Tupac's lyrics of "Keep Your Head Up," the message that African American women face adversity and should be treated with respect and be proud of their heritage. Sasha revealed for the first time her desire to have a man beat and control her. We discussed race, culture, and poverty and their relationship through the medium of rap music. Sasha began to identify positive traits about herself and a decrease in depressive symptoms, and she joined a Black Student Union at her school. Still she began engaging in self-harm and cutting behaviors, particularly following failures of her mother to follow through with visits. She experimented with drugs, engaged in a chat line, and reported having sex with an older man. In therapy, she began discussing past traumas and connecting her mother's past abuse by boyfriends, with her own desire to be hit, "kept in line," but then given an apology. She was engaging in more risky behaviors, possibly being sexually exploited, and finally made a suicide attempt through an overdose.

Psychological Assessment: Barbara

Kevin referred Sasha for a Therapeutic Assessment a few months following the crisis of Sasha's attempted suicide and a hospital stay of two weeks. She was oppositional with Miriam, seeking relationships with older men, and she had once disappeared for several days and reported later being drugged and sexually assaulted by an older boy. Miriam was further disturbed by an incident where a boy dragged Sasha around by her hair at a summer camp. Sasha did not tell the counselors, and later said, "My mom's boyfriend always hit her and she never cared, so why should I?" Both Kevin and Miriam wanted to know the cause and level of seriousness of Sasha's depression. Miriam wanted to know, "How can I parent Sasha? Why does she make herself the victim? How can I not get angry when she is disrespectful? How can I help her separate her anger at her mother from her anger at me?"

Sasha asked, "Why are my boyfriends always cheating on me?" (she often told her therapist that she enjoyed being hurt by boys and it made her feel wanted); "Why did my daddy leave me?"; and, "Why am I depressed? Will I hurt myself?" The hope we had was to understand the level of Sasha's depression and to help Miriam find ways to be closer and navigate her parenting of Sasha.

Their questions get to the heart of Sasha's problems with attachment and trauma as they speak to her ambivalence and dismissiveness of a new caring parent, her feelings of abandonment, and her disorganized self-destructive behavior with older boys. Dr. Stephen

Finn worked with Miriam to gather history, frame questions, and begin some assessment, while I, Barbara, did the assessment with Sasha. In the adolescent model of Therapeutic Assessment, in reflecting the task of adolescent development, one assessor works separately with the parent while the other works with the youth who can have private questions if desired. One of the goals in involving Miriam in the assessment is bringing in the test data to help her understand Sasha's depression and her developmental struggles.

In her therapy and during the assessment, Sasha vacillated between being minimizing, avoidant, and dissociative, and on the other hand, insightful and intensely expressive of her emotional experience. Living with her now adoptive mother, Auntie Miriam and having access to a better educational environment, she was capable of doing well in school. Her cognitive scores were average, her comprehension scores even superior. Her results suggested that her environment with Miriam supported her learning. Yet Sasha was having trouble concentrating in school, and her grades were declining. During the assessment, she told me about being one of the few African American girls in her classroom. When I wondered with her about this experience, she did not choose to discuss it further—not so surprising with a White clinician she barely knew. With her therapist, she reported a wish to be in a White family because African American families had drug problems and were violent. This sense of herself was reflected in her self-report Millon Adolescent Clinical Inventory (Millon, 1993) profile, with elevated self-demeaning tendencies and body disapproval, suggesting a negative self-image in a cultural context as a young African American female. She denied depressive symptoms on the Beck Depression Inventory, but endorsed suicidal items on the MACI.

Miriam, or Auntie's, own history played into their relationship. She herself was born to a teenage mother, and had assumed the role of holding it together for the family, to be a strong woman and caretaker in her community. Miriam had started her own artistic and spiritual program for African American women.

Sasha's biological mother was an intelligent woman capable of work and educational success who repeatedly pulled herself together and then slid back to drugs, victimization through domestic violence, and prostitution. Miriam was anxious and ambivalent about taking up the role of "mother" and struggling with whether to limit Sasha's involvement with her biological parent. While wanting to honor Sasha's biological mother, she often backed off from being the "real parent." In this context, if she anticipated rejection from Sasha, she too became dismissive of her own and Sasha's experience.

Assessment Results

Sasha's Rorschach showed a bright girl with a many strengths who intellectualizes to get through distress but who is overwhelmed nonetheless. She is insightful, reflective, yet highly vulnerable to emotional turmoil. Her coping style is to rely on herself; she tends to be a solo flyer and doesn't trust anyone to help her. She vacillates between being over-controlled and numbing herself, to reacting explosively. Her Rorschach reflected her over-control, yet her high score on a Depression Scale (Exner, 1993) and 5 MOR Scores convey how depressed she really is. Her Trauma Content Index is .61, against the normative sample of .06, and .33 in sexually abused women, and .55 in Dissociative disorders. With no evidence of psychosis or borderline diagnosis, her diagnosis was one of complex PTSD with severe depression.

Two themes were pervasive in her projective testing that I would like to stress: One was the intrusion of trauma into every story and response—what starts out as somewhat negative turns into something terrible. The second were issues around relationships and attachment.

Her themes in Rorschach content were rage and aggression, with strong flavors of suicidality and a struggle for balance. On Card I, she saw three people dancing, balancing on one person while the middle person tried to hold two figures together. Sasha looked for cooperation but it was in conflict. Her suicidal feeling was reflected in images of spirits, heaven, hell, and on Card X, after describing so much violence and "hell," going to a happy place where there was peace. Isolation was viewed as difficult but protective. There was a constant pull between succumbing to pain or escaping it.

Here are some of her Rorschach responses:

Card III: "A mom and dad fighting over a little child in the middle trying to get custody. The child is in pain cuz they're pulling on it."

Card III. : "Two people drawn together by each other's pain."

Card IV: "A monster a little kid dreams up … it's very hairy it's all dark like a kid being chased in the dark … "

Card IV: "The man is like drunk or something he's yelling, his arms are out he's coming down trying to hit him, the little boy is in the corner."

Card VI: "Like a child being pulled into darkness and trying to stay strong and not let the darkness overcome them."

Card VII: "This looks like a girl she's looking in the mirror at herself trying to see who she is what's her purpose in life."

Card IX: "This looks like the devil, a type of evil spirit. It's really scary. It's looking for people to bring looking for someone he can trap."

On the Rorschach extended inquiry (when I asked her to tell a story about any of her responses) she could articulate clearly her dilemmas. I was repeatedly amazed at her ability to describe her turmoil so clearly. She said of Card III:

Well it's me in the middle and it's actually my Auntie and my biological mom. I can't pick between the two and I don't want to choose. If I choose my Auntie over my real mom, she took care of me 'til now … I don't know what I'm supposed to do, who I'm supposed to be. Like a part of me is a little girl who used to live with her real mom and the other part is the little girl who hurt who doesn't live with her real mom.

Here are two Roberts cards with themes of powerlessness, anger, confusion, sexual exploitation, fear, and no access to affection. There are card series for a variety of ethnicities; this series is from the African American series:

Card 5: "This is a little girl, she lives with her mom and her mom's boyfriend. She doesn't like any boyfriend. Wants her dad back. She feels that mom is paying more attention to her boyfriend choosing her boyfriend over her. So the girl ran away and a man chased her and picked her up and made her a prostitute. She looks like she's living on the street."

Card 13: "Oh this is about a girl and she's angry. She has anger problems gets mad really fast over the smallest stuff. Her mom told her to clean up the house. She got mad one time she broke a glass her grandma gave her. Her mom told her to clean up the house. She's mad and she threw things. Her mom called the police and now she's in juvie. Her mom doesn't want her back in the house so they will put her in foster care and stuff."

Her projective drawings (Buck, 1966) showed a girl who looked righteously mad; a family drawing where she is with Auntie and her brother on the beach—she said her mother didn't deserve to be in the picture because she never followed through; and a fantasy animal, part cat with a heart on her forehead and part porcupine, capturing the affectionate but prickly part of her desire for relationships.

Her Trauma Symptom Checklist (Briere, 2011) revealed significant dissociation with an emphasis on sexual preoccupations and dissociative fantasy: that is, daydreaming/avoidance and thinking of being someone else or someplace else.

The Early Memory Procedure (Bruhn, 1992), accesses a child's memories of unresolved parental issues. We could see that the intensity of Sasha's trauma was constant, with the need to keep at bay unbearable aloneness and loss. The beginnings of ambivalent attachment were illustrated here when she described her half brother taken away by his father, with no one to take her, when the loss of hope for connectedness and childhood was lost. She went through her formative years with no happy memories, with the first memory of love at age 9. In the hospital for a suicide attempt the idea of victimization comes to the fore, with her dramatic behaviors being a way she can be cared for. Her primary defense was her need to wall off her heart and her emotions. Her first memory of Auntie spoke to her cognition becoming confused and disorganized: "It was weird," she said.

Sasha's first Early Memory at five years old described her mother's boyfriend attempting to throw her mother through a second story window:

> I remember a time we had to go to the hospital for my mom. And her and her boyfriend was fighting and he threw her, and she kicked her leg through the window and had to get stitches on her ankle.

What is the clearest part of the memory?

> Hearing her foot go through the window and then her scream and then being in the hospital waiting for her.

What is the strongest feeling in the memory?

I was scared. I didn't know what had happened. And I was hecka young.

If you could change the memory in any way, what would that be?

Um, well, um I wouldn't want to remember it. I just wouldn't want to remember it.

Her second memory was when her brother's father came to their foster home and:

> took my brother away from me … that's when he wanted to go live with him. It was like on my seventh birthday with a little purple balloon in his hand and then he asked where my brother was and I told him. And then he told my brother to come in and then told him to get his clothes and then he took him to the car. And I ended up letting go of my balloon and it floated up. I was sad. And kind of mad too cuz he got to leave and I didn't want to be there anymore either and I didn't see why I couldn't go with him.

Her third memory was a good one: her ninth birthday with Auntie, when she received a bike for her birthday and had a slumber party: "I was just very happy, excited. I felt so loved that day. It was so awesome."

A good memory of her mother was of a time they went to the market and ate and spent the whole day together: "That was one of the best times with her. We had one of those smoothies … I was really happy. I was just happy. I'd like to do it again."

The Adult Attachment Projective developed by Carol George, Malcolm L. West and Odile Pettem (1997-2007) assesses the attachment system and has been used by Dr. George with adolescents (George & West, 2012). A study from the National Child Traumatic Stress Network found that 95 percent of the children exposed to complex trauma have an insecure attachment style with less or no support from their primary caretaker (NCTSN n.d.). Insecure attachments, as well as community trauma and violence, are trauma intensifiers in children. All can lead to many of the symptoms we see in our clients: emotional dysregulation, negative self-image, dissociation, and tension reduction behaviors, including self-injury, suicidal and sexual acting out, and sexual exploitation. The distressing result is often the struggle of establishing close and trusting relationships in adolescence and adulthood and the perpetuation of intergenerational trauma.

In Sasha's protocol, we saw a girl with Unresolved or Disorganized Attachments characterized by dysregulation behaviors and a secondary coping strategy of Disconnection in relationships—that is, defending against the pain of closeness by pulling away. Sasha's experience with her biological mother (reinforced by Sasha's biological mother's own history of attachments and relationships), led her not to expect comfort from her mother, or from anyone, even if it was offered.

In these attachment stimuli, there are both *Alone* (one figure in the stimulus) and *Dyadic* (two figures in the stimulus) representations.

In an Alone stimulus of a girl standing and looking out a window, connections are blocked and there is no one brought in to help the lonely girl. The girl ultimately goes into her room and closes her door. Her parents are dismissive and preoccupied. The girl

on the bench (Figure 19.1) waits for her mother who never comes and then the man
picks her up and she goes missing:

Figure 19.1 BENCH

So this one is about a little girl and she's all by herself and her mom 'sposed to come
pick her up but her mom never showed up so she just went to sit on this little bench
and started crying and it was really really late and then this man came along in his
car and um axed her if she was okay and then she didn't say anything to the man
cuz she didn't know him and then the man got out of the car and took her away
and then she was missing … she's feeling very hurt and disappointed that her mom
didn't come cuz this wasn't the first time her mom never showed up but this is the
first time her mom never actually just showed up at all and forgot all about her. She's
feeling very forgotten and like nobody cares.

For this girl, as well as the man grieving for his wife (CEMETERY, a stimulus of a man
in a graveyard), and the boy, the victim of his father (CORNER; Figure 19.2), there is
only the agency to either shut the door alone, for the man to go home and kill himself,
or for the boy to yell at the dad in vain not to kill him because he doesn't want to die:

Figure 19.2 CORNER

And he's yelling at his dad not to hit him and um that he didn't do anything wrong
and the dad is not listening and he's about to hit him and the little boy is really
scared and um the little boy's been in the hospital like three times already for like
broken bones and bruises and stuff because of what his dad did so the little boy's
scared for his life that his dad might actually kill him this time. He's just really scared
he's thinking he's praying that his dad doesn't end up killing him. He doesn't want to

die. And his dad does actually kill him and then the dad goes to jail for um he gets life in prison for child abuse and then murder.

There is no resolution to attachment in these stories.

In Dyadic stories, she told to stimuli of DEPARTURE, BED, and AMBULANCE (Figure 19.3); there is comfort, but the boy is inconsolable due to the death of his mother. The grandmother can comfort him briefly but is too old to keep him:

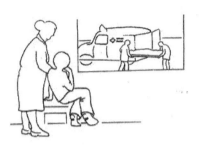

Figure 19.3 AMBULANCE

Okay so it's a little boy and his grandmother and they're at the little boy's house and he had just witnessed his um his mom being killed by his dad from she's been getting beaten from by him and by many nights for a long time and then finally the dad um had beat her too hard and hit her and he hit her so hard that she fell and um hit her head on the table and died. And so the little boy is very sad and um his grandma's over there to comfort him. And now the little boy has to go into foster care because his grandma is too old to take care of him … and wait to be adopted and he's very traumatized … he doesn't really understand what happened and he's scared cuz he doesn't know what's going to happen to him now. And um everybody's trying to comfort him and stuff and he just keeps crying and crying and then they take him to the foster home thing and he tries to run away cuz he doesn't understand like why he there and then um so then um, the police find him cuz he had run away … and then they took him back to the foster care and now he's um um under he has to be looked after like twenty-four seven so he won't try to run away or hurt hisself.

Reciprocal mutual enjoyment is melded with traumatizing events. The level of violence comes out of nowhere, and there are no connective links between experience and inner sense. In the Unresolved stories, the character's behaviors are dysregulated. The stories she tells are close to her life experiences, where social problems lead to drug abuse, domestic violence, prostitution, abandonment, and death.

Feedback and Follow-Up

In our feedback session with her therapist present, Sasha was overwhelmed and checked out. She didn't want to read the story I had written about an African princess named Malika who had two majestic mothers.

When she and her therapist finally read the story, she seemed confused and said, "What does this mean?" She was saying, as she said before, "I wish I didn't remember. I don't want to remember." Perhaps at this point, the story was more suited for her aunt. Five months following this assessment, Sasha said she no longer wanted therapy. Shortly before she terminated her therapy she was having significant conflict with her Auntie. She had run away, had been involved with an abusive boy whom she had told to beat her to keep her in line. She was seen on International Boulevard being hit by a purported pimp. She appeared to begin to hang out with people associated with gangs. A final event before termination was that she was robbed at gunpoint. This girl, with so many resources, was choosing to go it alone, to disconnect from those she had trusted. Her auntie, too, dropped out, and the family eventually moved out of Oakland.

The assessment in which she poured out the brutal parts of her experience were triggering of past trauma. While her therapist and the assessment process demonstrated attempts at understanding, support, and interest in aspects of her life outside her trauma experiences, the material flooded her and caused her further need to remove herself, to not have to think or remember. After beginning the assessment asking direct questions about her depression and self-abuse, by the end of the assessment she was reassuring us that she was "all better," no longer depressed. She was letting us know she didn't want to think about it anymore. The collage that she and Auntie did together in a Family Intervention session, combining images of strong African American women, promised only a fleeting elusive image of connection and feminine power.

Was the more positive relationship with her adoptive mother, her therapist, and the mirroring of her experience in the assessment enough to have any real impact? In this confusing picture, a girl began her life in a socially disadvantaged area, in a dope house, in poverty, with a mother who herself is marginalized and cannot take care of her, and where community violence and racial discrimination are the norm. Sasha was taken in and cared for—although it was, in her words, "weird" for her—by a strong woman who herself had suffered. At adolescence, her attachment needs re-surfaced and she longed for the mother she cannot have and sought relationships that mimicked her mother's self-destructive experience. Despite Sasha's intelligence, scholastic opportunities, capacity for friendships and relationships, and genuine engagement in treatment, these disorganized and traumatic attachments had their own life and pulled her away.

Therapy Second Phase: Kevin

Nine months following her termination, Sasha phoned me saying she wanted to return to therapy. She was again living in Oakland, where two of her friends had been murdered on the streets, and she was both fearful for her life, devastated by the loss, and afraid of further depression. This seemed like a genuine sign of Sasha's self-agency: that she was seeking comfort and activation in a nondestructive way from someone who would not hurt her, someone willing to understand, accept, and connect with her. What she said to me was simply, "I talk and you listen."

In this next phase of therapy, Sasha talked about fears for safety, worries about dying, and increased depression. She asked for the first time if I would be there for her when she turned 18. "I don't want to start this, and have you leave me in a year." With the new foster care bill passed in California, teens can be seen until 21. I assured her of our commitment to work with her. She expressed her desire to have therapy be for her alone, not for her family, her relief not to be judged, and to have a place to bring her feelings and "leave them here." We explored Sasha's desire to work with me on the deeper aspects of her trauma, yet there was reluctance to see herself as having been victimized because she didn't want to feel yet more powerless. In discussing this, we finally agreed on using the phrase, "That thing that happened to me." She continued to bring her relationship and sexual issues to therapy although she refused to work with her former case manager, or to think in terms of sexual exploitation. While some people working in the field of sexual exploitation believe that men should not work with sexually exploited girls, we trusted our relationship. I tried to approach the relationship with vulnerability and humility, not with an idea of being a rescuer. I asked if Sasha ever wondered about her views of being sexually exploited, and she talked about how she can determine trust in her relationships as well as others' intentions. I reiterated the therapist's role and boundaries.

She continued to sort through her difficult romantic relationships, her tendency to want to please her therapists, and her missing subsequent appointments. Although Sasha had developed more security in the therapy relationship, in times of need and crisis, she reverted to the dysregulated and insecure attachment style and had trouble accessing support. At the time of writing, she had disappeared, although texting continued to be a lifeline. I supposed she would return to therapy, yet I worried she would continue to expose herself to traumatic experiences. She wanted to show her therapist that she was "Okay." She had invited me to her high school graduation as a way of saying good-bye without having to terminate. She wanted to leave the door open. The emerging literature and research on sexually exploited minors has documented these phases of therapy and the repeated need to flee and then return to a safer haven (Rodarte 2013).

Conclusion

If we are to imagine change, we must listen to these repetitions of trauma and parenting tragedies from mother to daughter, not only as individual pathology but also as part of larger context of locale and community in our efforts to create greater equality in the emotional health of our citizens, and to hold the space and understanding in order to disavow that our kids are merely bad girls making bad choices. These rifts in relationships show us *in vivo* results of unresolved attachments and the desire for security, and in the context of community and generational trauma, how much time and effort it takes to begin to repair. If we cannot recognize these flights to danger as repeated attempts to master early parental rejections and to seek comfort that was originally tied to trauma rather than security, we, like the voice of an impatient society, ask why change does not happen more quickly. We must be witness to and tireless through the therapy relationship, the assessment data, and our growing knowledge about exploitation to begin to temper the wounds and give our traumatized youth a chance at productive lives.

214 *Barbara L. Mercer and Kevin Bunch*

References

Briere, J. (2011). *Trauma Symptom Inventory-2, professional manual.* Odessa, FL: Psychological Assessment Resources.
Bruhn, A. R. (1992). The Early Memories Procedure: A projective test of autobiographical memory: II. *Journal of Personality Assessment, 58*, 326–346.
Buck, J. N. (1966). *The House-Tree-Person Technique, revised manual.* Los Angeles: Western Psychological Services.
Exner, J. E. (1993). *The Rorschach: A comprehensive system, Vol 1: Basic foundations* (3rd ed.). New York: John Wiley & Sons, Inc.
Fisher, D. (October 18, 2012). Detroit tops the 2012 list of America's most dangerous cities. *Forbes.* Retrieved December 7, 2012. Retrieved from www.forbes.com/sites/danielfisher/2012/10/18/detroit-tops-the-2012-list-of-americas-most-dangerous-cities/.
George, C., West, M., & Pettem, O. (1997–2007). *The Adult Attachment Projective Picture System.* Unpublished coding and classification system, Mills College, Oakland, CA.
George, C. & West, M. L. (2012). *The Adult Attachment Projective Picture system.* New York: Guilford Press.
Jones, C. (2013) Recalling journey to promised land. *SF Chronicle*, June 15.
Kemet, M.O. (2010) Oakland B Mine. Oakland, CA, Runaway FilmworX, East West Productions
Lanktree, C. B., Breire, J., Godbout, N., Hodges, M., Chen, K., Trimm, L., Adams, B., Maida, C. A., & Freed, W. (2012). Treating multi-traumatized, socially marginalized children: Results of a naturalistic treatment outcome study. *Journal of Aggression, Maltreatment & Trauma, 21*(8), 813–828.
Lanktree, C.B. & Briere, J. (2013). Integrated treatment of complex trauma. In J.D. Ford and C.A. Courtois (Eds), *Treating complex traumatic stress disorders with children and adolescents: Scientific foundations and therapeutic models.* New York: Guilford Press.
McArthur, D. S. & Roberts, G. E. (1982). *Roberts Apperception Test for children: Manual.* Los Angeles: Western Psychological Services.
Millner, C. (2013) Staggering between greatness and misery. *SF Chronicle*, May 11.
Millon, T. (1993). *Millon Adolescent Clinical Inventory: Manual.* Minneapolis, MN: National Computer System.
NCTSN (National Child Traumatic Stress Network) (n.d.) Retrieved from http://www.nctsn.org.
Rodarte, A. (2013) Living with danger: Attachment, trauma and repair in Oakland. Paper presented at the Grand Rounds of West Coast Children's Clinic, Oakland, CA.
Rorschach, H. (1942). *Psychodiagnostics: A diagnostic test based on perception* (P. Lemkau & B. Kronenberg, Trans.). Berne, Switzerland: Huber (Originally published, 1921).
Tucker, J. (2013). Even-odds. *San Francisco Chronicle*, August 18–19, 2013.
van der Kolk, B. (2005). Developmental trauma disorder: Toward a relational diagnosis for children with complex trauma histories. *Psychiatric Annals, 35*, 401–408.
Youth Uprising (2011) East Oakland. Retrieved from http://www.youthuprising.org/issues-responses/east-oakland/

20 Shame

The Hidden Emotion with Tough Adolescents

Ankhesenamun Bal-Marioni

Adolescence is a complex time in any individual's life. Once characterized as a period of "storm and stress" by G. Stanley Hall (1904), many teens are faced with a plethora of burning questions, confusion about identity, and a strong desire to belong. They are learning to navigate the sting of intense emotions like rejection and shame. Shame, an innate emotional experience, underlies some of the complex choices and emotional turmoil that affect most teens (Lewis, 1971; Tangney & Dearing, 2002). Silvan Tomkins (1963, p. 351) described shame in this way:

> If distress is the affect of suffering, shame is the affect of indignity, of defeat, of transgression and of alienation … . While terror and distress hurt, they are wounds inflicted from outside which penetrate the smooth surface of the ego; but shame is felt as an inner torment, a sickness of the soul. It does not matter whether the humiliated one has been shamed by derisive laughter or whether he mocks himself. In any event, he feels himself naked, defeated, alienated, lacking in dignity or worth.

Essentially, shame is an innate emotion that sits on one end of a continuum. On the milder end, while still an intense internal experience, is shame; on the more extreme end lies humiliation. Research by Broucek (1991) indicated that there is a relationship among the experience of feeling efficacious or fulfilled and shame. Rather, shame occurs when there is the direct loss of feeling fulfilled or efficacious, leaving the person to feel exposed, defective, and/or useless. Outside of various experiences that cause shame, it seems that during points in our development, we are more susceptible to the experience of shame.

Shame peaks twice during one's lifetime: once during adolescence and again in old age (Orth, Robins, & Soto, 2010). A study conducted by Orth et al. sought to learn more about the effect of shame and guilt's effect on well-being later in life. In their findings, they discovered that "controlling for guilt increased the strength of the relation between shame and low-well being (high-depression, low self-esteem)"(2010, p.123). Rather, intense feelings of shame as an independent factor can lead to higher rates of depression and low self-esteem. Providing continued support from family, friends, and peer networks could help protect individuals from feelings of low self-worth or depression as a result of experiences of shame.

Some teens are lucky and grow up in stable and safe home and community environments where, in spite of having normative insecurities and doubts when it comes to the proverbial "who am I" or "where do I fit in?" they still have support to help them navigate through difficult experiences. While this is a normal period of confusion for most teens, distress, inconsistency, and lack of support can exacerbate normal life experiences and place them at risk. For teens at risk, the normative sense of insecurity and doubt is amplified to levels that obscure the ability to see past their present situation and into future possibilities. These are the teens that are generally seen at an urban community clinic. Many of the patients receiving services have been identified as at-risk and display significant acting-out behaviors or emotional disturbances. These children typically come from unstable home environments or foster care and lack a strong, stable, and consistent support team. As clinicians, mental health providers, paraprofessionals, teachers, and guardians, the child's behavior often captures our attention. The aggression, oppositionality, "attitude," and deep depression are all too common in this population; however, the underlying shame is often overlooked. With the help of Tanya, Earl, and April, I hope to illuminate how the tough exterior can be breached to allow for a healing therapeutic connection to emerge.

Tanya

Tanya was the stereotypical "reject," as she liked to call herself. She was a 16-year-old Latin American female. Born and raised in the tough streets of Richmond, California, she spent her first nine years living with her mother, who too often left her alone for days at time, sometimes without working electricity. Tanya had two younger siblings, both boys, whom she cared for in her mother's absence. When her mother was home, she often verbally and physically abused Tanya, telling her she was "Just like your father, worthless!" or "What are you good for? You can't do anything right!" Tanya told me that she used to have dreams of living with her father, despite not knowing who or where he was. Her dreams were shattered when her mother, in an angry fit, told her that her father was killed when she was five and that there was no one who wanted to take care of her. By the time she was eight years old, she had already begun hanging out with kids whose families were deep into drugs and gangs. With no parental guidance or objections, she was quickly accepted into the gang lifestyle.

Tanya's luck changed when she and her brothers were removed from their mother's care because of substantiated allegations of neglect. While Child and Family Services (CFS) investigated her mother on many instances for allegations of abuse and neglect over the previous five years, it was not until Tanya was 9 years old that CFS had enough information to remove the children. Tanya was sent to a different foster home from the brothers whom she had often cared for. Angry, sad, and confused, Tanya began to act out. She often skipped school and went to hang out with her "friends" in Richmond. By the time she was 13, she was already smoking marijuana and drinking alcohol. At 14, she was constantly getting into fights. Dispositional records indicated a criminal history where Tanya had been detained for possession of illegal drugs with an intent to sell, counts of assault against peers, and being in possession of stolen property. While she spoke of how she ran with the "gangtsa's from my hood," she never claimed to actually to be part of the gang; however, her tattoos boasted otherwise. Tanya believed that it was because of her "affiliation" with a well-known gang in Richmond that she was unable to visit her siblings, apparently "for safety reasons." Tanya lost touch with her brothers and bounced from foster home to foster home and from group home to group home before being returned to a foster home in Alameda County. Tanya had attended so many different schools that she had lost count. The only constant thing in her life was loss. By the time she reached 15, she had lost several family members to community violence and three of her closest friends to a drive by shooting, a stabbing, and a suicide.

In her last placement, she began working with the tenth social worker since entering into the system six years earlier. Her latest social worker was wonderful, showing genuine concern for Tanya. He worked with the schools to assist her in improving her grades and made efforts for her to reconnect with her siblings. Most importantly, he saw Tanya as a bright and capable young lady and wanted to see her succeed. It was this social worker that requested a psychological evaluation for Tanya.

When I met with Tanya she was immediately defensive. She refused to speak and when she did speak she was very dismissive and used lots of vulgar language. Connecting with dismissive clients can be hard but it's not impossible. After explaining the purpose and process of the assessment, she had not softened. Instead of continuing to push forward with the assessment, I connected with her by accepting her position. After ranting about how stupid this would be and how she wasn't going to do it, I agreed with her. "You're right; this probably is really stupid to you! Why even bother?" I was not sarcastic or degrading, but honest: Why should she bother if she found no real value? I added, "You feel like I can't teach you anything new and things in your life are fine the way they are, right? So what can I do for you?" Tanya agreed with everything except her life being fine, and that was my in. She told me that her life, "wasn't fine, it's f***ed up!" She went on to tell me that I would not be able to understand her, she had it hard, and that "You can't trust nobody in life, just yourself." After some time, we were able to turn these experiences into questions for the assessment. I reiterated the importance of being able to stop if she felt that she needed to. She appreciated this and agreed to give the testing a try. She did offer that she felt a little uncomfortable, but was interested in having answers to her questions.

Tanya hated the achievement tests. Any question I asked was met with, "I dunno" before it was even completed. While completing the task was important, it was equally important to explore the underlying forces driving this opposition. In between subtests and at the end of the session, we took time to discuss what she was thinking and feeling through each part of the testing. We also noticed together which tasks were more complicated for her. Tanya was able to tell me that she often struggled with reading because she had to spend so much time rereading words and paragraphs that she couldn't hold on to the meaning. Certain types of math questions made her think of being sent to new schools where she was behind and expected to know how to do "that type of math, when I never learned it." Writing and spelling made her feel "stupid, like I should know this stuff and I get angry when I don't." If I had just pressed on, I would never have known that every time she thought she answered something incorrectly, she would think that her mother was right—"What am I good for?" During such times it was extremely difficult not to become her cheerleader and tell her all of the great qualities that I thought she held, but I realized with support, and supervision, to trust my gut and really understand my countertransference responses before acting. Doing so allowed me to be able to sit with her in the despair and be genuinely supportive when necessary.

When Tanya became angry during the testing, I would never tell her not to be angry or that it would be okay. It was important for her to understand her triggers and what the anger was communicating. We spent many testing sessions just sitting with the anger and talking about what happens in her body and her mind, and what actions she wants to do because of it. Together we dissected the anger and looked at it as both an emotion and a means of communication. Even when she would get so angry that she would stand up and punch her hand or kick the cushions, we could be silent together in the anger and talk about what was happening. But most importantly, we could talk about what the anger meant. While it took many, "This is stupid" and "F*** this!" moments, she was eventually able to recognize that she would become angry when she thought that she was "dumber than or like I have this problem that can't never be fixed and it makes me worse than everyone else." While sitting in that space was extremely painful for Tanya and even quite scary we were able often to stay with the feelings. Some days it was too difficult, and so we did not push the issue. It was not until the last day of testing that Tanya was able to say she was glad that I could sit with her "scary anger," because most people couldn't.

Every bit of information that Tanya shared was important to the assessment process and helped illuminate the findings. She provided me several examples from her life that allowed me to synthesize the data in a way that was accessible to foster parents, family members, social workers, and academic institutions alike. While Tanya seemed to benefit from the assessment, it is important to note that she refused to attend her final feedback session. Throughout the testing she was on time or would notify the examiner if running late. However, for our last scheduled session, she did not appear. We rescheduled; then she canceled the morning of the appointment, and finally refused to come in. Even though it seemed that Tanya had come to enjoy our meetings, she was not interested in its ending. While I cannot say for certain, I assumed that we had made a connection. As long as we were working together the sting of loss remained far at bay. However, as the testing came to an end it seemed the pangs of loss that she once experienced were reawakened, which led to her subsequent avoidance.

While Tanya's case was complicated due to depression, post traumatic stress disorder, and learning difficulties, she nevertheless had grown quite accustomed to loss. Her best method for managing loss seemed to be avoidance. Her choice in not coming in for her final session sought to keep the sadness that she may have felt at a distance which allowed her, just for a little, to maintain the experience of feeling validated, useful, and seen.

I attended several meetings after the assessment (Individualized Education Plan meetings, collaboration with teachers and her therapist, and Team Decision Meetings) but each time Tanya did not want to speak with me about the assessment findings. She eventually did see me in passing and told me that she had indeed read her personal report (which is written in addition to the traditional report, which is just for her). In her most nonchalant voice she said, "It was cool, thank you!" Even though I didn't meet with Tanya again, I did find out a year later that she was doing better in her foster home and had recently been moved to a new high school where she would be part of program that supports teens in getting into college. There were still problems, and she continued to affiliate with her "gang buddies," but these small victories suggested that the assessment made a difference in her self-perception. While Tanya's anger had several sources, it was the feeling of being defective that was most striking in our work together. The collaborative assessment helped her recognize and name her shame in front of me while I took the position of a non-judgmental witness.

Research has shown that individuals tend to feel intense shame when they feel placed outside of a "context" that they wish to be considered part of (Schneider, 1997). In essence, not being part of the "in crowd" can lead to one feeling like they are less than or different. This was only one source of Tanya's pain, which she hid well behind her aggression. Other teens, like Earl, simply just hide.

Earl

Earl was a 14-year-old African American male. He was referred for a psychological assessment by his therapist due to concerns about self-harm, isolation, and intensifying suicidal ideation. His therapist was interested in knowing if there were any other underlying diagnostic concerns that could be exacerbating his depressive symptoms, as his improvement had taken a dive in recent months. Earl lived at home with his mother, father, and several siblings. His home life was chaotic. His younger sister was "fast" and highly sexualized, often bringing boys over to do "Lord knows what," as he would say. His older sister and father would fight with each other daily over trivialities and disappointments. If they weren't fighting, his mother and father's arguments would take their place, provided that his mother remained sober long enough to engage in an argument. Earl often hid away in his room in an attempt to block out the noise. His favorite escape was listening to hardcore "gangsta rap" music on his iPod. Although Earl loved his rap music, he didn't identify with a gang or as a gangbanger. Nonetheless, he used the "rap persona" to scare and intimidate other kids in his school. His size also made him seem like a formidable opponent. He enjoyed the aggression and the violent threats; "I thought they were creative," he told me.

Earl liked the idea of being feared because it made him feel superior to everyone else, but underneath it all he felt supremely inferior. When we met, he initially took the "hardcore bad boy" stance, but over time he seemed to be more than willing to talk about any and everything. From the beginning, however, he was reluctant when it came to discussing the issues that warranted the assessment or to talk about his family. Earl openly described the community violence that he was often exposed to (as they lived in a pretty rough side of town). He described witnessing a couple shot in a drive by, liquor stores on the corner being robbed, and teenagers fighting and stealing in the street. In spite of his hardcore stance, Earl agreed to the testing and completed many different tasks without complaint, but he wasn't willing to share how he felt about the tasks or what he thought about them.

Earl was generally a good kid: funny, engaging, but quite stubborn when it came to talking about anything "feelings" related. The therapist and I tried all sorts of techniques to help him open up so that he would complete the socio-emotional assessment tasks. We both agreed that it would be important to go back to the drawing board. What I hadn't realized at the time was that it wasn't simply the discussion about the feelings, but that feelings from his view were dangerous and could lead an individual to very dark places. When I revisited the affectively charged questions with Earl, I found it necessary to reassure him that his feelings were not stronger than his treatment team, that there was space for his feelings, and that his feelings could be contained. As we revisited the questions, Earl was slowly able to discuss feeling as if he was alone in the world and that he did not resonate with anyone. We were able to talk openly about his suicidal ideation and how discussing suicide did not mean that the "mental health police" were going to come and take him away. As he continued, the examiner was able to show him in the testing how his feelings were getting in the way of his performance cognitively, academically, and socially. Using the assessment data to help Earl understand how avoiding and denying his feelings were impacting his functioning was eye opening for him.

In subsequent sessions, and in our final feedback session, he was able to voice to his parents how deeply their fighting, drug and alcohol abuse, and lack of emotional connection had affected him. As Earl shared, his parents were able to take in his feelings and were encouraged to share their own. They both discussed their need to avoid talking about feelings with Earl because they feared it would cause him to "actually succeed in killing yourself." As the assessor, I was also able to explain to Earl's parents how his feelings were impacting his functioning and their relationship. Using the data from the testing, I told his parents what Earl was experiencing using his own words. Lastly, I was able to support the therapist in creating a treatment plan that allowed for continued discussion of their feelings, emotional containment, and growth.

While Earl was not involved in the "streets" like Tanya, he had plenty of experience with community and domestic violence. His behavior at school, defiance in the home, and reluctance to back down from a fight made him a tough case for many of the adults in his life. His size, along with his aggressive yet empty threats, served as a mask, which allowed him to hide the insecurity and vulnerability that he felt from the rest of the world. As Cassidy and Stevenson write, "Engagement in aggression among the youth … represents a reactive coping strategy in that it hides these boys' hyper-vulnerable qualities under a hyper-masculine façade" (Cassidy & Stevenson, 2005, p. 67). The assessment process allowed Earl to show sides of himself that he felt no one in his world could handle or wanted to see. By staying with the emotional content and facing those fears together, Earl was able to confront them. His feelings were no longer too big or too dangerous for anyone to manage. Normalizing his emotional experience also made it easier to challenge the experience of feeling broken or less than, due to such strong feelings. As with Tanya, allowing someone else to bear witness to the pain and fear that was hidden away allowed Earl to once again heal and grow.

April

April was a 17-year-old African American female. She came with a "rap sheet" longer than many I'd ever seen. She had been in and out of juvenile hall and detained several times for prostitution as well as possession of narcotics. At the time of the referral she was on probation for burglary in the second degree, for which she was an "accomplice" rather than an active participant. April also loved to play with fire. She diagnostically fit the criteria for pyromania; however, it was one of the only things that she was able to hide from everyone, the other being her sexual abuse history. Unlike many children that I worked with who had such extensive histories, April had family support. Her mother followed a similar path at April's age; she had also become enmeshed "in the life" and with drugs. She had April when she was 15 years old, but April was immediately removed from her care after being born drug exposed. April's mother began to work hard to straighten her life out when she was in her early 20s. By the time she reached her late 20s, she was stable, working, married, and starting a new family. That is when she began to reach out to April to establish a relationship. As expected, April was not interested and seemed to plunge deeper into the streets the more her mother reached out to provide support.

April's probation officer requested an assessment because there were significant concerns about April's cognitive functioning, reality testing, and her ability to live independently, as she was rapidly approaching adulthood. Records indicated that her early development was slightly delayed due to exposure to drugs and alcohol in utero. While she did not demonstrate any of the physical features of fetal alcohol syndrome (FAS), it was speculated by other providers that she demonstrated the Fetal Alcohol Effects (FAE). The records spoke of significant behavioral concerns from as early as three years old. The reports indicated "severe emotional outbursts" and "intense aggressive behavior." Information on her cognitive functioning ability was inconclusive as she often refused testing or failed to keep her appointments. Her school records indicated that April was absent at least three quarters of the year. Because she changed foster homes so frequently, the school reported that it was often difficult to keep up with "the party responsible for her well being." Like Tanya and many others in foster care, she had had several different social workers across her lifespan. April was a product of the system as having spent all her life in foster care. It was not until I received the referral that there was some push to shift that.

April was extremely inconsistent, manipulative, and argumentative during testing. Her presentation was often flat but on edge. She questioned everything and seemed to think that each question or activity was an affront to her well being. She absolutely hated that the examiner would not tell her if she answered a question correctly or not. Everything felt like a fight, even when the examiner complimented her on her outfit or nail polish, she would respond with, "What?! You think I ain't got good taste!" She often made comments like, "You think you're better than me!" Her comments were unprovoked (at least initially to me) and seemed to come out of left field. During one session, while doing the House-Tree-Person task she shouted, "I ain't stupid." I looked at her quizzically and exclaimed, "Huh?" She looked at the examiner with anger and repeated, "I ain't stupid, so don't call me stupid!" At first I tried to reassure her that I didn't say anything, which only led to her becoming more angry and saying, "You calling me a liar!?!" Everything that the examiner said seemed to be fuel for another attack. "Let's calm down," or "Maybe we should stop for today," was more fodder for "You telling me I'm angry" or "You think I can't do it because I'm stupid." After 35 minutes of a barrage of attacks, I said, "If I am such a horrible person who keeps attacking you, why are you still here?" For once she was silent. As with most of my clients, I reiterated that the she could choose not to participate. Again, the examiner was met with silence followed by tears. I was quite cautious of her reaction, as I was unsure if it was genuine or if she was being manipulative. April gathered her belongings and began to leave and stopped. She turned to me and said, "You are just like everyone else." Before I could think about my response, I stated, "Maybe you don't like the fact that you aren't." April exited the room, which made me think she was gone and not coming back, but much to my surprise, she returned ten minutes later with water and some snacks. I was chagrined that I had not trusted the connection that we had so painstakingly developed. When she entered, she asked, "What's next?" We tested for an hour and then I elected to spend the remaining time discussing our initial interaction during that session. April agreed that I was right. She described her day-to-day experience like window shopping, where she is the customer gazing in the store but everyone else is inside shopping. She talked about not being wanted and the confusion she felt with her mother wanting to be part of her life. I pointed out how her conflict with wanting to be wanted, and wanting to be protective, were playing out in her day-to-day life, using examples from the testing and from our initial interactions.

The conversation that day jumped from topic to topic. April eventually told me that she could "never be like everyone else" because she'd been sexually abused from five to seven years old and exploited for several years in her teens. The session felt as if it had shifted from being combative to supportive. The client was only able to hold that space for so long as she moved quickly into spilling about her feeling "stupid" because "I can't read good," to talking explicitly about her trauma experiences. April seemed to dissociate more and more, which led her to talking about her fascination with fire and how she enjoyed burning her arms and her thighs. I tried to support her by refocusing her attention to the factors that make her feel safe and calm.

While this helped, she had already gone too far and had revealed more than she wished. With only two sessions left, she went back to avoiding testing, and she arrived late to what was our last session. She was less combative during that session but remained defensive. I was unfortunately required to close her case as she did not turn up for her final session to hear the results of the evaluation. April's probation officer found the information to be useful and felt that she'd seen some shifts in April since the testing. In the report I wrote:

> April has a long history of loss which she has learned to manage through avoiding close connections. When she feels that she is becoming too close to others she is likely to sabotage the relationship through verbal attacks or avoiding people altogether. Intimacy is a risk, one that she is not yet willing to make, and for this reason she will maintain superficial relationships or none at all.

April's probation officer found those lines poignant because when she asked April why she wouldn't meet with the examiner for a feedback session, she reported, "I'm cool, she was done with me anyway right?!" Her probation officer stated that she was shocked because she'd spoken so highly of the assessment process before.

In each one of these stories the clients described feelings associated with shame. They all discussed feeling less than others or broken in some way. As a result, they often hid this vulnerable part of their psyche deep within the confines of their heart. People in their lives didn't notice the pain and anguish that these teens are experiencing because of their shame. Most are more focused on the problematic behaviors. When those behaviors don't shift, feelings of frustration emerge. I believe we clinicians get caught in a parallel process, where the child feels ineffectual in life and we then feel ineffectual in the treatment. The collaborative assessment, in my experience (along with very good supervision), has been the tool that allows me to observe the client's process from several angles, including my own negative transference experiences that hinder the necessary empathic process, which, in turn curtails further growth in treatment. By checking in with patients during our interactions, exploring their responses and their approach, I am able to learn more information about how their strengths and weaknesses impact them on a daily basis. I'd miss out if I simply relied on the data.

In addition to the many discoveries I have made with the clients, there have been major advances made with the treatment team and families. The assessment reports have been powerful tools in helping the adults in the teen's lives understand how they are being impacted by their feelings of shame. It is important to work through the shame so that it is no longer allowed to hide. I have seen many parents and treatment teams develop more empathy as a result of the findings gained from this process. Where empathy lives, healing can occur.

References

Broucek, F. J. (1991). *Shame and the self.* New York: The Guilford Press.

Cassidy, E. F. & Stevenson Jr, H. C. (2005). They wear the mask: Hypervulnerability and hypermasculine aggression among African American males in an urban remedial disciplinary school. *Journal of Aggression, Maltreatment & Trauma, 11*(4), 53–74.

Hall, G. S. (1904) *Adolescence: Its psychology and its relations to physiology, anthropology, sociology, sex, crime, religion, and education* (Vols I & II). New York: D. Appleton & Co.

Lewis, H. B. (1971). *Shame and guilt in neurosis.* New York: International Universities Press.

Orth, U., Robins, R., & Soto, C., (2010) Tracking the trajectory of shame, guilt, and pride across the lifespan. *Journal of Personality and Social Psychology, 99*(6), 1061–1071. doi: 10.1037/a0021342.

Schneider, C. (1977). *Shame, exposure, and privacy.* Boston: Beacon Press.

Tangney, J. P., & Dearing, R. L. (2002). *Shame and guilt.* New York: The Guilford Press.

Tomkins, S. (1963). *Affect imagery consciousness.* New York: Springer Publishing Company Inc.

Appendix A

Stories About Feelings

"Diary of a Grumpy Kid: A Story for Jay" by Margaret Owen-Wilson

My Name is Jay. I'm 12 years old and I just started middle school.

I guess I'm just your typical kid. I have a mom, a dad, and a brother. My parents are pretty cool and I love them both. I love my brother, too, but sometimes … just sometimes, he scares me …

I go to school, and like most typical kids, I don't like school much, but I do like my friends, and hanging out with them makes school less boring.

My mom says that I'm "handsome, smart, and caring." My dad agrees with my mom on that, so I guess that's true.

But my mom also notices that sometimes I get "irritable." My dad says that means "grumpy" … I guess that's true too.

I'm not really sure why I get "irritable" or "grumpy." My parents were not really sure either. I guess that's why they asked me to meet with this "doctor" person who gives tests.

It was kind of a bummer, 'cuz I already meet with a lot of doctors, and I already do a lot of tests at school. But after the tests, this testing doctor found out some things about me that she shared with my parents and me.

She told me that I was a "smart" kid. (Duh! I already knew that!) Anyway, she told me that even though I was a smart kid, there were a lot of things that got in the way of me doing well at school.

First, it was because I had a hard time paying attention. I told her I already knew that, and I had to drink medicine to help with that.

Then, she said that besides my difficulty with paying attention, I have a hard time because I'm thinking about things that happened to me that make me feel stressed out.

I don't like to really talk about these things, but maybe she's a little right. Some of these things have to do with my brother …

Like I said earlier, I love my brother but sometimes he does things that make me feel not safe. After he did something that made me feel not safe, he was taken away and he doesn't live with us right now … I guess I feel like it's sorta my fault that he got taken away. I know my mom and dad tell me that it's not my fault, and even this doctor says it's not my fault … . But I still feel bad that he doesn't live with us anymore—I really wish group homes were not invented! I guess I also miss our family being together like before … before my mom and dad split up. I know they both love me still, but I miss those fun times we had going out as a family together, like that time we went to a water park … I wish that things could go back to those days.

Then, there's this thing were I sometimes feel different from my friends, because of the other things I have a hard time with … that I don't want to talk about. But I'm working on it, and slowly I'm getting there.

This testing doctor said that all these things make me sad. But not like sad how my mom gets sad, but more like "grumpy." That means, that I get really irritable and annoyed and I don't want to talk to anybody. Sometimes, when I'm really grumpy, I also say things that I don't mean … and when I'm feeling grumpy, I don't feel so good about myself and I think about scary things like hurting myself.

Being grumpy really sucks! What sucks more is that I don't always feel like I have anyone to talk to about these things. You see, I really don't want to bug my mom and dad. I don't want them to worry about me. They have lots of stuff to worry about without me adding to their worries.

- Tip 1: Talk with my counselor about these sad and grumpy feelings. The testing doctor said it is important to remember that what happened with my brother is not my fault and that I should consider talking about this with my counselor.
- Tip 2: Try to talk with my parents about these feelings. Even if it might add to their worry, my parents love me and they don't want me to feel sad and grumpy
- Tip 3: Get some additional help at school. I'm smart, but it really is hard for me to pay attention. So doing things in a way that will keep my attention (like using art in my subjects) and taking breaks when I'm starting to feel antsy will help.
- Tip 4: Do after school fun activities, like track! I'm a really fast runner!
- Tip 5: Maybe get some family therapy to help our family communicate better.

I'm not really sure about all these tips and how they can help me, but feeling grumpy really sucks so I guess I can think about trying these tips. My mom and dad say they will help me follow these tips when I'm ready.

I have a lot of things going on right now, what with starting middle school. I guess if these tips will help make things easier and help me feel less grumpy, it's worth a try.

"EXO-MAN: A Story for Joe" by Ben Knipe

Meet Joe. Joe is a good football player, the **star** of his team, and he is **great** at making people laugh: he tells jokes, makes witty comments, or does silly things. Unfortunately, Joe lives in a dangerous place.

Luckily, he also has a special power … he has a **super exoskeleton** that can transform into many different forms. With his exoskeleton on, he becomes **EXO-MAN!!** He has a **super exoskeleton** that can transform into many different forms—with his exoskeleton on, he becomes **EXO-MAN!!**

EXO-MAN is very powerful, and keeps Joe **safe** in a dangerous land. Joe can even use the power of EXO-MAN to help other people.

Water can't stop him nor can fire. Joe only took off his exoskeleton to put on his football uniform and sometimes to make people laugh, but other than that, Joe **always** wore the exoskeleton for safety and **power.**

At first, he could let his **inner light** shine out **through** the exoskeleton, but the more time he spent as EXO-MAN, the less his light shined and the **darker** it felt inside the exoskeleton … and this caused a few problems since Joe spent all his time as EXO-MAN, nobody saw who he really was. This got lonely sometimes, but Joe thought EXO-MAN could handle anything, **even** the growing darkness and loneliness. The *other* glitch was that **Joe** couldn't always control the exoskeleton, and sometimes EXO-MAN would just explode and EXO-MAN would be **dangerous!**

This *didn't* make Joe *happy* but it seemed better than taking off the exoskeleton and not feeling safe, **but** as time went on and his light got dimmer, the **explosions** happened more **often**, and the harder Joe tried to **control** EXO-MAN the **bigger** the explosions got. Now the explosions were the only time Joe's light shined at all …

And **people** started to complain: "GET RID OF THAT THING!!!," "How could you DO that?!!!!?," "I demand a change!," "Get OUT of here!," "JERK," "Now listen here, buster … "

This isn't what Joe wanted … it made him mad. It wasn't **HIS** fault, he was just doing his best in a world that was **already dangerous**.

He **had** to do something … **but what to do??** It seemed all EXO-MAN could do anymore was **explode**. Then EXO-MAN met someone *else* with an exoskeleton. *His* inner light shone through clearly and *HE* could **control** *his* exoskeleton!

He offered to show Joe how to **control** his exoskeleton.

He said Joe didn't **have to** give up being EXO-MAN like people were demanding, but he did need to **choose** … whether he wanted to **only** be EXO-MAN who explodes all the time … **or** if he wanted to find Joe's **inner light** and **use** his inner light to master his exoskeleton.

This would mean Joe would have to figure out who **he** really is *inside himself* and let other people get to know him without the exoskeleton or his football uniform … **or** being funny.

This was hard at first. Joe didn't feel safe, and EXO-MAN still exploded sometimes, but in time, and with help from his new friend, Joe learned who he was, and let people get to know the REAL Joe so his **inner light** could grow **strong** again **and** he could **control** his exoskeleton so that he could use it to do the good things he **wanted** to do.

And he could **choose** when to be EXO-MAN and when to be Joe because he had found his strength within.

To view additional stories with illustrations, please see: www.routledge.com/9781138776289

Appendix B
Stories About Identity

"Many Colors of a Butterfly: A Story for Jael," by Lisa Greenberg

Once upon a time there was a young butterfly named Jael. He lived with his mother, sister, tios, and primos. Jael was kind and busy! He loved to play and to talk to other butterflies all around.

When Jael was a little boy, a man lived in Jael's home. He tried to hurt Jael and his family. He was mean and told Jael his butterfly colors were wrong.

Jael was really scared! He buzzed around, tried to hide back in his cocoon, and couldn't calm his body. Then the man was sent away. Jael and his family were safe!! But Jael didn't feel safe. He still worried things like bugs, noises, or mean animals could hurt him! He would get upset and fly all around.

He didn't like to think about these scary things. So he hid his feelings and pretended he could wave away his fears.

Jael was worried at school, too. Even though he is a smart butterfly and he likes school, it was hard to pay attention and learn. His teacher, Ms. Coco, helped him a lot.

His family saw that Jael was still scared. So they found Ellie and Rellie, the kind helper butterflies. Ellie found lots of people to help Jael, his mom, and sister. Jael talked and played. He started to tell Rellie his feelings and felt better.

"Rellie, I am sad and sometimes worried."

"Thanks for telling me, Jael. Your feelings will get smaller. You'll be okay."

"I don't want to talk about that now. I'm going into my cocoon."

Sometimes, Jael remembered the mean man and his mean words. It still scared him— he wanted to hide in his cocoon and talk about something else, like magic.

But he began to learn to tell his family, Ellie, and Rellie that he was scared or sad. When he told them, he didn't have to hold his feelings all by himself! And then he felt better! Jael also learned that the mean man was wrong about him. There was nothing wrong with his butterfly colors. Butterfly boys and girls are made of all kinds of colors!! Wow, look at all those cool colors!

His mom and family also saw that butterflies have different and beautiful colors. There were lots of ways and colors for a butterfly boy to be.

And now Jael the butterfly knows that he can be any kind of color. What kind of colors do you think he should be? Please color me how you think he should be?

"Miss Popular: A Story for V," by Margaret Owen-Wilson

In the city of Queens, New York, there lived a young girl named Vivian. Vivian was a smart, artistic, and pretty girl who lived with her two brothers and adoptive mother, Ms. Grace.

At school, Vivian was a cheerleader and she had both cheerleader friends and friends from her after-school clubs.

Even though Vivian was pretty, smart, and a cheerleader who had friends, she wasn't always very happy. You see, before she came to live with Ms. Grace, Vivian's birth family went through some very hard times. As a result, Vivian and her brothers lived with many different foster families starting at a very young age.

While at these foster families' homes, Vivian felt like she did not belong with these families because they could not understand the hard times she went through. What was worse was that Vivian felt that these families would never accept the real her.

At first, Vivian tried her best to be the "perfect girl" for the foster family, and everything would be great and Vivian felt loved and accepted. But the longer she stayed with a family, the harder it was for Vivian to be the "perfect" girl and not show the other parts of her, the parts that were sad and angry.

When she was sad and angry, Vivian would do things that would result in her being asked to leave her foster family—she would do things like throw tantrums, lie, and fight. Vivian's stay in each placement became shorter with every foster home she moved to. This made Vivian mad and sad because she didn't get to stay in many schools for long, and it became harder and harder to get to know people and be liked by people.

When Vivian met Grace, she felt a connection with Ms. Grace and she was happy that Ms. Grace seemed to truly like her. In true Vivian fashion, she tried her best to be the "perfect girl" when she first stayed with Ms. Grace, because she wanted Ms. Grace to like and accept her. Ms. Grace did like Vivian and even enrolled her in a good school. Vivian decided that she would continue her "perfect girl" persona by trying to be one of the most popular girls at school. She wanted to be known as "Miss Popular," because to Vivian, this meant that she was liked and accepted. Vivian tried her best to keep up the "good girl" face, but after a while it became hard, and soon she was acting out and getting into trouble at school. Vivian's grades were also suffering because of her acting out.

Despite Vivian's continued acting out, Ms. Grace decided to adopt Vivian and her brothers because she liked and cared about Vivian and her brothers. Vivian was so happy. She felt as though she could finally stay in one place and be accepted by someone who would care for her. So Vivian tried harder to put on her "good girl face" and become popular.

However, even Vivian's best efforts to be the "perfect girl," the pain of what happened to her before she met Ms. Grace would be in the back of her mind. What's more, that pain and the sadness and anger that comes from that pain got triggered in Vivian whenever she felt like she was being rejected, criticized, or told she could not do something. Vivian's goal of becoming "Miss Popular" backfired in a way because of her acting out. You see, Vivian was becoming "popular" at school, but she was becoming popular in a way that she did not want. She became known as the girl who would "pop-off" and get in fights.

Although Ms. Grace cared for Vivian, she grew weary of Vivian's behaviors and she worried that Vivian would get in to serious trouble at school. Ms. Grace worried about

Vivian's grades because she knew that Vivian was very smart and knew that Vivian could do better. Ms. Grace also worried that the arguments between her and Vivian got in the way of Vivian and Ms. Grace's quality mother-daughter time together. So, Ms. Grace decided to seek the help of a counselor named Violet to help Vivian with her behaviors. Ms. Grace's hope was that by getting Vivian some help, Vivian would be able to grow up and achieve her goals of being a productive, successful, and well-liked person in the community.

Vivian liked Violet. Vivian thought Violet was a nice person and she was starting to learn different ways to respond to people who upset her. However, Vivian still struggled with her acting out, and even though she was learning different ways to cope, it was hard for Vivian to use these new ways to cope and respond when she got angry and upset.

In order to continue to help Vivian, Ms. Grace and Violet called on a doctor that gave tests so that they could find a way to better help Vivian. Dr. May talked with Vivian and explained that Ms. Grace and Violet had questions about how they can help Vivian be successful in her life and get in trouble less, which is why they called upon Dr. May. Vivian said, "Can I have my questions answered too?" Dr. May smiled and said, of course.

Vivian had great questions for Dr. May. She wanted to know why it was so hard for her to sit still and why "people" were always "on her back." When Dr. May asked Vivian, "What would you like to see happen, if everything in your life was the way you wanted it to be?" Vivian answered with, "I want to get along better with my mom, Ms. Grace, and I want us to have fun and hang out together."

Vivian worked hard on the tests, even on days she didn't feel like doing them. After the tests were done, Dr. May spoke with Ms. Grace, Violet and Vivian about what the tests found. The tests found that Ms. Grace was right: Vivian was very smart, but that it was hard for Vivian to pay attention in school because Vivian sometimes thinks about all the bad things that happened to her. Other times, Vivian would feel that the teacher was being mean to and disrespecting her, and that made Vivian not want to do any work at all.

The test also found that because Vivian was used to "acting out" and doing things that got her into trouble when she was upset, it was very hard for Vivian to change and respond in a different way. The tests also indicated that for Vivian, not owning up to what she did was a way for her to protect herself not just from getting in trouble but from feeling really crummy about herself and her behaviors. Vivian felt that when Ms. Grace was scolding her or "getting on her back" that Ms. Vivian didn't like her anymore. This triggered those bad feelings from when Vivian used to be in her other foster homes.

Dr. May said to Vivian, "So you see Vivian, the reason you have a hard time sitting still and paying attention is because there are times when you daydream or think about the past. Other times, it's because you feel like your teacher doesn't like you and thinks you are 'not good' and so you want to get 'revenge' on your teacher by acting up and not doing your work. But doing that just gets you in trouble, and hurts your grades." Vivian was irritated after she heard this and said, "Well, what am I supposed to do then when she's being rude and when she thinks I'm dumb?" Dr. May smiled and said, "Well, you can prove her wrong by doing your work and getting a good grade, that is the best kind of 'revenge' you can dish out."

Vivian was still irritated, and she said, "Well, what about my other question? How can I get people off my back?" Dr. May said, "Well, I think, thinking about why they are 'on your back' to begin with is the key. Lets look at why Ms. Grace is 'on your back' about things. You see, Ms. Grace gets on you because she just wants you to be successful at school and at life. She gets sad and sometimes irritated when she sees how smart and likeable you are, and yet your grades are falling and you get in trouble at school."

Dr. May said, "Remember what you said you wanted?" Vivian nodded. "Do you know that Ms. Grace shared something similar?" Vivian looked at her mom and Ms. Grace said, "I would like us to all get along better and hang out more together too!"

Dr. May and Violet when on to talk with Vivian and Ms. Grace. They talked about strategies and ways to help Vivian get to her goals and get in to trouble at school less.

In counseling, Violet talked about continuing to help Vivian learn and practice new ways of coping and responding when Vivian was upset. One way was to write about her sad and angry feelings. Another way of coping was for Vivian to walk away from the situation that upset her and come back later and try to calmly talk about why she was upset.

Violet also worked with Vivian and Ms. Grace to begin set up a system where Violet can earn small rewards, like going to get ice cream with Ms. Grace and one-on-one "girl-time" with Ms. Grace for doing chores and getting in trouble at school less.

Vivian and Violet also began to talk about what it really means to be someone who is known as Miss Popular and how to make and keep friends who would be real friends to Vivian and really have "Vivian's back." Violet even explained that Vivian can be popular without having the title "Miss Popular," and more importantly, Vivian can be popular in a way that is not connected with getting in fights.

Finally, Ms. Grace, Violet, and Vivian began talking about Dr. May's final recommendation: the recommendation to have Vivian and Ms. Grace meet with Violet maybe one time every four or six weeks just to be able to check in with each other and get help on how to better communicate with each other and improve their relationship.

Vivian felt that this was a lot of work, and sometimes she just wanted to give up. But Vivian also cared about Ms. Grace and her relationship with Ms. Grace, and so she tried her best and worked hard in counseling. Vivian still had many days where her upset and angry feelings got the best of her, but Ms. Grace and Violet helped her by acknowledging all of Vivian's hard work and recognizing and applauding the times when Vivian was able to use her words and try a different way to respond when she became upset.

Vivian was hopeful that one day all her hard work and Ms. Grace's hard work with Violet will result in Vivian's goal and wish to be well liked by people, and most importantly, to improve her relationship with Ms. Grace and spend happy quality time with Miss Grace doing "fun stuff." The end … for now …

To view additional stories with illustrations, please see: www.routledge.com/9781138776289

Appendix C

Stories About Learning

"Julio el Patito Activo: A Story for Julio," by Kristin Moore

Había una vez un patito muy activo que se llamaba Julio.

Julio vivía con sus padres en una casita.

A Julio le gustaba pasar tiempo con sus padres, jugaban muchos juegos en casa.

En la primera escuela, Julio tenía problemas con los otros niños. No podía controlarse y les pegaba a los otros patitos. En una escuela, Julio le tiró un libro a otro niño y le cortó el ojo. Por eso, Julio tenía que cambiar de escuela.

En la segunda escuela Julio estaba contento, pero todavía tenia problemas. Julio hablaba patogués y los otros estudiantes y los maestros hablaban otra lengua. A veces no sabían lo que estaba diciendo. También, era muy difícil para Julio sentarse quieto.

A veces Julio le pegaba a los otros patitos y los maestros tenían que recordarle a Julio que eso no se hacía.

Un día los padres de Julio pensaron que a lo mejor Julio necesitaba ayuda de amigas muy especiales. Una amiga vino a la casa para ayudar a Julio a portarse mejor.

La otra amiga tenía una oficina cerca. En sus visitas con ella él tenía que contestar muchas preguntas y podiá jugar en la arena.

Los padres de Julio y sus amigas especiales trabajaron juntos para ayudar a Julio a sentirse y portarse mejor.

La primera idea era que Julio nesecitaba asistir a una escuela con estudiantes y maestros que hablan patogués como Julio y sus padres.

Julio sabía que todos lo querían mucho y estaban allí para ayudarle a seguir adelante.

"The Story of Naji," by Marianne Haydel, Barbara Mercer, and Erin Rosenblatt

There once was a puppy named Naji. Naji lived with his family—there were lots of dogs of all ages in his family. Naji loved his family very much.

Naji had long floppy ears and a waggly tail. Naji was very sweet and playful; he liked to run and roll in leaves and play with other puppies. But sometimes Naji was sad.

Not all his friends knew it, but Naji lost his sister because she'd gotten sick. He missed her very much.

The other thing that bothered Naji was that he was having trouble with his schoolwork even though he was a smart puppy. Sometimes this trouble at school made him feel like he couldn't do anything at all.

When Naji got upset, he liked to run away. One day, he ran away and put his nose in the stream and heard a loud croaking noise. Just as Naji was wondering what that noise was, out of the goo came a bunch of frogs: one, two, three frogs!

The frogs asked Naji why he was so sad.

Naji wasn't sure if he wanted to tell these frogs anything at all. But he told them that he felt sad because he just couldn't think sometimes.

The frogs talked to each other and asked him questions, had him count lily pads and asked him to write his letters.

After a while, the frogs said, "Maybe you just lost your thinking cap."

"We think we can help you make a new thinking cap."

At first, Naji wasn't sure the frogs could help him—he thought it might be much too hard to make a new thinking cap—but then they told him, "You'll need your mom's help—go and get her and together we can figure out how to make a new thinking cap."

Naji went to get his mom and told her about the frogs. He grabbed her paw and showed her the pond and the three frogs.

The frogs told his mom that even though Naji thinks he can't do a lot of things, and that he might try to run away when he thinks he can't do things, he is smart and he really can do a lot of things. The frogs told his mom, "Don't let him run away, help him keep trying until he gets it, because we know he can! That is how he'll start to make a new thinking cap!"

His mom told the frogs that she didn't want him to feel bad, cause she knows how hard some things can be for him, but the frogs told her that this is really going to help Naji feel better, so he knows he's smart.

Naji and his mom walked home together and decided to give it a try. Naji felt like running away, but his mom wouldn't let him. She gave him help and told him he could do it! Naji could tell that he was starting to get a new thinking cap and it was working really well.

Naji went to bed that night feeling happy about all the things he could do, and in the distance he could hear the frogs singing in the night air.

To view additional stories with illustrations, please see: www.routledge.com/9781138776289

Appendix D

Stories About Past Hurts

"Little Puppy's Adventures at the Zoo: A Story for Skip," by Margaret Husbands

Once upon a time, there was a cute, little puppy named Skippy. He loved to run and play ball with the other little puppies.

One day he woke up very, very, happy!!! Do you know why? Skippy was going to meet his teacher and the puppies from his class at the Zoo.

"Get up, Daddy!" He said. "Let's go! Let's go! I don't want to be late!"

When he got to the Zoo, he saw his teacher, Mrs. Smith, and his friends, and he yelped loudly, "There they are Daddy, there they are!" Then Skippy ran over to join them.

Mrs. Smith said, "Good morning, Skippy, Please stand in line quietly next to your friend, Flash."

But it was so very hard for Skippy to stand in line and be quiet. He was so happy to be at the Zoo. There were so many sounds, and smells, and so very much to see, too.

Sometimes it was also hard to be quiet in class. Sometimes he could pay attention and listen to his teacher. And sometimes, no matter how hard he tried in class, it was just too hard to pay attention.

As he looked around at the animals, he yelped to his friend Flash, "Look! Look! Do you see the penguins? And over there, look at the bear! And the monkey!!!" But when he turned to his friend, he saw that Flash was not there. Mrs. Smith was not there. The other puppies were all gone as well. *Where did they go?* thought Skippy.

Skippy had not paid attention and did not know where they went. He was alone. He did not like being alone. Skippy was so scared. He did not want to be lost and alone.

That was because when he was a little, little puppy, he was left with people who were mean and who hurt him, and made him afraid. Skippy did not want to be alone or hurt anymore. That's how he felt when he was in a new house or when he had to get to know a new Mommy or a new Daddy. Or when he did not have his sister to talk to or play with. When Skippy felt scared he could not be still. He ran around and jumped around. He ran and jumped and bumped into people and thought, *What do I do? Where do I go?*

Then, he heard his name. "SKIPPY!" He turned around and saw his teacher wagging her tail at him. "Thank you, Teacher! Thank you for finding me!" He said, jumping for joy. "You are welcome," Mrs. Smith yelped. "We care about you Skippy, and want you to be with us. We want you to be safe. Come and stay close to me, so that you don't get lost again."

Mrs. Smith then said to the class, "Now let's stay together, and let's go see the animals!!!!" Skippy yelped and wagged his tail happily as he went around the Zoo with his class.

THE END

"The Story of Oliver Good," by Cinthya Chin Herrera

There once lived a boy named Oliver Good.
He lived very deep in the dark, scary woods.
Oh the things he would see
And the things he would hear
Would give Oliver Good
A great sense of fear!
Late in the night the woods came alive.
Oliver shook with fright 'cause he was only five.
What if big monsters were hidden about?
There could be a wolf with a very long snout!
Lots of things happened to make Oliver feel scared
Like one time his sister fought a big angry bear!
And at night when the woods would quietly whisper
Oliver would secretly think of his sister.
When in the morning, the sun would come out.
Oliver wanted to yell or to shout
He was so happy
To have lived through the night
And that an end to the dark, scary night was in sight.
Still, those feelings inside did not go away
No, those feelings inside seemed to want to stay.
Running and jumping and even backflipping
Oliver just kept speeding and zipping.
"Settle down! Settle down,"
His momma would shout
But those feelings inside Oliver couldn't get out.
But then there were times when he would get hurt.
"Ouch!" He would shout when he fell in the dirt.
"Stupid dirt! YOU did this! You are the worst,"
Oliver hollered and shouted and cursed.
It felt really good to let all his feelings go.
Should he do it some more? He didn't know.
So Oliver went and chop-kicked a tree.
"Take THAT, you old tree! You can't get me!"
He kicked and he kicked
And still the tree stood.
But soon the sun started setting
And there was dark in the woods.
Oliver rushed home with all his might

Fearing all the monsters in the dark, woodsy night
Because who really knew how hard they could bite.
The thought of it all made Oliver shake with fright.
And so it repeated again and again.
Oliver would get scared every now and then.
So he found the old tree to hit, stomp, and kick
"One more for good measure! That did the trick!"
But suddenly one day Oliver saw something new.
The tree he had kicked 'til it was black and blue
Began talking aloud with a very sad voice,
"Please stop. Though I know you have a choice."
With marks all over from the kicking and hitting,
Oliver started to think about quitting.
"Who cares," he asked, a little angry and scared.
"I do! I do!" The tree answered prepared.
"To tell you a secret, I'm a little scared too.
"You might not believe me, but it really is true.
"The woods can be scary, and big and dark.
"The oceans, too, they're full of sharks!
"The jungles, no way! They're full of snakes!
"And don't even get me started on lakes.
"But one thing I know from my years as a tree
The thing that helps people feel happy and free
Is that feelings are scarier if you keep them inside.
"Those feelings can make you want to run and hide.
"Little Oliver, I know that your heart is good.
"And you're simply afraid of the dark, scary woods.
"They put feelings inside you that make you feel worried.
"And that's why your body won't stop feeling hurried.
"I care about you and want you to heal.
"Instead of kicking me, tell me how you feel.
"Your fears are real, but they can get better.
"And one thing is for sure, we can do it together."

"Princess Pinky," by Michelle Limon

Hi! My name is Princess Pinky!

Once upon a time … there was a little princess named Princess Pinky. She was a beautiful girl. She loved animals and the color pink.

Princess Pinky was a good girl but she came across some mean people who hurt her. She was mad because she couldn't stay safe and had to leave her castle. She didn't understand why people were so mean and hurtful.

She had to move to get away from the mean people. But she still felt confused about moving. She kept remembering the bad stuff and it made her worry so much that it made her stomach hurt, it made her say things that weren't always true, and she got confused a lot.

What was Princess Pinky to do? All she wanted was a family so that she could feel safe. She moved to a far-away land where someone tried to take care of her, love her, but sometimes didn't understand Princess Pinky when she became angry.

Princess Pinky would get in trouble and it would really hurt Princess Pinky's feelings. Princess Pinky started to do things that were hurtful to herself because she didn't know what to do.

All of a sudden, Princess Pinky had to move again! She didn't understand why this was happening again! Was it her fault? She was tired of feeling alone and not knowing what was going to happen next!

Princess Pinky moved to stay with this lady that loved her and took care of her. Princess Pinky felt like she could finally let go of some of her worries. She finally didn't feel alone and she felt like someone understood her.

Sometimes Princess Pinky would still get mad though. She didn't really know why. If she really thought about it, she knew that she was mad about the mean and hurtful things the people from her past did to her. She was still afraid that there were other people around who could hurt her. The nice lady who took care of her was worried. The nice lady brought her to a cottage to meet someone named Lion the Protector that might be able to help understand why Princess Pinky did what she did.

Princess Pinky found out that it was hard for her to trust, but Lion the Protector knew how to help her! Lion the Protector knew that she wanted to make sure that the people who were going to take care of her were going to keep her safe. He told her that she could be safe but that it would take a while to figure it out. He told her that there would be a home where she could be happy and feel safe. Even if she didn't stay with the nice lady who took care of her, Lion the Protector told her that the nice lady and Princess Pinky would always have a special connection between their hearts.

Princess Pinky had the strength inside of her heart that she needed to learn how to trust and feel safe. Princess Pinky always remembered her special connection to the nice lady and Lion the Protector, and learned to make new connections with other people who would do their best to take good care of her. One day, Princess Pinky would grow up and would have the strength to be happy and feel safe.

To view additional stories with illustrations, please see: www.routledge.com/9781138776289

Appendix E
Letters

Dear Lily,

I am writing you to tell you what I learned from talking and working with you.

Do you remember sitting in your room with me that day? You were so good at telling me how you were feeling and you worked really hard. The next day you didn't want to talk. That was OK, you had had enough.

Lily, thank you for talking with me. I liked being with you.

I liked seeing all your track and basketball trophies. I can see you playing sports and being really good,

I learned some things about you and I saw your strengths. I know you have been through a lot in your life and people have hurt you. You don't want to be hurt anymore. Sometimes you pull away from people to be sure they can't hurt you, like not talking or

going to your room. Sometimes you even run away to be sure they can't hurt you. Lily, I can see why you do this, but when you stop talking or run away, you are all alone. Being alone is hard, too. I would like you to have some help so you are not all alone.

Everyone is telling you lots of things right now, about going to school, turning 18, and getting a job. That is *a lot* of pressure. You told me you want *help* with these things (not just people telling you what to do). I think you are right and I think having one person, like a therapist, who will work with you would be good. I am going to talk with your social worker about finding you that person.

Lily, you are a talented, sweet person. I know you are trying really hard right now. You have stayed at your group home. You are going to school. Those are great things and a big deal.

I think about you a lot. Thank you again for talking with me. You can call me if you need to. I wish you all the best.

Letter to a Mother from Lisa Greenberg

Dear Ms. N.,

First, it was a pleasure to get to know you and your daughter. I really enjoyed the time I got to work with Millie. She was clearly interested in getting the evaluation and understanding more about herself, but she also seemed to enjoy the one-on-one time and the quiet of the office. It is clear that she benefits from time alone with caring adults in her life, and would also enjoy the process of individual therapy.

Before I answer your questions about your daughter, I wanted to let you know how much I appreciate your frankness and openness about what you and your family have been through. It takes courage to share difficult moments in your life with new people. Each time we discuss difficult events or feelings with new people, it is as if we are feeling some of the emotions again, which means we have to get through the feelings again. It seems that you work hard to handle your own difficult feelings and those of your children. I congratulate you for taking that on as it seems to strengthen you and your parenting of your children. Good for you!

I will try to answer your questions about Millie in a way that is clear and helpful to you. In answer to your question about her school challenges …

Millie is of average intelligence in comparison to kids her age. She is better with words than with visual thinking.

Millie has a very good memory. In fact, she has outstanding ability to remember a list of words when it is repeated to her several times. The conclusion here is that she can learn well and repetition helps.

Millie has a very slow rate of thinking and responding, similar to her slowness when eating, walking, or doing other activities. This does not mean that it is "hard" for her, it just means she needs time to think at her best.

Inattention: Her slowness means that she does not pick up everything that teachers or others say, especially when they talk about things she may not be so interested in or so good at. So her mind wanders or she turns to other distractions. Her slowness in following what people say also seems to affect her socially as it is hard for her to keep up with fast-talking, fast-moving girls her age.

Millie also has difficulty with organization, planning, shifting gears, and problem solving—the kinds of skills that she needs to get things done, do them in a timely manner, and to react when situations change.

In answer to your questions about her mood and social skills and her tendency to be careful around others …

Millie definitely seemed happier as the testing continued. She is clearly a kind person who tends to put other people first. She also has great ability to care for and love others, like she does for her brother.

Still, testing showed that Millie tends to have a lot of doubts about herself that keep coming up for her. She is also self-conscious about her body development (maybe because it seemed to happen so quickly from fourth grade to now) and the way she is dressed.

She also gets anxious about how she performs and about meeting new people. It seems that when she questions herself, it makes her more anxious.

Even though she doesn't talk directly about a lot of feelings and tends to avoid them, sad feelings came up in stories and pictures that she talked about. Depressive tendencies were also visible in her lack of interest in doing things, withdrawing from people, doing things in slow motion, and feeling tired a lot.

She has trouble feeling safe with peers and adults and feels uncomfortable in social situations. She tends to see people as aggressive or vulnerable in relationships. Some of this is related to losing important people in her life (like her grandmother) and some is related to being hurt or seeing her sisters getting hurt. She may also pull away because loud noises and a chaotic atmosphere really bother her.

The key recommendations to help Millie right now are:

She will need help getting organized, getting to school on time, planning her day the night before, and getting homework done. She just can't do this on her own yet and needs help with it.

She will benefit from continued family therapy and arranging individual therapy with her to help her have and talk about her feelings and to continue to build a sense of safety in relationships.

Continued one-on-one time with you, her mom, with Auntie, with Ms. M., and other safe adults also has a very positive impact on Millie.

To build her sense of trust in relationships, it will help to make sure that Millie is not put in a situation where she has to be around adults she does not feel safe with. This may make it uncomfortable if some of these adults are family members, but it will go a long way in supporting Millie's and others' sense of healthy relationships.

From the school she will need:

An evaluation and IEP and supportive services to address her slow thinking and her math difficulties, and to help her with daily homework support. Specific recommendations are provided in the school-based evaluation.

I would recommend giving the evaluation (Abridged Version for Educational Planning Purposes) to the principal and resource specialist at her school when she starts school and let them know you want to schedule an IEP, so that they can get her the help she needs. She really wants to be successful in school!

Ms. N., it has been a great pleasure to work with you and your family.

All the best to you and Millie and the rest of your family!

Index

Page numbers followed by *n* indicate note numbers.

ADHD. *See* Attention Deficit Hyperactivity Disorder
adoption, 136–7, 159–60
ADOS-2. *See* Autism Diagnostic Observation Schedule, Second Edition
Adult Attachment Projective, 209
Affordable Care Act, 16
African Americans, 21; case studies of shame in, 219–23; case study evaluation of pregnant youth, 71–3; case study of, 97–102; case study of a child with complex trauma, attachment, and repair, 202–14; case study of sexually exploited minors, 174–83; case study of youth for evaluation of hyperactivity and tantrums, 73–6; in foster care, 23; therapeutic assessment of a foster child in a community mental health setting, 143–58
aggression: case study of, 97–102
alcoholism, 84
Allport, Gordon, 119
Altman, Neil, 2, 3, 6, 23, 130, 132
American Counseling Association, 70
attachment: case study of an African-American child with complex trauma, attachment, and repair, 202–14
Attention Deficit Hyperactivity Disorder (ADHD), 198
Autism Diagnostic Observation Schedule, Second Edition (ADOS-2), 189–90

BASC-2. *See* Behavior Assessment System for Children, Second Edition
Bateson, Gregory, 1
Beery VMI, 177
behavior: case study of asssessment, 159–64
Behavior Assessment System for Children, Second Edition (BASC-2), 74, 85, 86, 177
Bion, Wilfred, 2, 20, 109–10, 153
Bowlby, John, 2
brave listening, 129–30

Briere, John, 202
Brown, Governor Jerry, 16
Burns, Ken, 11

California Verbal Learning Test—Child (CVLT-C), 75
CANS. *See* Child Assessment of Needs and Strengths
caretakers: Family Check-Up and, 53–4; in foster care, 96–7; screening requirements for, 27
CASA. *See* Court Appointed Special Advocate
case studies: of aggression, 97–102; of an African-American child with complex trauma, attachment, and repair, 202–14; of an African-American foster child in a community mental health setting, 143–58; of an African American youth for evaluation of hyperactivity and tantrums, 73–6; of an African American youth with countertransference reactions in collaborative assessments, 97–102; of an immigrant family, 80–8; of assessment intervention, 165–73; of assessment of a biracial child, 121–32; of behavior assessment, 159–64; of Hispanic youth, 184–95; of a pregnant African American youth, 71–3; of PTSD, 184–95; of racism, 184–95; of racist youth, 91–4; of sexually exploited minors, 174–83; of shame in African-American youth, 219–23; of shame in a Hispanic youth, 215–19; of training assessors in therapeutic assessment, 121–32; of trauma, 184–95; of traumatized and gender-nonconforming child, 192–201; of violence, 184–95
CAT. *See* Children's Apperception Test
Cattell-Horn-Carroll Theory (CHC), 34
C-Change program, 175
CCT. *See* Children's Category Test
CDI. *See* Childhood Depression Inventory

CELF-4. *See* Clinical Evaluation of Language Fundamentals, Fourth Edition
CFS. *See* Child and Family Services
CHC. *See* Cattell-Horn-Carroll Theory
Child and Family Feedback Form, 56–7
Child and Family Services (CFS), 216
Child Assessment of Needs and Strengths (CANS), 15, 48
Childhood Depression Inventory (CDI), 146
Child Protective Services (CPS), 85, 197
children: assessment-driven intervention for youth and families in community service delivery systems, 52–65; community mental health services for families of, 52–3
Children's Apperception Test (CAT), 24–5, 125, 147
Children's Category Test (CCT), 126
Child Welfare, 174
Chinese Americans, 90–1, 94
Civil Rights Movement, 14
Clinical Evaluation of Language Fundamentals, Fourth Edition (CELF-4), 75
Clinic for Therapeutic Assessment, 5
collaborative assessment model, 27–8, 69–78; case study of behavior assessment, 159–64; countertransference reactions to treatment team members in, 96–102; cross cultural dialogue with, 110–13; race and culture in, 89–95
Commercial Sexual Exploitation of Children (CSEC), 16, 174
communication, 16
community mental health, 1–2; of an African-American foster child in, 143–58; analysis of cognitive and Rorschach variables of children in, 31–51; assessment-driven intervention for youth and families in community service delivery systems, 52–65; assessment history of, 19; current state of assessment, 53; Family Check-Up and, 60–1; origins of, 13–14; psychological assessment of children in, 19–30; services for children and families in the United States, 52–3; therapeutic collaborative assessment model, 23–7
Community Mental Health Act, 13, 14
community psychology, 11–18; communication and policy, 16; description of, 1–2; entitlement, 11–13; mobile/systemic work, 14–15; model, 19–20; origins of, 13–14; overview, 1–7; "psychological mind" in, 2–3; relational psychology and, 20–2; theoretical foundations of, 1–6; therapeutic

collaborative assessment, 4–6; utilization and outcome, 15–16
conduct problems, 60
Conners' Continuous Performance Test, II (CPT-II), 74–5, 146
Continuous Performance Test-2 (CPT-2), 188
coping strategies, 72–3
Cornos, Dr. Francine, 22
countertransference, 90–1; in psychological assessment, 129–32; reactions to treatment team members in collaborative assessment, 96–102
Court Appointed Special Advocate (CASA), 97
CPS. *See* Child Protective Services
CPT-2. *See* Continuous Performance Test-2
CPT-II. *See* Conners' Continuous Performance Test, II
Crichton-Miller, Dr. Hugh, 2
critical race theory, 109–10
CSEC. *See* Commercial Sexual Exploitation of Children
culture: collaborative assessment and, 69–78; countertransference reactions to treatment team members in collaborative assessments, 96–102; fear of deportation, 12–13, 83; race in the assessment relationship, 89–95; supervision and, 105–13; training assessors in therapeutic assessment, 120–33; trauma for undocumented immigrants, 79–88
Cushman, Philip, 69
CVLT-C. *See* California Verbal Learning Test—Child

D-A-P. *See* Draw-A-Person
D-A-P-R. *See* Draw-A-Person-In-The-Rain
DAS-II. *See* Differential Ability Scales, Second Edition
Depression Scale, 206
development trauma disorder, 184–95
Differential Ability Scales, Second Edition (DAS-II), 34, 75, 99, 102n3, 126, 177
dilemmas of change, 127–9
DKEFS Tower subtest, 99
domestic violence, 123
Draw-A-Person (D-A-P), 146, 210–11
Draw-A-Person-In-The-Rain (D-A-P-R), 146, 147

Early and Periodic Screening, Diagnosis, and Treatment (EPSDT), 12
Early Memories Procedure (EMP), 147
Early Memory, 208–9
Early Steps Project, 58

EMDR. *See* Eye Movement Desensitization and Reprocessing
emotional functioning, 147; stories about past hurts, 233–6
EMP. *See* Early Memories Procedure
entitlement, 11–13; definition of, 11
Entitlement Act, 16
environment: stressors and, 14
EPSDT. *See* Early and Periodic Screening, Diagnosis, and Treatment
ethnicity: makeup of the population, 15
Everyday Parenting curriculum, 58
Exner Comprehensive System, 19, 34, 43
Eye Movement Desensitization and Reprocessing (EMDR), 193

FAE. *See* Fetal Alcohol Effects
family. *See also* mothers; parents: assessment-driven intervention for youth and families in community service delivery systems, 52–65; dilemmas of change, 127–9; history, 166–7; interventions, 128, 149–53, 180–2; model of family guidance, 2; psychologic assessment as family intervention, 170; trauma and, 3, 80–2
Family Check-Up (FCU), 53–61; child and family feedback form, 57; clinical example of, 58–9; in community mental health, 60–1; ecological assessment, 55–6; empirical support, 59–60; feedback and motivation, 56–8; goals of, 53–4; initial intake interview, 54–5; procedures, 54–8
FAS. *See* fetal alcohol syndrome
FCU. *See* Family Check-Up
fear: of deportation, 12–13; of undocumented immigrants, 79–88
feelings: stories about, 224–6
Fetal Alcohol Effects (FAE), 221
fetal alcohol syndrome (FAS), 221
FFA. *See* Foster Family Agency
Finn, Stephen, 1, 3, 5, 96, 99
Fischer, Constance, 1, 4–5
foster care: African Americans in, 23; of an African-American foster child in a community mental health setting, 143–58; analysis of cognitive and Rorschach variables of children in a community mental health clinic, 31–51; caregiver and, 96–7; case study of an African-American child with complex trauma, attachment, and repair, 202–14; case study of traumatized and gender-nonconforming child, 192–201; demographics and impact of, 23; feedback stories and, 26; trauma and, 24

Foster Family Agency (FFA), 97
Freud, Anna, 134
Freud, Sigmund, 2, 11

GCA. *See* General Conceptual Ability
gender. *See also* identity: case study of traumatized and gender-nonconforming child, 192–201; makeup of the population, 15
General Conceptual Ability (GCA), 34
government: funding for Medicaid, 12

Hardy, Dr. Kenneth, 99, 108
Head Start, 14
health care: universal, 5
Hispanic youth: case study of, 184–95; case study of shame in, 215–19; case study of traumatized and gender-nonconforming child, 192–201
House-Tree-Person (H-T-P), 146
H-T-P. *See* House-Tree-Person
Hughes, Langston, 105, 112–13
hyperactivity: case study of, 73–6

ICE. *See* US Immigration and Customs Enforcement
identity. *See also* gender: stories about, 227–30
immigrants: legal status of, 80; trauma for, 79–88; trusting the mental health system, 79–80; vulnerability of, 79
inner city: life in, 20
intake interview: for Family Check-Up, 54–5
interviews: with immigrant child, 82–3; intake, 54–5; play, 146
IQ, 34

Joint Commission on Mental Health and Illness, 13
Joint Commission on Mental Health and Mental Disabilities, 13

KABC-II Nonverbal Index, 85, 86
Kelly, Joan, 49
KFD. *See* Kinetic Family Drawing
Kinetic Family Drawing (KFD), 125
"kin-gap" bill, 15
Klein, Melanie, 134, 139

Lanktree, Cheryl, 202
Larry P. v. Riles, 107
learning: stories about, 231–2
Leary, Kimberlyn, 89, 94
legislation: Affordable Care Act, 16; Community Mental Health Act, 13, 14;

Entitlement Act, 16; "kin-gap" bill, 15; SB 855, 16; Social Security Act, 11
letters, 237–9; feedback, 73
level of care (LOC), 15
Life Timeline, 177
LOC. *See* level of care
loneliness, 134–6
Lyth, Menzies, 115

MACI. *See* Millon Adolescent Clinical Inventory
McFarlane, Alexander C., 1
Medicaid, 11, 12; government funding for, 12; policy for, 12
mental health: community, 1–2; criteria for, 52; immigrants' trust of the system, 79–80; of mothers, 165–73; principles of, 11–12; public face responders, 115; quality of services for, 52–3; stigma of, 12–13
Millon Adolescent Clinical Inventory (MACI), 177
Minnesota Multiphasic Personality Inventory, Adolescent (MMPI-A), 71
"miscuing," 162–3
MMPI-A. *See* Minnesota Multiphasic Personality Inventory, Adolescent
mobile/systemic work, 14–15
models: of collaborative assessment, 27–8, 69–78; of community psychology, 19–20; countertransference reactions to treatment team members in collaborative assessment, 96–102; Family Check-Up, 53–61; of family guidance, 2; therapeutic assessment, 4–5; of therapeutic collaborative assessment, 23–7; training model for therapeutic assessment, 124
mothers. *See also* family; parents: assessment questions, 167; evaluation of, 27; mental illness and, 165–73; referral for assessment of her son, 73; working with, 2–3

National Child Traumatic Stress Network, 209
NEPSY, 99, 101n2
Nonverbal Index (NVI), 85, 86
NVI. *See* Nonverbal Index

Parent Rating Scales, 177
parents. *See also* family; mothers: abilities of, 161; participation in therapeutic collaborative assessment model, 26–7; stress and, 59
Parks, Rosa, 107

past hurts: stories about, 233–6
phenomenology: description of, 4–5
policy, 16; advocacy in development and legislating of, 16; for Medicaid, 12
Post-Traumatic Stress Disorder (PTSD): case studies of, 184–95, 192–201
Preschool Language Scale-5 Spanish version, 85
professional realm: race in, 106–8; supervision and, 108–10
Projective Drawings, 87, 177
psyche, 2
psychological assessment: case study of an African-American child with complex trauma, attachment, and repair, 202–14; countertransference in, 129–32; as family intervention, 170; of urban youth, 31–2
PTSD. *See* Post-Traumatic Stress Disorder

race: in the assessment relationship, 89–95; case study of assessment of a biracial child, 121–32; critical race theory, 109–10; in the professional realm, 106–8; -related transference and countertransference, 90–1
racism: case studies of, 91–4, 184–95
RCMAS. *See* Revised Children's Manifest Anxiety Scale
relational theory, 109–10
Revised Children's Manifest Anxiety Scale (RCMAS), 146
Roberts Apperception Test, 125, 147, 177
Roberts cards, 151
Roosevelt, Franklin Delano, 11
Rorschach Comprehensive System, 75, 177, 189, 206–8
Rorschach Inkblot Method, 147
Rorschach research, 24; analysis of cognitive and Rorschach variables of children in a community mental health clinic, 31–51; limitations and future research, 48–9; methodology, 33–5; results, 35–43; study description, 43–8; with urban youth and trauma, 32–3
Rosenzweig Picture Frustration Study, 75, 98, 101n1
Rotter Sentence Completion, 177

SASH-Y. *See* Short Acculturation Scale for Hispanic Youth
SB 855, 16
SCAN-3 Test of Auditory Processing, 188
self: privileged versus subjugated, 108–9
SEM. *See* sexually exploited minors
sexually exploited minors (SEM), 32; case study of, 174–83

shame: case studies in an African-American youth, 219–23; case study in a Hispanic youth, 215–19; description of, 215
Short Acculturation Scale for Hispanic Youth (SASH-Y), 188
Simkus, Nora, 14
social cues: trauma and, 131–2
social justice: framework for collaborative assessment, 69–78
social psychology, 13
Social Security Act, 11
social workers, 1–2, 5–6; referral for assessment of youth, 71
stories, 25; about feelings, 224–6; about identity, 227–30; about learning, 231–2; about past hurts, 233–6; as assessment data, 170–1; from children in foster care, 26; feedback, 128–9, 149, 199–200, 211–12; feedback on adoption, 136–7; feedback on loneliness, 134–9; feedback on problematic behavior, 137–8; projective, 171; revising, 127–9; in therapeutic collaborative assessment model, 25–6
stressors, 14; parents and, 59
suicideal ideation, 219–20
supervision: culture and, 105–13; professional role of, 108–10; vicarious trauma, assessment and, 114–19

TA. *See* therapeutic assessment
Tagore, Rabinranath, v
tantrums: case study of, 73–6
TAT. *See* Thematic Apperception Test
Tavistock Clinic, 2
TBS. *See* Therapeutic Behavioral Services
TCA. *See* therapeutic collaborative assessment
Thematic Apperception Test (TAT), 23, 98
therapeutic assessment (TA): with an African-American foster child in a community mental health setting, 143–58; assessment data as therapeutic porthole, 170–1; assessment referral, 165–6; case study of an African-American child with complex trauma, attachment, and repair, 202–14; case study of assessment intervention, 165–73; case study of behavior assessment, 159–64; case study of sexually exploited minors, 174–83; case study of shame in a Hispanic youth, 215–19; case study of shame in an African-American, 219–20; feedback, 180–2; model, 4–5; observation, 167–8; questions, 146; of sexually exploited minor, 177–82; therapist's assessment questions, 166; training assessors in, 120–33; training model, 124; of traumatized and

gender-nonconforming child, 192–201; of a traumatized and gender-nonconforming child, 192–201
Therapeutic Behavioral Services (TBS), 97
therapeutic collaborative assessment (TCA), 23–7; cross cultural dialogue and, 110–13; demographics and impact of foster care, 23; feedback, 75–6, 172; feedback stories, 25–6; parent participation in, 26–7; structural and projective data, 23–5; use of data in, 25–7
therapist: assessment questions, 166; mother's assessment questions, 167
Tomkins, Silvan, 215
training: assessors in therapeutic assessment, 120–33; case study of, 121–32; structure of, 121
transference, 90–1
Transitional Age Youth Program/C-Change, 16
trauma, 2; case study of, 184–95; case study of an African-American child with complex trauma, attachment, and repair, 202–14; case study of traumatized and gender-nonconforming child, 192–201; distortion of social cues and, 131–2; exposure to, 15–16; with families, 3; foster care and, 24; Rorschach research with urban youth and, 32–3; secondary, 115–16; for undocumented immigrants, 79–88; vicarious, 114–19
Trauma Content Index, 206
Trauma Symptom Checklist for Children (TSCC), 177, 188–9, 208
TSCC. *See* Trauma Symptom Checklist for Children

US Immigration and Customs Enforcement (ICE), 80, 85

van der Kolk, Bessel A., 1
vicarious trauma, 114–19; clinician experience with, 116–17; protective strategies and, 119; supervisors' experience with, 117–18
Victims of Crime, 193–4
Vineland-II Communication Scale, 86, 177
violence, 92; case study of, 184–95; domestic, 123

War on Poverty, 14
WASI-II. *See* Wechsler Abbreviated Scale of Intelligence, Second Edition
WCST. *See* Wisconsin Card Sorting Test
Wechsler Abbreviated Scale of Intelligence, Second Edition (WASI-II), 71–2

Wechsler Adult Intelligence Test-III, 187
Wechsler Individual Achievement Test, Third
    Edition (WIAT-III), 75, 99, 102n4, 188
Wechsler Intelligence Scale for Children IV,
    34, 126
Weisaeth, Lars, 1
WestCoast Children's Clinic, 174–5
WIAT-III. *See* Wechsler Individual
    Achievement Test, Third Edition
Winnicott, D.W., 2, 3
Wisconsin Card Sorting Test (WCST), 74, 188

Women's Movement, 14
Woodcock-Johnson III Test of Achievement,
    147

Young Minds Advocacy Project, 11
youth: assessment-driven intervention for
    youth and families in community service
    delivery systems, 52–65; community
    mental health services for families of, 52–3;
    psychological assessment of urban, 31–2
Youth Uprising, 203

Taylor & Francis eBooks

Helping you to choose the right eBooks for your Library

Add Routledge titles to your library's digital collection today. Taylor and Francis ebooks contains over 50,000 titles in the Humanities, Social Sciences, Behavioural Sciences, Built Environment and Law.

Choose from a range of subject packages or create your own!

Benefits for you

» Free MARC records
» COUNTER-compliant usage statistics
» Flexible purchase and pricing options
» All titles DRM-free.

Benefits for your user

» Off-site, anytime access via Athens or referring URL
» Print or copy pages or chapters
» Full content search
» Bookmark, highlight and annotate text
» Access to thousands of pages of quality research at the click of a button.

REQUEST YOUR **FREE** INSTITUTIONAL TRIAL TODAY

Free Trials Available
We offer free trials to qualifying academic, corporate and government customers.

eCollections – Choose from over 30 subject eCollections, including:

Archaeology	Language Learning
Architecture	Law
Asian Studies	Literature
Business & Management	Media & Communication
Classical Studies	Middle East Studies
Construction	Music
Creative & Media Arts	Philosophy
Criminology & Criminal Justice	Planning
Economics	Politics
Education	Psychology & Mental Health
Energy	Religion
Engineering	Security
English Language & Linguistics	Social Work
Environment & Sustainability	Sociology
Geography	Sport
Health Studies	Theatre & Performance
History	Tourism, Hospitality & Events

For more information, pricing enquiries or to order a free trial, please contact your local sales team:
www.tandfebooks.com/page/sales

Routledge
Taylor & Francis Group

The home of
Routledge books

www.tandfebooks.com